MOTIVATION *and* MORALITY

MOTIVATION
and MORALITY
A Multidisciplinary Approach

Martha K. Berg and Edward C. Chang

EDITORS

AMERICAN PSYCHOLOGICAL ASSOCIATION

Published by
American Psychological Association
750 First Street, NE
Washington, DC 20002
https://www.apa.org

Order Department
https://www.apa.org/pubs/books
order@apa.org

In the U.K., Europe, Africa, and the Middle East, copies may be ordered from Eurospan
https://www.eurospanbookstore.com/apa
info@eurospangroup.com

Typeset in Charter and Interstate by Circle Graphics, Inc., Reisterstown, MD

Printer: Gasch Printing, Odenton, MD
Cover Designer: Beth Schlenoff Design, Bethesda, MD

Library of Congress Cataloging-in-Publication Data

Names: Berg, Martha K., editor. | Chang, Edward C. (Edward Chin-Ho), editor.
Title: Motivation and morality : a multidisciplinary approach / [edited by] Martha K. Berg and Edward C. Chang.
Description: Washington, DC : American Psychological Association, [2023] | Includes bibliographical references and index.
Identifiers: LCCN 2022035892 (print) | LCCN 2022035893 (ebook) | ISBN 9781433838729 (paperback) | ISBN 9781433838736 (ebook)
Subjects: LCSH: Moral development. | Motivation (Psychology)--Moral and ethical aspects. | Ethics--Psychological aspects. | BISAC: PSYCHOLOGY / Social Psychology | PSYCHOLOGY / Movements / Behaviorism
Classification: LCC BF723.M54 M75 2023 (print) | LCC BF723.M54 (ebook) | DDC 155.2/5--dc23/eng/20220919
LC record available at https://lccn.loc.gov/2022035892
LC ebook record available at https://lccn.loc.gov/2022035893

https://doi.org/10.1037/0000342-000

Printed in the United States of America

10 9 8 7 6 5 4 3 2 1

Contents

Contributors

Martha K. Berg, PhD, Department of Psychology, University of Michigan, Ann Arbor, MI, United States

Edward C. Chang, PhD, Department of Psychology and School of Social Work, University of Michigan, Ann Arbor, MI, United States

Jessica L. Engelbrecht, MA, Department of Psychology, New School for Social Research, New York, NY, United States

Oriel FeldmanHall, PhD, Department of Cognitive, Linguistic, and Psychological Sciences, Brown University, Providence, RI, United States

Bertram Gawronski, PhD, Department of Psychology, The University of Texas at Austin, Austin, TX, United States

Steven Hitlin, PhD, Department of Sociology and Criminology, University of Iowa, Iowa City, IA, United States

Anita Körner, PhD, Department of Psychology, University of Kassel, Kassel, Germany

Amrita Lamba, PhD, Department of Cognitive, Linguistic, and Psychological Sciences, Brown University, Providence, RI, United States

Kristin Laurin, PhD, Department of Psychology, The University of British Columbia, Vancouver, BC, Canada

Dillon M. Luke, MA, Department of Psychology, The University of Texas at Austin, Austin, TX, United States

Bertram F. Malle, PhD, Department of Cognitive, Linguistic, and Psychological Sciences, Brown University, Providence, RI, United States

Joan G. Miller, PhD, Department of Psychology, New School for Social Research, New York, NY, United States

Darcia Narvaez, PhD, Department of Psychology, University of Notre Dame, South Bend, IN, United States

Nancy E. Snow, PhD, Department of Philosophy, University of Kansas, Lawrence, KS, United States

Mary S. Tarsha, MA, Department of Psychology, University of Notre Dame, South Bend, IN, United States

Jordan E. Theriault, PhD, Department of Psychology, Northeastern University, Boston, MA, United States

Irein Ann Thomas, MA, Department of Psychology, The University of British Columbia, Vancouver, BC, Canada

Preface

The past few decades have seen a resurging interest in the science of morality. New methodologies, involving both technological advances and novel modeling approaches, have been used to test and expand on centuries-old theorizing about people's capacities for morality and immorality. Yet, as social scientists, we know that whether or not one really does act a certain way depends not only on one's capacity for it but also on one's motivation to do so. The present volume seeks to deeply explore this question of motivation and how it pertains to human morality. By gathering leading scholars across sociology, psychology, philosophy, and neuroscience, we aim to present an integrated account of how morality is motivated. We are deeply indebted to the scholars whose works constitute this volume, for their cutting-edge research that has powerfully shaped our current understanding of morality and for generously sharing their insights to help us drive this multidisciplinary science forward.

MOTIVATION
and MORALITY

INTRODUCTION

What Is Moral Motivation, and Why Does It Matter?

MARTHA K. BERG AND EDWARD C. CHANG

"Why did you do all this for me?" he asked.
"I don't deserve it. I've never done anything for you."

—E.B. White, *Charlotte's Web* (1952)

What drives us to do good things, or to avoid doing bad? This question has long sparked inquiry across multiple disciplines, and scholars have debated the answer to it both within and across fields. Yet morality as a topic of study has seen a resurgence in the past few decades, bringing this question back to the forefront of academic thought.

WHAT IS MORALITY?

To discuss moral motivation, we first must land on a working definition of morality. Although even this definition has elicited contention among moral scholars (Gert & Gert, 2020), for our purposes, we can conceptualize morality as *a framework that seeks to guide questions of right and wrong.*

https://doi.org/10.1037/0000342-001
Motivation and Morality: A Multidisciplinary Approach, M. K. Berg and E. C. Chang (Editors)

3

Immoral behavior, then, is that which is considered "wrong" (and moral behavior the opposite). To any given individual, moral rules are typically considered to be prescriptive, important, and generalizable across a range of similar situations (Wong, 2013). However, the extent to which there is a universal set of behaviors that are right and wrong (a *universalist* perspective) or many individualized or socially constructed ones (a *relativist* perspective) is itself disputed (Shweder & Bourne, 1984), and we return to this question throughout this volume. How can we study morally relevant behavior, though, if the bounds of this construct are potentially blurred? As we will see in the chapters of this volume, one approach is to consider morality from a *descriptive* perspective rather than a *normative* one; that is, rather than testing people's behaviors against a set of universal rules that are presumed to be the correct ones, we can construct and investigate moral frameworks based on the rules that people actually follow (which, of course, naturally lends itself to a relativist perspective, or at least one that allows for the possibility of relativism). In practice, then, *in studying morality, we study what people consider to be right and wrong, and how these rules guide behavior*.

WHY BE MORAL?

Once we have determined that a certain behavior is "moral," how can we understand *why* people engage in that behavior? Is it just because of its designation as moral (i.e., based on a motivation to act morally)? What about when there are other competing motivations at play, some of which may drive conflicting behaviors? What about when there are other competing behaviors to choose from, some of which also might be classified as moral, such as when one must decide between helping a stranger and helping a friend?

Broadly put, the question of motivation centers on the factors that lead people to initiate and persist in certain actions, moral or otherwise. In other words, out of all possible behaviors that a person could choose to do in a given scenario, why do they choose one specific behavior? Models of motivation have suggested that behavior ultimately is driven by unmet needs, whether these are survival needs (e.g., hunger, thirst) or psychological ones (e.g., belonging, consistency), whether they are distal (i.e., long term) or more proximal (i.e., immediate; Karniol & Ross, 1996; Locke, 1991; Pittman & Heller, 1987). Yet there are many ways of satisfying needs once they have been identified; for example, people can choose to eat a wide variety of foods to slake their hunger. To select a specific behavior among these options, people leverage their *values*, which have been proposed as the essence of motivation

(Locke, 1991). Returning to the previous example, one can imagine different food choices resulting from the value one places on, for example, sensory pleasure, dietary purity, or even animal rights. As such, values drive motivation toward specific goals to satisfy needs, but so too do other factors, such as perceptions of self-efficacy for meeting needs through a certain method, social expectations and comparisons (which also serve to inform values), and perceptions of the costs versus benefits of a certain course of action (Hattie et al., 2020). Furthermore, once an action is completed, outcomes (i.e., rewards or punishments for the behavior and the associated emotional responses) create a feedback loop; positive outcomes can motivate a continuation or repetition of the behavior, and negative outcomes can motivate a different behavioral solution the next time the same need arises (Locke, 1991; Pittman & Heller, 1987).

Thus, the range of motivations that might drive any given behavior is wide, and moral behaviors are no exception. Indeed, given the social relevance of moral and immoral behavior (both in terms of its distal relevance to social cooperation and its proximal relevance to everyday relationship dynamics), understanding *moral* motivations can be particularly tricky. When a person engages in a positive moral action, such as providing help to someone else, is it driven by a need to help the other person—for example, to fulfill a sense of debt or duty to others—or because this action benefits the self in some way, for example, by eliciting positive emotions in the self or affirming an identity to which morality is central? What are the central unmet needs that drive this helping behavior? These questions have been widely debated across multiple disciplines, and next we discuss some (but certainly not all) possible motivations for moral behavior.

To begin, we return to the opening quote, in which the speaker (Wilbur) implies that others help us because we have previously helped them. According to Kohlberg (1981), this idea of *reciprocal altruism* represents one of the early stages of moral development, in which people use reciprocal fairness norms to dictate their moral behavior. This motivation for moral behavior extends beyond early moral development; numerous studies have demonstrated the importance of reciprocity to social cooperation (Axelrod & Hamilton, 1981; Fehr & Fischbacher, 2003; Gintis, 2000), and it is theorized to be one of the universal components that give rise to morality (Curry et al., 2019; Gouldner, 1960; Henrich & Muthukrishna, 2021).

As reflected in the opening epigraph, however, there are times when reciprocity cannot explain moral behavior, which implies that there are other possible motives for moral behavior. The addressee of this quote (Charlotte) responds by indicating that she helped because Wilbur is a friend. In other words, Charlotte's moral behavior toward Wilbur is motivated not by his past moral behavior toward her but by the communal relationship they share (Clark & Mills, 1979). But what are the motivations within close relationships that drive moral behavior? Jacquette (2001) contended that in an Aristotelian view, the nature of close relationships both requires and reinforces virtuous behavior. In particular, virtue is a necessary precursor for friendship of the highest degree, meaning the kind of friendship in which each individual acts in the interest of the other's welfare rather than for self-interested or instrumental reasons. Moral behavior is required to attract similarly virtuous friends, and therefore the reward intrinsic to this type of friendship spurs us to act morally.

Scholars have also linked relationships to moral behavior through *empathy*, or the sharing of another person's mental state, which happens most frequently when the other person is relationally close or similar to the self (Gutsell & Inzlicht, 2012; Han, 2018). This aligns with one leading framework of morality that emphasizes the *ethic of care*, in which empathy is a critical component (Gilligan et al., 1988). Similar to moral emotions, empathy is thought to motivate helping and other moral behavior, acting as a spark to drive people to action (Coke et al., 1978; Hoffman, 1990). However, this empathy–altruism hypothesis sparked a decades-long debate that centered on the question of motivation. As noted, the original theorizing was that seeing another in distress led to other-oriented (i.e., empathic) concern, which in turn motivated altruistic behavior. However, others argued that because seeing another in distress sparked distress in the self, the helping behavior was instead motivated by self-oriented (i.e., egoistic) concerns, namely, the desire to alleviate one's own negative reaction (Cialdini et al., 1987).

More broadly, many have turned to moral emotions to explain how moral behavior is motivated. Perhaps most notably, Hume (2009) argued that, in line with his assertion that reason is the slave of the passions, moral reasoning is fundamentally shaped by emotions. Indeed, empirical work has demonstrated a robust link between emotions and moral behavior (Eisenberg, 2000; Haidt, 2001; Prinz & Nichols, 2010; Tangney et al., 2007). For example, experimentally inducing disgust (Schnall et al., 2008) or anger (Seidel & Prinz, 2013) increases the severity of individuals' moral judgments, whereas inducing happiness does the opposite (Seidel & Prinz, 2013).

Moral behavior may also be motivated by a sense of duty. Although some have argued that this comes in the form of a duty to adhere to the law (e.g., Kant, 1785), others have focused on one's duty to a higher power (e.g., James, 1982). These ideas are echoed in Kohlberg's (1981) stages of moral development, in which Stage 1 describes following rules in order to avoid punishment, but adherence to—and, eventually, critical reasoning about—societal principles are central throughout later stages of development. Morality motivated by religious beliefs has been posited as one of three universal ethics (Shweder et al., 2013), and it is further supported by public opinion; although there is national and regional variation, nearly half of people worldwide believe that religious beliefs are necessary for being moral (Tamir et al., 2020).

Finally, moral identity has been studied as a motivation for moral behavior. This idea has been most notably elaborated in Blasi's (1983) *self model* of moral functioning, which posits that when an individual judges a moral action to be central to their sense of self, they are motivated by self-consistency, or the desire to engage in behavior that is consistent with that sense of self. Moral identity may help to turn obligations (i.e., moral rules) into desires (Batson, 2011); whereas all individuals gain moral knowledge over the course of development, some argue that only those who internalize and endow that knowledge with personal relevance will be motivated to act morally (Nunner-Winkler, 1993). These ideas have been borne out in empirical evidence; the extent to which morality is central to one's identity predicts moral behavior across a range of domains (Aquino & Reed, 2002; Hardy & Carlo, 2011).

WHY DOES MOTIVATION MATTER?

The range of possible motivations for individuals' moral behavior sets the stage for the rest of this volume, in which we explore these motivations—including how they are shaped, how they are balanced against other motivations, and how we can assess them. But before we do so, we must ask: Why is this task important? Why should we care about the motivations that drive people's moral or immoral behavior?

To illustrate, we start with a classic thought experiment, introduced in Plato's (2007) *Republic*. The Ring of Gyges makes the wearer invisible and thus allows them to commit moral transgressions without detection. Why would the wearer *not* commit moral transgressions?

In the original text, Socrates answers by stating that, even if not detected, committing moral transgressions harms the soul and jeopardizes one's chance at an afterlife, an answer that echoes elements of both identity-based and religion-based motivation. In doing so, though, he draws a contrast between two courses of action that are differentiated by the underlying motives that drive them. In other words, in order to predict whether any given wearer would use the ring to do wrong, we would need to understand their underlying motivations. Are they motivated by the reward of appearing moral, or are they motivated by a desire to protect the sanctity of their character, regardless of who sees them?

On a more quotidian level, this thought experiment can generalize to any situation that affords the individual some sense of invisibility, whether that is due to a systemic lack of oversight or a coincidental window of opportunity to act unseen. Prior work has shown that when such an opportunity presents itself, people often choose actions metaphorically similar to wearing the Ring of Gyges: They act immorally, even though they know that what they are doing is wrong, because they think their transgression will go undetected (e.g., Batson, 2011; Valdesolo & DeSteno, 2007). Batson (2011) attributed this moral hypocrisy to "a relative lack of truly moral motivation" (p. 230), highlighting the centrality of motivation to understanding and predicting people's moral actions.

Understanding motivation is also critical from a moral education perspective. Wilson (1972) argued that encouraging moral behavior without interrogating the underlying motivations is akin to teaching children the answers to math problems without teaching them how to arrive at those answers. Learning how to navigate the reasons for moral action, including the various motivations we outlined in the previous sections, is important in the development of one's own moral framework. Furthermore, one could argue, as Wilson did, that these motivations do not carry equal moral value; if one wants to encourage acting on a certain moral motivation over others, for example, then understanding the range of what drives people is essential.

One compelling case for valuing certain motivations for morality over others, from a moral education standpoint, is that, in general, people tend to perceive behaviors differently based on the presumed underlying motivation. For example, in the previous section we discussed a religious motivation for moral behavior. Recent work has shown that when people perceive someone's moral behavior to be religiously motivated, they perceive that behavior as less moral (Gervais, 2014). Similarly, when helping behavior is done for self-oriented reasons, people rate the act as less altruistic (Carlson & Zaki, 2018). Thus, motivation for moral behavior is important because others think it is so; how our actions are received is dependent on our intentions (or, at least, what others believe them to be).

Finally, motivation has become an increasingly central component of how we model moral thought and action. For example, the social intuitionist model proposes that moral judgments are based on quick, intuitive, and emotion-driven evaluations that influence later deliberate reasoning (Greene et al., 2001; Haidt, 2001). This model is aligned with the broader concept of *motivated reasoning*; we reach certain conclusions not because we deliberately reason our way there but because we are motivated to reach certain conclusions, and we selectively apply rules and beliefs that help us to justify them (Ditto et al., 2009; Kunda, 1990). From this perspective, motivation is inherently linked to morality, and we as a multidisciplinary scientific community should prioritize investigating motivation as a critical step to expanding our understanding of human morality.

OVERVIEW OF THE PRESENT VOLUME

The goal of this volume is to cut across disciplines and modes of inquiry to answer central questions about moral motivation. The chapters explore how moral motivation is shaped socially, for example, through learning the expectancies of our social and cultural groups. They investigate how moral motivation differs from and is balanced against other motivations that drive behavior, and they describe how we measure these motivations as well as the challenges we face in measuring them. The volume is divided into three parts, each roughly corresponding to an overarching lens for human behavior—social, psychological, and neurobiological, respectively—but each enriched by the inclusion of leading scholars across multiple disciplines.

Part I, Social Contexts and Their Motivational Consequences, tackles the question of moral motivation from a social perspective, examining how communities, groups, and relationships motivate our moral frameworks and tendencies. In Chapter 1, Hitlin describes how sociology, a discipline concerned with collective human behavior, can shed light on what motivates morality at an individual level. He introduces key sociological constructs that speak to individuals' motives, which he argues can contribute toward a more transdisciplinary understanding of morality. In Chapter 2, Malle describes how context motivates moral behavior by way of social norms. He explains the ways in which norm violations are socially regulated, which results in patterns of moral behavior that allow a social group to flourish. In Chapter 3, Miller and Engelbrecht examine cultural variation in the social norms that motivate moral behavior. They describe and integrate two major approaches to studying morality across cultures—universalism and relativism—to draw conclusions about how culture shapes our moral motives.

Part II, Psychological Frameworks and Individual Differences, examines how individuals differ in their moral actions and the psychological factors that motivate them. In Chapter 4, Gawronski, Luke, and Körner explore three bases upon which individuals may make moral decisions: consequences, norms, and generalized inaction. They introduce the CNI model, which empirically differentiates among these motives, and they review what this model has revealed about the variation in motives across individuals. In Chapter 5,

Snow describes how the philosophical tradition of virtue ethics views moral, or virtuous, motivation as a necessary precursor to moral action. She builds on this philosophical stance by introducing whole trait theory, an empirically grounded model in which traits, including virtue, are assessed via the distribution of trait-appropriate responses in daily life. In Chapter 6, FeldmanHall and Lamba turn to the competing motivations we encounter, exploring how people learn to resolve these conflicts; specifically, they describe the mechanisms for social learning, including reinforcement learning and Bayesian models, that allow us to learn the social dynamics and reward contingencies that drive moral behavior.

Part III, Biological Origins and Markers of Moral Motivation, examines the ways in which the brain shapes, and can reveal insights about, our motivations for moral behavior. In Chapter 7, Tarsha and Narvaez describe the development of neurobiological systems that underpin moral motivation. They explain how the early satisfaction or nonsatisfaction of basic needs shapes our later well-being, including the moral mindsets that direct our behavior. In Chapter 8, Theriault introduces a novel account that posits that morality is motivated by a biological drive to optimize metabolic costs; specifically, he argues that we minimize the costs of information processing by behaving in line with others' expectations (e.g., by following moral norms), which in turn influences others to behave in similarly predictable (i.e., normative) ways.

Finally, we conclude with a broad synthesis of the social, psychological, and neurobiological approaches. In the Conclusion, Laurin and Thomas explore the nexus of these perspectives, drawing insights about the nature of moral motivation as well as important directions for future scholarship.

FINAL THOUGHTS

As a whole, this volume seeks to offer an integrative examination of the role of motivation in shaping morality. In bringing together leading researchers across sociology, philosophy, psychology, and neuroscience, we strive to represent the complex motivational aspects of morality, which represents a crucial step toward understanding how and why our moral choices arise and in turn can shape and guide how we engage in moral praxis.

REFERENCES

Aquino, K., & Reed, A., II. (2002). The self-importance of moral identity. *Journal of Personality and Social Psychology, 83*(6), 1423–1440. https://doi.org/10.1037/0022-3514.83.6.1423

Axelrod, R., & Hamilton, W. D. (1981, March 27). The evolution of cooperation. *Science, 211*(4489), 1390–1396. https://doi.org/10.1126/science.7466396

Batson, C. D. (2011). What's wrong with morality? *Emotion Review, 3*(3), 230–236. https://doi.org/10.1177/1754073911402380

Blasi, A. (1983). Moral cognition and moral action: A theoretical perspective. *Developmental Review, 3*(2), 178–210. https://doi.org/10.1016/0273-2297(83)90029-1

Carlson, R. W., & Zaki, J. (2018). Good deeds gone bad: Lay theories of altruism and selfishness. *Journal of Experimental Social Psychology, 75*, 36–40. https://doi.org/10.1016/j.jesp.2017.11.005

Cialdini, R. B., Schaller, M., Houlihan, D., Arps, K., Fultz, J., & Beaman, A. L. (1987). Empathy-based helping: Is it selflessly or selfishly motivated? *Journal of Personality and Social Psychology, 52*(4), 749–758. https://doi.org/10.1037/0022-3514.52.4.749

Clark, M. S., & Mills, J. (1979). Interpersonal attraction in exchange and communal relationships. *Journal of Personality and Social Psychology, 37*(1), 12–24. https://doi.org/10.1037/0022-3514.37.1.12

Coke, J. S., Batson, C. D., & McDavis, K. (1978). Empathic mediation of helping: A two-stage model. *Journal of Personality and Social Psychology, 36*(7), 752–766. https://doi.org/10.1037/0022-3514.36.7.752

Curry, O. S., Jones Chesters, M., & Van Lissa, C. J. (2019). Mapping morality with a compass: Testing the theory of "morality-as-cooperation" with a new questionnaire. *Journal of Research in Personality, 78*, 106–124. https://doi.org/10.1016/j.jrp.2018.10.008

Ditto, P. H., Pizarro, D. A., & Tannenbaum, D. (2009). Motivated moral reasoning. In B. H. Ross (Ed.), *Psychology of learning and motivation* (Vol. 50, pp. 307–338). Academic Press. https://doi.org/10.1016/S0079-7421(08)00410-6

Eisenberg, N. (2000). Emotion, regulation, and moral development. *Annual Review of Psychology, 51*(1), 665–697. https://doi.org/10.1146/annurev.psych.51.1.665

Fehr, E., & Fischbacher, U. (2003, October 23). The nature of human altruism. *Nature, 425*(6960), 785–791. https://doi.org/10.1038/nature02043

Gert, B., & Gert, J. (2020). The definition of morality. In E. N. Zalta (Ed.), *The Stanford encyclopedia of philosophy*. Metaphysics Research Laboratory, Stanford University. https://plato.stanford.edu/archives/fall2020/entries/morality-definition/

Gervais, W. M. (2014). Good for God? Religious motivation reduces perceived responsibility for and morality of good deeds. *Journal of Experimental Psychology: General, 143*(4), 1616–1626. https://doi.org/10.1037/a0036678

Gilligan, C., Ward, J. V., Bardige, B., & Taylor, J. M. (1988). *Mapping the moral domain: A contribution of women's thinking to psychological theory and education.* Harvard University Press.

Gintis, H. (2000). Strong reciprocity and human sociality. *Journal of Theoretical Biology, 206*(2), 169–179. https://doi.org/10.1006/jtbi.2000.2111

Gouldner, A. W. (1960). The norm of reciprocity: A preliminary statement. *American Sociological Review, 25*(2), 161–178. https://doi.org/10.2307/2092623

Greene, J. D., Sommerville, R. B., Nystrom, L. E., Darley, J. M., & Cohen, J. D. (2001, September 14). An fMRI investigation of emotional engagement in moral judgment. *Science, 293*(5537), 2105–2108. https://doi.org/10.1126/science.1062872

Gutsell, J. N., & Inzlicht, M. (2012). Intergroup differences in the sharing of emotive states: Neural evidence of an empathy gap. *Social Cognitive and Affective Neuroscience, 7*(5), 596–603. https://doi.org/10.1093/scan/nsr035

Haidt, J. (2001). The emotional dog and its rational tail: A social intuitionist approach to moral judgment. *Psychological Review*, *108*(4), 814–834. https://doi.org/10.1037/0033-295X.108.4.814

Han, S. (2018). Neurocognitive basis of racial ingroup bias in empathy. *Trends in Cognitive Sciences*, *22*(5), 400–421. https://doi.org/10.1016/j.tics.2018.02.013

Hardy, S. A., & Carlo, G. (2011). Moral identity: What is it, how does it develop, and is it linked to moral action? *Child Development Perspectives*, *5*(3), 212–218. https://doi.org/10.1111/j.1750-8606.2011.00189.x

Hattie, J., Hodis, F. A., & Kang, S. H. K. (2020). Theories of motivation: Integration and ways forward. *Contemporary Educational Psychology*, *61*, 101865. https://doi.org/10.1016/j.cedpsych.2020.101865

Henrich, J., & Muthukrishna, M. (2021). The origins and psychology of human cooperation. *Annual Review of Psychology*, *72*(1), 207–240. https://doi.org/10.1146/annurev-psych-081920-042106

Hoffman, M. L. (1990). Empathy and justice motivation. *Motivation and Emotion*, *14*(2), 151–172. https://doi.org/10.1007/BF00991641

Hume, D. A. (2009). *An enquiry concerning the principles of morals*. Merchant Books.

Jacquette, D. (2001). Aristotle on the value of friendship as a motivation for morality. *The Journal of Value Inquiry*, *35*(3), 371–389. https://doi.org/10.1023/A:1011873730850

James, W. (1982). *Essays in religion and morality* (F. Burkhardt, F. Bowers, & I. K. Skrupskelis, Eds.). Harvard University Press.

Kant, I. (1785). *Grounding for the metaphysics of morals* (J. W. Ellington, Trans.). Hackett.

Karniol, R., & Ross, M. (1996). The motivational impact of temporal focus: Thinking about the future and the past. *Annual Review of Psychology*, *47*(1), 593–620. https://doi.org/10.1146/annurev.psych.47.1.593

Kohlberg, L. (1981). *The philosophy of moral development: Moral stages and the idea of justice*. Harper & Row.

Kunda, Z. (1990). The case for motivated reasoning. *Psychological Bulletin*, *108*(3), 480–498. https://doi.org/10.1037/0033-2909.108.3.480

Locke, E. A. (1991). The motivation sequence, the motivation hub, and the motivation core. *Organizational Behavior and Human Decision Processes*, *50*(2), 288–299. https://doi.org/10.1016/0749-5978(91)90023-M

Nunner-Winkler, G. (1993). The growth of moral motivation. In G. G. Noam & T. E. Wren (Eds.), *The moral self* (pp. 269–291). MIT Press.

Pittman, T. S., & Heller, J. F. (1987). Social motivation. *Annual Review of Psychology*, *38*(1), 461–489. https://doi.org/10.1146/annurev.ps.38.020187.002333

Plato. (2007). *The republic* (D. Lee, Trans.).

Prinz, J. J., & Nichols, S. (2010). *Moral emotions*. In J. M. Doris & The Moral Psychology Research Group (Eds.), *The moral psychology handbook* (pp. 111–146). Oxford University Press.

Schnall, S., Haidt, J., Clore, G. L., & Jordan, A. H. (2008). Disgust as embodied moral judgment. *Personality and Social Psychology Bulletin*, *34*(8), 1096–1109. https://doi.org/10.1177/0146167208317771

Seidel, A., & Prinz, J. (2013). Mad and glad: Musically induced emotions have divergent impact on morals. *Motivation and Emotion*, *37*(3), 629–637. https://doi.org/10.1007/s11031-012-9320-7

Shweder, R. A., & Bourne, E. J. (1984). Does the concept of the person vary cross-culturally? In R. A. Shweder (Ed.), *Culture theory: Essays on mind, self and emotion* (pp. 97–138). Cambridge University Press.

Shweder, R. A., Much, N. C., Mahapatra, M., & Park, L. (2013). The "big three" of morality (autonomy, community, divinity) and the "big three" explanations of suffering. In A. M. Brandt & P. Rozin (Eds.), *Morality and health* (pp. 119–169). Routledge.

Tamir, C., Connaughton, A., & Salazar, A. M. (2020, July 20). *The global god divide*. Pew Research Center. https://www.pewresearch.org/global/2020/07/20/the-global-god-divide/

Tangney, J. P., Stuewig, J., & Mashek, D. J. (2007). Moral emotions and moral behavior. *Annual Review of Psychology, 58*(1), 345–372. https://doi.org/10.1146/annurev.psych.56.091103.070145

Valdesolo, P., & DeSteno, D. (2007). Moral hypocrisy: Social groups and the flexibility of virtue. *Psychological Science, 18*(8), 689–690. https://doi.org/10.1111/j.1467-9280.2007.01961.x

Wilson, J. (1972). Motivation and morality. *Journal of Moral Education, 2*(1), 25–29. https://doi.org/10.1080/0305724720020104

Wong, D. B. (2013). Definition of morality. In *International encyclopedia of ethics*. Wiley. https://doi.org/10.1002/9781444367072.wbiee671

I SOCIAL CONTEXTS AND THEIR MOTIVATIONAL CONSEQUENCES

1

SOCIOLOGICAL PERSPECTIVES ON MORAL MOTIVATION

STEVEN HITLIN

The surge in interdisciplinary research on morality in the past 2 decades has offered the possibility of empirically engaging classic philosophical debates about the nature of human action. Understandably, much of that research has been at the individual level, even as some classic scholars focused on the collective nature of moral life and how a society's priorities, culturally pre-scribed roles, socialization practices, and local moral orders shape individual motivation for moral (or not) behavior. Individuals certainly make choices, but they do so within structural and historical contexts not of their making. In this chapter, I offer a range of potential lenses to think about how individuals develop moral motivation within larger structures, ideally contributing to a more interdisciplinary focus on these issues.

Sociology, as a field, has a less explicit concern with motivation than might be expected for a discipline focused on social action. Theories of collective human behavior make necessarily simplified assumptions or elide the concept. Perhaps it is fairer to say that, in a field that attempts to model the cacopho-nous diversity of social forms, influences, and behaviors found in different societies and environments, and at different points in the life course, positing

https://doi.org/10.1037/0000342-002
Motivation and Morality: A Multidisciplinary Approach, M. K. Berg and E. C. Chang (Editors)

any specific motivation as "primary" will be viewed as simplistic. As Martin (2015) suggested, the first rule of sociology is "some do, some don't"; even processes that we would consider, if pressed, as universal (e.g., status and power) are interesting in their particulars, less so in the abstractions that can be generalized across time and place. These concepts, as I discuss here, may imply motivation, but turning to psychological theories of motivation is often unnecessary for developing larger theories of human social behavior. We are fundamentally social creatures, if being concerned with others' views and larger cultural proscriptions counts as motivation, alongside being sensitive to issues of fairness, status, power, and legitimacy. These forces, in any particular context, are filtered through cultural definitions of race, class, gender, and other salient social factors.

The volume of psychological research on moral motivation only partly filters into sociological work on morality, itself a reemerging field (Hitlin & Vaisey, 2013). With a broad overview, the surge in concern with "values" in sociology in the 1950s and 1960s led to a backlash about the totalizing nature of this work and a subsequent lessening of concern with morality for a few decades; precisely the time that Kohlberg's work (e.g., 1971) catalyzed a variety of psychological approaches to the topic, across subfields. Sociology has made only a few statements that directly address the nature of motivation (Turner, 1987; Vaisey, 2009), although motivations are implied in many of the different models posited about the social world. However, our diverse approaches to morality might inform more psychologically oriented work, offering some tools for thinking about the preconditions, contexts, and consequences of moral phenomena that can aid in the development of an interdisciplinary science of morality. Moral psychology has blossomed over the past 70 years or so, with Ellemers et al. (2019) concluding that this focus on core issues (social notions of right and wrong, the moral self, and moral thought and experience) has largely overlooked larger, shared social aspects of societal moral guidelines. This is where a sociological imagination can be instructive. Whereas the classic theorists (Kohlberg, notably) assumed a universal notion of moral motivation (Nunner-Winkler, 1993), more recent work has expanded on this, and sociological approaches attempt to confront the diversity of moral phenomena within and across societies.

We are motivated to seem plausibly, if not maximally, moral, within a range of sociological constructions of the idea of collective behavior. Others' views of us both define our senses of self and serve as correctives for how well our behavior, appearance, and utterances fit within larger sets of expectations. Much of sociology examines the construction and reproduction of those expectations, outside of needing to engage the mindsets of the people who internalize them. This, however, is changing, and in this chapter I aim to provide a partial road map to some sociological constructs that might be useful to a broader, transdisciplinary understanding of morality.

SOCIOLOGICAL PERSPECTIVES

In sociological parlance, the goal of encountering our field is to develop a sense of the *sociological imagination*, a counterintuitive (for Americans, at least) way of understanding the forces that shape our lives. C. Wright Mills (1959) coined the term, which is described as the intersection of personal history and public biography, or how personal troubles often reflect "public issues." This imagination tries to link one's individual circumstances to wider social trends; not finding a job during a recession, for example, feels like a personal failing, but it happens within a wider, more challenging context. As members of a discipline, sociologists want to develop the capacity for people to incorporate this wider conceptualization of social, economic, and cultural factors into shaping their worlds, choices, and outcomes.

Especially in individualistically oriented countries (like the United States), where cultural beliefs, media discussion, and personal orientations steer us toward the notion that the individual is a "master of their fate," many people blanch at the notion that their choices are circumscribed or that they often make choices to similar to those of other people who share their particular racial, geographic, religious (etc.) background. Collectivist countries, most often Asian nations (e.g., Japan, China), tend to have citizens who factor these larger forces and social groupings into their senses of self and their conceptualization of their bounded choice sets and the ramification of their actions. They are motivated, put more broadly, by a wider range of concerns than the self-focused, inwardly oriented ideal type represented by individualistic countries. We see self-focused motivation especially in America, where 2020 debates over "freedom" came to dominate individual responses to public health mandates, with significant portions of the population evidencing concern for personal comfort over potential inconveniences like wearing masks or staying out of crowded indoor spaces. The lodestone for such motivated behavior becomes what the self wants and less so what might be helpful to wider social groupings.

Mills also offered a skeptical take on social science's ability to understand human motivation; instead, and generations of sociologists have learned in this vein, he offered the notion of *vocabularies of motive* (Mills, 1940), or culturally acceptable articulations that describe motivation—but are not necessarily related to whatever one's "true" motivation is in a given situation—that must be learned and deployed properly according to societal standards within situations. I can tell you that I jaywalked because Zeus commanded me to do it, but that is not the proper vocabulary for this time and place, although at one point and place in human history that might have been accepted as a plausible motive.

Thus, a certain level of skepticism runs through the field about the capacity of scientists to determine the "true" motivations for any behavior as well as the fact that we typically problematize the notion that human behavior is "caused" by internal factors. There is not universal agreement on this point, but as a field sociologists share what Martin (2001) termed the *sociological hunch*, the belief that things outside of us shape our behaviors and whatever is inside of us. In this sense, findings about so-called moral hypocrisy (Batson et al., 1997, 2002) may be less surprising to sociologists, who do not expect much consistency between putatively internalized articulations behind action and actual behavior (see also Vaisey, 2009).

The dawn of sociological thinking is deeply intertwined with issues of morality and its connection to societal forms (Hodgkiss, 2013), with classical work seeking to explain (and sometimes justify) morality (Bykov, 2017). Over the past century, sociological study of morality declined greatly, in part because of the demise of a particular brand of reifying social patterns termed *structural functionalism* that overtook the field (Bargheer & Wilson, 2018). Emile Durkheim, one of the field's progenitors, was explicitly concerned with the ways societal institutions shaped individual morality, and the binding force of shared moral systems. He believed that the study of society *was* the study of morality (Lukes, 1985), but he used the term "sociology" to fit in with the development of the fledgling field across Europe around the turn of the last century.

Durkheim, like some classic psychologists, views humans as struggling between base impulses and higher moral needs shaped by society; morality is a top-down system in this corpus of work (Hookway, 2015). Morality, in Durkheim, has two basic elements: the duty and the good (Rosati & Weiss, 2015); it is not experienced as just a logical, duty-based Kantian code; we feel an imperative for those things we consider in or out of moral bounds (Hitlin, 2008). Durkheim viewed the sacred notion of the self as being rooted in religion, although trends in modernity render the religious basis superfluous (Joas, 2013). For Durkheim, morality is that aspect of society able to motivate the individual to transcend their own selfish interests (Hodgkiss, 2013). This echoes Adam Smith's notion that proper action requires "appropriate" sentiments alongside proper moral judgment (Thacher, 2015). Societal coherence was, for Durkheim, dependent on a shared "intellectual and moral community" (Durkheim, 1973); for him, "every society is a moral society" (Durkheim, 1984/1893).

Once central to inquiry into the nature of the social (Durkheim and Adam Smith treated "moral" and "social" as interchangeable), various paths of empirical and theoretical inquiry pushed concern with morality to the periphery of the discipline. Early sociological theory (see Hitlin, 2021) was, like its philosophical roots, centrally concerned with how the organization of a society shaped individuals' moral outlooks, motivations, and behaviors. The links between, say, the complexity of economic organization and people's senses of responsibility to others was a greater focus in those thinkers (e.g., Durkheim) who are considered progenitors of the sociological canon, then in some of the ancient philosophers, but notions of status, power, societal complexity, and historical accident (see work by Max Weber, e.g., 1921/1978) were discussed extensively as antecedents to contemporary action and moral frameworks.

As the field formalized, especially in the American context, the middle of the 20th century involved some notable models (largely by Talcott Parsons, whose perch at Harvard offered influence even as he tried to separate sociological analysis from the more prevalent field of economics) painted overly unified pictures of societies that, in practice, were riven with class, racial, and ethnic conflicts. For Parsons (1935), the quasimoral notion of "values" was a unifying force that explained a lot about the transmission of goals and behaviors across institutions, and generations, but this was interpreted as being an overly static conception of society (Wrong, 1961) that disturbed many in the field working from less lofty institutions and more engaged with on-the-ground civic struggles. Parsons exemplified a tendency still found in many fields of overgeneralizing traits to a population, although he allowed for more variation than his critics sometimes maintained. Regardless, his approach to society (termed *functionalism*) was viewed as being an apologia for social arrangements that favored and protected a few (e.g., those who went to Harvard) over the rest, and thus moral phenomena were seen as inherently conservative protectors of the current political order and fell out of fashion.

This is one part of a recurrent theme in the academic study of moral issues, the difficulty in trying to discover how people experience motivations toward moral issues that, from a nonacademic perspective, are fundamentally important and cannot maintain a supposedly "neutral" stance. Racism, genocide, and other issues can be studied clinically across the social sciences, but to do so can violate a scientist's own moral code. Other notables, such as

Marx—whose claim that societal morality was epiphenomenal to more structural, economic factors—embedded moral principles into their work while trying to stay purportedly "scientific" (Peffer, 2014). This captures an important divide in the field between those who feel one can study facts in a Weberian, value-free mode and those who feel any scientific inquiry implicates deep moral beliefs (Gorski, 2013, offered a solution to this antinomy).

Sociology has undergone a bit of a resurgence in terms of an interest in morality over the past decade (Abend, 2011, 2014; Hitlin & Vaisey, 2010, 2013; McCaffree, 2015), countering the protests about overly static, totalizing models of society with a focus on diversity, inequality, and proximate social context to understand moral phenomena. This draws heavily on advances in cognate social science disciplines. This reengagement stems from a few factors, not the least of which involved improved measurement and interest in psychology, as classic philosophical problems were translated into testable studies (e.g., Greene & Haidt, 2002; Haidt, 2001). At the same time, cultural sociologists were successfully adding to the field's central focus on social structural forces, highlighting the perceived imperatives that influence behavior, drawing on notions of ideologies, logics, and justifications to incorporate these collectively shaped normative constraints that shape individual orientations toward action.

SOME SOCIOLOGICAL CONCEPTS USEFUL FOR AN INTERDISCIPLINARY SCIENCE OF MORALITY

In a few pieces aimed at summarizing the recent resurgence of interest in the topic of morality in sociology, Hitlin and Vaisey (2010, 2013) have argued for a few principles that the field can contribute to the interdisciplinary exploration of the topic. Building on this call, I will discuss their concern with ecological validity; incorporation of issues of power and status; and a fuller sociological social psychology that incorporates broader understandings of identity, emotion, and self, as well as suggestions for how issues like culture and social networks can contribute to the field.

Perhaps the largest factor motivating (!) a sociological engagement with morality is to build on insights developed in the laboratory or the functional magnetic resonance imaging machine, to find out how actual people in actual situations living actual lives process moral issues alongside the myriad other concerns that a person has while living in the social world. This focus on ecological validity does not necessitate ethnographic specificity, although such studies are illuminating (e.g., Anderson, 2000; Baumgartner, 1989; Gengler,

2012; Kolb, 2014) but rather a multimethod focus on aspects of the contexts that surround and shape the kinds of processes often covered in laboratory research (although we do that, too: see Simpson & Willer, 2008; Simpson et al., 2013). More to the point, Abend (2014) delimited the science of morality as having three levels: (a) the level of practices, discussed earlier, with respect to interactional sociology; (b) the level of people's beliefs and judgments, captured largely in psychological work; and (c) what he termed "the moral background," the societally shaped "second-order elements that facilitate, support or enable" (p. 16) the first two levels of morality. As he put it, in our society it would be "crazy to morally evaluate a pig's behavior" (p. 30); a social community offers complex moral concepts and defines for its members who (or what) is subject to those moral prohibitions.

Social contexts delimit which moral forms are constructed and thus embedded in the local social action (Shadnam, 2015). For example, Altomonte (2020) introduced a notion of *moral polysemy* to demonstrate how situational ambiguity gives actors the freedom to construct situations aimed at different moral outcomes. In her case study, she showed that workers in a postacute care unit specializing in older patients must manage competing organizational goals to both discharge patients quickly while also trying to make sure they are safe enough not to be rehospitalized. Because of the importance given to being "home," and accordant linkages with the moral goal of autonomy, workers would use the ambiguity inherent in moral choices to juggle advocating for clients while also fulfilling organizational dictates. This captures a train of sociological work demonstrating how goods and ideals take on different moral meanings based on contexts and social relationships, such as organ donation (Healy, 2006) and life insurance (Zelizer, 1979), have shifted in moral meaning over time. Healy (2006) and Zelizer (1979) suggested that moral ambiguity is a part of economic life in ways that economics may obscure (Fourcade & Healy, 2007). Altomonte (2020) pointed out that, contrary to the notion that people engaging in interaction must agree on the meaning involved, some relationships function precisely because of moral polysemy, the fact that different parties can attribute different interpretations to the same interaction, allowing things to proceed smoothly.

Status and Power

The psychologist Susan Fiske (2011) posited that social status, represented by one's perceived place in the social (and, a sociologist would extend, economic) hierarchy, shapes the emotional experience people have; we tend to feel envy toward those above us and scorn toward those below. Less work has extended how these ideas extend to social action across the life course, but moral emotions are seen as one energizer for action; Turner (2007) suggested that they are the "teeth" that allow moral codes to have any power over individuals. Hitlin and Harkness (2018) demonstrated that one's culture, shaped by the level of economic inequality in a society, shapes the very tableau and meaning attached to these moral emotions. Kemper (2015) focused on the ways that some moral emotions (shame, guilt, contempt) favor the predominant social order while some others (he suggested anger and sadness/depression) may contribute to disorder.

Psychological evidence supports the notion that higher status people are more likely to engage in unethical behavior (Kraus et al., 2011; Piff et al., 2012) and to motivate less altruism (Piff et al., 2010). Empathy, as a moral motivator, appears to be less felt by upper class people (Côté et al., 2013). More relevant to this chapter, people from higher social classes are more likely to experience different positive emotions than others (Piff & Moskowitz, 2018); specifically, they experience self-motivated emotions (pride, contentment) as compared to the other-directed, bonding emotions (love, awe). Given how these moral emotions are the "teeth" for societal moral codes, more work can explore the motivational properties for action across the life course anchored by one's location in the economic structure.

People seem to rely on their own values in persuasion attempts and not consider the values of those they want to persuade (Feinberg & Willer, 2015). Values dictate how people want to experience the world, whereas emotions capture their actual experiences (Tamir et al., 2016). Morality explains a lot of variation in political orientation, more than basic demographic and religious predictors (Miles & Vaisey, 2015; see also Hofmann et al., 2014).

In the American context in particular, issues of status are intertwined with those of status characteristics like race and gender. Members of certain groups are privileged over others within interaction (Ridgeway, 2006, 2011), obtaining biased positive expectations that can, in turn, bring out more positive interactions. The cultural material that motivates these interactions have baked-in power differentials. Much of sociology engages these processes in different ways. I present one cross-national study by Lamont and colleagues (2016) as but one example of how this process becomes instantiated:

> Morality is salient in the boundary work of our respondents toward whites. (As we have seen, it was also salient when we asked respondents to define themselves.) This is in line with Lamont's (2000) finding that African American working-class men value a caring self, which they contrast with a more disciplined and domineering self among whites. (p. 56)

Thus, expectations for the kinds of people we judge and with whom we interact come from a common culture and, at a core level, this defines what to expect and how we evaluate behavior within the flow of interaction and simply when determining what "others" are like—something that matters for issues of voting and defining policies around in- versus outgroups:

> Taken together, the findings suggest White people's classification choices reflect a boundary-making strategy, not merely statistical inferences. Specifically, when White people perceive a threat to their group's status, they contract the boundary around Whiteness to expel claimants of ambiguous origin. (Abascal, 2020, p. 315)

Self and Identity

The study of self and identity spans social science disciplines, with sociologists focusing perhaps the most on the fact that people are embedded in social structures, organizations, networks, and cultures. This prism accomplishes a few things for thinking through motivation. For one thing, it suggests that motivations any person develops are shaped through encounters with significant others, including family, schools, media, and occupations. At one level, this problematizes the notions that any person has a simple, unified motivational structure, moral or otherwise. My motivations at home are, I hope, distinct from my work motivations, except at some unhelpful level of abstraction (being nice or good in both roles). This embeddedness also filters potential actions through a variety of filters (George Herbert Mead's "generalized other," or perhaps more familiarly, Freud's superego). Some people may develop moral motivation in harmony with their society, as if a society has a single motivation, and others may use an economic decision-making model in all parts of their lives, but most people juggle moral goods and ends while also trying to maintain relationships, live up to social expectations, follow the law, and so on. As mentioned all through this chapter, sociology problematizes the notion of the acontextual person just making random moral decisions about 1900s public transportation (the ubiquitous "trolley dilemma" of studying moral decisions).

Both the self, the myriad sets of feelings and beliefs that a social actor develops in their life, and the various identities that compose that self are relevant for understanding social behavior. Some of us incorporate morality as important in these processes, although much of the field can explain things outside of this domain. However, the notion of the self is a pivot for understanding motivation that involves an element of self-reflexivity in the process. It implies a notion of agency in the sense of not passively experiencing the world, although at the same time the alchemy of our cultural milieu and personal experience leads us to realize values within interaction that seem to be a priori sacred, not subject to personal whims (Joas, 2000). Values do empirically shape behavior (Hitlin, 2003; Miles, 2015) and are linked with specific identities (vaguely, internalized roles). Identities are a form of cultural content that gets internalized and anchors action within specific contexts (Miles, 2014).

One measure of the moral self outside of sociology, but fitting in with theories of identity and behavior, comes from Aquino and Reed (2002), who suggested that the *moral identity* motivates altruistic behavior. They view it more as a trait-based conception, whereas Stets and Carter (2006, 2011) have treated it as more interactionally developed. In both cases, however, the idea is that some people view morality as more of a motivating force than others, and this can be empirically captured using this developed scale. Using a different language, Colby and Damon (1993) suggested that some people unify their personal moral goals with a sense of self-interest to become more effortless moral exemplars. Nisan (1996) similarly suggested that moral motivation is grounded in the desire to present an identity as a good (or good-enough) person, and Godin et al. (2005) suggested that moral norms have more motivational force for some people than others. These different ways of saying similar things are useful steps toward a sociological cataloguing of (a) who develops such motivational aspects, (b) when they come into play, and (c) whether behavioral or life course outcomes differ for people with more or less of these internalized capacities.

From a sociological perspective, there is a level of self-reflexivity inherent in any account of motivation such that we can distinguish (analytically, at least), among impulses, self-reflective narratives (e.g., McAdams, 2013), and the larger cultural community that offers inputs for those individual-level phenomena. Moral motivation, in this view, has a lot of moving parts but requires a careful attention to context (Shadnam, 2015), and it is not something principally found within the actor playing out some sort of stable inner predisposition. In addition, people change over time because of life circumstances and biological aging (Gouveia et al., 2015). Rather than focusing only on internal moral preferences, people incorporate concepts like "identities" to explain how situations lead to various predictable behaviors (e.g., Burke & Stets, 2009; Miles, 2014). Frye (2017) found that cultural narratives shape people's actions through a construction of understandings of moral deservingness in evaluating others' behaviors, such that harsh punishment is seen in certain circumstances as legitimate.

Emotion

Emotions are core to understanding morality (Turner, 2007), and there is a great deal of work in both sociology and psychology on the nature of moral emotions (Haidt, 2003; Turner & Stets, 2006). There is little need to belabor the point here, except to point out the core sociological tenet of emotions: that they are socially shaped, channeled, and experienced. Regardless of the biological substrate, the timing, intensity, and meaning of emotions are shaped through cultural socialization and occurs within the flow of ongoing situations. The moral emotions represent the self-conscious emotions that our species has, to our knowledge, been alone in developing; they require the imaginative capacity to see one's actions through the actual or implied judgments of close others and the wider social community. Moral emotions range from the obvious candidates—shame, guilt, pride, and so forth—to the richer array of human experiences that Abend (2011) considered necessary for a "thick" understanding of morality, including notions like revenge, jealousy, and other concepts that are harder to identify within a magnetic resonance imaging machine. Other notable scholars of morality (e.g., Shweder & Haidt, 2000) have suggested even less uniformity across cultures.

Many people in the field of sociology would agree with, even if they are less aware of, the motivational properties of moral emotions (e.g., Blasi, 1999; Eisenberg, 2000). Specific emotions, such as guilt, motivate certain behaviors or, if left unattended, may contribute to maladaptive mental health. Even though some scholars problematize the possibility of finding a common notion of, say, shame, across cultures (Shweder, 2003), the more sociologically relevant concerns would be the social factors that lead to greater feelings of shame and how that emotion is interpreted in different contexts. Not only is shame considered worse in Western countries because it may motivate relationship restitution in more Eastern countries, but also the very prevalence of the emotion differs on the basis of a society's level of economic inequality (Hitlin & Harkness, 2018).

Boundaries

In any society, these taken-for-granted criteria for defining moral worth play a great role in creating and legitimating inequality (Lamont, 2017). One of the increasingly popular concepts in sociology is the notion of a *boundary* (Pachucki et al., 2007), the criteria group members use to distinguish themselves from others, and which groups are considered morally laudable. Boundaries contain categorial (classification) and behavioral dimensions (Wimmer, 2008) and influence how people sort their social worlds as well as what sorts of activities are considered admirable or detestable. Such boundaries, while operating at the cognitive level, are not generated by individuals but instead exist in a cultural, social space. Part of learning to be a member of any sort of collective involves internalizing this symbolic material, which in turn shapes individual outlooks, behaviors, and motivations.

Two boundaries, moral and cultural ones, are considered core in the ways people sort themselves into groups and define other groups (Lamont et al., 1996). *Moral boundaries* include perceived notions of honesty and selfishness and, like the voluminous psychological literature on in- and outgroups, these are positive criteria assigned to the ingroup. Lamont (2000) detailed, for example, how working-class men in France and America use moral boundaries, consisting of different criteria, to demonstrate how their own social locations have some superiority over those with economic advantages. *Cultural boundaries* involve the lines people use to feel culturally superior to others in terms of their tastes, education, and appreciation of the arts. Americans draw boundaries around salient issues like race and religion, but more compatibly than some theories suggest (Hartmann et al., 2011). People draw boundaries that are based on a constellation of factors (race, religion, language), and boundaries often end up representing the interest of majority groups in a society (Bail, 2008).

Pragmatism

If pressed to identify one growing trend for thinking about morality in the field (say, for a volume on motivation), I would point to the reinvigoration of the classic philosophical notion of American Pragmatism. Scholars consider Pragmatism as inseparable from its American philosophical orientation toward understanding reality as somewhat contingent and not aimed at finding truth as much as finding socially shared, workable notions that foster cooperation and communication, and it has recently been reengaged with sociological treatments of morality.

The foremost exposition on this comes intertwined with a study of bird watching (Bargheer, 2018) that grew into a statement of the nature of human moral experience. Bargheer (2018) demonstrated how we value activities (his use of bird-watching shows how seemingly banal activities can be suffused with this moral valuation) based on societal institutions and the practices they engender. He traced how Britain and Germany developed very different moral interpretations of the same, supposedly nonmoral, leisure activity; for Britain, bird watching is seen as a fun activity, "turning nature into a playground." In the German context at the same time, birds are seen as economic tools and treated more instrumentally. The key is that moral evaluation is embedded in action, established practices and institutions, that are not somehow outside of people's action but comprise behavior and judgment:

Taken together, the analysis of these three aspects gives considerable weight to the claim that morality is a central element of social life, yet it calls into doubt approaches that conceptualize morality as an analytically fixed category or operationalize it as a self-contained entity akin to a variable. The study shows that the boundaries of moral discourses and their relation to practices and institutions are contingent and should thus themselves be made the objects of empirical inquiry. (Bargheer, 2018, p. 256)

Alternatively, as the philosopher Charles Taylor (1989) posited, "Our moral motivations, I think, derive in large part not from abstract reason about what is right in general, but from concrete, highly immediate, and even embodied sensitivity to how our actions fit into the relationships we most value" (p. 262). Smetana (1995) made a similar argument, although in a much more psychologically based context.

In many ways, one might view a sociological perspective on the self and emotion through the lens posited by John Dewey, one of the core American Pragmatists whose reach has extended into modern life. Dewey viewed moral experience not as an abstraction, through which some esoteric fits-all-problems theory (e.g., utilitarianism, Kantianism) is somehow rigorously applied to a concrete situation. Instead, for Dewey, life presents itself as a series of uncertain situations with multiple, conflicting moral factors, and we need to use a cultivated moral imagination, anchored in community standards, to reconcile such issues and make decisions (Fesmire, 2014).

Moral Order

The concept of *moral order* is a distinctly sociological tradition, drawing from different approaches to interaction that can be merged into a general focus on the situated, local, interactional pressures that we feel to behave and follow broad expectations. The details differ, but later thinkers have imputed a moral pressure to the sheer force of expectations to conform, whether on the subway or in an elevator or at home. Perhaps the most prominent sociologist to advocate this technique of examining the microdetails of interaction to demonstrate the power of situations to shape behavior (and, implicitly, motivation), is Erving Goffman. His notion of *dramaturgy* has suffused across fields, but the simplest version is to consider social actors like actors in a play (Goffman, 1959). We analyze a play on the basis of the script, the costumes, and the audience reactions; social life is tantamount to playing roles, and if we "mess up" in a role, it is like stage actors trying to reclaim the collective illusion of the play. If a costume or a set falls apart, it damages the actors' and audience's capacity to maintain the collective fiction necessary for the play to work; regular life is like that, for Goffman, and we develop a great deal of techniques to help each other through the scenes that comprise life or to manage those aspects of ourselves that might seemingly disqualify us as "proper" players in the scene (Goffman, 1963).

The other contributor to this approach, although he felt his work quite distinct from Goffman's, was the ethnomethodologist Howard Garfinkel (1964, 1967). In short, in precisely the kind of summary that he and his crew viewed as anathema, Garfinkel was interested in the most microaspects of interaction. Before being able to talk meaningfully about abstractions like "identity" or "roles," Garfinkel and his students believed we need to study the actual movements people make, the cadences we use to communicate, and the vast range of ways we communicate and police intersubjective activity. There is an implied moral force to all the things we do, unconsciously and on end, to make interactions work smoothly and to fill in the gaps of interaction such that we are able to be mutually understood. For Garfinkel, the amount of work we perform and the moral imperative to do this work is evident when somebody commits a breach. He used to send his students home to do this intentionally, to play the game tic-tac-toe with somebody but instead of placing your "O" after they go first, you would erase their "X," move it to another space on the board, and then place your "O" where their "X" had been situated. This is an almost trivial act that, in practice, generates intense anger and bewilderment. If you sit next to somebody in a sparsely populated movie theater, or take something out of a stranger's grocery cart, you will encounter the kind of incredulity that, for ethnomethodologists, takes the polite veneer of social interaction away and shows how hard we all work to maintain the fiction of a society and the moral force underlying this collectively enacted, fundamentally vital fiction.

The most prolific current translator of these ideas in sociology is Anne Rawls, who for a few decades has consolidated these ideas about the *interaction order* into an accessible notion of the *moral order*. She argued that all societies have implicit rules for interacting necessarily have a mutually understood meaning and predictability and adhering to these tacit rules is itself a moral act (Rawls, 2015). She pulled together strands from Goffman's and Garfinkel's work to demonstrate how the social order, the taken-for-granted rules that members of a social community share and internalize, take on a moral force (Rawls, 2010). As we learn habits of thought, feeling, and behavior, these "automatic, habitual, and implicit processes confer a default status on existing patterns of social organization, whether deliberately designed or not" (Marsden, 2015, p. 321). This organization is taken as natural by socialized members of the community, but it is far from happenstance. These expectations are communicated verbally and nonverbally, and members of shared communities understand a variety of nuance and meaning inherent in all "normal" interaction (Turowetz & Maynard, 2010).

SOCIAL ASPECTS OF MORALITY IN OTHER FIELDS

What we term within sociology *classical theory* is replete with scholars, many of whom are from cognate fields like economics, psychology, and history, and develop Big Ideas about the nature of society and social life. Details vary widely, but in general sociologists begin with society (although what that means is not necessarily agreed on) and then root down into individual functioning. The sociologist Allan Johnson (e.g., Johnson, 2005) gave presentations about an unsubtle metaphor with the board game Monopoly whereby you can understand the game and the motivations of the players without knowing anything about any actual person playing the game. The motivations are inherent in the rules on the box, and the board and turn-taking are set up to encourage greed and attempts to bankrupt one's competitors (like I said, the analogy to capitalism is not subtle).

Modern sociology sees fewer (influential) attempts at Big Theory, treatments of ideas that capture the scope of human social organization, but if one looks around they can see the fruits of a century of focusing on the "social" within some attempts in evolutionary theory, political science, and psychology, with respect to moral motivation and its social aspects.

Biosociality and Evolutionary Arguments

Evolutionary theory is less popular in sociology, in part because of the issue of time frame (changes over the past 100 years of human society certainly outstrip our ability to simply link them to survival of the fittest or genetic changes), although some sociologists have argued that societies are tantamount to biological organisms. However, there is a burgeoning strand of evolutionary theory that places both "social" and "moral" at the center of the evolutionary processes that have shaped the current iteration of the human organism. Many versions of evolutionary logic have turned to the inextricably social processes whereby modern humans shaped their moral architecture, with the now-banal observation that "survival of the fittest" may refer also to groups and not simply individual members of a species. Henrich's (2016) conclusion that for about the last 2 million years "cultural evolutions became the primary driver of our species' genetic evolution" (p. 57) ultimately captures the inherent sociality necessary for a fuller evolutionary understanding explaining modern social life. We have evolved within communal frameworks and are not stuck in some prelinguistic biological state. Turner (2015) suggested that natural selection shapes primary emotions, and then social collectivities elaborate these feelings into forms that motivate social control and social–moral emotions such as shame and guilt. Sociologists tend to leave this sort of thing to other fields; society is complicated enough, and it evidences enough variation around the world in terms of how resources are allocated, people affiliate with others, and what creates status hierarchies that much of this work feels like "just-so" stories. Yet, these primary, prelinguistic aspects of social–emotional orientation are fundamental for understanding human behavior (de Waal, 2009; Flack & de Waal, 2000).

This logic extends to the interplay of biology and social structure through evolution, such that even "universal" processes, such as ingroup biases, seem to have been strengthened in collectivist societies and that, contrary to the popular (outside of academia, for the most part) notion that humans are naturally selfish, we have evolved in cooperative environments to be prewired with positive, binding moral systems (Christakis, 2019). The ability to understand that others are judging oneself through socially shared standards that situate one within the ingroup led to joint commitments and a notion of "we" that evolved well beyond other species (Tomasello, 2016). This sense of mutual agreement motivates altruistic (moral) behavior, in line with other species, but this contributes to a human sense of fairness, justice, and reciprocity that mark human moral motivation. These processes eventually became instantiated through the (sociological) concept of *roles* (Tomasello, 2020), socially created categories that embed social relations within larger societal processes. As people develop a sense of self, these roles become meaningful guiding forces for action, judgment, and feeling (e.g., Burke & Stets, 2009).

Relationship Regulation Models

One of the more structural theories about moral interaction comes from two nonsociologists, Alan Fiske and Tage Rai (2014; Rai & Fiske, 2011), who posited that most violence is morally motivated. Like others (Bandura, 2016; Hitlin, 2008; Luft, 2020) who focus on the mind's capacity to justify almost any actions, Fiske and Rai (2014), in developing *virtuous violence theory*, posited that human relationships are axiomatic to how people experience lives (this is core to sociological theories; see Emirbayer, 1997) and that "people are morally motivated to do violence to create, conduct, protect, redress, terminate, or mourn social relationship with the victim or with others" (pp. 1–2). Morality is about the treatment of others within social relationships (Leach et al., 2015).

Building on A. P. Fiske's (1992, 2004) previous notion of four elemental models of human relationships, people are strongly motivated to act within the precepts outlined by the type of interaction in which they find themselves. If one is acting in a "market" capacity, for example, certain types of behaviors are ruled in and out of bounds, and people expect to be treated differently than if they were a family member or an occupational superior. Put briefly, what one "should" do fits with the broad type of interaction— a core tenet of a century of sociological theorizing, but Fiske's great contribution is to delimit the kinds of structured interactions to four that he argues can be anthropologically determined across societies. This chapter builds on this to suggest that people are highly motivated to maintain important relationships and that much violence can be seen in this vein, potentially justifiable in the minds of perpetrators on that basis alone. Rather than random, Fiske suggests that people experience ruptures in relationships as necessarily leading to violent redress, that the actions that might appear immoral to another audience are fundamentally justified in the minds of the perpetrators. Relationships themselves are "intrinsically motivating" (A. P. Fiske & Haslam, 2005), with people looking to these structures for direction in how to coordinate their behaviors with others. Sunar (2009) offered a conceptual model linking this notion of motivation with Haidt's ubiquitous moral foundations theory (see Graham et al., 2013). Group life is a primary source of our internalized standards (Ellemers & van den Bos, 2012) that motivate social interaction. This is especially true for valued ingroups (Leach et al., 2007), although more so when one's group is widely perceived as putatively moral (Moscatelli et al., 2018).

East and West Cultural Orientations and Morality

The universality of moral emotions is a contested topic (e.g., Young & Saxe, 2011), with evidence supporting both the idea that humans have evolved to have a circumscribed potential moral emotional palate, and the notion that there are core societal differences that cannot ever be truly translated (Shweder, 2003). For example, Americans view anger as linked to shame more so than Asian Indians (Menon & Shweder, 1994).

Perhaps the most sweeping, and influential, model of these differences stems from Markus and Kitayama's (1991) distinction between the East and West. This theory covers all manner of cognition (Nisbett, 2004) and emotion, and I will not belabor it here. With respect to moral emotions, however, issues of guilt (for example) are suggested to be differentially experienced depending on which side of this putative divide one grows up

(Bedford & Hwang, 2003). Confucian societies, for example, experience the self as mutable and thus experience guilt as a potential motivator for self-improvement within a web of social obligations (Wong & Tsai, 2007). Motivation to lie, for example, might be due to a desire to keep smoother social relations in Eastern cultures (Wang et al., 2012). Some authors (e.g., Buchtel et al., 2015) have suggested that Eastern cultures, which are based more in Confucianism, are anchored in an interpersonal sense of duty rather than a more abstract, rights-based Western conception.

At a slightly lower level of abstraction, Shalom Schwartz (2013) provided evidence that countries are meaningful analytical units for studying culture, and this holds true for his influential study of values as well as other notable country-level examinations of moral phenomena that putatively motivate individual action. That said, there is more variance in values, a motivational aspect of self linked to social structure (e.g., Hitlin & Piliavin, 2004), within than across countries (Hanel et al., 2017), so sociologists are wary of over-generalization at the national level.

Recent explorations around the world have suggested that moral judgment is linked with societal structural characteristics in notable ways (Awad et al., 2018), demonstrating three moral clusters of countries (Western, Eastern, and Southern). In Awad et al.'s (2018) study, more unequal economies (measured with the Gini coefficient, an efficient and widely used measure of economic inequality at the societal level) predicted harsher judgment of poor people, and gender gaps in health predicted harsher judgment of imagined female characters.

Inglehart (2018) took a different approach to linking culture to individual motivation, arguing that "people's values and behavior are shaped by the degree to which survival is secure" (p. 1), thus connecting perceived social organization to the kinds of concerns individuals prioritize and are theoretically motivated to pursue. Another perspective that has recently been growing in popularity suggests cultures can be categorized as "tight" versus "loose," with different perceived binding strengths of social norms that motivate more (or less) conformity (Gelfand, 2018). The issue here is not to adjudicate which cultural-level theory is the most explanatory but merely to model a range of approaches (many of which are outside of sociology) that link societal culture to individual functioning, treating issues of moral (and other) motivation somewhat as a dependent, socially shaped variable. Nunner-Winkler (1998) posited two steps of moral development: (a) the obtaining of moral knowledge as something distinct from (b) the motivation to act morally. Keller et al. (1998) suggested that moral development lags behind moral knowledge in the global West and that these two aspects are merged earlier in Chinese education.

CONCLUSION

For some sociologists, in particular, those located at the more micro end of the spectrum focusing on interaction and internal experience, becoming acquainted with the field of motivation can help our work. Much of the field, however, has focused on larger patterns like organizations, family types, racialized cultural messages, and social networks have been quite successful relying on only rudimentary, often unarticulated notions of motivation. Perhaps egotistically, I might suggest we have some concepts and findings about socially organized phenomena that influence moral action, thought, and feeling, and some general perspectives that can aid interdisciplinary dialogue.

The issue is, given our epistemological priors, it is not easy to boil down what these helpful constructs might be, at least in terms of easily testable hypotheses that generalize across people and situations. Finding universal principles will be tricky, especially for a thick morality that is at the root of much sociological inquiry. From my perspective, I am partial to theories that try to incorporate specificity, cultural variation, and some general principles, such as the study of values or of status across cultures. Linking individual functioning to levels of economic and social inequality allows both for some general patterns to evolve without assuming all people represent the sorts of weird people that we in the West often study, like college sophomores (who statistically do not even represent Americans).

Sociology is largely in agreement on the distinction between what people think motivates them and what might actually motivate them. Vaisey's (2009) work incorporated a simplified notion of the ubiquitous dual-process psychology to demonstrate that, when asked the reasons for quasi-moral behavior, American adolescents offer often incoherent predictions and justifications. However, some broad survey items that tap into implicit worldviews are strong, temporal predictors of such behavior. This lends a note of caution to interpreting any findings, statistical or otherwise, through one's favorite theory. People may act in line with theories of rational actors, or status-seeking ones, but often they act in ways that are surprising, and the best theories often explain only a relatively small portion of an R^2. Given the parameter that people have multiple and conflicting identities, goals, and accordant motivation (Hitlin, 2008), if you want to identify one, you can likely find evidence for it. But that does not mean it is the central, or only, causal factor.

Morality, in this broad perspective, has some universal properties, but much of the variation in motivation and behavior is culturally determined and, within that, shaped by the amount of power and status an individual has, in both society and the situation under study. Depending on one's perspective, morality is either a subset of human action, or any society is shaped by the notion that adhering to local norms is itself moral behavior. Psychologists term much of this as "conventional" norms—those that elide issues of harm—but fairness, justice, and other core properties may or may not constitute the realm of morality, depending on one's perspective. Wearing the proper clothes to a funeral, or not wearing a protective mask on an airplane, or heckling a professional athlete, may be seen by some as moral violations and by others as simply personal choices.

This review ultimately offers little in terms of easily digestible take-away points; if anything, the sociology of morality revolves around a notion that people are complicated. The environment, broadly understood to include cultural beliefs, structural patterns and resources, a historical era, and local situated pressures, is a powerful influence on moral behavior, motivation, and justification. Human beings may or may not evidence consistency; sometimes they act in line with personal dictates and at other times in line with situational pressures. Often, we do not know why we behave as we do. Social and political conflicts revolve precisely around differences in definition and judgment about the realm of morality (e.g., Lamont, 2000); the sociological interesting issues involve how to capture this, through the lens that most people most of the time believe they have the right motivations. It complicates the development of a universalistic set of claims. What sociologists can offer are theories and strategies of measurement for concepts that are referenced, if not centered, in the study of morality: culture, society, social class, identity, and so forth.

A sociology of morality points toward avenues of exploration and measurement to get some handle on this variance. Social class matters, for example, in some patterned ways across societies. Gender is a powerful influence on the development of motivation. People with power tend to be unaware of how that power shapes their moral behavior, and most people justify their actions with a range of culturally available moral precepts. Ideally, some of the work discussed in this chapter can be explored in the context of other research agendas, in the service of truly developing an interdisciplinary understanding of human morality.

REFERENCES

Abascal, M. (2020). Contraction as a response to group threat: Demographic decline and Whites' classification of people who are ambiguously white. *American Sociological Review, 85*(2), 298–322. https://doi.org/10.1177/0003122420905127

Abend, G. (2011). Thick concepts and the moral brain. *Archives Européennes de Sociologie, 52*(1), 143–172. https://doi.org/10.1017/S0003975611000051

Abend, G. (2014). *The moral background: An inquiry into the history of business ethics*. Princeton University Press. https://doi.org/10.1515/9781400850341

Altomonte, G. (2020). Exploiting ambiguity: A moral polysemy approach to variation in economic practices. *American Sociological Review, 85*(1), 76–105. https://doi.org/10.1177/0003122419895986

Anderson, E. (2000). *Code of the street: Decency, violence, and the moral life of the inner city*. W. W. Norton.

Aquino, K., & Reed, A., II (2002). The self-importance of moral identity. *Journal of Personality and Social Psychology, 83*(6), 1423–1440. https://doi.org/10.1037/0022-3514.83.6.1423

Awad, E., Dsouza, S., Kim, R., Schulz, J., Henrich, J., Shariff, A., Bonnefon, J.-F., & Rahwan, I. (2018). The Moral Machine experiment. *Nature, 563*(7729), 59–64. https://doi.org/10.1038/s41586-018-0637-6

Bail, C. A. (2008). The configuration of symbolic boundaries against immigrants in Europe. *American Sociological Review, 73*(1), 37–59. https://doi.org/10.1177/000312240807300103

Bandura, A. (2016). *Moral disengagement: How people do harm and live with themselves*. Worth.

Bargheer, S. (2018). *Moral entanglements: Conserving birds in Britain and Germany*. University of Chicago Press. https://doi.org/10.7208/chicago/9780226543963.001.0001

Bargheer, S., & Wilson, N. H. (2018). On the historical sociology of morality. *European Journal of Sociology, 59*(1), 1–12. https://doi.org/10.1017/S0003975618000012

Batson, C. D., Kobrynowicz, D., Dinnerstein, J. L., Kampf, H. C., & Wilson, A. D. (1997). In a very different voice: Unmasking moral hypocrisy. *Journal of Personality and Social Psychology, 72*(6), 1335–1348. https://doi.org/10.1037/0022-3514.72.6.1335

Batson, C. D., Thompson, E. R., & Chen, H. (2002). Moral hypocrisy: Addressing some alternatives. *Journal of Personality and Social Psychology, 83*(2), 330–339. https://doi.org/10.1037/0022-3514.83.2.330

Baumgartner, M. P. (1989). *The moral order of a suburb*. Oxford University Press.

Bedford, O., & Hwang, K.-K. (2003). Guilt and shame in Chinese culture: A cross-cultural framework from the perspective of morality and identity. *Journal for the Theory of Social Behaviour, 33*(2), 127–144. https://doi.org/10.1111/1468-5914.00210

Blasi, A. (1999). Emotions and moral motivation. *Journal for the Theory of Social Behaviour, 29*(1), 1–19. https://doi.org/10.1111/1468-5914.00088

Buchtel, E. E., Guan, Y., Peng, Q., Su, Y., Sang, B., Chen, S. X., & Harris, M. (2015). Immorality East and West: Are immoral behaviors especially harmful, or especially uncivilized? *Personality & Social Psychology Bulletin, 41*(10), 1382–1394. https://doi.org/10.1177/0146167215595606

Burke, P. J., & Stets, J. E. (2009). *Identity theory*. Oxford University Press. https://doi.org/10.1093/acprof:oso/9780195388275.001.0001

Bykov, A. (2017). Altruism: New perspectives of research on a classical theme in sociology of morality. *Current Sociology, 65*(6), 797–813. https://doi.org/10.1177/0011392116657861

Christakis, N. A. (2019). *Blueprint: The evolutionary origins of a good society*. Hachette Book Group.

Colby, A., & Damon, W. (1993). The uniting of self and morality in the development of extraordinary moral commitment. In T. E. Wren & G. G. Noam (Eds.), *The moral self* (pp. 149–174). MIT Press.

Côté, S., Piff, P. K., & Willer, R. (2013). For whom do the ends justify the means? Social class and utilitarian moral judgment. *Journal of Personality and Social Psychology, 104*(3), 490–503. https://doi.org/10.1037/a0030931

de Waal, F. (2009). *The age of empathy: Nature's lessons for a kinder society.* Crown.

Durkheim, E. (1973). *Emile Durkheim on morality and society* (R. N. Bellah, Ed.). University of Chicago Press.

Durkheim, E. (1984). *The division of labor in society* (S. Lukes, Ed.). Free Press. (Original work published 1893) https://doi.org/10.1007/978-1-349-17729-5

Eisenberg, N. (2000). Emotion, regulation, and moral development. *Annual Review of Psychology, 51*(1), 665–697. https://doi.org/10.1146/annurev.psych.51.1.665

Ellemers, N., & van den Bos, K. (2012). Morality in groups: On the social-regulatory functions of right and wrong. *Social and Personality Psychology Compass, 6*(12), 878–889. https://doi.org/10.1111/spc3.12001

Ellemers, N., van der Toorn, J., Paunov, Y., & van Leeuwen, T. (2019). The psychology of morality: A review and analysis of empirical studies published from 1940 through 2017. *Personality and Social Psychology Review, 23*(4), 332–366. https://doi.org/10.1177/1088868318811759

Emirbayer, M. (1997). Manifesto for a relational sociology. *American Journal of Sociology, 103*(2), 281–317. https://doi.org/10.1086/231209

Feinberg, M., & Willer, R. (2015). From gulf to bridge: When do moral arguments facilitate political influence? *Personality and Social Psychology Bulletin, 41*(12), 1665–1681. https://doi.org/10.1177/0146167215607842

Fesmire, S. (2014). *Dewey.* Routledge. https://doi.org/10.4324/9780203816899

Fiske, A. P. (1992). The four elementary forms of sociality: Framework for a unified theory of social relations. *Psychological Review, 99*(4), 689–723. https://doi.org/10.1037/0033-295X.99.4.689

Fiske, A. P. (2004). Relational models theory 2.0. In N. Haslam (Ed.), *Relational models theory: A contemporary overview* (pp. 3–25). Erlbaum.

Fiske, A. P., & Haslam, N. (2005). The four basic social bonds: Structures for coordinating interaction. In M. W. Baldwin (Ed.), *Interpersonal cognition* (pp. 267–298). Guilford Press.

Fiske, A. P., & Rai, T. S. (2014). *Virtuous violence: Hurting and killing to create, sustain, end, and honor social relationships.* Cambridge University Press. https://doi.org/10.1017/CBO9781316104668

Fiske, S. T. (2011). *Envy up, scorn down: How status divides us.* Russell Sage Foundation.

Flack, J. C., & de Waal, F. B. M. (2000). "Any animal whatever": Darwinian building blocks of morality in monkeys and apes. *Journal of Consciousness Studies, 7*(1–2), 1–29.

Fourcade, M., & Healy, K. (2007). Moral views of market society. *Annual Review of Sociology, 33*(1), 285–311. https://doi.org/10.1146/annurev.soc.33.040406.131642

Frye, M. (2017). Cultural meanings and the aggregation of actions: The case of sex and schooling in Malawi. *American Sociological Review, 82*(5), 945–976. https://doi.org/10.1177/0003122417720466

Garfinkel, H. (1964). Studies of the routine grounds of everyday activities. *Social Problems, 11*(3), 225–250. https://doi.org/10.2307/798722

Garfinkel, H. (1967). *Studies in ethnomethodology*. Prentice Hall.

Gelfand, M. J. (2018). *Rule makers, rule breakers: How culture wires our minds, shapes our nations, and drives our differences*. Constable & Robinson.

Gengler, A. M. (2012). Defying (dis)empowerment in a battered women's shelter: Moral rhetorics, intersectionality, and processes of control and resistance. *Social Problems*, *59*(4), 501–521. https://doi.org/10.1525/sp.2012.59.4.501

Godin, G., Conner, M., & Sheeran, P. (2005). Bridging the intention–behaviour "gap": The role of moral norm. *British Journal of Social Psychology*, *44*(4), 497–512. https://doi.org/10.1348/014466604X17452

Goffman, E. (Ed.). (1959). *The presentation of self in everyday life*. Doubleday.

Goffman, E. (Ed.). (1963). *Stigma: Notes on the management of spoiled identity*. Prentice Hall.

Gorski, P. S. (2013). Beyond the fact/value distinction: Ethical naturalism and the social sciences. *Society*, *50*(6), 543–553. https://doi.org/10.1007/s12115-013-9709-2

Gouveia, V. V., Vione, K. C., Milfont, T. L., & Fischer, R. (2015). Patterns of value change during the life span: Some evidence from a functional approach to values. *Personality and Social Psychology Bulletin*, *41*(9), 1276–1290. https://doi.org/10.1177/0146167215594189

Graham, J., Haidt, J., Koleva, S., Motyl, M., Iyer, R., Wojcik, S. P., & Ditto, P. H. (2013). Moral foundations theory: The pragmatic validity of moral pluralism. *Advances in Experimental Social Psychology*, *47*, 55–130. https://doi.org/10.1016/B978-0-12-407236-7.00002-4

Greene, J., & Haidt, J. (2002). How (and where) does moral judgment work? *Trends in Cognitive Sciences*, *6*(12), 517–523. https://doi.org/10.1016/S1364-6613(02)02011-9

Haidt, J. (2001). The emotional dog and its rational tail: A social intuitionist approach to moral judgment. *Psychological Review*, *108*(4), 814–834. https://doi.org/10.1037/0033-295x.108.4.814

Haidt, J. (2003). The moral emotions. In R. J. Davidson, K. R. Scherer, & H. H. Goldsmith (Eds.), *Handbook of affective sciences* (pp. 852–870). Oxford University Press.

Hanel, P., Vione, K., Hahn, U., & Maio, G. R. (2017). Value instantiations: The missing link between values and behavior? In S. Roccas & L. Sagiv (Eds.), *Values and behavior* (pp. 175–190). Springer. https://doi.org/10.1007/978-3-319-56352-7_8

Hartmann, D., Winchester, D., Edgell, P., & Gerteis, J. (2011). How Americans understand racial and religious differences: A test of parallel items from a national survey. *The Sociological Quarterly*, *52*(3), 323–345. https://doi.org/10.1111/j.1533-8525.2011.01209.x

Healy, K. (2006). *Last best gifts: Altruism and the market for human blood and organs*. University of Chicago Press. https://doi.org/10.7208/chicago/9780226322384.001.0001

Henrich, J. (2016). *The secret of our success: How culture is driving our evolution, domesticating our species, and making us smarter*. Princeton University Press. https://doi.org/10.1515/9781400873296

Hitlin, S. (2003). Values as the core of personal identity: Drawing links between two theories of the self. *Social Psychology Quarterly*, *66*(2), 118–137. https://doi.org/10.2307/1519843

Hitlin, S. (2008). *Moral selves, evil selves: The social psychology of conscience*. Palgrave Macmillan. https://doi.org/10.1057/9780230614949

Hitlin, S. (2021). Morality and sociological theory. In S. Abrutyn & O. Lizardo (Eds.), *Handbook of classical sociological theory* (Vol. 2, pp. 631–649). Springer. https://doi.org/10.1007/978-3-030-78205-4_29

Hitlin, S., & Harkness, S. K. (2018). *Unequal foundations: Inequality, morality, and emotions across cultures*. Oxford University Press.

Hitlin, S., & Piliavin, J. A. (2004). Values: Reviving a dormant concept. *Annual Review of Sociology, 30*, 359–393. https://doi.org/10.1146/annurev.soc.30.012703.110640

Hitlin, S., & Vaisey, S. (2010). Back to the future: Reviving the sociology of morality. In S. Hitlin & S. Vaisey (Eds.), *Handbook of the sociology of morality* (pp. 3–14). Springer. https://doi.org/10.1007/978-1-4419-6896-8_1

Hitlin, S., & Vaisey, S. (2013). The new sociology of morality. *Annual Review of Sociology, 39*(1), 51–68. https://doi.org/10.1146/annurev-soc-071312-145628

Hodgkiss, P. (2013). A moral vision: Human dignity in the eyes of the founders of sociology. *The Sociological Review, 61*(3), 417–439. https://doi.org/10.1111/1467-954X.12049

Hofmann, W., Wisneski, D. C., Brandt, M. J., & Skitka, L. J. (2014, September 12). Morality in everyday life. *Science, 345*(6202), 1340–1343. https://doi.org/10.1126/science.1251560

Hookway, N. (2015). Moral decline sociology: Critiquing the legacy of Durkheim. *Journal of Sociology, 51*(2), 271–284. https://doi.org/10.1177/1440783313514644

Inglehart, R. F. (2018). *Cultural evolution: People's motivations are changing, and reshaping the world*. Cambridge University Press. https://doi.org/10.1017/9781108613880

Joas, H. (Ed.). (2000). *The genesis of values*. Polity Press.

Joas, H. (2013). *The sacredness of the person: A new genealogy of human rights*. Georgetown University Press.

Johnson, A. G. (2005). *The gender knot: Unraveling our patriarchal legacy*. Temple University Press.

Keller, M., Edelstein, W., Schmid, C., Fang, F. X., & Fang, G. (1998). Reasoning about responsibilities and obligations in close relationships: A comparison across two cultures. *Developmental Psychology, 34*(4), 731–741. https://doi.org/10.1037/0012-1649.34.4.731

Kemper, T. (2015). Status, power and social order. In E. J. Lawler, S. R. Thye, & J. Yoon (Eds.), *Order on the edge of chaos: Social psychology and the problem of social order* (pp. 208–226). Cambridge University Press. https://doi.org/10.1017/CBO9781139924627.012

Kohlberg, L. (1971). Stages of moral development. *Moral Education, 1*(51), 23–92.

Kolb, K. H. (2014). *Moral wages: The emotional dilemmas of victim advocacy and counseling*. University of California Press. https://doi.org/10.1525/9780520958661

Kraus, M. W., Piff, P. K., & Keltner, D. (2011). Social class as culture: The convergence of resources and rank in the social realm. *Current Directions in Psychological Science, 20*(4), 246–250. https://doi.org/10.1177/0963721411414654

Lamont, M. (2000). *The dignity of working men: Morality and the boundaries of gender, race and class*. Harvard University Press. https://doi.org/10.4159/9780674039889

Lamont, M. (2017). *Prisms of inequality: Moral boundaries, exclusion, and academic evaluation*. Praemium Erasmianum Foundation. https://scholar.harvard.edu/

lamont/publications/prisms-inequality-moral-boundaries-exclusion-and-academic-evaluation

Lamont, M., Schmalzbauer, J., Waller, M., & Weber, D. (1996). Cultural and moral boundaries in the United States: Structural position, geographic location, and lifestyle explanations. *Poetics*, *24*(1), 31–56. https://doi.org/10.1016/0304-422X(96)00005-8

Lamont, M., Silva, G. M., Welburn, J., Guetzkow, J., Mizrachi, N., Herzog, H., & Reis, E. (2016). *Getting respect: Responding to stigma and discrimination in the United States, Brazil, and Israel.* Princeton University Press. https://doi.org/10.2307/j.ctv346qr9

Leach, C. W., Bilali, R., & Pagilaro, S. (2015). Groups and morality. In M. Mikulincer, P. R. Shaver, J. F. Dovidio, & J. A. Simpson (Eds.), *APA handbook of personality and social psychology: Vol. 2. Group processes* (pp. 123–149). American Psychological Association. https://doi.org/10.1037/14342-005

Leach, C. W., Ellemers, N., & Barreta, M. (2007). Group virtue: The importance of morality (vs. competence and sociability) in the positive evaluation of in-groups. *Journal of Personality and Social Psychology*, *93*(2), 234–249. https://doi.org/10.1037/0022-3514.93.2.234

Luft, A. (2020). Theorizing moral cognition: Culture in action, situations, and relationships. *Socius*, *6*, 237802312091612. https://doi.org/10.1177/2378023120916125

Lukes, S. (1985). *Emile Durkheim: His life and work; a historical and critical study.* Stanford University Press.

Markus, H., & Kitayama, S. (1991). Culture and the self: Implications for cognition, emotion, and motivation. *Psychological Review*, *98*(2), 224–253. https://doi.org/10.1037/0033-295X.98.2.224

Marsden, P. V. (2015). Social order from the bottom up? In E. J. Lawler, S. R. Thye, & J. Yoon (Eds.), *Order on the edge of chaos: Social psychology and the problem of social order* (pp. 309–322). Cambridge University Press. https://doi.org/10.1017/CBO9781139924627.017

Martin, J. L. (2001). On the limits of sociological theory. *Philosophy of the Social Sciences*, *31*(2), 187–223. https://doi.org/10.1177/004839310103100203

Martin, J. L. (2015). *Thinking through theory.* W. W. Norton.

McAdams, D. P. (2013). The psychological self as actor, agent, and author. *Perspectives on Psychological Science*, *8*(3), 272–295. https://doi.org/10.1177/1745691612464657

McCaffree, K. (2015). *What morality means: An interdisciplinary synthesis for the social sciences.* Springer.

Menon, U., & Shweder, R. A. (1994). Kali's tongue: Cultural psychology and the power of shame in Orissa, India. In S. Kitayama & H. R. Markus (Ed.), *Emotion and culture: Empirical studies of mutual influence* (pp. 241–282). American Psychological Association. https://doi.org/10.1037/10152-007

Miles, A. (2014). Addressing the problem of cultural anchoring: An identity-based model of culture in action. *Social Psychology Quarterly*, *77*(2), 210–227. https://doi.org/10.1177/0190272514524062

Miles, A. (2015). The (re)genesis of values: Examining the importance of values for action. *American Sociological Review*, *80*(4), 680–704. https://doi.org/10.1177/0003122415591800

Miles, A., & Vaisey, S. (2015). Morality and politics: Comparing alternate theories. *Social Science Research*, *53*, 252–269. https://doi.org/10.1016/j.ssresearch.2015.06.002

Mills, C. W. (1940). Situated actions and vocabularies of motive. *American Sociological Review*, 5(6), 904–913. https://doi.org/10.2307/2084524

Mills, C. W. (Ed.). (1959). *The sociological imagination*. Oxford University Press.

Moscatelli, S., Menegatti, M., Albarello, F., Pratto, F., & Rubini, M. (2018). Can we identify with a nation low in morality? The heavy weight of (im)morality in international comparison. *Political Psychology*, 40(1), 93–110. https://doi.org/10.1111/pops.12504

Nisan, M. (1996). Personal identity and education for the desirable. *Journal of Moral Education*, 25(1), 75–83. https://doi.org/10.1080/0305724960250108

Nisbett, R. (2004). *The geography of thought: How Asians and Westerners think differently . . . and why*. Simon & Schuster.

Nunner-Winkler, G. (1993). The growth of moral motivation. In G. G. Noam & T. E. Wren (Eds.), *The moral self* (pp. 269–291). MIT Press.

Nunner-Winkler, G. (1998). The development of moral understanding and moral motivation. *International Journal of Educational Research*, 27(7), 587–603. https://doi.org/10.1016/S0883-0355(97)00056-6

Pachucki, M. A., Pendergrass, S., & Lamont, M. (2007). Boundary processes: Recent theoretical developments and new contributions. *Poetics*, 35(6), 331–351. https://doi.org/10.1016/j.poetic.2007.10.001

Parsons, T. (1935). The place of ultimate values in sociological theory. *The International Journal of Ethics*, 45(3), 282–316.

Peffer, R. G. (2014). *Marxism, morality, and social justice*. Princeton University Press.

Piff, P. K., Kraus, M. W., Côté, S., Cheng, B. H., & Keltner, D. (2010). Having less, giving more: The influence of social class on prosocial behavior. *Journal of Personality and Social Psychology*, 99(5), 771–784. https://doi.org/10.1037/a0020092

Piff, P. K., & Moskowitz, J. P. (2018). Wealth, poverty, and happiness: Social class is differentially associated with positive emotions. *Emotion*, 18(6), 902–905. https://doi.org/10.1037/emo0000387

Piff, P. K., Stancato, D. M., Côté, S., Mendoza-Denton, R., Keltner, D. (2012). Higher social class predicts increased unethical behavior. *Proceedings of the National Academy of Sciences*, 109(11), 4086–4091. https://doi.org/10.1073/pnas.1118373109

Rai, T. S., & Fiske, A. P. (2011). Moral psychology is relationship regulation: Moral motives for unity, hierarchy, equality, and proportionality. *Psychological Review*, 118(1), 57–75. https://doi.org/10.1037/a0021867

Rawls, A. W. (2010). Social order as moral order. In S. Hitlin & S. Vaisey (Eds.), *Handbook of the sociology of morality* (pp. 95–121). Springer. https://doi.org/10.1007/978-1-4419-6896-8_6

Rawls, A. W. (2015). Interaction order: The making of social facts. In E. J. Lawler, S. R. Thye, & J. Yoon (Eds.), *Order on the edge of chaos: Social psychology and the problem of social order* (pp. 227–247). Cambridge University Press. https://doi.org/10.1017/CBO9781139924627.013

Ridgeway, C. (2006). Status construction theory. In P. J. Burke (Ed.), *Contemporary social psychological theories* (pp. 301–323). Stanford University Press. https://doi.org/10.1515/9780804768047-015

Ridgeway, C. L. (2011). *Framed by gender: How gender inequality persists in the modern world*. Oxford University Press. https://doi.org/10.1093/acprof:oso/9780199755776.001.0001

Rosati, M., & Weiss, R. (2015). Tradition and authenticity in post-conventional world: A Durkheimian reading. *Sociologias, 17*(39), 110–159. https://doi.org/10.1590/15174522-017003904

Schwartz, S. H. (2013). National culture as value orientations: Consequences of value differences and cultural distance. In V. A. Ginsburgh & D. Throsby (Eds.), *Handbook of the economics of art and culture* (Vol. 2, pp. 547–586). Elsevier. https://doi.org/10.1016/B978-0-444-53776-8.00020-9

Shadnam, M. (2015). Theorizing morality in context. *International Review of Sociology, 25*(3), 456–480. https://doi.org/10.1080/03906701.2015.1050309

Shweder, R. A. (2003). Toward a deep cultural psychology of shame. *Social Research, 70*(4), 1110–1129. https://doi.org/10.1353/sor.2003.0035

Shweder, R. A., & Haidt, J. (2000). The cultural psychology of the emotions: Ancient and new. In M. Lewis & J. M. Haviland-Jones (Eds.), *Handbook of emotions* (pp. 397–414). Guilford Press.

Simpson, B., Harrell, A., & Willer, R. (2013). Hidden paths from morality to cooperation: Moral judgments promote trust and trustworthiness. *Social Forces, 91*(4), 1529–1548. https://doi.org/10.1093/sf/sot015

Simpson, B., & Willer, R. (2008). Altruism and indirect reciprocity: The interaction of person and situation in prosocial behavior. *Social Psychology Quarterly, 71*(1), 37–52. https://doi.org/10.1177/019027250807100106

Smetana, J. G. (1995). Morality in context: Abstractions, ambiguities and applications. In R. Vasta (Ed.), *Annals of child development* (Vol. 10, pp. 83–130). Jessica Kingsley.

Stets, J. E., & Carter, M. J. (2006). The moral identity: A principle level identity. In K. McClelland & T. J. Fararo (Eds.), *Purpose, meaning, and action: Control system theories in sociology* (pp. 293–316). Palgrave Macmillan. https://doi.org/10.1007/978-1-137-10809-8_12

Stets, J. E., & Carter, M. J. (2011). The moral self: Applying identity theory. *Social Psychology Quarterly, 74*(2), 192–215. https://doi.org/10.1177/0190272511407621

Sunar, D. (2009). Suggestions for a new integration in the psychology of morality. *Social and Personality Psychology Compass, 3*(4), 447–474. https://doi.org/10.1111/j.1751-9004.2009.00191.x

Tamir, M., Schwartz, S. H., Cieciuch, J., Riediger, M., Torres, C., Scollon, C., Dzokoto, V., Zhou, X., & Vishkin, A. (2016). Desired emotions across cultures: A value-based account. *Journal of Personality and Social Psychology, 111*(1), 67–82. https://doi.org/10.1037/pspp0000072

Taylor, C. (Ed.). (1989). *Sources of the self: The making of the modern identity.* Harvard University Press.

Thacher, D. (2015). The perception of value: Adam Smith on the moral role of social research. *European Journal of Social Theory, 19*(1), 94–110. https://doi.org/10.1177/1368431014567267

Tomasello, M. (2016). *A natural history of human morality.* Harvard University Press. https://doi.org/10.4159/9780674915855

Tomasello, M. (2020). The role of roles in uniquely human cognition and sociality. *Journal for the Theory of Social Behaviour, 50*(1), 2–19. https://doi.org/10.1111/jtsb.12223

Turner, J. H. (1987). Toward a sociological theory of motivation. *American Sociological Review, 52*(1), 15–27. https://doi.org/10.2307/2095389

Turner, J. H. (2007). *Human emotions: A sociological theory*. Routledge. https://doi.org/10.4324/9780203961278

Turner, J. H. (2015). The evolutionary biology and sociology of social order. In E. J. Lawler, S. R. Thye, & J. Yoon (Eds.), *Order on the edge of chaos: Social psychology and the problem of social order* (pp. 18–42). Cambridge University Press. https://doi.org/10.1017/CBO9781139924627.003

Turner, J. H., & Stets, J. E. (2006). Moral emotions. In J. H. Turner & J. E. Stets (Eds.), *Handbook of the sociology of emotions* (pp. 544–566). Springer.

Turowetz, J. J., & Maynard, D. W. (2010). Morality in the social interactional and discursive world of everyday life. In S. Hitlin & S. Vaisey (Eds.), *Handbook of the sociology of morality* (pp. 503–526). Springer. https://doi.org/10.1007/978-1-4419-6896-8_27

Vaisey, S. (2009). Motivation and justification: A dual-process model of culture in action. *American Journal of Sociology, 114*(6), 1675–1715. https://doi.org/10.1086/597179

Wang, X.-L., Bernas, R., & Eberhard, P. (2012). When a lie is not a lie: Understanding Chinese working-class mothers' moral teaching and moral conduct. *Social Development, 21*(1), 68–87. https://doi.org/10.1111/j.1467-9507.2011.00619.x

Weber, M. (1978). *Economy and society*. University of California Press. (Original work published 1922)

Wimmer, A. (2008). The making and unmaking of ethnic boundaries: A multilevel process theory. *American Journal of Sociology, 113*(4), 970–1022. https://doi.org/10.1086/522803

Wong, Y., & Tsai, J. (2007). Cultural models of shame and guilt. In J. L. Tracy, R. W. Robins, & J. P. Tangney (Eds.), *The self-conscious emotions: Theory and research* (pp. 209–223). Guilford Press.

Wrong, D. H. (1961). The oversocialized conception of man in modern sociology. *American Sociological Review, 26*(2), 183–193. https://doi.org/10.2307/2089854

Young, L., & Saxe, R. (2011). Moral universals and individual differences. *Emotion Review, 3*(3), 323–324. https://doi.org/10.1177/1754073911402383

Zelizer, V. A. (1979). *Morals and markets: The development of life insurance in the United States*. Transaction Books. https://doi.org/10.7312/zeli92046

2 WHAT ARE NORMS, AND HOW IS NORM COMPLIANCE REGULATED?

BERTRAM F. MALLE

Most great apes lived in hierarchical groups, often engaging in fierce battles for position (Boehm, 1999). Even though a few exceptions, like the bonobos, exist today, the main line of our ancestors lived by power and domination. Sometime in the past 2 million years, a remarkable change occurred: The *homo* evolution moved toward social group living that substantially increased cooperation, joint action, teaching, and learning (Boehm, 2000; Tomasello & Vaish, 2013). Perhaps precursors to empathy helped (de Waal & Preston, 2017), but empathy is reactive and local (Bloom, 2016) and can conflict with fairness and justice (Decety & Cowell, 2015). By itself, empathy does not provide a social organization that can sustain a group's success in the most uncertain and harshest environments. Norms do.

Norms are guides to action. They constrain an individual's options in a given context to act in ways that benefit the group, and groups that have a well-functioning norm system function well as groups (Bicchieri, 2006; Chudek & Henrich, 2011; Wilson, 2002). Norms provide organization and regulation of group members' actions that can sustain a group's success even in the face of serious threats—through ice ages, natural catastrophes, and wars.

https://doi.org/10.1037/0000342-003

Motivation and Morality: A Multidisciplinary Approach, M. K. Berg and E. C. Chang (Editors)

But although norms enable group success—and thus, ultimately, individual success—they impose costs on the individual, thus tempting them to avoid those costs. Two questions therefore arise. First, what motivates individuals to resist this temptation and comply with the group's norms? Second, how does the group strengthen compliance? To answer these questions, I first clarify what norms are. I then examine how norms regulate behavior at the individual level, how they regulate behavior at the social level, and how these levels are intimately entwined.

WHAT ARE NORMS?

The importance of norms has long been recognized in sociology and economics (Elster, 1989; Hechter & Opp, 2001; Horne & Mollborn, 2020; Schelling, 1960). These fields aim to explain how human cooperation is possible despite the individual's self-interest. Norms are therefore treated as an external force that constrains human action. But the social sciences have rarely addressed how norms operate cognitively, in such a way that enables norms (as external forces) to succeed at guiding behavior. A person complying with norms must have something in their mind that allows their action to conform to the norm; they must have a *norm representation*. A few empirical studies have examined the automatic activation of such norm representations by situation cues—for example, garbage on the floor triggers the "Don't litter" norm (Cialdini et al., 1990), or the sight of a library triggers the "Be quiet" norm (Aarts & Dijksterhuis, 2003). But exactly what is activated?

Definition

A cognitive and social model of norms must clarify what norms are. The following definition integrates several overlapping proposals (Bicchieri, 2006; Brennan et al., 2013; Cialdini et al., 1991; Malle et al., 2017, 2021):

> A norm N is a directive, in a given social community S, to (not) perform an action A in a given context C, provided that (i) a sufficient number of individuals in the community demand of each other, with a certain deontic force D^f, to follow the directive and (ii) a sufficient number of individuals in the community do follow it with prevalence P.

Using this definition, we can differentiate norms, norm representations, and norm-based motivation. First, for something to be a norm N of A in C, conditions (i) and (ii) must hold true. Second, for a community member to have a representation of N, the person must believe (consciously or not) that conditions (i) and (ii) hold. Third, for someone to have a norm-based motivation to *A* in *C*, the person must both believe conditions (i) and (ii) and try to (not) *A* because of conditions (i) and (ii).

Elaboration

A norm directs action, and this directive can be a *prescription* (directing the person to act a certain way) or a *prohibition* (directing the person to not act a certain way; see Folger & Whiting, 2020; Janoff-Bulman & Carnes, 2013; McNamara, 2006). In either case, people may not be aware that a norm influences their action, or the norm can be so internalized that it feels like (or cognitively becomes) a personal goal. In some cases, people are fully aware of the norm, such as when they struggle with a conflict between norms or between personal goals and norms.

Every norm has a deontic force D^f, indicating how strongly people demand of each other to (not) perform *A* (Horne & Mollborn, 2020; Malle, 2020). For example, a prescription may be weak (as in a suggestion) or strong (as in a requirement). The motivation to comply with norms will therefore vary in a roughly proportional way to the norm's deontic force. Compliance also varies with the *prevalence* of a norm—the (perceived) frequency with which community members actually follow the norm. High prevalence facilitates norm activation (Cialdini et al., 1990; Lindenberg, 2013) and signals the presence of a norm's deontic force (Eriksson & Strimling, 2015). Seeing that everybody stands in line to order ice cream makes the strength of that norm clear; seeing that hardly any bicyclist stops at the stop sign highlights the weakness of that norm (Cullum et al., 2012). People can misperceive prevalence or deontic force (Prentice & Miller, 1996), which illustrates that behavior is caused by norm representations, not by some objective force of norms themselves.

Community Specificity

Norms are rarely[1] universal—most of them exist relative to a social community *S*, at a certain time and place. For example, the social norm of wearing a mask in public varies widely (as of this writing) in different regions of the

---

[1]Or never. Some authors have proposed that a norm of reciprocity is universal and innate (e.g., Krebs & Janicki, 2004), but reciprocity is more akin to a principle or a social process than a norm. It would be meaningless as a concrete action direction: "Reciprocate!" How? To what? To make it meaningful would require context constraints because reciprocating is not always prescribed (e.g., not when the other's favor is strategic or when the other does something immoral), and many constraints vary according to culture (e.g., rules of gift giving and matching).

United States. Moreover, communities are nested, such that norms vary across nations, across states within nations, urban and rural regions within states, neighborhoods within regions, and so on. Even within any given community, individuals will vary to some degree—because of different learning histories, different competing personal interests, or different sensitivities to community demands. However, for a norm to exist, enough community members must reasonably agree on D^f for A in C.

Context Specificity

Being on the phone is forbidden in a train's quiet car but required on the trading floor; killing another person, prohibited in many contexts, is permitted in self-defense and prescribed in war and executions (for communities that allow them). What varies here, *context*, is a fascinating and complex construct. We can think of it as bundles of features that include time (e.g., evening, religious holiday), physical environments (e.g., bathroom, hallway), role (e.g., friend, colleague), interaction type (e.g., first date, business negotiation), and more. Norm compliance therefore requires a refined knowledge of contexts and the ability to recognize them quickly and accurately as well as the norms that are governed by them (Malle et al., 2017). Thus, a norm violation can stem from a misperception of the context one is in (e.g., an informal dinner vs. an extended job interview) rather than from an intention to flout the norm.

Related Concepts

Norms differ from other action guides, such as preferences, goals, and collective habits. The key distinguishing feature is the deontic force condition (i), which ensures that the action in question reflects the community's demands and interests, not merely the individual's desires or benefits. Putting milk in one's coffee is a widespread preference, not a norm, because people do not demand it of each other, and they do it for their own pleasure, not others'. By contrast, getting in line to order coffee is a norm, because that is what people demand of each other, even though each individual would rather place their order without having to wait.

Norms also differ from virtues and values, which have a deontic force but lack other properties of norms. *Virtues* (e.g., generosity or courage) are personality dispositions that a community appreciates in its members, but they are more like ideals than required traits, and as dispositions they lack action and context specificity. *Values* (e.g., fairness, freedom, respect) also lack action and context specificity because they govern large classes of possible actions and outcomes across a wide range of contexts (Serramia et al.,

2018), and it is difficult to teach them by instruction, as most norms can be. However, sets of norms can reflect or implement broader values, such as when sharing norms implement fairness or when politeness norms implement respect (Stohr, 2012).

Features Not Included in the Norm Definition

To define a concept means setting boundaries, excluding certain features that are not part of the defined concept. In this section, I discuss three features that have been proposed as defining features of norms but that I believe should not be part of the definition.

Moral Versus Conventional

The first feature not included in the norm definition just given is the distinction between *moral norms* on one side and *social* or *conventional norms* on the other side (Aharoni et al., 2012; Turiel, 1983). The proposed definition applies to both classes of norms, and the bundle of features traditionally meant to distinguish norms from conventions (e.g., universality, authority independence) are loose and ill defined (Shoemaker, 2014). Moreover, claims of norm universality seem untenable because what is treated as moral rather than merely social–conventional varies significantly across time and communities (Kelly et al., 2007). Mild conventions in one group, such as regarding food or dress, are moral in other groups (e.g., orthodox religious communities). The primary distinguishing feature of moral and conventional norms is deontic force. "Moral" norms are consistently higher in deontic force and, because of that force, other features follow (e.g., that an authority cannot simply cancel the norm). We may want to treat moral norms and social conventions as two prototypes, but the definition of norms offered earlier would seem to hold for both; cognitively, the two prototypes still fall under a common construct (Roughley, 2019).

The Role of Sanctions

The second feature not included in the definition of norms is the presence of *sanctions* (e.g., blaming, shaming, punishment), which some have described as a defining feature of norms (Bendor & Swistak, 2001; Horne & Mollborn, 2020). Sanctions are undoubtedly important. They can be informative in revealing a norm's deontic force (e.g., the most severe punishment is often reserved for violations of the strongest norms), and many communities use sanctions to respond to norm violations. However, sanctions are not the only method to communicate the deontic force of a norm—for example, proactive exhortations or modeling costly compliance (e.g., in rituals), among others, help convey the strength of a norm. And even in response to violations, communities have other tools beside sanctions (see the Alternative Regulation Methods section). Although it would therefore seem misleading to make sanctions part of the *definition* of norms, sanctions are certainly one core element of the regulation and enforcement of norms, as I discuss shortly.

Injunctive and Descriptive Norms

The third feature not included in the definition of norms is the distinction between *injunctive* and *descriptive norms* (Borsari & Carey, 2003; Cialdini et al., 1991; Lapinski & Rimal, 2005). The core of this distinction is between "people's beliefs about what ought to be done" (injunctive) and "beliefs about what is actually done by most others in one's social group" (descriptive; Lapinski & Rimal, 2005, p. 130). Reflecting this important distinction, the norm definition given earlier contains the two conditions of (a) *deontic force* (corresponding to the injunctive property) and (b) *prevalence* (corresponding to the descriptive property). However, these are two properties of norms, not two kinds of norms. If the prevalent pattern of behavior in a group (descriptive norm) is a norm at all, it will have to come with some deontic force; otherwise, it is a mere statistical regularity, perhaps promising cues for personal benefits. Telling a homeowner that neighbors use 20% less energy (a classic descriptive norm) will not activate a genuine norm unless the homeowner infers that saving energy is the right thing to do (deontic force) and they should therefore try harder. Thus, what researchers have studied as descriptive norms is prevalence information about a norm that allows people to infer its deontic force. By contrast, telling a homeowner that neighbors spend 20% less money by shopping at the nearby grocery store is merely descriptive information, not a norm (and therefore not a descriptive norm) because it is beneficial to spend less money, not something (typically) demanded by the community.

REGULATION OF NORM COMPLIANCE

With this conceptual grounding of what norms are, I turn to the question of what regulation mechanisms motivate individuals to comply with norms. A fundamental conflict necessitates this regulation: Following norms may benefit the community but often imposes a cost on the individual (e.g., freedom, time, effort, money; Cooter, 2000), even though it can also benefit the individual, in the end (compared with a situation in which everybody is out for themselves). If community members already tend to do something, there is no reason for a norm to emerge—there are no norms that encourage eating or sleeping, going to restaurants or movie theaters. But if a community benefit carries some cost for the individual, norms may have to come into play, such as for being quiet in a movie theater or (in the United States) for tipping the waitstaff in a restaurant. Because of these costs to the individual, norm compliance requires mechanisms of regulation.

We might draw a distinction between regulation at the individual level (e.g., guilt) and regulation at the social level (e.g., ostracism), even though the subsequent discussion shows that individual mechanisms are very much the product of social processes and that social processes cannot succeed without the individual's psychological readiness (e.g., a need to belong to groups, which makes reintegration valuable). Another distinction may be useful to bring some organization to norm regulation mechanisms, namely, those that are proactive (encouraging compliance in advance) and those that are reactive (responding to violations after they occur). Figure 2.1 shows a selection of regulation mechanisms within this space of individual–social and proactive–reactive groupings that I discuss in the following sections.

Compliance Regulation at the Individual Level

I begin with three regulation mechanisms that occur primarily at the individual level, namely, internalization of norms, feelings of guilt, and justification of norm-compliant actions.

Internalization
Among proactive individual regulation mechanisms, one phenomenon has received a considerable amount of attention in the literature: the internalization of norms. With some variations, most scholars cast internalization as a process of adopting and embracing a social or moral norm so that it becomes an intrinsically motivating personal standard, to which people commit even if explicit demands or sanctioning possibilities are low (Bandura, 1991; Gintis,

FIGURE 2.1. Select Mechanisms That Regulate Compliance With Norms

	Individual	Social
Proactive	Internalization, anticipatory guilt, justification	Norm activation, inducing guilt, demanding justification
Reactive	Guilt, justification	Sanctions, forgiveness, reintegration

2003; Horne, 2003; Schwartz, 1977). Communities have an interest in seeing norms get internalized (Gavrilets & Richerson, 2017), because individuals are more likely not only to follow internalized norms but also to enforce them in others (Hannah et al., 2016; Peysakhovich & Rand, 2016). *Socialization*, the community's teaching of norms, is therefore very much focused on internalization (Grusec & Kuczynski, 1997). If the community can get most individuals to be intrinsically motivated to act the "right" way, then the expected community benefits are likely to obtain.

The success of internalization attempts stems in part from the original norm-learning situation. Kochanska and Aksan (2006) identified *committed compliance* as the willing, eager stance toward social (often parental) influence, such as when an adult teaches a new rule. This receptive stance predicts later internalization—that is, sustained compliance with a norm even when no audience enforces the norm (Kochanska et al., 1995). Internalization has its limits, because there is virtually always some level of personal benefit that can tempt a person into breaking a strongly endorsed norm (Baron & Leshner, 2000). Internalization can also go overboard, when it becomes an inflexible, intolerant moral conviction (Skitka et al., 2021), of which we have seen ample evidence in recent decades in the form of political polarization in the United States.

It is apparent that norm internalization, even though it is in one way a psychological mechanism at the individual level, is deeply entwined with the community's socialization practices and facilitates the social process of communal norm enforcement, which the internalizers are more willing to take on.

Guilt

A second mechanism of individual-level compliance regulation is guilt, which can be reactive or proactive. *Reactive guilt* is the feeling of discomfort after a norm violation (Kochanska & Aksan, 2006; McGraw, 1987), and such feelings predict subsequent prosocial behavior—not only restitution for the one whom one wronged but even benevolence toward others (Freedman et al., 1967). Meta-analyses have shown that guilt induces norm compliance across a wide range of conditions and with a strong and robust effect size (Boster et al., 2016; O'Keefe, 2000). Guilt is *proactive* when a person considers a potential action that would violate a norm and imagines feeling guilty if they were to take the action. This form of *anticipated* guilt has been shown to be impactful in blocking various processes that lead to transgressive behavior, such as moral disengagement (Bandura et al., 1996) or the influence of deviant peers (Svensson et al., 2013). Anticipated guilt is parallel to the role of anticipated regret in nonmoral decision making (Zeelenberg, 2018), but whereas regret is largely a personal emotion, guilt has a strong social component. For one thing, anticipated guilt can activate internalized norms (De Groot & Steg, 2009; Schwartz, 1977), which reflect, as discussed, the impact of social forces. In addition, guilt often co-occurs with shame (Ferguson et al., 2007; Tangney & Dearing, 2002). As a result, anticipated guilt over one's potential norm violation may also invoke anticipated shame, which incorporates other people's evaluations and one's perceived social standing (Maibom, 2010).

Justification

All forms of justification—when reactive for a performed action, or proactive for a planned action—build on the fundamental human tendency to explain intentional actions with reasons, which are the beliefs and desires that provide grounds for acting a particular way (Davidson, 1963; Malle, 2004). In order for reasons to *justify* an action they have to meet a normative criterion—they have to show that the action is somehow in compliance with social–moral norms. Demands for justification arise only when an action in question violates a norm. The agent will try to demonstrate that, in the given context, the norm was suspended (e.g., injuring another person was justified in the context of self-defense) or that the action upheld norms that are more important than the one it violated. For example, yelling at a person in a group conversation may be justified if the person told a racist joke and the norm to resist racism is more important than the norm to not yell at people.

Who decides whether a given explanation justifies the action in question? Often it is the relevant moral community, such as the audience to whom the agent offers the justification. If the audience denies that the context suspends the violated norm or that the action upholds more important norms, the justification will fail. An audience, or moral community, thus provides a check on the agent's proffered justification.

At other times, justifications take place in the mind of the decision maker. They may still be guided by the social community, such as when the person imagines what reasons a relevant moral community would find justifiable (Scanlon, 1998). Such imagined responses, however, can be inaccurate, and the decision maker may rely solely on their own subjective judgment of whether a particular course of action is justifiable. In this case, self-serving and potentially community-damaging justifications may take hold (Bandura, 1999; Mullen & Monin, 2016). For example, decision makers might suppose that everybody else is acting the same way (misrepresenting norm prevalence), that it is not their duty to protect the other (misrepresenting deontic force), or that they have already done a lot of good things ("licensing" the action in question; Green, 1991; Polman et al., 2013; Shalvi et al., 2011).

Justification becomes here the enemy of guilt, and only a challenge from the community may correct that.

Even when justifications pass the challenge by a relevant community, a moral decision may be considered justified by one community and wholly unjustified by another (Cohen & Nisbett, 1994). Human history is full of examples in which members of one group justify acts of oppression, discrimination, or terror that they inflict on another group (Fiske & Rai, 2015). Thus, justifications represent a core tool of regulation, but their value and impact are a function of the particular community's norm system.

Compliance Regulation at the Social Level

Just as we have seen that individual processes of regulating norm compliance rely on social processes, so do social processes rely on individual ones. Among these social processes, I discuss measures of activating norms, instilling guilt, and the sanctions of blame and punishment, along with some alternatives to sanctions.

Norm Activation

For context-specific norms to operate efficiently, they need to be cognitively accessible when the person enters relevant contexts but not in other contexts (e.g., the prescription to talk when meeting someone for coffee but not during a poetry reading). Somehow, the context must activate the relevant norms (Aarts & Dijksterhuis, 2003; Cialdini et al., 1991; Malle et al., 2017; Schwartz, 1977). Internalized norms might be reliably activated even when the person is merely thinking about the context. Other norms may need help from the environment, through physical or symbolic means, or from other people.

What does the activating? The most obvious triggers are physical signs like "Don't lean out the window" or "The line begins here." People also offer verbal reminders ("What's the magic word?" or "This is a no-shoes household"), and they model norm compliance for each other; even just two people queuing will typically suffice to trigger compliance (at least in London). Less obvious triggers lie in the presence of certain objects (e.g., a basket of kippahs at the entrance of a Jewish temple) or the physical arrangements of objects in space (e.g., chairs that indicate where and how far apart to sit).

What is being activated? In most cases, context activates a mental representation of the prescribed or prohibited action, and if the norm representation as a whole is reinstated, then the norm's deontic force will be activated as well. The individual may sense (not necessarily consciously) this deontic force (Folger & Whiting, 2020; Heider, 1958), and the motivational pull toward prescribed actions, or away from prohibited actions, can emerge fast and with a strong (dis)value association (Cushman, 2013; Folger & Whiting, 2020). In these cases, the person will comply with the norm, with little further reasoning, especially when the costs of compliance are low (Diekmann & Preisendörfer, 2003). Many everyday situations are of this kind. We enter a coffee shop and swiftly join the end of the order line; a colleague says, "Good morning," and we immediately return the greeting.

Inducing Guilt

Earlier we saw that guilt as a within-person process relies heavily on social factors. Conversely, the social process of inducing guilt succeeds only if individuals are receptive to such intervention. Guilt induction can be used proactively to persuade others to do what the persuader desires (O'Keefe, 2000), including not to commit a planned transgression ("You will regret this your entire life!"). More common are reactive attempts to make the transgressor feel guilty about a past transgression, often with the aim of deterring the person from committing it again. Either way, inducing guilt is akin to a test: If the person responds as desired (with concern, remorse, perhaps an apology), the deterrence attempt was successful and blame is mitigated (Darby & Schlenker, 1989); if the person does not respond as desired, the planned or repeat transgressions are likely to occur, and more serious interventions may be needed. It is important to note that guilt inductions have teeth only if the moral decision maker in principle shares the relevant norm or cares about the inducer's disapproval. As a result, guilt induction succeeds primarily in smaller communities and in closer relationships (Baumeister et al., 1994). Guilt induction also has its risks (Baumeister et al., 2001), and it can be dysfunctional (Rakow et al., 2011), but modeling, evoking, and nurturing guilt in measured ways is part of ordinary socialization (Abell & Gecas, 1997).

Sanctions

When proactive deterrence fails, when no valid justifications are offered, and neither guilt nor an apology is forthcoming, people turn to *sanctions*. Here I focus on the primary moral sanctioning mechanisms featured in the literature: punishment and blame.[2] Even though the two are often treated as highly similar, in reality they are quite distinct (Baumard, 2011; Buckholtz

---

[2]Although rewards are sometimes used to regulate behavior, mere norm compliance is not normally rewarded (unless it is the first compliance after one or more violations). We would have to reward people nearly all the time for complying with norms; in reality, reward applies to actions that exceed the normative expectations.

et al., 2015; Malle, 2021). I first consider punishment, then blame, as potential forces that respond to norm violations and reinstate compliance.

The Prospects of Punishment for Regulating Norm Compliance

A widely touted proposal is that informal punishment, or even just the threat of punishment, fosters cooperation (Fehr & Gächter, 2000; Gintis, 2000; Yamagishi, 1986). Much of the evidence for this proposal comes from behavioral economics studies, in which people play monetary games that pit self-interest against prosociality. In the public goods game, for example, individuals in small groups have an endowment and can spend any part of it to invest in a group payoff. When most group members contribute, each contributor benefits because investments are multiplied. Free riders benefit even more, but when too many members free-ride, investors lose money, and soon nobody contributes or gains. Yamagishi (1986) showed that instituting punishment as a sanction for free-riding increased cooperation and payoffs. The effect of punishment, however, was far greater in groups composed of low-trusting individuals (who were skeptical of others' cooperation) than in high-trust groups. In another type of game, the Ultimatum game, a "proposer" receives a monetary endowment (e.g., $10) and offers a "responder" a cut of that endowment (say, $3). If the responder accepts the proposer's offer, both receive the allotted money ($3 for the responder and $7 for the proposer); if the responder rejects the offer, neither of them receives any money. Such rejections are infrequent but increase with unfair offers (e.g., 8:2 or 9:1 splits). Rejections are taken to be expressions of costly punishment because people respond to the proposer's norm violation (e.g., a 9:1 split) by foregoing a small amount ($1) themselves and causing the proposer to lose a large amount ($9).

The evidence from behavioral economics games must be met with caution, however, both because of its monetary focus and because of the absence of social interaction or relationships (Pedersen et al., 2013). For punishment to be a major norm regulation mechanism outside of economic games, two things must be true: (a) The punishment must be frequent enough to do the hypothesized regulatory work, and (b) it must be effective enough at fostering norm compliance. There are reasons to doubt both of these propositions. First, consider frequency.

How frequent is punishment? Before humans settled down about 12,000 years ago, they lived in small groups of nomadic hunter–gatherers (Boehm, 1999; Knauft, 1991). The few remaining hunter–gatherer bands studied in the 20th century use little to no punishment to regulate behavior (Baumard, 2010; Guala, 2012). They respond to norm violations with criticism, ridicule, or temporary ostracism rather than with punishment (Wiessner, 2005). In the everyday life of modern societies, punishment is infrequent as well. Using daily surveys to study naturally occurring norm violations, Molho et al. (2020) measured people's motivation to engage in various kinds of punishment, including verbal or physical confrontation, gossip, and withdrawal. People were generally unmotivated to engage in confrontation and somewhat more motivated to gossip or exclude the transgressor. In a cross-cultural study of individuals recalling an instance in which they had witnessed (as a third party) an attack, insult, or other mistreatment (Pedersen et al., 2020), rates of cost-imposing punishment (e.g., yelling, insulting, pushing, hitting) were extremely low, between 1% and 6%, with variations primarily due to caring about the victim of the violation. Hofmann et al. (2018) assessed people's desire to punish a norm violator, a variable that should lead to higher rates than actual punishment behavior because fear of retaliation and other obstacles do not depress the rate of punishment desire. However, whether as victim or third party, people indicated weak desires to punish, from a mean of just over 2 (on a 0–6 scale) when the violator was a romantic partner to just over 3 when the violator was a stranger.

Returning to behavioral economics experiments, which have provided the best evidence for people endorsing and sometimes executing punishment, research increasingly suggests that people have little natural inclination to punish if alternatives to punishment are available (which the original experiments did not offer). For example, when given a choice between punishing the perpetrator and compensating the victim, people prefer the latter (Chavez & Bicchieri, 2013; Ohtsubo et al., 2018). This finding also is also observed in real life, where people who witness a restaurant customer mistreat wait-staff will support the victim rather than directly confront the perpetrator (Hershcovis & Bhatnagar, 2017). Likewise, when given a choice not to punish but to warn others who will interact with the transgressor, people select the latter path (Feinberg, Willer, et al., 2012). People will also try to get out of punishing a perpetrator if they can do so without losing face (Kriss et al., 2016). In the limited cases when people do punish others, they do so as the victim of the transgression or as a close ingroup member to the victim (Bernhard et al., 2006; Pedersen et al., 2018). Even victims of unfair offers in the Ultimatum game will often refrain from punishing the proposer when they are granted an opportunity to communicate their disapproval by sending a note (Xiao & Houser, 2005). Finally, it should be noted that people reject unfair offers even when the proposer does not learn they received a punishment or when the rejection has no monetary impact on the proposer. This pattern suggests that people's rejection of unfair offers does not primarily function as inflicting punishment on the transgressor but as a signal to themselves and others that they are no suckers, that they have dignity. However, this signal can be sent just as well with a note of disapproval.

Punishment also does not elicit much social support. People who punish an unfair player are not trusted more by other participants in a subsequent game (Patil et al., 2021); victims who punish are not seen positively, whereas victims who forego punishing the perpetrator are seen as moral, trustworthy, and altruistic (Heffner & FeldmanHall, 2019). Kiyonari and Barclay (2008) showed that, in an economic game context, when given a choice between rewarding or punishing other players, punishers were not rewarded; instead, people overwhelmingly assigned rewards to both cooperators and rewarders of cooperators; the only group that was punished were nonrewarders of cooperators. In a real life setting of a staged act of littering (Balafoutas et al., 2014), only 17% of participants confronted a stranger who littered; they preferred indirect punishment by subsequently withholding help from the violator when he dropped some books. In addition, experimenter-staged punishers of the original norm violator were not rewarded (received no more help than did control individuals). It should be noted that the observed rates of "punishment," low as they already were, relied on a very lenient punishment definition. Participants' response counted as punishment if they "explicitly asked the violator to pick up the cup or expressed disapproval of the norm violation" (Balafoutas et al., 2014, p. 15927), and the experimental manipulation of punishment behavior amounted to a speech act of "Would you please pick up your garbage? The platform is not a garbage bin."

In sum, in presettlement human history and modern life, punishment is infrequent because people prefer other responses to norm violations: compensating victims, rewarding cooperators, warning community members. If they engage with the perpetrator at all, they prefer mild expressions of disapproval, such as verbal criticism, and often they simply ignore or stop interacting with the person (Baumard, 2010; Martin & Cushman, 2015). Whether the latter is self-protection or punishment depends on whether there are any costs to the perpetrator (e.g., true ostracism would carry such costs; Williams, 2009).

How effective is punishment? The second assumption underlying the hypothesized significance of punishment for moral regulation is that it works, that it halts ongoing violations and deters future violations. We saw earlier that weak, low-cost punishment via monetary fines can increase cooperation (Fehr & Gächter, 2000; Yamagishi, 1986), but often it does not (Xiao, 2018), and it can lead to retaliation (Bone et al., 2016). Punishment in behavioral economics games works best when the punishment expresses community norms (Balliet & Van Lange, 2013; Xiao, 2018)—a function, however, that can also be achieved by nonpunishing interventions (Xiao & Houser, 2005).

Research on whether everyday punishment deters repeat violations comes primarily from the educational and developmental literature. To be effective, punishment must have clear and reliable outcome contingencies (Cipani, 2004). Under these conditions, when a child chooses between a compliant action and a violating action, the compliant one (resulting in desired benefits) will be dominant, and punishment rarely has to be applied. When punishment does have to be applied, its form matters. Physical punishment is reliably ineffective (Gershoff & Lee, 2020), whereas fines, withheld benefits, and simultaneous teaching of norms can be effective (e.g., Azrin & Powers, 1975). For both child and adult transgressors, confidence in the prospect of punishment, should the norm violation occur, increases norm compliance (Cipani, 2004; Kura et al., 2015). However, if norm internalization is the ultimate goal, disciplining children must be gentle, deemphasize power assertions, and incorporate positive feelings (Kochanska & Aksan, 2006).

Further evidence for the lack of success of cost-imposing punishment comes from the justice system. Numerous studies on recidivism have demonstrated clear failures of deterrence (Wright & Khade, 2017). Three to 5 years after being released from prison, 30% to 47% of past offenders are rearrested, and 25% to 43% are reimprisoned (compared with the base rate of imprisonment in the United States as a whole of 0.4%; Wagner & Sawyer, 2018). Research on the death penalty, too, shows a lack of deterrent effects (Nagin & Pepper, 2012). In fact, the U.S. South has the highest rate of executions and the highest murder rate; the U.S. Northeast has the lowest rate of executions and the lowest murder rate (Death Penalty Information Center, 2019).

Thus, we face a paradox: If punishment is rare and ineffective, why does it have such a long and brutal human history (Lyons, 2017)? Part of the answer lies in the instrumental benefits of punishment. In a strongly hierarchical society, the powerful defend their power: Rulers pass laws to their advantage, and the majority imposes selectively harsh punishments on the minority (as amply demonstrated in the United States; Tonry, 2009). In addition, over the course of history, the agents of norm enforcement and conflict resolution have shifted from community members to sovereign institutions (Cushman, 2015). This shift may help prevent blood feuds among communities, but, perhaps more important, it allows ordinary people to condemn violators and support their punishment without having to get their hands dirty and their conscience tainted. It is far easier to cheer on the torturer or vote for "tough on crime" policies than it is to break the offender's arm oneself or stand guard at a solitary confinement cell. No doubt there are vigilantes, militias, guards, and police officers who welcome opportunities for brutal submission, but most people are averse to harming others (Grossman, 1996; McDonald et al., 2017). They prefer to leave punishment to professionals and institutions, but violence abounds if the latter remain unchecked.

The systematic delegation of harsh punishment to institutions also explains why people are commonly portrayed as *retributivists*—desiring proportional, and often painful, punishment of norm violators, even when it has no deterrent function (Carlsmith et al., 2002; Keller et al., 2010). What the research actually shows is that people recommend or endorse proportional punishment for crimes. People mimic the familiar institutional punishment tendencies because that is what they have learned all their lives and presumably think is the proper response. People's real attitudes toward punishment and their own punishment behavior may tell a different story. When there is less priming of crime and punishment institutions, people want a *response* from the perpetrator (Funk et al., 2014; Gollwitzer et al., 2011) and want the perpetrator to *learn* something (Cushman, 2015). People don't necessarily want everyday norm violators to suffer deeply if a lesser intervention promises norm compliance. However, when people consider those who assault, rape, and kill others, they see severe punishment as an acceptable response (O'Hear & Wheelock, 2020).

To summarize, evidence suggests that everyday punishment is infrequent, unpopular, and effective only under specific conditions. Thus, punishment is unlikely to be the primary social regulator of norm compliance in everyday life. Punishment, which has arisen over the past 12,000 years, may enjoy popular support, not because people are deep-seated retributivists but because they have adopted the logic and practice of institutional punishment. As a threat, punishment sometimes works (Gächter et al., 2008)—people do slow down (briefly) when they see a police car on the highway; however, a standard legal punishment is surprisingly ineffective (National Institute of Justice, 2016; Yukhnenko et al., 2020) and appears to serve more the continued affirmation of dominance hierarchies than the successful social regulation of norm compliance (Sidanius & Pratto, 1999).

The Prospects of Moral Criticism for Regulating Norm Compliance

The term *blaming* is often used to refer to unjustified, unfair attacks, such as in the "blame game" (Knobloch-Westerwick & Taylor, 2008), in which accusations of others are used to deflect fault from oneself. Dysfunctional forms of blame certainly exist (Douglas, 1995; Furlong & Young, 1996), but this is not the meaning of blaming I focus on here. The question I pursue is whether blaming as functional moral criticism, grounded in considerations of facts at hand (Malle et al., 2014), can and does regulate norm compliance.

Whereas punishment is a more recent phenomenon that emerged as part of the hierarchies and legal systems after human settlement, blame is an older form of regulation that predominated in small hunter–gatherer societies and continues to exist prominently today. We have seen that punishment is typically coercive regulation, often institutionally anchored, to correct or incapacitate transgressors. Blame is socially expressed moral criticism, often among equals, typically with room for explanation, corrective action, and reconciliation (Voiklis & Malle, 2018). This gentler, more cooperative tool of regulation stems in part from the social demands in small groups. In a band of 30, each member is needed, and debilitating sanctions hurt the community. Furthermore, an egalitarian social structure forbids assertations of power by coercively punishing a norm violator and instead favors communication, sometimes ridicule, and thus a threat to social reputation (Wiessner, 2005). Repeat offenders are ignored, isolated, or, as a last measure, expelled from the group.

This more measured approach to communicate moral criticism is grounded in blame judgments, which appear to be the most complex and well-calibrated moral judgments (Malle, 2021; Monroe & Malle, 2019). They are formed from a range of information: the norm that was violated; the agent's causal contribution to the violation; whether the contribution was intentional; if it was perceived as intentional, what the person's reasons were and their potential justification; and if it was perceived as unintentional, whether the agent should have and could have prevented the violation (Alicke, 2000; Laurent et al., 2016; Malle et al., 2014). Being sensitive to all this information enables blame to be a graded and evidence-based moral judgment.

My colleagues and I have proposed that part of the reason for the evidence-based information processing in blame judgments is the fact that people appreciate that even modest blame is costly (Malle et al., 2014, 2022). Costs for the perpetrator include loss of status, damage to a relationship, and bad feelings; costs for the blamer include risk of retaliation and embarrassment if blame is misplaced; and even for other community members, costs arise from the burden of damaged relationships within the group and the potential for unfair treatment (e.g., false accusations) that would be toxic to the community. In light of these costs, the community puts demands on expressed blame, namely, that blame is backed by evidence and is proportional to the violation and its circumstances. When challenged, a blamer has to be able to present the relevant evidence and thus offer *warrant* for the act of blaming (Malle et al., 2014; Voiklis & Malle, 2018)—to specify, through evidence, why the perpetrator deserves the judged amount of blame. Valid evidence lies in the information that people process when arriving at blame judgments, such as causality, intentionality, reasons, and so on. Such evidence can be contested by the blamer's audience (including the perpetrator)—for example, that the violation was not intentional, or that it was intentional but done for justified reasons. In the course of debating the evidence, the judgment can become refined, further attuned to the facts of the case. If demands for warrant hold, then blame judgments have what, in the law, has been called *procedural fairness* (Tyler & Jost, 2007) and hold promise for effective regulation of norm compliance.

How frequent is blame? Researchers sometimes call "punishment" what seems, on closer inspection, to be moral criticism. In Molho et al.'s (2020) study, when participants recalled their responses to acts they deemed morally wrong, they reported confronting the perpetrator 35% of the time. However, about 78% of the confronting acts were communications, requests, or explanations, and the rest were shouting and yelling and, in one case, withdrawal of help (see Molho et al., 2020, supplementary materials, pp. 23–24). Contrast this with Pedersen et al.'s (2020) recall study, in which the rates of more explicit third-person punishment (e.g., hitting, insulting) ranged from 1% to 6%. In studies that have observed naturally occurring moral criticism, rates vary greatly by context. When alone in facing a stranger who littered, 4% of people in Greece (Balafoutas & Nikiforakis, 2012), and 17% in Germany (Balafoutas et al., 2014), asked the norm violator to pick up the garbage. In greater safety, around others in a train's silent car, 50% of people told a stranger to turn off their music (Przepiorka & Berger, 2016). And when in a crowd, 19% in Greece (Balafoutas & Nikiforakis, 2012), but up to 75% in Germany (Wolbring et al., 2013), verbally intervened when a stranger blocked an escalator's fast left lane. Once more, the most common interventions were requests or demands to move, verbally or with a tap on the shoulder.

Third-person blaming refers to telling other people about a norm violation when the norm violator is absent. Molho et al. (2020) found that people who witnessed a violation preferred to talk about it with others (gossip) over confronting the violator, especially when they had less power and when the norm violations were severe. People who gossip to make norm followers known to others can guide community members' own partner choice (Feinberg, Willer, et al., 2012; Smith, 2014). However, such warnings may veer into punishment when they actively damage reputation and impose opportunity costs (Feinberg, Cheng, & Willer, 2012).

How effective is blame? The behavioral economics literature shows positive effects of blame in the form of expressed disapproval. In a voluntary-contribution game, such expressions raised cooperation as much as monetary "punishment" (Masclet et al., 2003); in a coordination game, expressed disapproval led to near-optimal collective outcomes (Dugar, 2010); and in the Ultimatum game discussed earlier, even just anticipating communication between proposer and responder increased proposers' offer levels, presumably to avert potential moral criticism (Capizzani et al., 2017). Such anticipated blame is powerful in smaller communities, where a potential norm violator will interact with, and be criticized by, potential future witnesses or victims. In such communities, the power of gossip and reputation encourage people to selectively choose cooperators and ostracize defectors, which can bring those defectors back to normal levels of cooperation (Feinberg et al., 2014).

Dersley and Wootton (2000) reported that 95% of second-person complaints (many of which can be classified as blaming) are, to some degree, contested, and Alberts (1989) found that 65% of spousal responses to their partner's complaints were denials and justifications. Such contested communication between victim and perpetrator can have benefits, however, because the purpose of blame is not only to change the other's behavior but also to mark a problem, reaffirm norms, and reconcile.

Individual Requirements for the Success of Sanctions

In the foregoing discussion it should have become clear that social sanctions, in the form of punishment or blame, by no means automatically alter the perpetrator's course of action. The individual must be sensitive to the sanction— fearing punishment, feeling hurt by criticism, worrying about their reputation. Indeed, except for psychopaths, people value being accepted in social communities, as they have a "need to belong" (Baumeister & Leary, 1995), strive to be "morally adequate" (Steele, 1988), and suffer pain from social rejection (Eisenberger et al., 2003; Williams, 2009). This, in short, is the contract: Behave according to our norms, and we will value you as one of us; violate our norms, and we will take from you what you value: us.

Alternative Regulation Methods

I have extensively discussed punishment and moral criticism, in part because research has devoted so much attention to these two social regulation responses and in part because they do appear predominant in modern life. However, there are historic, indigenous, and novel social and legal practices that offer alternatives but are only slowly being recognized in the literature.

One of the more frequently discussed mechanisms is forgiveness. Rather than demanding punishment, the victim or community expresses their grievance but forgives the perpetrator and allows victim–perpetrator relationships to be restored (Gobodo-Madikizela, 2008). There is evidence that forgiving a transgressor actually reduces the likelihood of repeat transgressions (Wallace et al., 2008), but acknowledgment of the wrongdoing appears to be necessary in many cases before forgiveness is granted (Hamber, 2007; Vollhardt et al., 2014). In addition, for some atrocities, feelings of hurt and revenge on the victim's side simply do not allow forgiveness (Kurgan, 2001). When forgiveness is possible, it often has benefits for the victim: Those who forgive feel a sense of justice (Wenzel & Okimoto, 2010), are seen as moral and trustworthy (Heffner & FeldmanHall, 2019), and receive more support from community members (Hershcovis & Bhatnagar, 2017).

A second mechanism is *restorative justice*, which has a good track record in lowering recidivism in the legal domain (Kennedy et al., 2019) and in improving psychological outcomes among crime victims (Goodmark, 2015; Lloyd & Borrill, 2020). Its success may in part stem from its reliance on the structure of moral criticism in its best form, where acknowledgement of the violation, norm affirmation, and reconciliation replace damaging penalties— practices that overlap with a number of indigenous justice systems (Chartrand & Horn, 2016; Wielenga et al., 2020). It should be noted that restorative justice still imposes costs on the perpetrator, such as facing the victim, addressing the violation and the damage that violation caused, experiencing guilt, and sometimes providing compensation. In this sense, restorative justice is not free of retribution (Goodwin & Gromet, 2014), and some "retributive" measures (but not classic punishment) may actually improve its outcomes (Gromet & Darley, 2006).

A final alternative, probably the least known and most ambitious, is *transformative justice* (Barrie, 2020; Generation FIVE, 2007). Like restorative justice, it rejects the destructive and ineffective carceral system and considers the perpetrator as part of a larger community. It goes further by aiming to not only restore but also transform the relationships among perpetrator, victim, and community (Barrie, 2020). Transformative justice does not force the victim to reconcile with or forgive the perpetrator; instead, it demands insight, accountability, and change, not only from the perpetrator but also from the community. It thereby tries to change the broader causal nexus that enabled the violation in the first place (Howe, 2018), often with a longer term perspective, such as ending child sexual abuse within five generations (Generation FIVE, 2007). The transformative process includes reflecting on community norms, both identifying norms that are harmful (e.g., those that enable child sexual abuse) and those that create accountability, safety, and healing (Ansfield & Colman, 2012). Transformative justice may not be a standard mechanism of regulating norm compliance, but it offers a community-level analysis that the common discourse of sanctions rarely considers.

CONCLUSION

No human community can exist without norms. As mental representations of directives that the community puts on individuals, norms steer their actions toward community benefits, with small sacrifices asked of the individual. These sacrifices may at times feel natural, even desirable, in the case of internalized norms, but the tension between individual and community interests generally requires regulation to motivate individuals to comply with norms. In this chapter, I have discussed norm internalization and norm activation; guilt, felt and anticipated by the individual and encouraged by the community; action justifications, offered by the individual and challenged by the community; and sanctions and their alternatives, enacted by the community and enabled by the individual's valuing of community reintegration. All of these mechanisms are imperfect, and some are outright counterproductive. However, from the early, perhaps simpler beginnings of hunter–gatherer groups, human norm regulation has evolved to uphold social benefits even as our society of strangers has become larger and stranger.

Humans are deeply social learners; not merely in the sense that they excel in social forms of learning but also in the sense that they so easily learn what it means to be social, to respect and live within the norms of one's community.

REFERENCES

Aarts, H., & Dijksterhuis, A. (2003). The silence of the library: Environment, situational norm, and social behavior. *Journal of Personality and Social Psychology, 84*(1), 18–28. https://doi.org/10.1037/0022-3514.84.1.18

Abell, E., & Gecas, V. (1997). Guilt, shame, and family socialization: A retrospective study. *Journal of Family Issues, 18*(2), 99–123. https://doi.org/10.1177/019251397018002001

Aharoni, E., Sinnott-Armstrong, W., & Kiehl, K. A. (2012). Can psychopathic offenders discern moral wrongs? A new look at the moral/conventional distinction. *Journal of Abnormal Psychology, 121*(2), 484–497. https://doi.org/10.1037/a0024796

Alberts, J. K. (1989). A descriptive taxonomy of couples' complaint interactions. *The Southern Communication Journal, 54*(2), 125–143. https://doi.org/10.1080/10417948909372751

Alicke, M. D. (2000). Culpable control and the psychology of blame. *Psychological Bulletin, 126*(4), 556–574. https://doi.org/10.1037/0033-2909.126.4.556

Ansfield, B., & Colman, T. (2012). Confronting sexual assault: Transformative justice on the ground in Philadelphia. *Tikkun, 27*(1), 41–44. https://doi.org/10.1215/08879982-2012-1018

Azrin, N. H., & Powers, M. A. (1975). Eliminating classroom disturbances of emotionally disturbed children by positive practice procedures. *Behavior Therapy, 6*(4), 525–534. https://doi.org/10.1016/S0005-7894(75)80009-8

Balafoutas, L., & Nikiforakis, N. (2012). Norm enforcement in the city: A natural field experiment. *European Economic Review*, *56*(8), 1773–1785. https://doi.org/10.1016/j.euroecorev.2012.09.008

Balafoutas, L., Nikiforakis, N., & Rockenbach, B. (2014). Direct and indirect punishment among strangers in the field. *Proceedings of the National Academy of Sciences of the United States of America*, *111*(45), 15924–15927. https://doi.org/10.1073/pnas.1413170111

Balliet, D., & Van Lange, P. A. M. (2013). Trust, punishment, and cooperation across 18 societies: A meta-analysis. *Perspectives on Psychological Science*, *8*(4), 363–379. https://doi.org/10.1177/1745691613488533

Bandura, A. (1991). Social cognitive theory of moral thought and action. In W. M. Kurtines & J. L. Gewirtz (Eds.), *Handbook of moral behavior and development: Vol. 1. Theory* (pp. 45–103). Erlbaum.

Bandura, A. (1999). Moral disengagement in the perpetration of inhumanities. *Personality and Social Psychology Review*, *3*(3), 193–209. https://doi.org/10.1207/s15327957pspr0303_3

Bandura, A., Barbaranelli, C., Caprara, G. V., & Pastorelli, C. (1996). Mechanisms of moral disengagement in the exercise of moral agency. *Journal of Personality and Social Psychology*, *71*(2), 364–374. https://doi.org/10.1037/0022-3514.71.2.364

Baron, J., & Leshner, S. (2000). How serious are expressions of protected values? *Journal of Experimental Psychology: Applied*, *6*(3), 183–194. https://doi.org/10.1037/1076-898X.6.3.183

Barrie, H. (2020). No one is disposable: Towards feminist models of transformative justice. *Journal of Law and Social Policy*, *33*(1), 65–92.

Baumard, N. (2010). Has punishment played a role in the evolution of cooperation? A critical review. *Mind & Society*, *9*(2), 171–192. https://doi.org/10.1007/s11299-010-0079-9

Baumard, N. (2011). Punishment is not a group adaptation. *Mind & Society*, *10*(1), 1–26. https://doi.org/10.1007/s11299-010-0080-3

Baumeister, R. F., & Leary, M. R. (1995). The need to belong: Desire for interpersonal attachments as a fundamental human motivation. *Psychological Bulletin*, *117*(3), 497–529. https://doi.org/10.1037/0033-2909.117.3.497

Baumeister, R. F., Stillwell, A. M., & Heatherton, T. F. (1994). Guilt: An interpersonal approach. *Psychological Bulletin*, *115*(2), 243–267. https://doi.org/10.1037/0033-2909.115.2.243

Baumeister, R. F., Stillwell, A. M., & Heatherton, T. F. (2001). Interpersonal aspects of guilt. In W. G. Parrott (Ed.), *Emotions in social psychology: Essential readings* (pp. 295–305). Psychology Press.

Bendor, J., & Swistak, P. (2001). The evolution of norms. *American Journal of Sociology*, *106*(6), 1493–1545. https://doi.org/10.1086/321298

Bernhard, H., Fischbacher, U., & Fehr, E. (2006, August 24). Parochial altruism in humans. *Nature*, *442*(7105), 912–915. https://doi.org/10.1038/nature04981

Bicchieri, C. (2006). *The grammar of society: The nature and dynamics of social norms*. Cambridge University Press.

Bloom, P. (2016). *Against empathy: The case for rational compassion*. Ecco.

Boehm, C. (1999). *Hierarchy in the forest: The evolution of egalitarian behavior*. Harvard University Press. https://doi.org/10.4159/9780674028449

Boehm, C. (2000). The origin of morality as social control. *Journal of Consciousness Studies, 7*(1–2), 149–183.

Bone, J. E., Wallace, B., Bshary, R., & Raihani, N. J. (2016). Power asymmetries and punishment in a prisoner's dilemma with variable cooperative investment. *PLOS ONE, 11*(5), e0155773. https://doi.org/10.1371/journal.pone.0155773

Borsari, B., & Carey, K. B. (2003). Descriptive and injunctive norms in college drinking: A meta-analytic integration. *Journal of Studies on Alcohol, 64*(3), 331–341. https://doi.org/10.15288/jsa.2003.64.331

Boster, F. J., Cruz, S., Manata, B., DeAngelis, B. N., & Zhuang, J. (2016). A meta-analytic review of the effect of guilt on compliance. *Social Influence, 11*(1), 54–67. https://doi.org/10.1080/15534510.2016.1142892

Brennan, G., Eriksson, L., Goodin, R. E., & Southwood, N. (2013). *Explaining norms.* Oxford University Press. https://doi.org/10.1093/acprof:oso/9780199654680.001.0001

Buckholtz, J. W., Martin, J. W., Treadway, M. T., Jan, K., Zald, D. H., Jones, O., & Marois, R. (2015). From blame to punishment: Disrupting prefrontal cortex activity reveals norm enforcement mechanisms. *Neuron, 87*(6), 1369–1380. https://doi.org/10.1016/j.neuron.2015.08.023

Capizzani, M., Mittone, L., Musau, A., & Vaccaro, A. (2017). Anticipated communication in the ultimatum game. *Games, 8*(3), 29. https://doi.org/10.3390/g8030029

Carlsmith, K. M., Darley, J. M., & Robinson, P. H. (2002). Why do we punish? Deterrence and just deserts as motives for punishment. *Journal of Personality and Social Psychology, 83*(2), 284–299. https://doi.org/10.1037/0022-3514.83.2.284

Chartrand, L., & Horn, K. (2016). *A report on the relationship between restorative justice and indigenous legal traditions in Canada.* Department of Justice Canada. https://www.justice.gc.ca/eng/rp-pr/jr/rjilt-jrtja/index.html

Chavez, A. K., & Bicchieri, C. (2013). Third-party sanctioning and compensation behavior: Findings from the ultimatum game. *Journal of Economic Psychology, 39*, 268–277. https://doi.org/10.1016/j.joep.2013.09.004

Chudek, M., & Henrich, J. (2011). Culture–gene coevolution, norm-psychology and the emergence of human prosociality. *Trends in Cognitive Sciences, 15*(5), 218–226. https://doi.org/10.1016/j.tics.2011.03.003

Cialdini, R. B., Kallgren, C. A., & Reno, R. R. (1991). A focus theory of normative conduct: A theoretical refinement and reevaluation of the role of norms in human behavior. In M. P. Zanna (Ed.), *Advances in experimental social psychology* (Vol. 24, pp. 201–234). Academic Press. https://doi.org/10.1016/S0065-2601(08)60330-5

Cialdini, R. B., Reno, R. R., & Kallgren, C. A. (1990). A focus theory of normative conduct: Recycling the concept of norms to reduce littering in public places. *Journal of Personality and Social Psychology, 58*(6), 1015–1026. https://doi.org/10.1037/0022-3514.58.6.1015

Cipani, E. (2004). *Punishment on trial.* Context Press.

Cohen, D., & Nisbett, R. E. (1994). Self-protection and the culture of honor: Explaining Southern violence. *Personality and Social Psychology Bulletin, 20*(5), 551–567. https://doi.org/10.1177/0146167294205012

Cooter, R. (2000). Do good laws make good citizens? An economic analysis of internalized norms. *Virginia Law Review, 86*(8), 1577–1601. https://doi.org/10.2307/1073825

Cullum, J., O'Grady, M., Armeli, S., & Tennen, H. (2012). The role of context-specific norms and group size in alcohol consumption and compliance drinking during natural drinking events. *Basic and Applied Social Psychology*, *34*(4), 304–312. https://doi.org/10.1080/01973533.2012.693341

Cushman, F. (2013). Action, outcome, and value: A dual-system framework for morality. *Personality and Social Psychology Review*, *17*(3), 273–292. https://doi.org/10.1177/1088868313495594

Cushman, F. (2015). Punishment in humans: From intuitions to institutions. *Philosophy Compass*, *10*(2), 117–133. https://doi.org/10.1111/phc3.12192

Darby, B. W., & Schlenker, B. R. (1989). Children's reactions to transgressions: Effects of the actor's apology, reputation and remorse. *British Journal of Social Psychology*, *28*(4), 353–364. https://doi.org/10.1111/j.2044-8309.1989.tb00879.x

Davidson, D. (1963). Actions, reasons and causes. *The Journal of Philosophy*, *60*(23), 685–700. https://doi.org/10.2307/2023177

Death Penalty Information Center. (2019). *Murder rates by state by region*. https://deathpenaltyinfo.org/facts-and-research/murder-rates/murder-rates-by-state-by-region

Decety, J., & Cowell, J. M. (2015). Empathy, justice, and moral behavior. *AJOB Neuroscience*, *6*(3), 3–14. https://doi.org/10.1080/21507740.2015.1047055

De Groot, J. I. M., & Steg, L. (2009). Morality and prosocial behavior: The role of awareness, responsibility, and norms in the norm activation model. *The Journal of Social Psychology*, *149*(4), 425–449. https://doi.org/10.3200/SOCP.149.4.425-449

Dersley, I., & Wootton, A. (2000). Complaint sequences within antagonistic argument. *Research on Language and Social Interaction*, *33*(4), 375–406. https://doi.org/10.1207/S15327973RLSI3304_02

de Waal, F. B. M., & Preston, S. D. (2017). Mammalian empathy: Behavioural manifestations and neural basis. *Nature Reviews Neuroscience*, *18*(8), 498–509. https://doi.org/10.1038/nrn.2017.72

Diekmann, A., & Preisendörfer, P. (2003). Green and greenback: The behavioral effects of environmental attitudes in low-cost and high-cost situations. *Rationality and Society*, *15*(4), 441–472. https://doi.org/10.1177/1043463103154002

Douglas, T. (1995). *Scapegoats: Transferring blame*. Routledge.

Dugar, S. (2010). Nonmonetary sanctions and rewards in an experimental coordination game. *Journal of Economic Behavior & Organization*, *73*(3), 377–386. https://doi.org/10.1016/j.jebo.2009.11.003

Eisenberger, N. I., Lieberman, M. D., & Williams, K. D. (2003). Does rejection hurt? An fMRI study of social exclusion. *Science*, *302*(5643), 290–292. https://doi.org/10.1126/science.1089134

Elster, J. (1989). Social norms and economic theory. *The Journal of Economic Perspectives*, *3*(4), 99–117. https://doi.org/10.1257/jep.3.4.99

Eriksson, K., & Strimling, P. (2015). Injunctive versus functional inferences from descriptive norms: Comment on Gelfand and Harrington. *Journal of Cross-Cultural Psychology*, *46*(10), 1330–1332. https://doi.org/10.1177/0022022115605387

Fehr, E., & Gächter, S. (2000). Cooperation and punishment in public goods experiments. *The American Economic Review*, *90*(4), 980–994. https://doi.org/10.1257/aer.90.4.980

Feinberg, M., Cheng, J. T., & Willer, R. (2012). Gossip as an effective and low-cost form of punishment. *Behavioral and Brain Sciences*, *35*(1), 25–25. https://doi.org/10.1017/S0140525X11001233

Feinberg, M., Willer, R., & Schultz, M. (2014). Gossip and ostracism promote cooperation in groups. *Psychological Science, 25*(3), 656–664. https://doi.org/10.1177/0956797613510184

Feinberg, M., Willer, R., Stellar, J., & Keltner, D. (2012). The virtues of gossip: Reputational information sharing as prosocial behavior. *Journal of Personality and Social Psychology, 102*(5), 1015–1030. https://doi.org/10.1037/a0026650

Ferguson, T. J., Brugman, D., White, J., & Eyre, H. L. (2007). Shame and guilt as morally warranted experiences. In J. L. Tracy, R. W. Robins, & J. P. Tangney (Eds.), *The self-conscious emotions: Theory and research* (pp. 330–348). Guilford Press.

Fiske, A. P., & Rai, T. S. (2015). *Virtuous violence.* Cambridge University Press.

Folger, R., & Whiting, S. W. (2020). HR research and practice from a deonance perspective. In M. R. Buckley, A. R. Wheeler, J. E. Baur, & J. R. B. Halbesleben (Eds.), *Research in personnel and human resources management* (Vol. 38, pp. 259–283). Emerald.

Freedman, J. L., Wallington, S. A., & Bless, E. (1967). Compliance without pressure: The effect of guilt. *Journal of Personality and Social Psychology, 7*(2, Pt. 1), 117–124. https://doi.org/10.1037/h0025009

Funk, F., McGeer, V., & Gollwitzer, M. (2014). Get the message: Punishment is satisfying if the transgressor responds to its communicative intent. *Personality and Social Psychology Bulletin, 40*(8), 986–997. https://doi.org/10.1177/0146167214533130

Furlong, M., & Young, J. (1996). Talking about blame. *Australian and New Zealand Journal of Family Therapy, 17*(4), 191–200. https://doi.org/10.1002/j.1467-8438.1996.tb01098.x

Gächter, S., Renner, E., & Sefton, M. (2008, December). The long-run benefits of punishment. *Science, 322*(5907), 1510–1510. https://doi.org/10.1126/science.1164744

Gavrilets, S., & Richerson, P. J. (2017). Collective action and the evolution of social norm internalization. *Proceedings of the National Academy of Sciences of the United States of America, 114*(23), 6068–6073. https://doi.org/10.1073/pnas.1703857114

Generation FIVE. (2007). *Toward transformative justice: A liberatory approach to child sexual abuse and other forms of intimate and community violence.* http://www.generationfive.org/wp-content/uploads/2013/07/G5_Toward_Transformative_Justice-Document.pdf

Gershoff, E. T., & Lee, S. J. (Eds.). (2020). *Ending the physical punishment of children: A guide for clinicians and practitioners.* American Psychological Association. https://doi.org/10.1037/0000162-000

Gintis, H. (2000). Strong reciprocity and human sociality. *Journal of Theoretical Biology, 206*(2), 169–179. https://doi.org/10.1006/jtbi.2000.2111

Gintis, H. (2003). The hitchhiker's guide to altruism: Gene–culture coevolution and the internalization of norms. *Journal of Theoretical Biology, 220*(4), 407–418. https://doi.org/10.1006/jtbi.2003.3104

Gobodo-Madikizela, P. (2008). Transforming trauma in the aftermath of gross human rights abuses: Making public spaces intimate through the South African Truth and Reconciliation Commission. In A. Nadler, T. E. Malloy, & J. D. Fisher (Eds.), *The social psychology of intergroup reconciliation* (pp. 57–75). Oxford University Press.

Gollwitzer, M., Meder, M., & Schmitt, M. (2011). What gives victims satisfaction when they seek revenge? *European Journal of Social Psychology, 41*(3), 364–374. https://doi.org/10.1002/ejsp.782

Goodmark, L. (2015). "Law and justice are not always the same": Creating community-based justice forums for people subjected to intimate partner abuse. *Florida State University Law Review, 42*(3), 707–763.

Goodwin, G. P., & Gromet, D. M. (2014). Punishment. *WIREs Cognitive Science, 5*(5), 561–572. https://doi.org/10.1002/wcs.1301

Green, R. M. (1991). When is "everyone's doing it" a moral justification? *Business Ethics Quarterly, 1*(1), 75–93.

Gromet, D. M., & Darley, J. M. (2006). Restoration and retribution: How including retributive components affects the acceptability of restorative justice procedures. *Social Justice Research, 19*(4), 395–432. https://doi.org/10.1007/s11211-006-0023-7

Grossman, D. (1996). *On killing: The psychological cost of learning to kill in war and society*. Little, Brown.

Grusec, J. E., & Kuczynski, L. (1997). *Parenting and children's internalization of values: A handbook of contemporary theory* (Vol. J). Wiley.

Guala, F. (2012). Reciprocity: Weak or strong? What punishment experiments do (and do not) demonstrate. *Behavioral and Brain Sciences, 35*(1), 1–15. https://doi.org/10.1017/S0140525X11000069

Hamber, B. (2007). Forgiveness and reconciliation: Paradise lost or pragmatism? *Peace and Conflict, 13*(1), 115–125. https://doi.org/10.1037/h0094027

Hannah, S. T., Schaubroeck, J. M., & Peng, A. C. (2016). Transforming followers' value internalization and role self-efficacy: Dual processes promoting performance and peer norm-enforcement. *Journal of Applied Psychology, 101*(2), 252–266. https://doi.org/10.1037/apl0000038

Hechter, M., & Opp, K.-D. (Eds.). (2001). *Social norms*. Russell Sage Foundation.

Heffner, J., & FeldmanHall, O. (2019). Why we don't always punish: Preferences for non-punitive responses to moral violations. *Scientific Reports, 9*(1), 13219. https://doi.org/10.1038/s41598-019-49680-2

Heider, F. (1958). Ought and value. In F. Heider, *The psychology of interpersonal relations* (pp. 218–243). Wiley. https://doi.org/10.1037/10628-008

Hershcovis, M. S., & Bhatnagar, N. (2017). When fellow customers behave badly: Witness reactions to employee mistreatment by customers. *Journal of Applied Psychology, 102*(11), 1528–1544. https://doi.org/10.1037/apl0000249

Hofmann, W., Brandt, M. J., Wisneski, D. C., Rockenbach, B., & Skitka, L. J. (2018). Moral punishment in everyday life. *Personality and Social Psychology Bulletin, 44*(12), 1697–1711. https://doi.org/10.1177/0146167218775075

Horne, C. (2003). The internal enforcement of norms. *European Sociological Review, 19*(4), 335–343. https://doi.org/10.1093/esr/19.4.335

Horne, C., & Mollborn, S. (2020). Norms: An integrated framework. *Annual Review of Sociology, 46*(1), 467–487. https://doi.org/10.1146/annurev-soc-121919-054658

Howe, R. (2018). Community-led sexual violence and prevention work: Utilising a Transformative Justice framework. *Social Work & Policy Studies, 1*(001), Article 001. https://openjournals.library.sydney.edu.au/index.php/SWPS/article/view/12525

Janoff-Bulman, R., & Carnes, N. C. (2013). Surveying the moral landscape: Moral motives and group-based moralities. *Personality and Social Psychology Review, 17*(3), 219–236. https://doi.org/10.1177/1088868313480274

Keller, L. B., Oswald, M. E., Stucki, I., & Gollwitzer, M. (2010). A closer look at an eye for an eye: Laypersons' punishment decisions are primarily driven by retributive motives. *Social Justice Research, 23*(2–3), 99–116. https://doi.org/10.1007/s11211-010-0113-4

Kelly, D., Stich, S. P., Haley, K. J., Eng, S. J., & Fessler, D. M. T. (2007). Harm, affect, and the moral/conventional distinction. *Mind & Language, 22*(2), 117–131. https://doi.org/10.1111/j.1468-0017.2007.00302.x

Kennedy, J. L. D., Tuliao, A. P., Flower, K. N., Tibbs, J. J., & McChargue, D. E. (2019). Long-term effectiveness of a brief restorative justice intervention. *International Journal of Offender Therapy and Comparative Criminology, 63*(1), 3–17. https://doi.org/10.1177/0306624X18779202

Kiyonari, T., & Barclay, P. (2008). Cooperation in social dilemmas: Free riding may be thwarted by second-order reward rather than by punishment. *Journal of Personality and Social Psychology, 95*(4), 826–842. https://doi.org/10.1037/a0011381

Knauft, B. M. (1991). Violence and sociality in human evolution. *Current Anthropology, 32*(4), 391–409. https://doi.org/10.1086/203975

Knobloch-Westerwick, S., & Taylor, L. D. (2008). The blame game: Elements of causal attribution and its impact on siding with agents in the news. *Communication Research, 35*(6), 723–744. https://doi.org/10.1177/0093650208324266

Kochanska, G., & Aksan, N. (2006). Children's conscience and self-regulation. *Journal of Personality, 74*(6), 1587–1618. https://doi.org/10.1111/j.1467-6494.2006.00421.x

Kochanska, G., Aksan, N., & Koenig, A. L. (1995). A longitudinal study of the roots of preschoolers' conscience: Committed compliance and emerging internalization. *Child Development, 66*(6), 1752–1769. https://doi.org/10.2307/1131908

Krebs, D. L., & Janicki, M. (2004). Biological foundations of moral norms. In M. Schaller & C. S. Crandall (Eds.), *The psychological foundations of culture* (pp. 125–148). Erlbaum.

Kriss, P. H., Weber, R. A., & Xiao, E. (2016). Turning a blind eye, but not the other cheek: On the robustness of costly punishment. *Journal of Economic Behavior & Organization, 128*, 159–177. https://doi.org/10.1016/j.jebo.2016.05.017

Kura, K. M., Shamsudin, F., & Chauhan, A. (2015). Does self-regulatory efficacy matter? Effects of punishment certainty and punishment severity on organizational deviance. *SAGE Open, 5*(2), 2158244015591822. https://doi.org/10.1177/2158244015591822

Kurgan, L. (2001). Memories, healing, reconciliation and forgiveness. *Psycho-Analytic Psychotherapy in South Africa, 9*(1), 1–10.

Lapinski, M. K., & Rimal, R. N. (2005). An explication of social norms. *Communication Theory, 15*(2), 127–147. https://doi.org/10.1111/j.1468-2885.2005.tb00329.x

Laurent, S. M., Nuñez, N. L., & Schweitzer, K. A. (2016). Unintended, but still blameworthy: The roles of awareness, desire, and anger in negligence, restitution, and punishment. *Cognition and Emotion, 30*(7), 1271–1288. https://doi.org/10.1080/02699931.2015.1058242

Lindenberg, S. (2013). How cues in the environment affect normative behaviour. In L. Steg, A. E. van den Berg, & J. I. M. de Groot (Eds.), *Environmental psychology: An introduction* (pp. 119–128). BPS Blackwell.

Lloyd, A., & Borrill, J. (2020). Examining the effectiveness of restorative justice in reducing victims' post-traumatic stress. *Psychological Injury and Law, 13*, 77–89. https://doi.org/10.1007/s12207-019-09363-9

Lyons, L. (2017). *The history of punishment*. Amber Books.

Maibom, H. L. (2010). The descent of shame. *Philosophy and Phenomenological Research*, *80*(3), 566–594. https://doi.org/10.1111/j.1933-1592.2010.00341.x

Malle, B. F. (2004). *How the mind explains behavior: Folk explanations, meaning, and social interaction*. MIT Press. https://doi.org/10.7551/mitpress/3586.001.0001

Malle, B. F. (2020). Graded representations of norm strength. In S. Denison, M. Mack, Y. Xu, & B. C. Armstrong (Eds.), *Proceedings of the 42nd Annual Meeting of the Cognitive Science Society* (pp. 3342–3348). Cognitive Science Society.

Malle, B. F. (2021). Moral judgments. *Annual Review of Psychology*, *72*(1), 293–318. https://doi.org/10.1146/annurev-psych-072220-104358

Malle, B. F., Austerweil, J. L., Chi, V. B., Kenett, Y., Beck, E. D., Thapa, S., & Allaham, M. (2021). Cognitive properties of norm representations. *Proceedings of the Annual Meeting of the Cognitive Science Society*, *43*, 819–825. https://escholarship.org/uc/item/0cr0x2b3

Malle, B. F., Guglielmo, S., & Monroe, A. E. (2014). A theory of blame. *Psychological Inquiry*, *25*(2), 147–186. https://doi.org/10.1080/1047840X.2014.877340

Malle, B. F., Guglielmo, S., Voiklis, J., & Monroe, A. E. (2022). Cognitive blame is socially shaped. *Current Directions in Psychological Science*, *31*(2), 169–176. https://doi.org/10.1177/09637214211068845

Malle, B. F., Scheutz, M., & Austerweil, J. L. (2017). Networks of social and moral norms in human and robot agents. In M. I. Aldinhas Ferreira, J. Silva Sequeira, M. O. Tokhi, E. E. Kadar, & G. S. Virk (Eds.), *A world with robots: International Conference on Robot Ethics: ICRE 2015* (pp. 3–17). Springer.

Martin, J. W., & Cushman, F. (2015). To punish or to leave: Distinct cognitive processes underlie partner control and partner choice behaviors. *PLoS One*, *10*(4), e0125193. https://doi.org/10.1371/journal.pone.0125193

Masclet, D., Noussair, C., Tucker, S., & Villeval, M.-C. (2003). Monetary and nonmonetary punishment in the voluntary contributions mechanism. *The American Economic Review*, *93*(1), 366–380. https://doi.org/10.1257/000282803321455359

McDonald, M. M., Defever, A. M., & Navarrete, C. D. (2017). Killing for the greater good: Action aversion and the emotional inhibition of harm in moral dilemmas. *Evolution and Human Behavior*, *38*(6), 770–778. https://doi.org/10.1016/j.evolhumbehav.2017.06.001

McGraw, K. M. (1987). Guilt following transgression: An attribution of responsibility approach. *Journal of Personality and Social Psychology*, *53*(2), 247–256. https://doi.org/10.1037/0022-3514.53.2.247

McNamara, P. (2006). Deontic logic. In D. M. Gabbay & J. Woods (Eds.), *Handbook of the history of logic* (pp. 197–288). North-Holland.

Molho, C., Tybur, J. M., Van Lange, P. A. M., & Balliet, D. (2020). Direct and indirect punishment of norm violations in daily life. *Nature Communications*, *11*(1), 3432. https://doi.org/10.1038/s41467-020-17286-2

Monroe, A. E., & Malle, B. F. (2019). People systematically update moral judgments of blame. *Journal of Personality and Social Psychology*, *116*(2), 215–236. https://doi.org/10.1037/pspa0000137

Mullen, E., & Monin, B. (2016). Consistency versus licensing effects of past moral behavior. *Annual Review of Psychology*, *67*(1), 363–385. https://doi.org/10.1146/annurev-psych-010213-115120

Nagin, D. S., & Pepper, J. V. (Eds.). (2012). *Deterrence and the death penalty*. National Research Council.

National Institute of Justice. (2016, June 5). *Five things about deterrence*. https://nij.ojp.gov/topics/articles/five-things-about-deterrence

O'Hear, M., & Wheelock, D. (2020). Violent crime and punitiveness: An empirical study of public opinion. *Marquette Law Review, 103*(3), 1035–1071.

O'Keefe, D. J. (2000). Guilt and social influence. *Annals of the International Communication Association, 23*(1), 67–101. https://doi.org/10.1080/23808985.2000.11678970

Ohtsubo, Y., Sasaki, S., Nakanishi, D., & Igawa, J. (2018). Within-individual associations among third-party intervention strategies: Third-party helpers, but not punishers, reward generosity. *Evolutionary Behavioral Sciences, 12*(2), 113–125. https://doi.org/10.1037/ebs0000107

Patil, I., Dhaliwal, N., & Cushman, F. (2021). Reputational and cooperative benefits of third-party compensation. *Organizational Behavior and Human Decision Processes, 164*, 27–51. https://doi.org/10.1016/j.obhdp.2021.01.003

Pedersen, E. J., Kurzban, R., & McCullough, M. E. (2013). Do humans really punish altruistically? A closer look. *Proceedings. Biological Sciences, 280*(1758), 20122723.

Pedersen, E. J., McAuliffe, W. H. B., & McCullough, M. E. (2018). The unresponsive avenger: More evidence that disinterested third parties do not punish altruistically. *Journal of Experimental Psychology: General, 147*(4), 514–544. https://doi.org/10.1037/xge0000410

Pedersen, E. J., McAuliffe, W. H. B., Shah, Y., Tanaka, H., Ohtsubo, Y., & McCullough, M. E. (2020). When and why do third parties punish outside of the lab? A cross-cultural recall study. *Social Psychological & Personality Science, 11*(6), 846–853. https://doi.org/10.1177/1948550619884565

Peysakhovich, A., & Rand, D. G. (2016). Habits of virtue: Creating norms of cooperation and defection in the laboratory. *Management Science, 62*(3), 631–647. https://doi.org/10.1287/mnsc.2015.2168

Polman, E., Pettit, N. C., & Wiesenfeld, B. M. (2013). Effects of wrongdoer status on moral licensing. *Journal of Experimental Social Psychology, 49*(4), 614–623. https://doi.org/10.1016/j.jesp.2013.03.012

Prentice, D. A., & Miller, D. T. (1996). Pluralistic ignorance and the perpetuation of social norms by unwitting actors. In M. P. Zanna (Ed.), *Advances in experimental social psychology* (Vol. 28, pp. 161–209). Academic Press. https://doi.org/10.1016/S0065-2601(08)60238-5

Przepiorka, W., & Berger, J. (2016). The sanctioning dilemma: A quasi-experiment on social norm enforcement in the train. *European Sociological Review, 32*(3), 439–451. https://doi.org/10.1093/esr/jcw014

Rakow, A., Forehand, R., Haker, K., McKee, L. G., Champion, J. E., Potts, J., Hardcastle, E., Roberts, L., & Compas, B. E. (2011). Use of parental guilt induction among depressed parents. *Journal of Family Psychology, 25*(1), 147–151. https://doi.org/10.1037/a0022110

Roughley, N. (2019). Normative guidance, deontic statuses, and the normative animal thesis. In N. Roughley & K. Bayertz (Eds.), *The normative animal?* (pp. 321–337). Oxford University Press. https://doi.org/10.1093/oso/9780190846466.003.0016

Scanlon, T. (1998). *What we owe to each other* (pp. 169–175). Harvard University Press.

Schelling, T. C. (1960). *The strategy of conflict.* Harvard University Press.

Schwartz, S. H. (1977). Normative influences on altruism. In L. Berkowitz (Ed.), *Advances in experimental social psychology* (Vol. 10, pp. 221–279). Academic Press.

Serramia, M., López-Sánchez, M., Rodríguez-Aguilar, J. A., Wooldridge, M., Morales, J., & Ansótegui, C. (2018). Moral values in norm decision making. In M. Dastani, G. Sukthankar, E. André, & S. Koenig (Eds.), *Proceedings of the 17th International Conference on Autonomous Agents and Multiagent Systems* (pp. 1294–1302). International Foundation for Autonomous Agents and Multiagent Systems.

Shalvi, S., Dana, J., Handgraaf, M. J. J., & De Dreu, C. K. W. (2011). Justified ethicality: Observing desired counterfactuals modifies ethical perceptions and behavior. *Organizational Behavior and Human Decision Processes, 115*(2), 181–190. https://doi.org/10.1016/j.obhdp.2011.02.001

Shoemaker, D. W. (2014). Psychopathy, responsibility, and the moral/conventional distinction. In T. Schramme (Ed.), *Being amoral: Psychopathy and moral incapacity* (pp. 247–274). MIT Press.

Sidanius, J., & Pratto, F. (1999). *Social dominance: An intergroup theory of social hierarchy and oppression.* Cambridge University Press. https://doi.org/10.1017/CBO9781139175043

Skitka, L. J., Hanson, B. E., Morgan, G. S., & Wisneski, D. C. (2021). The psychology of moral conviction. *Annual Review of Psychology, 72*(1), 347–366. https://doi.org/10.1146/annurev-psych-063020-030612

Smith, E. R. (2014). Evil acts and malicious gossip: A multiagent model of the effects of gossip in socially distributed person perception. *Personality and Social Psychology Review, 18*(4), 311–325. https://doi.org/10.1177/1088868314530515

Steele, C. M. (1988). The psychology of self-affirmation: Sustaining the integrity of the self. In L. Berkowitz (Ed.), *Advances in experimental social psychology* (Vol. 21, pp. 261–302). Academic Press. https://doi.org/10.1016/S0065-2601(08)60229-4

Stohr, K. (2012). *On manners.* Routledge. https://doi.org/10.4324/9780203859803

Svensson, R., Weerman, F. M., Pauwels, L. J. R., Bruinsma, G. J. N., & Bernasco, W. (2013). Moral emotions and offending: Do feelings of anticipated shame and guilt mediate the effect of socialization on offending? *European Journal of Criminology, 10*(1), 22–39. https://doi.org/10.1177/1477370812454393

Tangney, J. P., & Dearing, R. L. (2002). *Shame and guilt.* Guilford Press.

Tomasello, M., & Vaish, A. (2013). Origins of human cooperation and morality. *Annual Review of Psychology, 64*(1), 231–255. https://doi.org/10.1146/annurev-psych-113011-143812

Tonry, M. (2009). Explanations of American punishment policies: A national history. *Punishment & Society, 11*(3), 377–394. https://doi.org/10.1177/1462474509334609

Turiel, E. (1983). *The development of social knowledge: Morality and convention.* Cambridge University Press.

Tyler, T. R., & Jost, J. T. (2007). Psychology and the law: Reconciling normative and descriptive accounts of social justice and system legitimacy. In A. W. Kruglanski & E. T. Higgins (Eds.), *Social psychology: Handbook of basic principles* (2nd ed., pp. 807–825). Guilford Press.

Voiklis, J., & Malle, B. F. (2018). Moral cognition and its basis in social cognition and social regulation. In K. Gray & J. Graham (Eds.), *Atlas of moral psychology* (pp. 108–120). Guilford Press.

Vollhardt, J. R., Mazur, L. B., & Lemahieu, M. (2014). Acknowledgment after mass violence: Effects on psychological well-being and intergroup relations. *Group Processes & Intergroup Relations, 17*(3), 306–323. https://doi.org/10.1177/1368430213517270

Wagner, P., & Sawyer, W. (2018). *States of incarceration: The global context 2018.* Prison Policy Initiative. https://www.prisonpolicy.org/global/2018.html

Wallace, H. M., Exline, J. J., & Baumeister, R. F. (2008). Interpersonal consequences of forgiveness: Does forgiveness deter or encourage repeat offenses? *Journal of Experimental Social Psychology, 44*(2), 453–460. https://doi.org/10.1016/j.jesp.2007.02.012

Wenzel, M., & Okimoto, T. G. (2010). How acts of forgiveness restore a sense of justice: Addressing status/power and value concerns raised by transgressions. *European Journal of Social Psychology, 40*(3), 401–417. https://doi.org/10.1002/ejsp.629

Wielenga, C., Batley, M., & Murambadoro, R. (2020). Beyond restorative justice: Understanding justice from an African perspective. *African Journal of Peace and Conflict Studies, 9*(1), 43–69. https://doi.org/10.31920/2050-4950/2020/9n1a3

Wiessner, P. (2005). Norm enforcement among the Ju/'hoansi Bushmen: A case of strong reciprocity? *Human Nature, 16*(2), 115–145. https://doi.org/10.1007/s12110-005-1000-9

Williams, K. D. (2009). Ostracism: A temporal need–threat model. In M. P. Zanna (Ed.), *Advances in experimental social psychology* (Vol. 41, pp. 275–314). Elsevier Academic Press.

Wilson, D. S. (2002). *Darwin's cathedral: Evolution, religion, and the nature of society.* University of Chicago Press. https://doi.org/10.7208/chicago/9780226901374.001.0001

Wolbring, T., Bozoyan, C., & Langner, D. (2013). "Links gehen, rechts stehen!": Ein Feldexperiment zur Durchsetzung informeller Normen auf Rolltreppen ["Walk left, stand right!": A field experiment on the enforcement of informal norms on escalators]. *Zeitschrift für Soziologie, 42*(3), 239–258. https://doi.org/10.1515/zfsoz-2013-0305

Wright, K. A., & Khade, N. (2017). Offender recidivism. In V. H. Woodward & O. H. Griffin III (Eds.), *Routledge handbook of corrections in the United States* (pp. 494–502). Routledge. https://doi.org/10.4324/9781315645179-45

Xiao, E. (2018). Punishment, social norms, and cooperation. In J. C. Teitelbaum & K. Zeiler (Eds.), *Research handbook on behavioral law and economics* (pp. 155–173). Edward Elgar. https://doi.org/10.4337/9781849805681.00014

Xiao, E., & Houser, D. (2005). Emotion expression in human punishment behavior. *Proceedings of the National Academy of Sciences of the United States of America, 102*(20), 7398–7401. https://doi.org/10.1073/pnas.0502399102

Yamagishi, T. (1986). The provision of a sanctioning system as a public good. *Journal of Personality and Social Psychology, 51*(1), 110–116. https://doi.org/10.1037/0022-3514.51.1.110

Yukhnenko, D., Sridhar, S., & Fazel, S. (2020). A systematic review of criminal recidivism rates worldwide: 3-year update. *Wellcome Open Research, 4.* https://doi.org/10.12688/wellcomeopenres.14970.3

Zeelenberg, M. (2018). Anticipated regret: A prospective emotion about the future past. In G. Oettingen, A. T. Sevincer, & P. Gollwitzer (Eds.), *The psychology of thinking about the future* (pp. 276–295). Guilford Press.

3 CULTURAL NORMS IN MORAL MOTIVATION

JOAN G. MILLER AND JESSICA L. ENGELBRECHT

Morality is central to culture. As Shweder (1999) observed, culture involves "community-specific ideas about what is *true, good* [emphasis added], beautiful and efficient that are . . . constitutive of different ways of life and play a part in the self-understanding of members of the community" (p. 212). Despite this recognition that culture influences people's outlook on what is good and true, mainstream psychological approaches to morality typically have downplayed cultural variation.

UNIVERSALISM IN WORK ON MORALITY

An embracement of universalism characterizes psychological theory and research on morality. This embrace reflects the contrasting theoretical agendas and methodological commitments of the mainstream traditions of developmental and social psychological work on this topic.

https://doi.org/10.1037/0000342-004
Motivation and Morality: A Multidisciplinary Approach, M. K. Berg and E. C. Chang (Editors)

Developmental Models

Models of morality that have emerged in developmental psychology share a concern with avoiding what they see as the flaws of *moral relativism*, which they associate with views that morality can be defined as whatever the group or the individual considers it to be. To achieve this, theoretical frameworks are formulated that distinguish, on what they see as philosophically justifiable grounds, between (a) issues that are inherently moral in nature and thus that can be claimed as universal and (b) issues of social convention and personal choice that are nonmoral. Whereas the latter issues are recognized to vary in content cross-culturally, the content of morality itself is considered nonculturally relative.

Cognitive Developmental Theory

Kohlberg's (1969, 1971, 1981) cognitive developmental theory of moral development presented an early highly influential model that was part of the cognitive revolution in psychology. According to Kohlberg's theory, morality is based on objective standards that are universal in nature. Kohlberg (1981) rejected social learning approaches to morality (e.g., Bandura's, 1969) because he viewed them as embodying an extreme cultural relativism that provided no basis for appraising a practice as immoral to the extent the practice was socially accepted and normative in a given society.

Kohlberg defined morality as centered exclusively on justice and individual rights. This definition was based on the philosopher John Rawls's (1971) concept of a *veil of ignorance*, which bases morality on the perspective of a hypothetical individual considered independently of their social position, personal inclinations, or other distinctive attributes. Kohlberg assumed that the individual self-constructs this moral endpoint through rational processes of logical deduction in which they cognitively reflect on their social experiences.

As a cognitive developmental theorist, Kohlberg formulated a stage model that distinguished between an early emerging preconventional stage, which was based on the preferences of the individual; a more advanced conventional stage, which was based on the perspectives of the social group; and the most advanced and only truly moral stage, which was based on an assumed objective natural law that transcends group or individual subjectivity. Work in the Kohlbergian tradition assessed moral outlooks using methods that required individuals to give sophisticated verbal justifications for their appraisals of hypothetical vignette situations, such as the Heinz dilemma, a case in which the only way to save one's dying wife involved stealing a drug. Results gained by using these methods yielded marked cross-cultural and developmental variation. Kohlberg found that not only that young children fail to reach the conventional stage but that most of the world's adult populations outside of the United States and western Europe reaches only the conventional stage, with adults from small-scale tribal cultural groups reaching only the preconventional stage (Kohlberg, 1969). Despite this bias in favor of WEIRD (Western, educated, industrialized, rich, and democratic) populations (Henrich et al., 2010) in the observed results, mainstream psychological theorists treated such cultural skewness as expected, interpreting it as evidence that certain sociocultural environments are more cognitively stimulating than others and therefore more effective in promoting moral development. Although contemporary cultural critics have argued that Kohlberg's model was culturally skewed in its neglect of communitarian concerns and of the spiritual aspects of moral outlooks (e.g., Simpson, 1974; Snarey, 1985; Vasudev & Hummel, 1987), mainstream psychological theorists were not swayed by this cultural critique; instead, psychologists continued for decades to fully embrace Kohlbergian theory and its conclusion that the outlooks observed among non-Western adult populations resemble the outlooks of Western children.

Distinct Domain Theory

Developed originally by Turiel (1983), the *distinct domain perspective* was part of a larger theoretical and methodological turn in developmental psychology, one that adopted more child-centered methods and that yielded findings that challenged stage models of cognitive development (e.g., Donaldson, 1978; Gelman, 1978). This turn highlighted early child competencies and pointed to no fundamental developmental changes as occurring in either cognitive or moral outlooks. The distinct domain perspective remains one of the most influential contemporary perspectives on morality in developmental psychology (e.g., Smetana, 2006; Turiel, 1998a; Turiel et al., 1991).

Like Kohlberg, distinct domain theorists assume that morality is centered on justice and individual rights universally (Turiel, 1998b, 2002). Going beyond the Kohlbergian claims, distinct domain theorists identified ways that morality can be self-constructed through a cognitively simple inductive process in which individuals observe the consequences of actions. It is assumed that, through such an inferential process, people come to distinguish between moral issues that involve justice or individual rights, as compared with social conventional issues that involve social coordination, as compared with personal choice issues that involve neither of these considerations.

Distinct domain theorists adopted methods for assessing moral outlooks that made fewer cognitive and linguistic demands than had occurred in the case of the Kohlbergian methods. In a common methodology used in the distinct domain perspective, individuals are asked short-answer questions that tap their appraisals of simply worded vignettes involving different types of social rules, such as in research contrasting a prototypical moral violation that involves harm (e.g., deliberately pushing a friend off a chair) with a prototypical conventional violation that involves social coordination (e.g., wearing pajamas to a restaurant; Turiel, 1983). Short-answer questions are administered to assess a person's application of abstract criteria to distinguish among the different types of social rules. Behaviors are categorized as *moral violations* if they are appraised as not rule contingent (i.e., wrong regardless of whether there are rules against doing them) and as generalizing across social contexts (e.g., wrong if done in a different group or context). They are categorized as *social conventions* if they are appraised as rule contingent (i.e., dependent on the existence of a rule against doing them) and as contextually relative (acceptable if done in another group or community). Finally, they are categorized as *matters of personal choice* if they are appraised as illegitimate to regulate (i.e., unacceptable to have rules about) and as personally contingent (okay if an individual wants to do them).

A major contribution of distinct domain theory has been to highlight the heterogeneity of outlooks, with the distinct domain approach establishing that a multifaceted view of social rules is held at all ages and universally. Instead of focusing on young children attaining moral understandings only in late adolescence or as adults (e.g., Kohlberg, 1969), findings gained from the distinct domain perspective provide evidence that children as young as 2 or 3 years old (e.g., Smetana et al., 1993, 2018) are able to distinguish, on the basis of these formal criteria, among issues of morality, convention, and personal choice. Work in this tradition also has provided evidence indicating that, in all cultural populations, people distinguish among matters of morality, matters of convention, and matters of personal choice (e.g., Ardila-Rey & Killen, 2001; Song et al., 1987).

Research conducted from the distinct domain perspective, however, has tended to use prototypical vignettes that do not involve culturally variable issues and thus cannot conclusively rule out cultural variation. Distinct domain researchers also have dismissed evidence by cultural researchers who have presented evidence for cultural variation in moral outlooks (e.g., of orthodox Hindu Indians but not Americans considering it a moral violation for a son to get a haircut or to eat chicken the day after his father's death; Shweder et al., 1987). Distinct domain theorists argue that such cultural variation reflects contrasting epistemological assumptions held in the cultural communities under consideration, such as beliefs in purity and pollution, rather than cultural variation in the morality of justice and individual rights (Turiel et al., 1987). This latter assumption, however, neglects to take into account nonrational premises that may underlie cultural variation in moral outlooks.

Social Psychological Models

Contemporary models of morality that have emerged in social psychology share the same assumption as the developmental traditions, that is, that the content of morality is universal. This reflects the long-standing emphasis in mainstream social psychology traditions on forwarding theory that is universally applicable and that has both parsimony and predictive power (e.g., Higgins & Kruglanski, 1996).

Moral Grammar Theory

The *moral grammar perspective* of Hauser and his colleagues (Hauser, 2006; Hauser et al., 2007) constitutes an influential contemporary perspective on morality in social psychology. This perspective shares with the mainstream developmental approaches a view of morality as centering universally on justice and individual rights. It also resembles developmental approaches in that it draws heavily on philosophical theorizing for insight into morality and in that it has close ties to contemporary work in cognitive development. Just as the Kohlberg's stage model reflected Piagetian stage theory, and the distinct domain model reflected contemporary approaches in cognitive development uncovering cognitive competence among young children, the moral grammar approach reflects the contemporary emphasis on *nativism* in research (e.g., Baillargeon et al., 2015, 2016; Thomsen & Carey, 2013; Spelke, 2017). In the area of language, nativist theories specify the constraints that individuals bring with them and to which, it is argued, they must adhere in learning their culture's particular language (Pinker, 1984). In a process analogous to that underlying language learning, moral grammar is seen as involving inborn heuristics that constrain individuals' moral outlooks as they come to acquire their particular culture's distinctive moral views.

Moral grammar theorists argue that a small set of innate computational mechanisms structure morality. Three examples of such mechanisms include the following heuristics: (a) harm caused by action is worse than harm caused by omission, (b) intended harm is worse than harm that arises as a side effect, and (c) harm involving physical contact is worse than harm involving no physical contact (Cushman et al., 2006). These types of heuristics are seen as implicit and in many cases, but not all, as operating outside of conscious awareness. In this respect, moral appraisal resembles language, with people able to speak grammatically even as they have limited awareness of grammatical rules.

The appeal of moral grammar theory rests on its parsimony and predictive power. The theory is compatible with work in the fields of linguistics and cognitive science as well as with evolutionary theory. Like the developmental perspectives discussed earlier, theorists who take a moral grammar perspective do not ignore cultural variation but instead minimize its significance. Although the moral grammar model has been linked to cultural relativism by certain theorists (e.g., Pinker, 2008), moral grammar theorists reject this assertion, arguing that any culturally specific moral content that an individual adopts is so fully constrained by the inborn moral grammar that it does not give rise to fundamental cultural variation in moral outlooks (Banerjee et al., 2010).

Cultural research undertaken from a moral grammar perspective has involved culturally constrained samples and a limited range of situations. For example, a large-scale investigation, conducted by Banerjee et al. (2010), examined cross-cultural variation in moral outlooks in a large sample of participants ($N = 8,778$). Although Banerjee and her colleagues portrayed their investigation as providing a rigorous test of the universality of moral grammar theory, they sampled only small numbers of Muslims, Buddhists, and Hindus, and the sample was limited to populations with internet access who could respond in English. Banerjee et al. assessed responses to the Moral Sense Test, a measure that includes the types of conflict situations portrayed in the trolley dilemma. Based on a thought experiment that originated in philosophy (Foot, 1967), the trolley dilemma, in its classic form, presents a hypothetical situation involving a runaway trolley that is about to hit five people tied up on a track, with the observer having the option to either do nothing or to pull a lever to divert the trolley onto a side track, where it will kill only one person. Responses to this dilemma are seen as providing a way to distinguish between a *deontological* moral outlook, by choosing to not do anything, in order to avoid taking a human life, versus a *utilitarian* moral outlook, by choosing the option that results in only one life, rather than five lives, being lost.

Banerjee and her colleagues (2010; Hauser et al., 2010) have argued that the "unfamiliarity" of these vignette situations make them culturally fair and even recommended their adoption as a standardized measure in future research. However, the vignettes in the Moral Sense Test portray contrived life-and-death situations unlikely to be experienced in peoples' everyday lives and thus have limited external validity. The scenarios also focus on justice and do not include any examples of the types of community or spiritual concerns that cultural critics identified as missing from developmental theories of morality (e.g., Snarey, 1985; Snarey & Keljo, 1991).

From a moral grammar perspective, theorists tend to interpret any cross-cultural variation that is observed in one of three ways: (a) as of limited theoretical significance, (b) as arising from nonmoral processes, or (c) as an adaptation to particular ecological pressures. Thus, for example, Banerjee et al. (2010) characterized the group differences observed in their cross-cultural research as spurious effects with small effect sizes. Moral grammar theorists have produced evidence that in their view calls into question the universality of the *act/omission heuristic*—for example, that Mayans judge harms resulting from omissions to be just as serious as harms resulting from commissions (Abarbanell & Hauser, 2010). However, Banerjee et al. portrayed this finding as a rare phenomenon that represents an adaptation to conditions of life in small-scale societies and thus does not challenge the fundamental universality of moral grammar theory. In an argument that resembles the one made by distinct domain theorists (Turiel et al., 1987), moral grammar theorists also offer an informational interpretation of the cross-cultural differences in outlooks regarding spiritual issues that cultural theorists, such as Shweder et al. (1987), have identified. They argue that such differences arise from contrasting culturally based epistemological assumptions and not from variation in moral outlook (Hauser et al., 2010). Put more generally, they assert that any cultural differences related to individualism–collectivism can be explained as adaptations to ecological pressures and thus do not challenge claims made about a universal moral grammar.

Moral Foundations Theory

In a highly influential early model, Shweder and his colleagues formulated the Big Three Ethics framework (Shweder et al., 1997). In the framework, Shweder argued for the existence of qualitatively distinct moral orientations involving autonomy, community, and divinity. The ethics of autonomy pertains to justice and individual rights; the ethics of community to one's membership in society; and the ethics of divinity to spiritual concerns. Shweder offered rich descriptions of how the orientations inform each other as well as reflect specific local epistemological assumptions. To give an example, Shweder and Much (1987) noted how orthodox Hindu Indian respondents intermixed spiritual, community, and autonomy concerns in arguing, in response to the Heinz dilemma, that it would be wrong for Heinz to save his wife's life in that it would violate *dharma* and lead to suffering in cycles of future rebirth. Notably, whereas Shweder presented the three types of moral concerns as ones that he anticipated would be observed universally, he assumed that they take culturally variable forms and did not treat the ethics as mutually exclusive or attempt to assess them on Likert scale measures.

Moral foundations theory (MFT) was developed by Haidt and his colleagues (e.g., Haidt & Joseph, 2007) as an extension of the Big Three ethics framework. Haidt and his colleagues expanded the Big Three to include a larger number of concerns and portrayed the ethics as having an evolutionary grounding (Haidt & Joseph, 2007). Proponents of MFT view morality as based on five foundations that evolved in response to different adaptive demands experienced by early humans and their nonhuman primate ancestors (Graham et al., 2011; Haidt & Joseph, 2007). These foundations include (a) harm/ care, (b) fairness/reciprocity, (c) ingroup/loyalty, (d) authority/respect, and (e) purity/sanctity.[1] In terms of their evolutionary propensities, the harm/care foundation involves protecting and caring for young, vulnerable, or injured kin; the fairness/reciprocity foundation involves benefiting from dyadic cooperation with non-kin; the ingroup/loyalty foundation involves securing group cooperation; the authority/respect foundation involves negotiating hierarchy and maintaining group cohesion; and the purity/sanctity foundation involves avoiding microbes and parasites. Most of the empirical research in the MFT tradition has used the Moral Foundations Questionnaire (MFQ), an individual-difference measure that is intended to tap the "full range of moral concerns" (Graham et al., 2011, p. 366).

MFT has been applied to politics and religion because it is relevant to understanding America's "culture wars" (Haidt, 2012). Findings that have been obtained using the MFQ show that politically liberal Americans rely mostly on the harm/care and fairness/reciprocity foundations while placing less emphasis on the ingroup/loyalty, authority/respect, and purity/sanctity foundations. In contrast, politically conservative Americans rely heavily on all five moral foundations (Graham et al., 2009; Haidt & Graham, 2007; Haidt & Joseph, 2007). Cross-cultural differences on the MFQ, however, are minimal. Asian participants endorse ingroup and purity concerns more strongly than do participants from North America and western Europe and are only slightly more concerned than these Western populations with harm/care, fairness/reciprocity, and authority/respect (Graham et al., 2011). Although MFT theorists interpret these findings as congruent with the universality of the moral foundations, the number of observed cross-cultural differences are fewer than expected. For example, as Graham and his colleagues (2011)

---

[1]Although these five foundations remain central to the model, in recent years MFT theorists have introduced an additional foundation focused on liberty and indicated an openness to identifying additional moral foundations (Graham et al., 2018).

acknowledged, the finding of few or no cultural differences in endorsement of authority is surprising given the evidence of greater sensitivity to social hierarchy in Eastern as compared with Western cultures.

The limited sensitivity of the MFT to cross-cultural differences is notably congruent with its aim. The goal of the theory is not to elucidate cross-cultural differences in moral reasoning but to tap moral orientations at a highly general level that is shared among individuals whose specific moral outlooks differ. Thus, for example, to assess the harm/care foundation, MFT includes moral "relevance" items that make no mention of the particular individuals targeted or of the specific nature of the harm involved (e.g., as seen in items such as "whether or not someone suffered emotionally" and "whether or not someone was cruel"). Likewise, on the portion of the MFT that taps moral "judgments," the harm items involve abstract behaviors about which there is cross-cultural agreement (e.g., as seen in items such as "It can never be right to kill a human being").

Note that the adoption of such a methodological approach is congruent with the larger goal of psychology to identify psychological universals in a parsimonious way. This type of stance involves a search for deep structural explanatory mechanisms. As Higgins and Kruglanski (1996) explained,

> A discovery of lawful principles governing a realm of phenomena is a fundamental objective of scientific research. . . . A scientific analysis needs to probe beneath the surface. In other words, it needs to get away from the "phenotypic" manifestations and strive to unearth the "geneotypes" that may lurk beneath. (p. vii)

In this widely held view in social psychology, cultural considerations are viewed as mere content effects that should be held constant in order to focus on isolating more fundamental underlying psychological mechanisms (Malpass, 1988).

Even with its inclusion of predominately highly abstract items, the MFQ also contains items that are culturally biased toward the United States. The ingroup/loyalty, purity/sanctity, and authority/respect items are not fully abstract but rather sample content that is associated with U.S. conservative political and religious viewpoints. Thus, for example, the ingroup/loyalty items on the MFQ involve the politically sensitive issue of "love for his or her country," the authority/respect items involve the politically sensitive issue of "respect for authority," and the purity/sanctity items involve the culturally specific religious concern of acting "in a way that God would approve of." In these cases, the items are likely to be particularly salient to right-wing orthodox groups in the United States—which may contribute to the finding that endorsement of such items is associated with political and religious conservatism. However, had the MFQ included content that appeals to liberals, such as environmentalism, liberal cultural groups might have shown greater endorsement of other moral foundations beyond harm/care and fairness/reciprocity, such as sanctity-related concerns (see Suhler & Churchland's, 2011, argument).

Although the MFQ succeeds in tapping certain distinctions between American political and religious groups, this is a result of the scale construction process and a feature that does not detract from its fundamental theoretical commitment to assessing abstract universals. The focus of the MFQ is on tapping constructs at a highly global level that glosses over the subtlety and contextual dependence of cultural outlooks. It also adopts an emic perspective that avoids any reference to culturally specific concepts for which there is no ready term or notion in English. Note that it would not be feasible to construct a psychological scale measure that succeeds in tapping the full range of moral concerns found cross-culturally. Such a scale would be unwieldy, if not unbounded, in the range of items it sampled, and it would likely include items that would not be meaningful or that would be construed in nonequivalent ways among different cultural populations.

Theory of Dyadic Morality

In a challenge to the claim that the content of morality is multiple, the *theory of dyadic morality* (TDM), developed by Gray and his colleagues (Gray et al., 2012; Schein & Gray, 2018a), portrays morality as centering on harm. According to this view, moral cognition is based on an internalized cognitive template in which the individual perceives an intentional agent to be causing damage to a vulnerable patient. People are seen as appraising actions as wrong to the extent that they perceive the actions as harmful, with greater perceived harm leading the actions to be viewed as more immoral. From this perspective, moral cognition is based on the complementary perceptual processes of *dyadic comparison* and *dyadic completion* (Gray et al., 2014). In dyadic comparison, acts are compared with an internalized cognitive template of harm, and an assessment of the extent to which they match this cognitive template is made. Once the recognition of harm has occurred, dyadic completion follows, with the harm perceptually linked to the damage or hurt it has caused to a suffering patient. Processes of dyadic comparison and of dyadic completion are seen as forming a mutually reinforcing feedback cycle. For example, an individual's perception that an act of theft involves harm is associated with identification of the target of this harm, which increases perceptions of the level of harm involved and may broaden the range of targets recognized as suffering from the harm. As Schein and

Gray (2018a) argued, "harmification" leads to moralization; moralization in turn leads to more "harmification" (p. 365).

TDM challenges the claims MFT makes about the existence of diverse moral codes. As discussed, MFT considers morality as encompassing distinct moral modules that include not only harm/care but also modules based on fairness/reciprocity, ingroup/loyalty, authority/respect, and purity/sanctity. TDM challenges this view and calls into question the existence of non–harm-based moralities. From this perspective, claims made in MFT that there exists a morality of disgust (e.g., Haidt, 2001) are challenged by findings that such appraisals are more strongly related to perceived harm. To give an example, although moral condemnation of sacrilegious thoughts empirically predict disgust, these ratings are fully mediated by perceptions of harm (Schein et al., 2016; see also Gray & Keeney, 2015).

TDM resembles the mainstream psychological theories of morality discussed earlier that also identify morality exclusively with harm. Both in Kohlberg's cognitive developmental theory and Turiel's distinct domain perspective, moral judgment is identified with content that involves harm, whereas in moral grammar theory the innate heuristic computational mechanisms involve inferences about harm. In contrast to these theoretical viewpoints that privilege actual instances of harm, the focus of TDM, however, is on perceptions of harm. However, TDM does not embrace a pluralistic view of moral content but instead asserts that any evidence of qualitative variation in moral outlooks can be reduced ultimately to harm. To give an example, TDM theorists reject Shweder et al.'s (1987) claim that it constitutes a violation of the morality of divinity for members of a highly orthodox Hindu Indian community to consider it spiritually polluting for a son to eat chicken the day after his father's death. Instead, from the perspective of TDM, this type of case is seen as based fundamentally on harm, given the Hindu Indian cultural belief that eating meat will pollute the recently deceased father's soul, thereby condemning the father to endless suffering (Shweder, 2012). This same argument notably resembles that made by Turiel and his colleagues (1987), who likewise asserted that the type of cultural differences Shweder et al. identified result from contrasting culturally based epistemological assumptions bearing on perceived harm. In this way, TDM adopts a universalistic approach to morality that downplays the existence of any fundamental cultural variation in moral outlooks (e.g., Schein & Gray, 2015).

Empirical challenges have been raised by critics of TDM who maintain that perceiving intentional action as causing harm is neither necessary nor sufficient for moral appraisal (Royzman & Borislow, 2022). Royzman and Borislow (2022) identified situations in which harm is perceived to exist but an action is considered morally justified, such as in cases involving "virtuous violence," such as engaging in p-hacking as a way to achieve social status in one's peer group (e.g., Fiske & Rai, 2014), as well as situations in which an action is not seen as causing harm but nonetheless constitutes a moral violation, such as in a bystander not intervening to help someone in need. In addition, the claim that perceived harm invariably mediates moral appraisal has been empirically challenged, with, for example, findings that concerns with desecration, and not pain, predict moral condemnation of painting desert rocks (Frimer et al., 2015). As Royzman and Borislow noted, Schein and Gray (2018b) began to soften their assertions by portraying the claims in probabilistic rather than certain terms, arguing that harming is only "*typically necessary* for judging an act as immoral" (p. 43, italics added).

Beyond these empirical challenges, however, conceptual limitations may be noted in the analytic approach adopted in TDM. Schein and Gray (2018b) framed their model as congruent with claims Shweder (1982) made that ideas such as harm and justice reflect abstract universals. They also claimed that TDM is even more pluralistic than MFT in its recognition that both morality and harm are sensitive to cultural construction. However, the approach adopted in TDM differs fundamentally from the monistic stance adopted by Shweder and other theorists in cultural psychology who, while acknowledging the existence of abstract universals related to such concepts as harm, justice, personhood, and territories of the self, recognize the impoverished explanatory stance of such universals. As the philosopher Hart (1961), cited in Shweder (1982, p. 44) observed: "Treat like cases alike and different cases differently" is the central element in the idea of justice but it is by itself incomplete and "cannot afford any determinate guide to conduct." Likewise, Miller (2005) argued that it is "ultimately reductive and untrue to everyday phenomenal experience to partition out . . . (cultural) . . . influences to tap a measure of 'pure' moral outlook" (p. 385). As Shweder (1982) explained, "It is necessary to go beyond such abstractions as duty, harm, and justice. One must examine some rather concrete, culture-specific ideas about what is a vice and what is a virtue" (p. 45). In giving no theoretical attention to culturally variable meanings that inform concrete moral judgments, TDM is unable to predict or explain the basis of group variability in everyday moral reasoning. Whereas the contrasting moral judgments that eating a cow represents a moral violation versus a matter of personal choice may be related to differences in levels of perceived harm, such an empirical demonstration provides no insight into why such actions are seen as varying in harmfulness or into meanings other than harm that they have. TDM has predictive power but limited explanatory force in accounting for specific cultural differences in everyday moral reasoning.

BRINGING CULTURE TO WORK ON MORALITY

In this section, we consider ways to understand culture and its impact on moral appraisals. We then discuss challenges facing psychologists in giving greater weight to culture in research on morality.

Understanding Culture

Psychology theorists have historically embraced ecological views that treat culture as adapted to the objective adaptive affordances and constraints of the environment (e.g., Berry, 1976; Nisbett et al., 2001; Whiting & Whiting, 1975). An ecological perspective on culture is congruent with the field's long-standing embrace of evolutionary models and with the emphasis more broadly in psychology on universal laws of behavior. Ecological approaches support the mainstream psychological stance of assuming that culture represents mere content and does not contribute anything new to psychological theory beyond the attention already given to situational or individual difference influences on behavior.

Whereas ecological views of culture are important, one must also recognize that cultures involve symbolic meanings that are not based purely on adaptive affordances and constraints (D'Andrade, 1984; Geertz, 1973; Sahlins, 1976). From a symbolic perspective, culture is recognized to include non-rational meanings that define and thus bring into being certain social realities (Searle, 1969). To give an example from work on morality, the assumption made in the Kohlbergian tradition that only humans are entitled to protection from harm neglects conceptions of personhood held in certain groups, such as Hindu Indian outlooks that accord value to all life, not just human life (Vasudev & Hummel, 1987). In another example, work by Smetana (1981) shows that whether an abortion is regarded as a moral violation versus as a matter of personal choice depends on culturally variable conceptions of the point at which personhood begins.

From a symbolic perspective, it is further recognized that cultural change is patterned by historical shifts and not merely by adaptive processes. Inglehart and Baker (2000), for example, showed that the cultural heritage of a society, such as whether it maintains Confucian or Protestant cultural traditions, affects outlooks even with modernization and globalization (DiMaggio, 1994). From this perspective, it is recognized that the outcomes associated with objective conditions of life vary depending on cultural community and ethnicity and are not predicted merely by objective affordances and constraints related to wealth or socioeconomic status (Kusserow, 1999; Lareau, 2003).

Culture, it may be seen, provides a code that guides but does not fully determine an individual's conduct, just as language provides a code for individual speech. Assessing culture then requires the identification of symbolic meanings that are embodied in practices and that affect the meanings accorded to everyday activities. To illustrate, Shweder and his colleagues (1995) identified cultural variability in everyday parent–infant sleeping practices, with this variability associated with contrasting moral meanings. Whereas middle-class American parents consider independent sleeping arrangements important in supporting the child's growing autonomy, cultures such as Japan and India disparage that as harmful. In another example, Tobin and his colleagues (1989) showed that both American and Japanese teachers recognize that having a high teacher–student ratio in preschool classrooms affords more individual attention to students from the teacher. However, whereas American teachers value a high teacher–student ratio as a means of supporting each child's creativity, Japanese teachers disparage the practice as detracting from the child's capacity to gain experiences as a member of a peer community. One must recognize that there is not a one-to-one relationship between a cultural practice and its meanings, with the same practice having, in cases, divergent meanings in different cultural communities.

Challenges

Cultural approaches tend to be not only downplayed but actively rejected by mainstream theories of morality. Beyond the concern with cultural relativism, theorists tend to view cultural concerns in social psychology as antithetical to the goal of developing models that have explanatory power and parsimony.

It is important for mainstream theorists of morality to better account for everyday morality. For example, just as it is recognized that inborn grammars give rise to a multiplicity of real-world languages, one must recognize that any inborn moral grammar has limited predictive power to explain everyday moral reasoning. Issues with external validity, for example, arise in the use of trolley dilemmas as a measure of moral outlooks. This method has become a standard way to assess morality in social psychology. It has theoretical appeal in tapping into philosophical concepts, such as the distinction between deontological and utilitarian outlooks. As recent critics have pointed out (e.g., Bauman et al., 2014), however, the type of quandary portrayed in the trolley dilemma is unrepresentative of the moral situations people experience in real-world settings and may even be met with amusement by respondents, despite the fact that it portrays a life-and-death decision.

Beyond giving greater attention to real-world moral judgments, it is also important to consider a wider range of cultural outlooks in theory and construct development. Many mainstream psychology research hypotheses are based on informal observations made by researchers about behavioral effects they have observed or personally experienced. As Moscovici (1972) once commented about social psychology,

> The real advance made by American social psychology was . . . that it took for its theme of research and for the content of its theories the issues of its own society. Its merit was as much in its techniques as in translating the problems of American society into sociopsychological terms and in making them an object of scientific inquiry. (p. 19)

This kind of stance of adopting methods with limited cultural inclusiveness, as noted earlier, may be seen in MFQ items that do not capture culturally variable moral outlooks, beyond constructs linked to U.S. political culture. It is important to work toward enhancing not only the construct validity of measures but also their cultural validity. To the extent that items included in scale measures are based on constructs that are particularly salient in the United States or in other Western cultures, or that are framed in a highly abstract way intended to tap universals, they are likely to provide limited insight into the cultural variability that exists in moral outlooks.

One way to incorporate a wider range of cultural sensibilities in the formulation and testing of psychological constructs is through collaborations among researchers from different cultural backgrounds, who each draw from their own real life experiences, not merely from global claims associated with such dichotomies as the individualism–collectivist distinction. Making greater use of open-ended measures that provide study participants with opportunities to freely express their outlooks as opposed to merely responding to preset response alternatives also would be valuable.

CULTURAL INFLUENCES ON MORALITY AND MOTIVATION

Research has uncovered cultural variability in moral and motivational outlooks, even as it also reveals certain cross-cultural commonalities. In this section, we provide an overview of this cultural work and its theoretical significance.

Justice and Harm

A concern with justice and harm exists universally; however, whereas all cultural groups maintain a global concept of justice, in endorsing general propositions to avoid harm and to treat like cases alike (Shweder, 1982), marked cultural variation exists in reasoning about justice in specific situations.

This variation arises from such factors as contrasting interpretations of what constitutes harm, which entities are considered entitled to protection from harm, how expansively to define the territories of the self that are viewed as deserving protection from harm, and the weight given to contextual factors.

In an investigation that compared responses of an orthodox Brahmin Indian population with responses of a secular American population, Shweder et al. (1987) showed that the moral appraisal of justice reflects culturally variable conceptions of personhood. In endorsing a hierarchical view of gender relations, the Brahmin Indian informants considered an unequal inheritance between males and females as morally right, whereas American respondents, who hold more egalitarian gender norms, considered an unequal inheritance as morally wrong. In another example, only the Brahmin Indian informants, and not the American informants, extended protection from harm to non-human animals in deeming the consumption of beef morally wrong.

This program of research also demonstrated that issues of individual rights depend on cultural meanings; what is considered a moral violation in one culture is considered a matter of individual rights in another. To illustrate, whereas Brahmin Indians considered it morally wrong for a widow to eat fish after her husband dies, in judging that such an action would be polluting and thus interfere with her spiritual salvation, Americans treated the issue as a matter of individual rights, arguing that all people have the right to eat whatever they want, when they want (Shweder et al., 1987). In contrast to distinct domain theorists' claim that matters of personal choice are self-constructed by individuals on the basis of the identification of issues involving the absence of harm (Nucci, 1997, 2014), this work shows that personal choice categorization is affected by cultural meanings, with culturally variable outlooks entailed in the judgment that no harm has occurred.

Cultural variation has also been observed to be affected by the priority given to justice relative to competing interpersonal considerations. Within mainstream theories of morality, as well as in Kantian philosophy (Gert, 1988), justice obligations are considered duties that can be realized completely merely by not engaging in harm or rights violations. On this basis, they are assumed to take precedence over helping or meeting interpersonal responsibilities, which are considered too unbounded in scope to be realized completely. This claim, however, does not take into account cultural variation in the moral salience of interpersonal expectations. Cross-cultural commonality has been shown in the priority given to justice obligations over competing interpersonal expectations in cases involving life-and-death consequences (Miller & Bersoff, 1992). However, the research further showed that whereas Americans give priority to justice obligations over competing interpersonal responsibilities in a range of non–life-threatening situations that include family, friend, and stranger relationships, Indians give priority to meeting inter-personal responsibilities (Miller & Bersoff, 1992). This pattern is illustrated in responses to a hypothetical vignette that presented a conflict situation in which the only way to reach one's best friend's wedding in time to deliver the rings was to steal a train ticket that had been left unattended at a train station. Whereas Americans considered it morally obligatory to not steal the ticket, Indians considered stealing the ticket as morally obligatory given that it was the only way to fulfill the interpersonal expectation. These findings challenge the assumption of moral grammar theory that harm caused by action is invariably worse than harm caused by inaction, given that Indians judged inaction (e.g., failing to arrive at the wedding in time to deliver the rings) more negatively than action (e.g., theft of the train ticket). They also point to cultural variation in the weighting of justice obligations relative to competing interpersonal expectations in cases beyond the type of life-and-death situations privileged in the trolley dilemma.

Cultural variation in the weight given to contextual factors may also influ-ence moral judgment. To categorize a behavior as a moral or conventional violation, the agent must be seen as sufficiently in control of their behavior that they could have acted otherwise. This contrast is reflected in the distinc-tion between an *action*, which is under the agent's voluntary control (e.g., deliberately hitting someone) versus an *occurrence*, which is involuntary (e.g., one's body hitting someone after a bus swerves). Research conducted among American and Indian populations indicates that this distinction is made universally, with both cultural groups appraising an action that is fully outside the agent's control as something for which they should not be held morally accountable (e.g., a man shattering his friend's glass shelf after the ladder on which he is standing breaks; Bersoff & Miller, 1993). How-ever, in cases in which the agent is under situational pressures but still has some control over their actions, Indians, more frequently than Americans, absolved agents of moral accountability for justice breaches. In particular, when a justice violation was undertaken in the context of such potentially extenuating circumstances as the agent's emotional duress or immaturity, Indians showed a greater tendency than did Americans to judge that the agent should not be held morally accountable for their behavior. To illustrate, one emotional duress vignette involves a man striking two strangers in a park after becoming irate when they mocked his facial deformity, whereas one of the agent-immaturity vignettes involved a young child taking a small toy out of a store without paying for it. In these cases, Indians, more frequently than Americans, judged that the agent could not totally control their behavior and thus that social expectations did not apply. These results could not be explained in terms of contrasting moral appraisals of the issues themselves.

Thus, in an experimental condition that presented only the standard social domain distinctions, without any response option to absolve the agent of accountability, Indians more frequently judged the breaches as moral violations than did Americans.

The present considerations highlight the need to take into account nonmoral beliefs and values in understanding real life moral reasoning. One must recognize that cultural groups may differ in their application of moral rules to situations even when they agree about the moral status of the issues under consideration. Cultural variation in moral judgment about concrete situations then may result from nonmoral attributions made about situational influences on behavior.

Interpersonal Responsibilities

Interpersonal responsibilities involve expectations to help that are based, in part, on the agent's connection to the needy party, such as their role relationship or personal bond. In mainstream theories of morality, interpersonal responsibilities, such as commitments to one's parents based on filial piety, have tended either to be considered as nonmoral in nature or to be neglected entirely. Thus, for example, in mainstream developmental theories of morality such outlooks have been viewed as having only a social conventional or preconventional rather than moral status, on the basis of the assumption that interpersonal responsibilities involve partiality and thus lack the generality associated with moral laws.

The argument that interpersonal responsibilities had been mischaracterized in Kohlberg's cognitive developmental model was first made by Gilligan (1977, 1982) in her claims about the existence of a morality of caring. Gilligan has argued that the morality of caring represents an alternative to the morality of justice in that the former is based on relationship ties and that involves bonds of caring rather than being impartial and rational in nature. Gilligan portrayed the morality of caring as universal while viewing it as relied on more by females than by males—a claim later challenged by empirical evidence showing that males rely on caring to as great an extent as females (Walker, 1984, 1991). In turn, in mainstream social psychology, interpersonal responsibilities have been neglected, even in an approach such as MFT that purports to offer a comprehensive approach that captures all moral outlooks on a worldwide scale.

In terms of limitations, whereas Gilligan claimed that interpersonal responsibilities are fully moral in nature, she and her colleagues did not provide evidence that the morality of caring is distinct from beneficence, other than in its relationship dependence. This may be seen in an example she gave in which an 11-year-old girl describes the discretionary nature of the morality of caring:

> If you have a responsibility with somebody else, then you should keep it to a certain extent, but to the extent that it is really going to hurt you or stop you from doing something that you really, really want, then I think maybe you should put yourself first. (Gilligan, 1982, pp. 35–36)

As can be seen in this example, the morality of caring resembles beneficence in that it is a discretionary commitment rather than a matter of obligation.

A program of cross-cultural research that Miller et al. (1990) undertook among European American and Hindu Indian populations provides evidence that Indians hold a form of interpersonal morality that is as obligatory as justice expectations. In terms of commonalities, the research showed that both Americans and Indians share the view that it is desirable to help family and friends (Miller et al., 1990); however, Americans consider helping family and friends a matter of personal decision, whereas Indians consider it a moral duty that extends to a broad range of need and role situations, including to cases involving self-sacrifice (Miller, 1994; Miller & Bersoff, 1995). The nature of these cultural differences in interpersonal morality are illustrated in open-ended responses given by European American and Indian respondents to the case of an adult son not looking after his elderly parents in his own home but arranging for their care elsewhere. Appraising such behavior as the son's failure to perform his moral duty, an Indian respondent argued that "It's a son's duty—birth duty—to take care of his parents. . . . Even if the parents had not [done] so much for the son, still he is expected to have a certain responsibility toward his parents" (Miller & Luthar, 1989, p. 253). In contrast, an American respondent categorized this as a matter of personal choice in arguing: "It's up to the individual to decide. . . . It wasn't a life-and-death-situation, and their needs were being taken care of. Beyond that, it's a personal choice" (Miller & Luthar, 1989, p. 253).

Cross-cultural research also challenges Gilligan's (1977, 1982) claim that the morality of caring is undiminished by the self-serving affective considerations that exist in close relationships. Miller and Bersoff (1998) demonstrated that only Americans, and not Indians, treat interpersonal responsibilities as contingent on personal affinity and liking. Thus, for example, whereas Americans considered it acceptable to decline to help one's brother if an individual does not particularly like or enjoy spending time with that brother, Indians considered the duty to help one's brother as undiminished by personal affinity and liking.

Within-culture comparisons involving the methodological strategy of triangulation (Kitayama et al., 2006; Medin et al., 2007; Miller, 1984) made it possible for researchers to evaluate whether the cross-cultural differences they observed could be fully explained from an evolutionary perspective in terms of the lesser societal wealth and exposure to globalization processes in India as compared with the United States. Within-culture comparisons showed that no differences occurred in moral outlook between Indian groups of high versus low socioeconomic status (Miller et al., 1990; Miller & Bersoff, 1992; see also Miller, 1984). Such findings call into question claims that differences between individualistic versus collectivist cultural populations can be fully explained as adaptations to different objective conditions of life.

Other types of cross-cultural differences have been observed in interpersonal responsibilities (for a review, see Miller & Källberg-Shroff, 2020). For example, research among Japanese samples has uncovered a perspective on interpersonal morality that centers on *omoiyari* (empathy) and that takes into account the concerns of others in the situation (Shimizu, 2001). Such a stance may be seen in the following response of an adolescent who refrained from reporting a case of student vandalism, in empathizing with the student's desire to retain a supportive relationship with his mother, the school nurse:

> You see, if I became their enemy by accusing them, they would be uncomfortable to see my mother . . . although they destroy school property, I would feel bad for them if they lost someone with whom they could talk about their problems. (Shimizu, 2001, p. 463)

In another example, research with Finnish adolescents uncovered a form of interpersonal morality that gives priority to promoting the welfare of citizens in the larger community (Vainio, 2015).

Spiritual Outlooks

A contribution of cross-cultural research is the highlighting of the importance of attending to spiritual outlooks that are reflected in everyday activities. For example, research has found that purity concerns contribute to the tendency to moralize food practices and health activities among both Americans and other cultural groups (e.g., Rozin, 1990; Rozin & Singh, 1999). Likewise, in work conducted among U.S. fundamentalist Baptist communities, Jensen (1997) documented ways that outlooks on marriage are framed in terms of spiritual concerns, with respondents considering divorce a sacrilege that "breaks down the very essence of religion" (p. 342). Spiritual concerns are also salient in socialization practices, such as those seen in the response of an 8-year-old Hindu Indian boy who described fearing divine sanctions for his transgressions: "If we do good for God, God will also do good for us.

But if we have broken his idol by mistake and if we don't tell everyone, then God will be upset and angry" (Pandya & Bhangaokar, 2015, p. 33).

An additional contribution of cross-cultural research on spiritual concerns is the highlighting of the nonrational beliefs that underlie moral outlooks. For example, Shweder et al. (1987) showed that orthodox Hindu Indian populations consider it a moral violation for a wife to dine with her husband's elder brother or for a widow to eat fish, with their reasoning influenced by such spiritually based epistemological premises as that "The husband is a moving god and should be treated with comparable respect" and "The body is a temple with a spirit dwelling in it. . . . Therefore, impure things must be kept out of and away from the body" (pp. 76–77). The cross-cultural differences associated with these types of epistemological assumptions cannot be fully reconciled with reason and evidence or meaningfully abstracted from moral appraisal. For example, assumptions that the universe is ordered by a forgiving god, by immutable laws of karma, or by random processes of chance, represent conceptual premises that inform moral appraisals (White et al., 2019). From the present perspective, the goal of work in cultural psychology is to gain insight into psychological processes at the level of lived experience, and not merely at an abstract level or as an ideal type. In contributing to basic theory in the discipline, and in offering empirically testable predictions that consider situational influences on behavior, work in cultural psychology achieves the theoretical and methodological rigor of psychology even as it continues to be downplayed.

Implications for Motivation

In the sections that follow, we present examples of ways that culturally variable moral outlooks motivate behavior. For illustrative purposes, we discuss findings in three different content areas: (a) lying, (b) internalization of helping norms, and (c) norms of reciprocity.

Lying
Cultural work has identified culturally variable outlooks on lying that are motivated by distinctive moral concerns. Fu et al. (2001) demonstrated that Chinese show a greater tendency than Canadians to approve of lying in prosocial situations. This may be seen, for example, in one of the prosocial vignettes they presented to participants, which portrayed a child lying to his teacher about having given lunch money to a fellow student. In this type of situation, involving taking credit for a prosocial action, Chinese endorsed lying, whereas Canadians considered it wrong to lie. These culturally variable outlooks on

lying were motivated by contrasting moral concerns, with Canadians basing their stance that lying was wrong in this situation on the moral values of honesty and self-responsibility and Chinese basing their stance that lying was desirable in this situation on their moral sense that it is immodest to acknowledge one's good deeds. Lee et al. (1997, 2001) have established that this cultural difference in lying was evident among children as young as age 7 years and increased in extent over the age range from 7 to 16 years.

Subsequent research (Dmytro et al., 2014, Lau et al., 2013) has established that Chinese children rated lying more positively in situations that involved helping a collective and harming an individual, whereas Canadian children showed the reverse contextual effect, with these cross-cultural differences increasing with the size of the collective involved (e.g., class vs. national teams). Of note is that Canadian children justified their outlooks largely on the basis of moral concerns about harm. In contrast, Chinese justified their judgments on the basis of the moral importance of showing loyalty to social collectives, with these moral outlooks congruent with moral education in Chinese schools and with Confucian ethical values.

Internalization of Helping Norms
In terms of helping norms, cultural work has shown that the degree to which norms to help friends and family are experienced in agentic terms is related to culturally variable moral outlooks on helping. Miller et al. (2011) showed that Americans associated a lesser sense of choice and satisfaction with helping in situations when it is strongly socially expected as compared with when social expectations to help are low. In contrast, Indians associated a strong sense of duty with helping family and friends that did not vary as a function of how strongly the help was socially expected (see also Miller & Bersoff, 1994). These cross-cultural differences in agentic motivation notably were related to cross-cultural differences in moral reasoning. Miller et al. (1990) demonstrated that whereas Indians tended to categorize helping family and friends as role related moral duties, Americans tended to categorize them in "personal–moral" terms, in which they considered helping as simultaneously a moral obligation and a discretionary matter of person decision making. This moral stance reflects the conflicting attitude toward meeting social role expectations held more generally among Americans (see also Markus & Kitayama, 1994), which considers meeting social expectations as in conflict with one's personal preferences. From the perspective of self-determination theory, it is assumed that environments that are characterized by unclear or conflicting social expectations are less fully internalized than are environments in which social expectations are more consistently endorsed (Deci & Ryan,

1987). In categorizing helping family and friends in this conflictual way as a moral obligation that is discretionary to fulfill, it was predicted and observed that role-related helping expectations would be less fully internalized in the United States than in India.

This cultural work also has implications for how role obligations are treated methodologically in self-determination theory. Self-determination theorists assume that once role related expectations have been fully internalized, the individual is motivated exclusively from internalized psychological orientations, such as in feeling that a particular way of behaving is personally important to them or congruent with their personal values (Deci & Ryan, 1987; Ryan & Deci, 2017). Self-determination theory measures thus score items that involve acting out of a sense of obligation or duty as external motivational orientations that are no different from items that reference sanctions or other controlling influences. Current cultural work on motivation shows, however, that the sense of role-related duty that underlies a felt moral duty to be responsive to the needs of family and friends among Indians represents a fully internalized motivational stance that should be scored this way on self-determination theory scale measures. More broadly, the research challenges claims made in certain social psychological works (e.g., Bontempo et al., 1990; Iyengar & Lepper, 1999) that a lesser sense of agency is associated with the strong sense of obligation associated with collectivism (Oyserman et al., 2002) or that collectivism entails the subordination of the self to the group (e.g., Singelis, 1994; Triandis, 1995).

Norms of Reciprocity

Obligations to help are also motivationally linked with culturally variable norms of reciprocity. A recent cross-cultural investigation has revealed that the obligation to help family and friends reflects culturally variable norms of reciprocity (Miller et al., 2014, 2017). Molm et al. (2007) showed that Americans rely, in regard to social support, on a form of non–market-based exchange norm that involves a felt obligation to reciprocate help received soon after receiving a benefit. This form of exchange involves not only a sense of indebtedness but also of gratitude, and it supports the closeness found in family and friend relationships (Adams & Miller, 2022). In contrast, Indians feel an obligation to be responsive to the needs of the help giver and, when future needs arise, with reciprocity, assuming a communal form that is based on need-based mutual responsiveness.

These culturally variable norms of reciprocity have further been shown to influence how the obligation to help is affected by the passage of time (Goyal & Miller, 2018). In maintaining communal norms, the obligation to help among Indians is unaffected by reciprocation and does not vary with the passage of time. In contrast, the obligation to help among Americans decreases after reciprocation according to two contrasting patterns involving, respectively, immunity and expiration, which are associated with the expectation for short-term reciprocation associated with exchange. Americans, but not Indians, feel less obligated to aid a benefactor who asks for help years in the future if they have achieved immunity from any further reciprocation in having made a short-term reciprocation for earlier help they received from this benefactor. Likewise, the obligation to reciprocate to a benefactor is less if the opportunity for reciprocation occurs years after one has received a benefit as compared with only a few months after receiving a benefit because this period extends beyond the short-term reciprocation time window and the expectation to reciprocate has expired.

Note that the interrelationship between the obligation to help and norms of reciprocity has implications for adaptation. In the case of India, the reliance on communal norms implies that the strong sense of moral duty to family and friends Indians feel is not a selfless stance; instead, the stance involves mutuality, with the felt moral duty to help family and friends supported by the understanding that the help giver can expect to receive help themselves should they ever be in need. In contrast, among Americans the interpersonal trust that exists in close relationships depends on reciprocating in a time-sensitive manner. Research also has demonstrated the existence of cross-cultural commonalities in helping ingroup members and has highlighted the distinctive ways community is achieved across cultures. In the short-term time condition of Goyal and Miller's (2018) study, Indians and Americans reported similar levels of obligation to aid a friend who was in need, which was supported by their culturally variable norms of reciprocity and distinctive moral outlooks on helping.

CONCLUSION

In this chapter, we have underscored the respects in which cultural approaches to morality are underappreciated in mainstream theories of morality within developmental and social psychology. This stance has resulted from concerns with moral relativism as well as from a commitment to the natural science ideal of explanation.

The critique of relativism, in particular within mainstream developmental work on morality, we note, has been directed at an extreme form of relativism in which all cultural practices are treated as equally morally acceptable. However, this constitutes a straw man argument that does not reflect the position embraced by cultural psychologists; instead, the position adopted in cultural psychology work involves moral pluralism and cultural contextualization (Miller et al., 2019). It constitutes a position that highlights the importance of more fully taking into account local cultural meanings in psychological theory and of recognizing the significant, though not unbounded, diversity that exists in moral outlooks. It is also a position that supports social change while rejecting the premise that social change can take only the form of a focus on universal human rights, as assumed by various feminists and other contemporary social theorists (see Menon's, 2002, argument).

The concern raised by work in cultural psychology, however, is that the product of this type of approach is a reification of existing psychological theory and the adoption of methods that are insensitive to cultural variation. For example, the heavy reliance on forms of the trolley dilemma in contemporary work on morality in mainstream social psychology entails a culturally narrow focus centered exclusively on deontological versus utilitarian justice issues and applied in extreme situations. Although this type of standardization of methods might be welcome, in particular because it involves the adoption of easily administered assessment tools, it glosses over cultural differences in moral viewpoints about issues other than abstract justice concerns and has low ecological validity in predicting everyday moral reasoning.

Work on morality in cultural psychology accepts the existence of moral universals at an abstract level and in relation to clear-cut cases. It also rejects extreme forms of moral relativism, in which the possibility of identifying moral abuse is denied. However, it raises concerns that important cultural variation is being glossed over in present theoretical approaches and obscured in the use of methodological approaches that are highly constraining of the responses observed. Just as cultural psychologists acknowledge the important universals that exist in moral outlooks, they call for greater attention to the significant cultural variation that remains to be explored as an important frontier for future work.

REFERENCES

Abarbanell, L., & Hauser, M. D. (2010). Mayan morality: An exploration of permissible harms. *Cognition*, *115*(2), 207–224. https://doi.org/10.1016/j.cognition.2009.12.007

Adams, M., & Miller, J. G. (2022). The flexible nature of everyday reciprocity: Reciprocity, helping and relationship closeness. *Motivation and Emotion*, *46*, 461–475. https://doi.org/10.1007/s11031-022-09949-y

Ardila-Rey, A., & Killen, M. (2001). Middle class Colombian children's evaluations of personal, moral, and social-conventional interactions in the classroom. *International Journal of Behavioral Development*, *25*(3), 246–255. https://doi.org/10.1080/01650250042000221

Baillargeon, R., Scott, R. M., & Bian, L. (2016). Psychological reasoning in infancy. *Annual Review of Psychology, 67*(1), 159–186. https://doi.org/10.1146/annurev-psych-010213-115033

Baillargeon, R., Scott, R. M., He, Z., Sloane, S., Setoh, P., Jin, K.-S., Wu, D., & Bian, L. (2015). Psychological and sociomoral reasoning in infancy. In M. Mikulincer, P. R. Shaver, E. Borgida, & J. A. Bargh (Eds.), *APA handbook of personality and social psychology: Vol. 1. Attitudes and social cognition* (pp. 79–150). American Psychological Association. https://doi.org/10.1037/14341-003

Bandura, A. (1969). Social learning of moral judgments. *Journal of Personality and Social Psychology, 11*(3), 275–279. https://doi.org/10.1037/h0026998

Banerjee, K., Huebner, B., & Hauser, M. (2010). Intuitive moral judgments are robust across variation in gender, education, politics and religion: A large-scale web-based study. *Journal of Cognition and Culture, 10*(3–4), 253–281. https://doi.org/10.1163/156853710X531186

Bauman, C. W., McGraw, A. P., Bartels, D. M., & Warren, C. (2014). Revisiting external validity: Concerns about trolley problems and other sacrificial dilemmas in moral psychology. *Social and Personality Psychology Compass, 8*(9), 536–554. https://doi.org/10.1111/spc3.12131

Berry, J. W. (1976). *Human ecology and cognitive style*. Halsted Press.

Bersoff, D. M., & Miller, J. G. (1993). Culture, context, and the development of moral accountability judgments. *Developmental Psychology, 29*(4), 664–676. https://doi.org/10.1037/0012-1649.29.4.664

Bontempo, R., Lobel, S., & Triandis, H. (1990). Compliance and value internalization in Brazil and the U.S. *Journal of Cross-Cultural Psychology, 21*(2), 200–213. https://doi.org/10.1177/0022022190212004

Cushman, F., Young, L., & Hauser, M. (2006). The role of conscious reasoning and intuition in moral judgment: Testing three principles of harm. *Psychological Science, 17*(12), 1082–1089. https://doi.org/10.1111/j.1467-9280.2006.01834.x

D'Andrade, R. G. (1984). Cultural meaning systems. In R. A. Shweder & R. A. LeVine (Eds.), *Culture theory: Essays on mind, self, and emotion* (pp. 88–119). Cambridge University Press.

Deci, E. L., & Ryan, R. M. (1987). The support of autonomy and the control of behavior. *Journal of Personality and Social Psychology, 53*(6), 1024–1037. https://doi.org/10.1037/0022-3514.53.6.1024

DiMaggio, P. (1994). Culture and economy. In N. J. Smelser & R. Swedberg (Eds.), *Handbook of economic sociology* (pp. 27–52). Princeton University Press.

Dmytro, D., Lo, J., O'Leary, J., Fu, G., Lee, K., & Cameron, C. A. (2014). Development of cultural perspectives on verbal deception in competitive contexts. *Journal of Cross-Cultural Psychology, 45*(8), 1196–1214. https://doi.org/10.1177/0022022114535485

Donaldson, M. (1978). *Children's minds*. W. W. Norton.

Fiske, A. P., & Rai, T. S. (2014). *Virtuous violence: Hurting and killing to create, sustain, end, and honor social relationships*. Cambridge University Press. https://doi.org/10.1017/CBO9781316104668

Foot, P. (1967). The problem of abortion and the doctrine of the double effect. *Oxford Review, 5*, 5–15. https://doi.org/10.1093/0199252866.003.0002

Frimer, J. A., Tell, C. E., & Haidt, J. (2015). Liberals condemn sacrilege too: The harmless desecration of Cerro Torre. *Social Psychological & Personality Science, 6*(8), 878–886. https://doi.org/10.1177/1948550615597974

Fu, G., Lee, K., Cameron, C. A., & Xu, F. (2001). Chinese and Canadian adults' categorization and evaluation of lie- and truth-telling about prosocial and anti-social behaviors. *Journal of Cross-Cultural Psychology, 32*(6), 720–727. https://doi.org/10.1177/0022022101032006005

Geertz, C. (1973). *The interpretation of cultures.* Basic Books.

Gelman, R. (1978). Cognitive development. *Annual Review of Psychology, 29*(1), 297–332. https://doi.org/10.1146/annurev.ps.29.020178.001501

Gert, B. (1988). *Morality: A new justification of the moral rules.* Oxford University Press.

Gilligan, C. (1977). In a different voice: Women's conceptions of self and of morality. *Harvard Educational Review, 47*(4), 481–517. https://doi.org/10.17763/haer.47.4.g6167429416hg5l0

Gilligan, C. (1982). *In a different voice: Psychological theory and women's development.* Harvard University Press.

Goyal, N., & Miller, J. G. (2018). The importance of timing in reciprocity: An investigation of reciprocity norms among Indians and Americans. *Journal of Cross-Cultural Psychology, 49*(3), 381–403. https://doi.org/10.1177/0022022117746239

Graham, J., Haidt, J., Motyl, M., Meindl, P., & Iskiwitch, C. (2018). On the advantages of moral pluralism over moral monism. In K. Gray & J. Graham (Eds.), *Atlas of moral psychology* (pp. 211–222). Guilford Press.

Graham, J., Haidt, J., & Nosek, B. A. (2009). Liberals and conservatives rely on different sets of moral foundations. *Journal of Personality and Social Psychology, 96*(5), 1029–1046. https://doi.org/10.1037/a0015141

Graham, J., Nosek, B. A., Haidt, J., Iyer, R., Koleva, S., & Ditto, P. H. (2011). Mapping the moral domain. *Journal of Personality and Social Psychology, 101*(2), 366–385. https://doi.org/10.1037/a0021847

Gray, K., & Keeney, J. E. (2015). Impure or just weird? Scenario sampling bias raises questions about the foundation of morality. *Social Psychological & Personality Science, 6*(8), 859–868. https://doi.org/10.1177/1948550615592241

Gray, K., Schein, C., & Ward, A. F. (2014). The myth of harmless wrongs in moral cognition: Automatic dyadic completion from sin to suffering. *Journal of Experimental Psychology: General, 143*(4), 1600–1615. https://doi.org/10.1037/a0036149

Gray, K., Young, L., & Waytz, A. (2012). Mind perception is the essence of morality. *Psychological Inquiry, 23*(2), 101–124. https://doi.org/10.1080/1047840X.2012.651387

Haidt, J. (2001). The emotional dog and its rational tail: A social intuitionist approach to moral judgment. *Psychological Review, 108*(4), 814–834. https://doi.org/10.1037/0033-295X.108.4.814

Haidt, J. (2012). *The righteous mind: Why good people are divided by politics and religion.* Pantheon.

Haidt, J., & Graham, J. (2007). When morality opposes justice: Conservatives have moral intuitions that liberals may not recognize. *Social Justice Research, 20*(1), 98–116. https://doi.org/10.1007/s11211-007-0034-z

Haidt, J., & Joseph, C. (2007). The moral mind: How 5 sets of innate moral intuitions guide the development of many culture-specific virtues, and perhaps even modules. In P. Carruthers, S. Laurence, & S. Stich (Eds.), *The innate mind* (pp. 367–391). Oxford University Press.

Hart, H. L. A. (1961). *The concept of law.* Oxford University Press.

Hauser, M. (2006). *Moral minds: How nature designed our universal sense of right and wrong.* HarperCollins.

Hauser, M., Cushman, F., Young, L., Jin, R. K.-X., & Mikhail, J. (2007). A dissociation between moral judgments and justifications. *Mind & Language, 22*(1), 1–21. https://doi.org/10.1111/j.1468-0017.2006.00297.x

Hauser, M. D., Huebner, B., & Lee, J. J. (2010). The moral–conventional distinction in mature moral competence. *Journal of Cognition and Culture, 10*(1–2), 1–26. https://doi.org/10.1163/156853710X497149

Henrich, J., Heine, S. J., & Norenzayan, A. (2010). The weirdest people in the world? *Behavioral and Brain Sciences, 33*(2–3), 61–83. https://doi.org/10.1017/S0140525X0999152X

Higgins, E. T., & Kruglanski, A. W. (1996). *Social psychology: Handbook of basic principles*. Guilford Press.

Inglehart, R., & Baker, W. E. (2000). Modernization, cultural change, and the persistence of traditional values. *American Sociological Review, 65*(1), 19–51. https://doi.org/10.2307/2657288

Iyengar, S. S., & Lepper, M. R. (1999). Rethinking the value of choice: A cultural perspective on intrinsic motivation. *Journal of Personality and Social Psychology, 76*(3), 349–366. https://doi.org/10.1037/0022-3514.76.3.349

Jensen, L. A. (1997). Different worldviews, different morals: America's culture war divide. *Human Development, 40*(6), 325–344. https://doi.org/10.1159/000278737

Kitayama, S., Ishii, K., Imada, T., Takemura, K., & Ramaswamy, J. (2006). Voluntary settlement and the spirit of independence: Evidence from Japan's "Northern frontier." *Journal of Personality and Social Psychology, 91*(3), 369–384. https://doi.org/10.1037/0022-3514.91.3.369

Kohlberg, L. (1969). Stage and sequence: The cognitive–developmental approach to socialization. In D. A. Goslin (Ed.), *Handbook of socialization theory* (pp. 347–380). Rand McNally.

Kohlberg, L. (1971). From is to ought: How to commit the naturalistic fallacy and get away with it in the study of moral development. In T. Mischel (Ed.), *Cognitive development and epistemology* (pp. 151–235). Academic Press. https://doi.org/10.1016/B978-0-12-498640-4.50011-1

Kohlberg, L. (1981). *The philosophy of moral development: Moral stages and the idea of justice* (Vol. 1). Harper & Row.

Kusserow, A. S. (1999). De-homogenizing American individualism: Socializing hard and soft individualism in Manhattan and Queens. *Ethos, 27*(2), 210–234. https://doi.org/10.1525/eth.1999.27.2.210

Lareau, A. (2003). *Unequal childhoods: Class, race, and family life*. University of California Press.

Lau, Y. L., Cameron, C. A., Chieh, K. M., O'Leary, J., Fu, G., & Lee, K. (2013). Cultural differences in moral justifications enhance understanding of Chinese and Canadian children's moral decisions. *Journal of Cross-Cultural Psychology, 44*(3), 461–477. https://doi.org/10.1177/0022022112453315

Lee, K., Cameron, C. A., Xu, F., Xu, G., & Board, J. (1997). Chinese and Canadian children's evaluations of lying and truth telling: Similarities and differences in the context of pro- and antisocial behaviors. *Child Development, 68*(5), 924–934. https://doi.org/10.2307/1132042

Lee, K., Xu, F., Fu, G., Cameron, C. A., & Chen, S. (2001). Taiwan and Mainland Chinese and Canadian children's categorization and evaluation of lie- and truth-telling: A modesty effect. *British Journal of Developmental Psychology, 19*(4), 525–542. https://doi.org/10.1348/026151001166236

Malpass, R. S. (1988). Why not cross-cultural psychology?: A characterization of some mainstream views. In M. H. Bond (Ed.), *The cross-cultural challenge to social psychology: Cross-cultural research and methodology series* (pp. 29–35). Sage.

Markus, H. R., & Kitayama, S. (1994). A collective fear of the collective: Implications for selves and theories of selves. *Personality and Social Psychology Bulletin, 20*(5), 568–579. https://doi.org/10.1177/0146167294205013

Medin, D. L., Unsworth, S. J., & Hirschfeld, L. (2007). Culture, categorization, and reasoning. In S. Kitayama & D. Cohen (Eds.), *Handbook of cultural psychology* (pp. 615–644). Guilford Press.

Menon, U. (2002). Neither victim nor rebel: Feminism and the morality of gender and family life in a Hindu temple town. In R. A. Shweder, M. Minow, & H. R. Markus (Eds.), *Engaging cultural differences: The multicultural challenge in liberal democracies* (pp. 288–308). Russell Sage Foundation.

Miller, J. G. (1984). Culture and development of everyday social explanation. *Journal of Personality and Social Psychology, 46*(5), 961–978. https://doi.org/10.1037/0022-3514.46.5.961

Miller, J. G. (1994). Cultural diversity in the morality of caring: Individually oriented versus duty-based interpersonal moral codes. *Cross-Cultural Research, 28*(1), 3–39. https://doi.org/10.1177/106939719402800101

Miller, J. G. (2005). Insights into moral development from cultural psychology. In M. Killen & J. Smetana (Eds.), *Handbook of moral development* (pp. 375–398). Erlbaum.

Miller, J. G., Akiyama, H., & Kapadia, S. (2017). Cultural variation in communal versus exchange norms: Implications for social support. *Journal of Personality and Social Psychology.* https://doi.org/10.1037/pspi0000091

Miller, J. G., & Bersoff, D. M. (1992). Culture and moral judgment: How are conflicts between justice and interpersonal responsibilities resolved? *Journal of Personality and Social Psychology, 62*(4), 541–554. https://doi.org/10.1037/0022-3514.62.4.541

Miller, J. G., & Bersoff, D. M. (1994). Cultural influences on the moral status of reciprocity and the discounting of endogenous motivation. *Personality and Social Psychology Bulletin, 20*(5), 592–602. https://doi.org/10.1177/0146167294205015

Miller, J. G., & Bersoff, D. M. (1995). Development in the context of everyday family relationships: Culture, interpersonal morality and adaptation. In M. Killen & D. Hart (Eds.), *Morality in everyday life: A developmental perspective* (pp. 259–282). Cambridge University Press.

Miller, J. G., & Bersoff, D. B. (1998). The role of liking in perceptions of the moral responsibility to help: A cultural perspective. *Journal of Experimental Social Psychology, 34*(5), 443–469. https://doi.org/10.1006/jesp.1998.1359

Miller, J. G., Bersoff, D. M., & Harwood, R. L. (1990). Perceptions of social responsibilities in India and in the United States: Moral imperatives or personal decisions? *Journal of Personality and Social Psychology, 58*(1), 33–47. https://doi.org/10.1037//0022-3514.58.1.33

Miller, J. G., Bland, C., Källberg-Shroff, M., Tseng, C.-Y., Montes-George, J., Ryan, K., Das, R., & Chakravarthy, S. (2014). Culture and the role of exchange vs. communal norms in friendship. *Journal of Experimental Social Psychology*, *53*, 79–93. https://doi.org/10.1016/j.jesp.2014.02.006

Miller, J. G., Das, R., & Chakravarthy, S. (2011). Culture and the role of choice in agency. *Journal of Personality and Social Psychology*, *101*(1), 46–61. https://doi.org/10.1037/a0023330

Miller, J. G., & Källberg-Shroff, M. (2020). Culture and the development of moralities of community. In L. Jensen (Ed.), *The Oxford handbook of moral development* (pp. 52–70). Oxford University Press.

Miller, J. G., & Luthar, S. (1989). Issues of interpersonal responsibility and accountability: A comparison of Indians' and Americans' moral judgments. *Social Cognition*, *7*(3), 237–261. https://doi.org/10.1521/soco.1989.7.3.237

Miller, J. G., Wice, M., & Goyal, N. (2019). Cultural psychology of moral development. In S. Kitayama & D. Cohen (Eds.), *Handbook of cultural psychology* (2nd ed., pp. 424–446). Guilford Press.

Molm, L. D., Schaefer, D. R., & Collett, J. L. (2007). The value of reciprocity. *Social Psychology Quarterly*, *70*(2), 199–217. https://doi.org/10.1177/019027250707000208

Moscovici, S. (1972). Society and theory in social psychology. In J. Israel & H. Tajfel (Eds.), *The context of social psychology: A critical assessment* (pp. 17–69). Academic Press.

Nisbett, R. E., Peng, K., Choi, I., & Norenzayan, A. (2001). Culture and systems of thought: Holistic versus analytic cognition. *Psychological Review*, *108*(2), 291–310. https://doi.org/10.1037/0033-295X.108.2.291

Nucci, L. (1997). Culture, universals, and the personal. In H. D. Saltzstein (Ed.), *Culture as a context for moral development: New perspectives on the particular and the universal* (pp. 5–22). Wiley.

Nucci, L. P. (2014). The personal and the moral. In M. Killen & J. G. Smetana (Eds.), *Handbook of moral development* (2nd ed., pp. 538–558). Psychology Press. https://doi.org/10.4324/9780203581957.ch25

Oyserman, D., Coon, H. M., & Kemmelmeier, M. (2002). Rethinking individualism and collectivism: Evaluation of theoretical assumptions and meta-analyses. *Psychological Bulletin*, *128*(1), 3–72. https://doi.org/10.1037/0033-2909.128.1.3

Pandya, N., & Bhangaokar, R. (2015). Divinity in children's moral development: An Indian perspective. In L. A. Jensen (Ed.), *Moral development in a global world: Research from a cultural–developmental perspective* (pp. 20–45). Cambridge University Press. https://doi.org/10.1017/CBO9781139583787.003

Pinker, S. (1984). *Language learnability and language development*. Harvard University Press.

Pinker, S. (2008, January 13). The moral instinct. *The New York Times Magazine*. https://www.nytimes.com/2008/01/13/magazine/13Psychology-t.html

Rawls, J. (1971). *A theory of justice*. Harvard University Press. https://doi.org/10.4159/9780674042605

Royzman, E. B., & Borislow, S. H. (2022). The puzzle of wrongless harms: Some potential concerns for dyadic morality and related accounts. *Cognition*, *220*, 104980. https://doi.org/10.1016/j.cognition.2021.104980

Rozin, P. (1990). Social and moral aspects of food and eating. In I. Rock (Ed.), *The legacy of Solomon Asch: Essays in cognition and social psychology* (pp. 97–110). Erlbaum.

Rozin, P., & Singh, L. (1999). The moralization of cigarette smoking in the United States. *Journal of Consumer Psychology, 8*(3), 321–337. https://doi.org/10.1207/s15327663jcp0803_07

Ryan, R. M., & Deci, E. L. (2017). *Self-determination theory: Basic psychological needs in motivation, development, and wellness.* Guilford Press. https://doi.org/10.1521/978.14625/28806

Sahlins, M. (1976). *Culture and practical reason.* University of Chicago Press.

Schein, C., & Gray, K. (2015). The unifying moral dyad: Liberals and conservatives share the same harm-based moral template. *Personality and Social Psychology Bulletin, 41*(8), 1147–1163. https://doi.org/10.1177/0146167215591501

Schein, C., & Gray, K. (2018a). Moralization: How acts become wrong. In K. Gray & J. Graham (Eds.), *Atlas of moral psychology* (pp. 363–370). Guilford Press.

Schein, C., & Gray, K. (2018b). The theory of dyadic morality: Reinventing moral judgment by redefining harm. *Personality and Social Psychology Review, 22*(1), 32–70. https://doi.org/10.1177/1088868317698288

Schein, C., Ritter, R. S., & Gray, K. (2016). Harm mediates the disgust–immorality link. *Emotion, 16*(6), 862–876. https://doi.org/10.1037/emo0000167

Searle, J. R. (1969). *Speech acts: An essay in the philosophy of language.* Cambridge University Press. https://doi.org/10.1017/CBO9781139173438

Shimizu, H. (2001). Japanese adolescent boys' senses of empathy (*omoiyari*) and Carol Gilligan's perspectives on the morality of care: A phenomenological approach. *Culture and Psychology, 7*(4), 453–475. https://doi.org/10.1177/1354067X0174003

Shweder, R. A. (1982). Beyond self-constructed knowledge: The study of culture and morality. *Merrill–Palmer Quarterly, 28*(1), 41–69.

Shweder, R. A. (1999). Cultural psychology. In R. A. Wilson & F. C. Keil (Eds.), *The MIT encyclopedia of the cognitive sciences* (pp. 211–213). MIT Press.

Shweder, R. A. (2012). Relativism and universalism. In D. Fassin (Ed.), *A companion to moral anthropology* (pp. 85–102). Wiley. https://doi.org/10.1002/9781118290620.ch5

Shweder, R. A., Jensen, L. A., & Goldstein, W. M. (1995). Who sleeps by whom revisited: A method for extracting the moral goods implicit in practice. *New Directions for Child and Adolescent Development, 67*, 21–39. https://doi.org/10.1002/cd.23219956705

Shweder, R. A., Mahapatra, M., & Miller, J. G. (1987). Culture and moral development. In J. Kagan & S. Lamb (Eds.), *The emergence of morality in young children* (pp. 1–83). University of Chicago Press.

Shweder, R. A., & Much, N. C. (1987). Determinants of meaning: Discourse and moral socialization. In W. M. Kurtines & J. L. Gewirtz (Eds.), *Moral development through social interaction* (pp. 197–244). Wiley.

Shweder, R. A., Much, N. C., Mahapatra, M., & Park, L. (1997). The "big three" of morality (autonomy, community, divinity) and the "big three" explanations of suffering. In A. M. Brandt & P. Rozin (Eds.), *Morality and health* (pp. 119–169). Taylor & Francis/Routledge.

Simpson, E. L. (1974). Moral development research: A case study of scientific cultural bias. *Human Development, 17*(2), 81–106. https://doi.org/10.1159/000271335

Singelis, T. M. (1994). The measurement of independent and interdependent self-construals. *Personality and Social Psychology Bulletin, 20*(5), 580–591. https://doi.org/10.1177/0146167294205014

Smetana, J. (1981). Reasoning in the personal and moral domains: Adolescent and young adult women's decision-making regarding abortion. *Journal of Applied Developmental Psychology, 2*(3), 211–226. https://doi.org/10.1016/0193-3973(81)90002-2

Smetana, J. (2006). Social–cognitive domain theory: Consistencies and variations in children's moral and social judgments. In M. Killen & J. G. Smetana (Eds.), *Handbook of moral development* (pp. 119–153). Erlbaum.

Smetana, J. G., Ball, C. L., Jambon, M., & Yoo, H. N. (2018). Are young children's preferences and evaluations of moral and conventional transgressors associated with domain distinctions in judgments? *Journal of Experimental Child Psychology, 173*, 284–303. https://doi.org/10.1016/j.jecp.2018.04.008

Smetana, J. G., Schlagman, N., & Adams, P. W. (1993). Preschool children's judgments about hypothetical and actual transgressions. *Child Development, 64*(1), 202–214. https://doi.org/10.2307/1131446

Snarey, J. R. (1985). Cross-cultural universality of social–moral development: A critical review of Kohlbergian research. *Psychological Bulletin, 97*(2), 202–232. https://doi.org/10.1037/0033-2909.97.2.202

Snarey, J., & Keljo, K. (1991). In a *Gemeinschaft* voice: The cross-cultural expansion of moral development theory. In W. M. Kurtines & J. L. Gewirtz (Eds.), *Handbook of moral behavior and development: Vol. 1. Theory* (pp. 395–424). Erlbaum.

Song, M., Smetana, J. G., & Kim, S. Y. (1987). Korean children's conceptions of moral and conventional transgressions. *Developmental Psychology, 23*(4), 577–582. https://doi.org/10.1037/0012-1649.23.4.577

Spelke, E. S. (2017). Core knowledge, language, and number. *Language Learning and Development, 13*(2), 147–170. https://doi.org/10.1080/15475441.2016.1263572

Suhler, C. L., & Churchland, P. (2011). Can innate, modular "foundations" explain morality? Challenges for Haidt's Moral Foundations Theory. *Journal of Cognitive Neuroscience, 23*(9), 2103–2116. https://doi.org/10.1162/jocn.2011.21637

Thomsen, L., & Carey, S. (2013). Core cognition of social relations. In M. R. Banaji & S. A. Gelman (Eds.), *Navigating the social world: What infants, children, and other species can teach us* (pp. 17–22). Oxford University Press. https://doi.org/10.1093/acprof:oso/9780199890712.003.0004

Tobin, J. J., Wu, D. Y. H., & Davidson, D. H. (1989). *Preschool in three cultures: Japan, China, and the United States*. Yale University Press. https://doi.org/10.1093/acprof:oso/9780199890712.003.0004

Triandis, H. C. (1995). *Individualism and collectivism*. Westview Press.

Turiel, E. (1983). *The development of social knowledge: Morality and convention*. Cambridge University Press.

Turiel, E. (1998a). The development of morality. In N. Eisenberg (Ed.), *Handbook of child psychology: Vol. 3. Social, emotional, and personality development* (pp. 863–892). Wiley.

Turiel, E. (1998b). Notes from the underground: Culture, conflict, and subversion. In J. Langen & M. Killen (Eds.), *Piaget, evolution, and development* (pp. 271–296). Erlbaum.

Turiel, E. (2002). *The culture of morality: Social development, context, and conflict*. Cambridge University Press.

Turiel, E., Killen, M., & Helwig, C. C. (1987). Morality: Its structure, functions, and vagaries. In J. Kagan & S. Lamb (Eds.), *The emergence of morality in young children* (pp. 155–243). University of Chicago Press.

Turiel, E., Smetana, J. G., & Killen, M. (1991). Social contexts in social cognitive development. In W. M. Kurtines & J. L. Gewirtz (Eds.), *Handbook of moral behavior and development, Vol. 2: Research* (pp. 307–332). Erlbaum.

Vainio, A. (2015). Finnish moral landscapes: A comparison of nonreligious, liberal religious, and conservative religious adolescents. In L. A. Jensen (Ed.), *Moral development in a global world: Research from a cultural–developmental perspective* (pp. 46–68). Cambridge University Press. https://doi.org/10.1017/CBO9781139583787.004

Vasudev, J., & Hummel, R. C. (1987). Moral stage sequence and principled reasoning in an Indian sample. *Human Development, 30*(2), 105–118. https://doi.org/10.1159/000273170

Walker, L. J. (1984). Sex differences in the development of moral reasoning: A critical review. *Child Development, 55*(3), 677–691. https://doi.org/10.2307/1130121

Walker, L. J. (1991). Sex differences in moral reasoning. In W. M. Kurtines & J. L. Gewirtz (Eds.), *Handbook of moral behavior and development: Vol. 2. Research* (pp. 333–364). Erlbaum.

White, C. J. M., Kelly, J. M., Shariff, A. F., & Norenzayan, A. (2019). Supernatural norm enforcement: Thinking about karma and God reduces selfishness among believers. *Journal of Experimental Social Psychology, 84*, 103797. https://doi.org/10.1016/j.jesp.2019.03.008

Whiting, B. B., & Whiting, J. W. (1975). *Children of six cultures: A psycho-cultural analysis.* Harvard University Press. https://doi.org/10.4159/harvard.9780674593770

II

PSYCHOLOGICAL FRAMEWORKS AND INDIVIDUAL DIFFERENCES

4

CONSEQUENCES, NORMS, AND GENERAL ACTION TENDENCIES

Understanding Individual Differences in Moral Dilemma Judgments

BERTRAM GAWRONSKI, DILLON M. LUKE, AND ANITA KÖRNER

A few years before the COVID-19 pandemic killed more than 6 million people around the world, an outbreak of the Ebola virus disease in West Africa stirred a heated debate in the United States. The debate was ignited by the case of Dr. Kent Brantly, an American physician who contracted the Ebola virus in Liberia (Blinder & Grady, 2014). It soon became clear that Brantly would die if he did not receive advanced medical treatment in his home country, but returning him involved a risk of causing an Ebola outbreak in the United States. In the weeks before Brantly was returned and cured, some people claimed a moral duty to save Brantly's life by returning him to the United States for treatment; others argued that it would be better to let him die in Liberia to avoid the potential death of a larger number of people.

The two conflicting views in this debate illustrate two philosophical ideas about morality. From a deontological view, the moral status of a behavioral option depends on its consistency with moral norms. This view is reflected in the argument that returning Brantly to the United States is morally right because it conforms to a moral duty to save his life. In contrast, from a utilitarian view, the moral status of a behavioral option depends on its consequences

https://doi.org/10.1037/0000342-005
Motivation and Morality: A Multidisciplinary Approach, M. K. Berg and E. C. Chang (Editors)

for the greater good. This view is reflected in the argument that not returning Brantly to the United States is morally right because it prevents the potential death of a larger number of people. Inspired by the distinction between deontology and utilitarianism, a substantial amount of research has investigated people's responses to moral dilemmas that pit one philosophical idea against the other (for a review, see Bartels et al., 2015). In addition to identifying various contextual factors that influence people's preference for utilitarian versus deontological judgments (e.g., Suter & Hertwig, 2011; Valdesolo & DeSteno, 2006), this research revealed a wide range of individual-difference variables that are systematically related to moral dilemma judgments (e.g., Gleichgerrcht & Young, 2013; Moore et al., 2011; Patil, 2015; van den Bos et al., 2011). The latter findings suggest that conflicting views in societal debates about the right course of action in real-world dilemmas (e.g., the debate about Brantly's return for medical treatment) may reflect deeper psychological differences between people.

In this chapter, we illustrate the value of a mathematical modeling approach in understanding individual differences in moral dilemma judgments. Toward this end, we first explain the traditional approach to studying moral dilemma judgments and its limitations. We then describe the CNI model of moral decision making (Gawronski et al., 2017), which quantifies three determinants of moral dilemma judgments: sensitivity to consequences (C), sensitivity to moral norms (N), and general preference for inaction versus action (I). In the remainder of the chapter, we review research that has used the CNI model to investigate the nature of individual differences in moral dilemma judgments. Our central argument is that, by identifying individual differences along the three dimensions, research using the CNI model provides more nuanced insights into the roots of societal controversies about the right course of action in real-world dilemmas.

THE TRADITIONAL DILEMMA APPROACH

In the traditional approach to studying moral dilemma judgments, participants are presented with a brief scenario with two response options, one of which is morally right from a utilitarian view and morally wrong from a deontological view, the other of which is morally right from a deontological view and morally wrong from a utilitarian view. The most well-known example is the *trolley dilemma*, a scenario in which a runaway trolley is on course to kill a group of five workers unless a particular action is performed that would kill one person instead of five (see Chapter 3, this volume). In a variant known as the *switch dilemma*, participants are asked if it would be acceptable to pull a switch to redirect the trolley to another track where it would kill only one person instead of five (Foot, 1967). In a variant known as the *footbridge dilemma*, participants are asked if it would be acceptable to push a person from a footbridge to their death in order to obstruct the path of the trolley (Thomson, 1976). If participants judge the described action as acceptable, they are said to have made a characteristically utilitarian judgment (i.e., a judgment that maximizes the greater good; see Conway et al., 2018). Conversely, if participants judge the described action as unacceptable, they are said to have made a characteristically deontological judgment (i.e., a judgment that is consistent with the moral norm that one should not kill innocent people; see Conway et al., 2018).

Although the trolley dilemma and similar sacrificial dilemmas have been used in hundreds of studies, this research has been criticized for multiple reasons. One criticism is that the scenarios used in this research are rather implausible, which has been found to promote norm-congruent judgments (Körner et al., 2019). This is especially problematic for studies that compare responses across dilemmas that differ in terms of their plausibility. For example, although both the switch and the footbridge variants of the trolley dilemma seem rather implausible, many participants find the footbridge dilemma especially implausible (Körner & Deutsch, 2022). This difference poses a challenge to the widespread assumption that stronger preferences for deontological judgments in the footbridge dilemma are the result of direct physical contact with the target of one's harmful action (i.e., killing a person by pushing the person from a bridge vs. killing a person by pulling a switch), which has been claimed to enhance negative emotional reactions to the idea of causing harm (Greene et al., 2001). Given that (a) participants find the footbridge dilemma less plausible than the switch dilemma (Körner & Deutsch, 2022) and (b) low plausibility promotes norm-congruent judgments (Körner et al., 2019), different responses to these two dilemmas could also be due to differences in their perceived plausibility.

The low plausibility of the trolley dilemma and its variants also has important implications for research on individual differences in moral dilemma judgments. If (a) willingness to entertain implausible assumptions buffers the tendency to make norm-congruent judgments in implausible scenarios and (b) people systematically differ in their willingness to entertain implausible assumptions, people may show systematic differences in their responses to implausible dilemmas in the absence of genuine differences in moral preferences. These considerations call for scenarios with greater plausibility and real-world relevance compared with the artificial scenarios commonly used in moral dilemma research (see also Bauman et al., 2014).

In addition to the ambiguities that arise from low dilemma plausibility, the traditional approach includes two structural confounds that further undermine interpretations of findings obtained with this approach. First, the traditional approach confounds the measurement of outcome maximization and norm adherence in that accepting one option implies rejecting the other (Conway & Gawronski, 2013). Thus, it is impossible to determine whether differences in moral dilemma judgments are driven by differences in the tendency to maximize outcomes, differences in the tendency to adhere to moral norms, or differences in both. Second, the traditional approach typically conflates outcome maximization with action and norm adherence with inaction, leading to a confound with general action tendencies (Crone & Laham, 2017). This confound can be illustrated with the introductory example of Brantly's Ebola infection, where the action–inaction mapping is directly opposite to the one in the trolley dilemma. In the trolley dilemma and all of its variants, outcome maximization suggests action (e.g., pulling the lever, pushing the person), whereas norm adherence suggests inaction (e.g., not pulling the lever, not pushing the person). In contrast, in the case of Brantly's Ebola infection, outcome maximization suggests inaction (e.g., not returning him to the United States for treatment), whereas norm adherence suggests action (e.g., returning him to the United States for treatment). Because research using the traditional approach rarely controls for action–inaction mappings, whether differences in moral dilemma judgments reflect differences in outcome maximization, norm adherence, or general action tendencies remains ambiguous.

THE CNI MODEL

The CNI model of moral decision making is a formal model that resolves the two structural confounds in the traditional approach (Gawronski et al., 2017). Toward this end, the CNI model identifies patterns of responses across four types of dilemmas that vary in terms of whether (a) the consequences of the focal action for the greater good are either greater or smaller than the costs and (b) the focal action is either proscribed by a proscriptive norm or prescribed by a prescriptive norm (for an example, see Table 4.1). By exclusively relying on scenarios inspired by societal debates about real-world dilemmas (see Gawronski et al., 2017; Körner et al., 2020), research using the CNI model also addresses concerns about potential artifacts resulting from low dilemma plausibility.

Using a multinomial modeling approach (Hütter & Klauer, 2016), the CNI model quantifies the extent to which participants' judgments in a set of moral

TABLE 4.1. Example of a Moral Dilemma Involving Either a Proscriptive or a Prescriptive Norm Where the Benefits of Action Are Either Greater or Smaller Than the Costs of Action

	Benefits of action greater than costs	Benefits of action smaller than costs
Proscriptive norm prohibits action	You are the director of a hospital in a developing country. A foreign student who is volunteering in the country got infected with a rare virus. The virus is highly contagious and deadly to seniors and children. The only medication that can effectively stop the virus from spreading has severe side effects. Although the virus will not kill her, the student suffers from a chronic immune deficiency that will make her die from these side effects. Would you give the student the medication in this case?	You are the director of a hospital in a developing country. A foreign student who is volunteering in the country got infected with a rare virus. The virus is highly contagious and can cause severe stomach cramps. The only medication that can effectively stop the virus from spreading has severe side effects. Although the virus will not kill her, the student suffers from a chronic immune deficiency that will make her die from these side effects. Would you give the student the medication in this case?
Prescriptive norm prescribes action	You are the director of a hospital in a developing country. A foreign student who is volunteering in the country got infected with a rare virus. The virus is highly contagious and can cause severe stomach cramps. The student suffers from a chronic immune deficiency that will make her die from the virus if she is not returned to her home country for special treatment. However, taking her out of quarantine involves a considerable risk that the virus will spread. Would you take the student out of quarantine to return her to her home country for treatment in this case?	You are the director of a hospital in a developing country. A foreign student who is volunteering in the country got infected with a rare virus. The virus is highly contagious and deadly to seniors and children. The student suffers from a chronic immune deficiency that will make her die from the virus if she is not returned to her home country for special treatment. However, taking her out of quarantine involves a considerable risk that the virus will spread. Would you take the student out of quarantine to return her to her home country for treatment in this case?

Note. From "Consequences, Norms, and Generalized Inaction in Moral Dilemmas: The CNI Model of Moral Decision-Making," by B. Gawronski, J. Armstrong, P. Conway, R. Friesdorf, and M. Hütter, 2017, *Journal of Personality and Social Psychology, 113*(3), p. 371 (https://doi.org/10.1037/pspa0000086). Copyright 2017 by the American Psychological Association.

dilemmas reflect (a) a response pattern that is sensitive to consequences (first row in Figure 4.1), (b) a response pattern that is sensitive to moral norms (second row in Figure 4.1), or (c) a response pattern of general inaction versus general action (third and fourth rows in Figure 4.1). Each response pattern is captured by a model parameter that can range from a value of 0 to 1. Sensitivity to consequences is captured by the model's C parameter, with higher scores reflecting a greater impact of consequences on responses; sensitivity to moral norms is captured by the model's N parameter, with higher scores reflecting a greater impact of moral norms on responses; and general preference for inaction versus action is captured by the model's I parameter, with scores above .50 reflecting a greater general preference for inaction responses and scores below .50 reflecting a greater general preference for action responses.

Because the statistical underpinnings of the CNI model were explained in detail by Gawronski et al. (2017), here we only summarize the main steps in analyzing moral dilemma responses with the CNI model. On the basis of the processing tree depicted in Figure 4.1, the CNI model provides four mathematical equations that include the three model parameters as unknowns and the observed probabilities of action (vs. inaction) responses on the four kinds of dilemmas as known values (see Gawronski et al., 2017, Appendix B). Numerical scores for the three parameters are estimated via maximum likelihood statistics with the aim of minimizing the discrepancy between the empirically observed probabilities of action (vs. inaction) responses on the four types of dilemmas and the probabilities of action (vs. inaction) responses predicted by the model equations using the identified parameter estimates. The adequacy of the model in describing the data can be evaluated by means of goodness-of-fit statistics, such that poor model fit would be reflected in a significant deviation between the empirically observed probabilities and the probabilities predicted by the model. Differences in parameter estimates across groups can be tested by enforcing equal estimates for a given parameter across groups. If setting a given parameter equal across groups leads to a significant reduction in model fit, one can infer that the parameter estimates for the two groups are significantly different. To the extent that the number of dilemmas completed by each participant is sufficiently large, associations between the three parameters and individual-difference measures can be investigated by fitting the CNI model to the responses from each participant (see Körner et al., 2020).

The value of the CNI model in resolving the ambiguities of findings with the traditional approach can be illustrated with the results of multiple regression analyses using the three parameters as predictors and responses on traditional dilemmas as the criterion. Traditional dilemmas are scenarios where

FIGURE 4.1. The CNI Model of Moral Decision Making Predicting Action Versus Inaction Responses in Moral Dilemmas With Proscriptive and Prescriptive Norms and Consequences Involving Benefits of Action That Are Either Greater or Smaller Than the Costs of Action

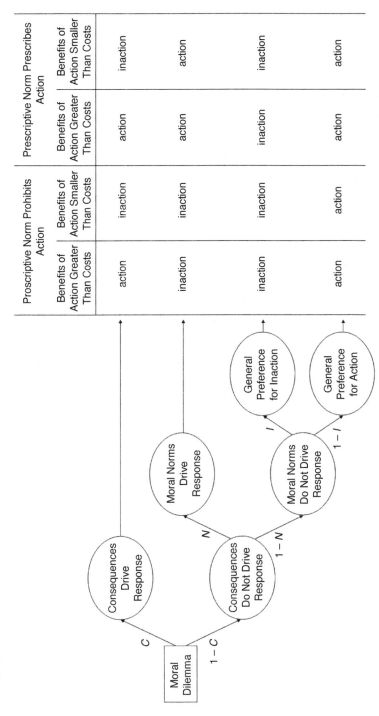

Note. From "Consequences, Norms, and Generalized Inaction in Moral Dilemmas: The CNI Model of Moral Decision-Making," by B. Gawronski, J. Armstrong, P. Conway, R. Friesdorf, and M. Hütter, 2017, *Journal of Personality and Social Psychology, 113*(3), p. 347 (https://doi.org/10.1037/pspa0000086). Copyright 2017 by the American Psychological Association.

an action is prohibited by a moral norm but produces benefits for overall well-being that are greater than the costs (in line with the structure of the trolley dilemma). In the traditional approach, action responses to this type of dilemma maximize overall outcomes and have therefore been interpreted as characteristically utilitarian judgments (see Conway et al., 2018). Conversely, inaction responses conform to moral norms and have therefore been interpreted as characteristically deontological judgments (see Conway et al., 2018). On the basis of this conceptualization, the relative preference for action over inaction on this type of dilemma can be described as the relative preference for utilitarian over deontological judgments. Consistent with the concern that this preference score conflates multiple distinct factors, multiple regression analyses revealed systematic relations with all three parameters of the CNI model. Controlling for mere mathematical dependence,[1] preference for utilitarian over deontological judgments on traditional dilemmas has been found to be (a) positively associated with sensitivity to consequences on the C parameter, (b) negatively associated with sensitivity to moral norms on the N parameter, and (c) negatively associated with general preference for inaction versus action on the I parameter (Gawronski et al., 2020). Research by Luke and Gawronski (2022) further suggests that individual differences in sensitivity to consequences and moral norms are highly stable over a period of 1 month, showing test–retest correlations that are comparable to those of the Big Five personality traits ($rs = .81$ and $.84$, respectively). The temporal stability of general action tendencies was found to be significantly lower ($r = .41$). The latter finding seems partly due to the lower internal consistency of scores on the I parameter compared with the C and the N parameters (see Gawronski et al., 2020; Luke & Gawronski, 2022).

INDIVIDUAL DIFFERENCES IN MORAL DILEMMA JUDGMENTS

Research using the traditional approach has identified a wide range of individual-difference variables that are associated with moral dilemma judgments. However, as we explained earlier, the theoretical meaning of

---

[1]Because responses to traditional dilemmas are used in the CNI model equations to estimate numerical values for the three parameters, Gawronski et al. (2020) ensured mathematical independence of predictors and outcomes by using CNI model parameters for dilemmas with odd item numbers to predict traditional scores for dilemmas with even item numbers. Conversely, CNI model parameters for dilemmas with even item numbers were used to predict traditional dilemma scores for dilemmas with odd item numbers.

these findings is ambiguous because the observed associations may be driven by individual differences in (a) sensitivity to consequences, (b) sensitivity to moral norms, or (c) general preference for inaction versus action (or any combination of the three). In the following sections, we review research that has used the CNI model to gain deeper insights into the nature of individual differences in moral dilemma judgments. Toward this end, we first describe evidence regarding the relation of a given variable with moral dilemma judgments in research that has used the traditional approach, and then we review the more nuanced results obtained in research that has used the CNI model. Because the dilemmas in the latter work have been designed to be more plausible compared with the artificial scenarios in prior work that has taken the traditional approach, we also discuss whether the findings of previous research that has used the traditional approach can be replicated with the more plausible scenarios in research that has used the CNI model. Although different findings in the two lines of work may be due to multiple factors, one potential reason is that the low plausibility of the dilemmas in prior research produces artificial associations that may not reflect genuine differences in moral preferences (see Körner et al., 2019). Such artifacts may emerge when a given individual-difference variable is associated with systematic differences in the willingness to entertain implausible assumptions, such as the implausible assumptions in the trolley dilemma.

Empathic Concern

Prior research that has adopted the traditional approach has found a negative association between individual differences in empathic concern and preference for utilitarian over deontological judgments (e.g., Gleichgerrcht & Young, 2013). This finding was replicated in several studies using the more plausible dilemmas for research with the CNI model (Körner et al., 2020). Further analyses suggest that this relation is driven by a positive association between empathic concern and sensitivity to moral norms. Some studies also found a positive association between empathic concern and general preference for inaction versus action (Körner et al., 2020); however, this association seems less reliable compared with the association with sensitivity to moral norms. A potential reason for the mixed findings with the I parameter is that scores on this parameter tend to show lower estimates of internal consistency (Gawronski et al., 2020; Luke & Gawronski, 2022), which can reduce statistical power for the detection of associations that actually exist. Nevertheless, the reliable association between empathic concern and the N parameter suggests that previous findings obtained with the traditional approach are driven by a stronger sensitivity to moral norms among individuals high in empathic concern (instead of a weaker sensitivity to consequences).

Need for Cognition

Some studies have found a positive association between individual differences in need for cognition and preference for utilitarian over deontological judgments (e.g., Wiech et al., 2013), but this association has been somewhat unreliable across studies (e.g., Patil et al., 2021). It also did not replicate in studies that have used the more plausible dilemmas for research with the CNI model (Körner et al., 2020). If anything, these studies suggest a negative association between need for cognition and preference for utilitarian over deontological judgments. Further analyses using the CNI model suggest that this negative relation is driven by a positive association between need for cognition and sensitivity to moral norms. A conceptually similar link has been found in studies that have used reaction times as an indicator of cognitive elaboration, showing that longer reaction times are associated with greater sensitivity to moral norms (Kroneisen & Steghaus, 2021). A potential explanation for the conflicting findings is that low plausibility of the dilemmas in prior research produces artificial associations that do not reflect genuine differences in moral preferences (see Körner et al., 2019). To the extent that (a) low plausibility promotes norm-congruent judgments and (b) individuals high in need for cognition are more willing to entertain the implausible assumptions of artificial dilemmas, need for cognition may show an artificial positive association with preference for utilitarian over deontological judgments, but this association may not be reflective of genuine differences in moral preferences. Thus, if such artifacts are controlled by means of plausible dilemmas with high real-world relevance, associations between need for cognition and moral dilemma judgments may look very different, as shown in studies that have used the more plausible dilemmas for research with the CNI model (Körner et al., 2020). This conclusion is consistent with other findings suggesting that the impact of cognitive deliberation on moral dilemma judgments is much more complex than suggested by the widespread assumption that high levels of deliberation invariably increase concerns about outcomes (e.g., Byrd & Conway, 2019; Körner & Volk, 2014).

Moral Identity Internalization

Some studies that have used the traditional approach have found a negative association between individual differences in self-importance of moral identity internalization (for the sake of brevity, hereafter called *moral identity internalization*) and preference for utilitarian over deontological judgments (e.g., Glenn et al., 2010). This finding was replicated in several studies that used the more plausible dilemmas for research with the CNI model (Körner et al., 2020). It is interesting to note that further analyses using the CNI model have revealed that moral identity internalization is positively associated with sensitivity to consequences as well as sensitivity to moral norms. Although the two associations should have compensatory effects on the relation between moral identity internalization and preference for utilitarian over deontological judgments, the N parameter has consistently shown a stronger association with moral identity internalization compared with the C parameter, leading to a negative "net" relation between moral identity internalization and preference for utilitarian over deontological judgments. These findings indicate that the confounds in the traditional approach can conceal complex associations that remain hidden in standard data analytic methods, and these associations can be uncovered with the CNI model.

Utilitarian Beliefs

Kahane et al. (2018) proposed a two-dimensional model that distinguishes between two kinds of utilitarian beliefs: (a) *impartial beneficence* (IB), which refers to an impartial concern for the greater good; and (b) *instrumental harm* (IH), which refers to a permissive attitude toward instrumental harm. Using a newly developed scale measuring individual differences along the two dimensions, Kahane et al. found that impartial beneficence and instrumental harm are both positively associated with preference for utilitarian over deontological judgments. Both of these associations were replicated in several studies using the more plausible dilemmas for research with the CNI model (Körner et al., 2020). However, counter to the idea that impartial beneficence and instrumental harm are linked to individual differences in utilitarian responding, further analyses using the CNI model did not find any evidence for positive associations between the C parameter and the two dimensions; instead, both IB and IH showed significant negative associations with the N and the I parameters; that is, higher scores on each dimension were associated with (a) a weaker sensitivity to moral norms and (b) a weaker general preference for inaction versus action. Although further research is needed to understand the psychological underpinnings of these findings, they suggest that the two dimensions of utilitarian beliefs may serve to rationalize a preference for norm-violating actions regardless of the specific situation (see Haidt, 2001) instead of promoting a maximization of outcomes in a utilitarian sense.

Behavioral Activation and Inhibition

Prior research that has taken the traditional approach suggests that preference for utilitarian over deontological judgments is positively associated with individual differences in behavioral activation (BAS; e.g., Moore et al., 2011) and negatively associated with individual differences in behavioral inhibition (BIS; e.g., van den Bos et al., 2011). Conceptually, these findings may point to the role of general action tendencies in moral dilemma judgments in that BAS may be associated with a general preference for action, whereas BIS may be associated with a general preference for inaction. With the traditional measure of preference for utilitarian over deontological judgments, these associations should produce a negative association with BIS and a positive association with BAS; however, the available evidence for these predictions has been somewhat mixed across studies that have used the traditional approach (see Moore et al., 2011; van den Bos et al., 2011). In line with the mixed evidence, the obtained associations with BAS and BIS were not consistently replicated in studies that have used the more plausible dilemmas for research with the CNI model (Körner et al., 2020). The latter work also did not obtain any reliable associations with the three CNI parameters.

Religiosity

Prior research with the traditional approach has found a negative association between religiosity and preference for utilitarian over deontological judgments (e.g., Szekely et al., 2015). This finding was not replicated in studies that used the more plausible dilemmas for research with the CNI model (Körner et al., 2020); however, further analyses using the CNI model obtained a pattern consistent with prior findings in that religiosity showed a reliable negative association with sensitivity to consequences. Of interest is that there was no evidence for a positive association between religiosity and sensitivity to moral norms, which speaks against the hypothesis that the negative association between religiosity and preference for utilitarian over deontological judgments in previous studies might be driven by a greater concern about moral norms among religious individuals.

Political Orientation

Prior research with the traditional approach suggests that conservatives show a weaker preference for utilitarian over deontological judgments than liberals (e.g., Hannikainen et al., 2017). This finding was replicated in several studies that used the more plausible dilemmas for research with the CNI model (Luke & Gawronski, 2021a). Further analyses using the CNI model revealed that the obtained association is driven by a weaker sensitivity to consequences among conservatives compared with liberals. This difference is consistent with accounts suggesting that conservatives are less willing to accept consequentialist arguments about the greater good than liberals (see Piazza & Sousa, 2014). There is no evidence for an association between political ideology and sensitivity to moral norms, disconfirming the hypothesis that conservatives are more concerned about norm violations than liberals (see Young et al., 2013). Moreover, there was no evidence for an association between political ideology and general preference for inaction over action, disconfirming the hypothesis that conservatives are more concerned about actions that interfere with current states of affairs than liberals (i.e., the status quo bias; see Samuelson & Zeckhauser, 1988).

Basic Personality Traits

We are not aware of any published research that has investigated associations between basic personality traits (e.g., Big Five, HEXACO) and moral dilemma judgments using the traditional approach. Using the CNI model to investigate associations between moral dilemma judgments and the Big Five personality traits (i.e., Extraversion, Agreeableness, Conscientiousness, Neuroticism, and Openness; see Soto & John, 2017), Luke and Gawronski (2022) found that (a) sensitivity to consequences was negatively associated with Extraversion and positively associated with Openness, (b) sensitivity to moral norms was positively associated with Agreeableness and Openness, and (c) general preference for inaction versus action was positively associated with Openness. Kroneisen and Heck (2020) investigated the associations between moral dilemma judgments and a selected subset of the HEXACO personality traits (i.e., Honesty–Humility, Emotionality, Conscientiousness; see Ashton & Lee, 2007) and found a positive association between sensitivity to consequences and Emotionality, a positive association between sensitivity to moral norms and Honesty–Humility, and a positive association between general preference for inaction versus action and Emotionality.[2]

---

[2]Kroneisen and Heck (2020) focused on only six of the 18 possible relations between the three CNI parameters and the six HEXACO traits. Thus, there may be more significant associations in the data set than reported in their article.

Testosterone

Prior research that has taken the traditional approach has found a positive association between individual differences in endogenous testosterone levels and preference for utilitarian over deontological judgments, and this association remained robust when controlling for gender (Carney & Mason, 2010). This finding did not replicate in a study that used the more plausible dilemmas for research with the CNI model (Brannon et al., 2019); however, further analyses using the CNI model revealed a pattern consistent with the association obtained in prior research in that endogenous testosterone levels showed a significant negative association with sensitivity to moral norms. An experimental manipulation of exogenous testosterone paradoxically showed the opposite pattern in that intranasal administration of testosterone increased (rather than decreased) sensitivity to moral norms compared with a placebo condition. The latter finding raises questions about whether the obtained associations between endogenous testosterone and moral dilemma judgments reflect a genuine causal effect of testosterone. A potential alternative is that these associations are driven by other variables that tend to be associated with both endogenous testosterone levels and moral dilemma judgments (e.g., psychopathy).

Psychopathy

Prior research that has used the traditional approach has found a positive association between psychopathy and preference for utilitarian over deontological judgments (for a meta-analysis, see Marshall et al., 2018). This finding was replicated in several studies that used the more plausible dilemmas for research with the CNI model (e.g., Gawronski et al., 2017; Körner et al., 2020; Luke & Gawronski, 2021b). However, further analyses using the CNI model revealed a much more complex pattern in that psychopathy showed negative associations with all three parameters (but see Luke et al., 2022). To be specific, individuals high (vs. low) in psychopathy showed (a) a weaker sensitivity to consequences, (b) a weaker sensitivity to moral norms, and (c) a weaker general preference for inaction versus action. A particularly noteworthy finding is the negative association between psychopathy and sensitivity to consequences. Counter to the association obtained with the traditional approach, this finding suggests that individuals high in psychopathy are less (not more) utilitarian than individuals low in psychopathy (cf. Bartels & Pizarro, 2011; Kahane et al., 2015).

Research by Luke and Gawronski (2021b) further suggests that some of the obtained associations are driven by a poor understanding of societal standards about right and wrong among individuals high in psychopathy (see Blair, 1995; Blair et al., 1995). For other associations, the results suggest that individuals high in psychopathy are aware of societal standards about right and wrong, but they do not care about using these standards in their personal judgments (see Aharoni et al., 2012, 2014; Cima et al., 2010). First, the negative association between psychopathy and the C parameter seems to be driven by differences in the understanding of societal conventions about the significance of morally relevant consequences. Second, the negative association between psychopathy and the I parameter seems to be driven by differences in the personal level of general action aversion, with individuals high and low in psychopathy showing a similar understanding of societal conventions regarding the moral status of actions versus inactions (e.g., difference between killing someone vs. letting someone die). Third, the negative association between psychopathy and the N parameter seems to be driven by both (a) differences in the understanding of societal conventions involving moral norms and (b) differences in personal standards about the acceptability of norm-incongruent actions (Luke & Gawronski, 2021b). These results have important implications for understanding the underpinnings of unethical behavior among psychopaths and demonstrate the value of the CNI model in providing nuanced insights that cannot be gained with the traditional approach.

CONCLUSION

The findings we have reviewed in this chapter suggest that conflicting views in societal debates about real-world moral dilemmas may reflect deeper psychological differences between people. However, it would be ill advised to reduce these psychological differences to a simple bipolar dimension with *outcome maximization* on one end and *norm adherence* on the other. After all, conflicting views may be driven by individual differences in (a) sensitivity to consequences, (b) sensitivity to moral norms, or (c) general preference for inaction versus action (or any combination of the three). Compared with the traditional dilemma approach, a major advantage of the CNI model is that it allows researchers to quantify the three determinants of moral dilemma judgments. Although research using the traditional dilemma approach has identified a wide range of individual-difference variables that are systematically associated with moral dilemma judgments, research using the CNI model suggests that the obtained associations differ in terms of their psychological underpinnings. Some associations are driven by differences in the sensitivity to consequences, some are driven by differences in the sensitivity to moral norms, and some are driven by differences in general action tendencies. Indeed, some individual-difference variables show complex patterns of associations with more than one factor, with some of the identified associations remaining undetected in the traditional dilemma approach (e.g., a positive association between sensitivity to consequences and moral identity internalization, a negative association between sensitivity to consequences and psychopathy). Thus, by identifying individual differences along the three dimensions, research using the CNI model offers nuanced insights into the roots of societal debates about the right course of action in real-world dilemmas, providing a more informed foundation for their potential resolution.

An important question for future research concerns the mental processes underlying associations between the three dimensions of moral dilemma judgments and established individual-difference constructs (see Fleeson & Jayawickreme, 2021). What are the cognitive, affective, and motivational mechanisms that account for the obtained associations? A central aspect related to the topic of this book is the role of motivational factors, which thus far have received relatively little attention in research on moral dilemma judgment. Although some researchers claim that individual differences in moral dilemma judgments primarily reflect differences in antisocial motivations (e.g., Kahane et al., 2018), others suggest that individual differences in moral dilemma judgments can arise from differences in either prosocial or antisocial motivations (e.g., Conway et al., 2018). Still others claim that differences in moral dilemma judgments could even stem from differences in self-focused motivations (e.g., Miller et al., 2014; Sarlo et al., 2014). Empirical evidence regarding these claims is still scarce. By disentangling sensitivity to consequences, sensitivity to moral norms, and general action tendencies, the CNI model may be a helpful tool to gain deeper insights into the understudied role of motivational processes in moral dilemma judgments.

REFERENCES

Aharoni, E., Sinnott-Armstrong, W., & Kiehl, K. A. (2012). Can psychopathic offenders discern moral wrongs? A new look at the moral/conventional distinction. *Journal of Abnormal Psychology, 121*(2), 484–497. https://doi.org/10.1037/a0024796

Aharoni, E., Sinnott-Armstrong, W., & Kiehl, K. A. (2014). What's wrong? Moral understanding in psychopathic offenders. *Journal of Research in Personality, 53*, 175–181. https://doi.org/10.1016/j.jrp.2014.10.002

Ashton, M. C., & Lee, K. (2007). Empirical, theoretical, and practical advantages of the HEXACO model of personality structure. *Personality and Social Psychology Review, 11*(2), 150–166. https://doi.org/10.1177/1088868306294907

Bartels, D. M., Bauman, C. W., Cushman, F. A., Pizarro, D. A., & McGraw, A. P. (2015). Moral judgment and decision making. In G. Keren & G. Wu (Eds.), *The Wiley-Blackwell handbook of judgment and decision making* (pp. 478–515). Wiley. https://doi.org/10.1002/9781118468333.ch17

Bartels, D. M., & Pizarro, D. A. (2011). The mismeasure of morals: Antisocial personality traits predict utilitarian responses to moral dilemmas. *Cognition, 121*(1), 154–161. https://doi.org/10.1016/j.cognition.2011.05.010

Bauman, C. W., McGraw, A. P., Bartels, D. M., & Warren, C. (2014). Revisiting external validity: Concerns about trolley problems and other sacrificial dilemmas in moral psychology. *Social and Personality Psychology Compass, 8*(9), 536–554. https://doi.org/10.1111/spc3.12131

Blair, R. J. R. (1995). A cognitive developmental approach to mortality: Investigating the psychopath. *Cognition, 57*(1), 1–29. https://doi.org/10.1016/0010-0277(95)00676-P

Blair, R. J. R., Jones, L., Clark, F., & Smith, M. (1995). Is the psychopath "morally insane"? *Personality and Individual Differences, 19*(5), 741–752. https://doi.org/10.1016/0191-8869(95)00087-M

Blinder, A., & Grady, D. (2014, August 2). American doctor with Ebola arrives in U.S. for treatment. *New York Times.* https://www.nytimes.com/2014/08/03/us/kent-brantley-nancy-writebol-ebola-treatment-atlanta.html

Brannon, S. M., Carr, S., Jin, E. S., Josephs, R. A., & Gawronski, B. (2019). Exogenous testosterone increases sensitivity to moral norms in moral dilemma judgements. *Nature Human Behaviour, 3*(8), 856–866. https://doi.org/10.1038/s41562-019-0641-3

Byrd, N., & Conway, P. (2019). Not all who ponder count costs: Arithmetic reflection predicts utilitarian tendencies, but logical reflection predicts both deontological and utilitarian tendencies. *Cognition, 192,* 103995. https://doi.org/10.1016/j.cognition.2019.06.007

Carney, D. R., & Mason, M. F. (2010). Moral decisions and testosterone: When the ends justify the means. *Journal of Experimental Social Psychology, 46*(4), 668–671. https://doi.org/10.1016/j.jesp.2010.02.003

Cima, M., Tonnaer, F., & Hauser, M. D. (2010). Psychopaths know right from wrong but don't care. *Social Cognitive and Affective Neuroscience, 5*(1), 59–67. https://doi.org/10.1093/scan/nsp051

Conway, P., & Gawronski, B. (2013). Deontological and utilitarian inclinations in moral decision making: A process dissociation approach. *Journal of Personality and Social Psychology, 104*(2), 216–235. https://doi.org/10.1037/a0031021

Conway, P., Goldstein-Greenwood, J., Polacek, D., & Greene, J. D. (2018). Sacrificial utilitarian judgments do reflect concern for the greater good: Clarification via process dissociation and the judgments of philosophers. *Cognition, 179,* 241–265. https://doi.org/10.1016/j.cognition.2018.04.018

Crone, D. L., & Laham, S. M. (2017). Utilitarian preferences or action preferences? De-confounding action and moral code in sacrificial dilemmas. *Personality and Individual Differences, 104,* 476–481. https://doi.org/10.1016/j.paid.2016.09.022

Fleeson, W., & Jayawickreme, E. (2021). Whole traits: Revealing the social–cognitive mechanisms constituting personality's central variable. *Advances in Experimental Social Psychology, 63,* 69–128. https://doi.org/10.1016/bs.aesp.2020.11.002

Foot, P. (1967). The problem of abortion and the doctrine of double effect. *Oxford Review*, *5*, 5–15. https://doi.org/10.1093/0199252866.003.0002

Gawronski, B., Armstrong, J., Conway, P., Friesdorf, R., & Hütter, M. (2017). Consequences, norms, and generalized inaction in moral dilemmas: The CNI model of moral decision-making. *Journal of Personality and Social Psychology*, *113*(3), 343–376. https://doi.org/10.1037/pspa0000086

Gawronski, B., Conway, P., Hütter, M., Luke, D. M., Armstrong, J., & Friesdorf, R. (2020). On the validity of the CNI model of moral decision-making: Reply to Baron and Goodwin (2020). *Judgment and Decision Making*, *15*, 1054–1072.

Gleichgerrcht, E., & Young, L. (2013). Low levels of empathic concern predict utilitarian moral judgment. *PLOS ONE*, *8*(4), e60418. https://doi.org/10.1371/journal.pone.0060418

Glenn, A. L., Koleva, S., Iyer, R., Graham, J., & Ditto, P. H. (2010). Moral identity in psychopathy. *Judgment and Decision Making*, *5*, 497–505.

Greene, J. D., Sommerville, R. B., Nystrom, L. E., Darley, J. M., & Cohen, J. D. (2001). An fMRI investigation of emotional engagement in moral judgment. *Science*, *293*(5537), 2105–2108. https://doi.org/10.1126/science.1062872

Haidt, J. (2001). The emotional dog and its rational tail: A social intuitionist approach to moral judgment. *Psychological Review*, *108*(4), 814–834. https://doi.org/10.1037/0033-295X.108.4.814

Hannikainen, I. R., Miller, R. M., & Cushman, F. A. (2017). Act versus impact: Conservatives and liberals exhibit different structural emphases in moral judgment. *Ratio*, *30*(4), 462–493. https://doi.org/10.1111/rati.12162

Hütter, M., & Klauer, K. C. (2016). Applying processing trees in social psychology. *European Review of Social Psychology*, *27*(1), 116–159. https://doi.org/10.1080/10463283.2016.1212966

Kahane, G., Everett, J. A. C., Earp, B. D., Caviola, L., Faber, N. S., Crockett, M. J., & Savulescu, J. (2018). Beyond sacrificial harm: A two-dimensional model of utilitarian psychology. *Psychological Review*, *125*(2), 131–164. https://doi.org/10.1037/rev0000093

Kahane, G., Everett, J. A. C., Earp, B. D., Farias, M., & Savulescu, J. (2015). "Utilitarian" judgments in sacrificial moral dilemmas do not reflect impartial concern for the greater good. *Cognition*, *134*, 193–209. https://doi.org/10.1016/j.cognition.2014.10.005

Körner, A., & Deutsch, R. (2022). Deontology and utilitarianism in real life: A set of moral dilemmas based on historic events. *Personality and Social Psychology Bulletin*. Advance online publication. https://doi.org/10.1177/01461672221103058

Körner, A., Deutsch, R., & Gawronski, B. (2020). Using the CNI model to investigate individual differences in moral dilemma judgments. *Personality and Social Psychology Bulletin*, *46*(9), 1392–1407. https://doi.org/10.1177/0146167220907203

Körner, A., Joffe, S., & Deutsch, R. (2019). When skeptical, stick with the norm: Low dilemma plausibility increases deontological moral judgments. *Journal of Experimental Social Psychology*, *84*, 103834. https://doi.org/10.1016/j.jesp.2019.103834

Körner, A., & Volk, S. (2014). Concrete and abstract ways to deontology: Cognitive capacity moderates construal level effects on moral judgments. *Journal of Experimental Social Psychology*, *55*, 139–145. https://doi.org/10.1016/j.jesp.2014.07.002

Kroneisen, M., & Heck, D. W. (2020). Interindividual differences in the sensitivity for consequences, moral norms, and preferences for inaction: Relating basic personality traits to the CNI model. *Personality and Social Psychology Bulletin, 46*(7), 1013–1026. https://doi.org/10.1177/0146167219893994

Kroneisen, M., & Steghaus, S. (2021). The influence of decision time on sensitivity for consequences, moral norms, and preferences for inaction: Time, moral judgments, and the CNI model. *Journal of Behavioral Decision Making, 34*(1), 140–153. https://doi.org/10.1002/bdm.2202

Luke, D. M., & Gawronski, B. (2021a). Political ideology and moral dilemma judgments: An analysis using the CNI model. *Personality and Social Psychology Bulletin, 47*(10), 1520–1531. https://doi.org/10.1177/0146167220987990

Luke, D. M., & Gawronski, B. (2021b). Psychopathy and moral dilemma judgments: A CNI model analysis of personal and perceived societal standards. *Social Cognition, 39*(1), 41–58. https://doi.org/10.1521/soco.2021.39.1.41

Luke, D. M., & Gawronski, B. (2022). Temporal stability of moral dilemma judgments: A longitudinal analysis using the CNI model. *Personality and Social Psychology Bulletin, 48*(8), 1191–1203. https://doi.org/10.1177/01461672211035024

Luke, D. M., Neumann, C. S., & Gawronski, B. (2022). Psychopathy and moral dilemma judgment: An analysis using the four-factor model of psychopathy and the CNI model of moral decision-making. *Clinical Psychological Science, 10*(3), 553–569. https://doi.org/10.1177/21677026211043862

Marshall, J., Watts, A. L., & Lilienfeld, S. O. (2018). Do psychopathic individuals possess a misaligned moral compass? A meta-analytic examination of psychopathy's relations with moral judgment. *Personality Disorders, 9*(1), 40–50. https://doi.org/10.1037/per0000226

Miller, R. M., Hannikainen, I. A., & Cushman, F. A. (2014). Bad actions or bad outcomes? Differentiating affective contributions to the moral condemnation of harm. *Emotion, 14*(3), 573–587. https://doi.org/10.1037/a0035361

Moore, A. B., Stevens, J., & Conway, A. R. (2011). Individual differences in sensitivity to reward and punishment predict moral judgment. *Personality and Individual Differences, 50*(5), 621–625. https://doi.org/10.1016/j.paid.2010.12.006

Patil, I. (2015). Trait psychopathy and utilitarian moral judgement: The mediating role of action aversion. *Journal of Cognitive Psychology, 27*(3), 349–366. https://doi.org/10.1080/20445911.2015.1004334

Patil, I., Zucchelli, M. M., Kool, W., Campbell, S., Fornasier, F., Calò, M., Silani, G., Cikara, M., & Cushman, F. (2021). Reasoning supports utilitarian resolutions to moral dilemmas across diverse measures. *Journal of Personality and Social Psychology, 120*(2), 443–460. https://doi.org/10.1037/pspp0000281

Piazza, J., & Sousa, P. (2014). Religiosity, political orientation, and consequentialist moral thinking. *Social Psychological & Personality Science, 5*(3), 334–342. https://doi.org/10.1177/1948550613492826

Samuelson, W., & Zeckhauser, R. (1988). Status quo bias in decision making. *Journal of Risk and Uncertainty, 1*(1), 7–59. https://doi.org/10.1007/BF00055564

Sarlo, M., Lotto, L., Rumiati, R., & Palomba, D. (2014). If it makes you feel bad, don't do it! Egoistic rather than altruistic empathy modulates neural and behavioral responses in moral dilemmas. *Physiology & Behavior, 130*, 127–134. https://doi.org/10.1016/j.physbeh.2014.04.002

Soto, C. J., & John, O. P. (2017). Short and extra-short forms of the Big Five Inventory–2: The BFI–2–S and BFI–2–XS. *Journal of Research in Personality*, *68*, 69–81. https://doi.org/10.1016/j.jrp.2017.02.004

Suter, R. S., & Hertwig, R. (2011). Time and moral judgment. *Cognition*, *119*(3), 454–458. https://doi.org/10.1016/j.cognition.2011.01.018

Szekely, R. D., Opre, A., & Miu, A. C. (2015). Religiosity enhances emotion and deontological choice in moral dilemmas. *Personality and Individual Differences*, *79*, 104–109. https://doi.org/10.1016/j.paid.2015.01.036

Thomson, J. J. (1976). Killing, letting die, and the trolley problem. *The Monist*, *59*(2), 204–217. https://doi.org/10.5840/monist197659224

Valdesolo, P., & DeSteno, D. (2006). Manipulations of emotional context shape moral judgment. *Psychological Science*, *17*(6), 476–477. https://doi.org/10.1111/j.1467-9280.2006.01731.x

van den Bos, K., Müller, P. A., & Damen, T. (2011). A behavioral disinhibition hypothesis of interventions in moral dilemmas. *Emotion Review*, *3*(3), 281–283. https://doi.org/10.1177/1754073911402369

Wiech, K., Kahane, G., Shackel, N., Farias, M., Savulescu, J., & Tracey, I. (2013). Cold or calculating? Reduced activity in the subgenual cingulate cortex reflects decreased emotional aversion to harming in counterintuitive utilitarian judgment. *Cognition*, *126*(3), 364–372. https://doi.org/10.1016/j.cognition.2012.11.002

Young, O. A., Willer, R., & Keltner, D. (2013). "Thou shalt not kill": Religious fundamentalism, conservatism, and rule-based moral processing. *Psychology of Religion and Spirituality*, *5*(2), 110–115. https://doi.org/10.1037/a0032262

5

MOTIVATION TO ACT VIRTUOUSLY

NANCY E. SNOW

This chapter is different from the others in this volume. The aim is to give a philosophical overview, or *excursus*, into theories of motivation used in the philosophical subfield of ethical theory known as *virtue ethics*. The motivations to act virtuously explored here are found in different versions of virtue ethics and virtue theory—a distinction I introduce and explain later in the Virtue Ethics and Virtue Theory section. These motivations differ from those found in other types of philosophical theories of ethics, such as deontology, consequentialism, natural law theory, and divine command theory. A second respect in which this chapter differs from others in this volume is that it does not include many references to empirical studies.[1] This is because

---

[1]Recently, much interesting work has been done on morality and character by psychologists. From the field of person perception, see, for example, Pizarro and Tannenbaum (2012), Uhlmann et al. (2015), Goodwin et al. (2014, 2015), Piazza et al. (2014), and Goodwin (2015). More generally, see, for example, Strohminger and Nichols (2014), Cushman (2013), Ellemers (2017), Ellemers et al. (2019). This interesting and valuable work is not reviewed here because the aim of the chapter is to provide an overview of accounts of motivation found in recent work in philosophical virtue ethics and virtue theories. Points of overlap and intersection no doubt exist, but examining them is beyond the scope of this chapter.

https://doi.org/10.1037/0000342-006
Motivation and Morality: A Multidisciplinary Approach, M. K. Berg and E. C. Chang (Editors)

philosophers typically do not seek to support their theories with empirical data. Many, though not all, of us believe that empirical work is best left to those with the expertise to do it—our colleagues in the social sciences. With these observations in hand, let us turn to philosophical theorizing about virtue.

Most philosophers who theorize about virtue use a common, or what might be called *ecumenical* conception of virtue. They believe that virtues are entrenched dispositions of character that comprise three central components: (a) virtuous motivations; (b) practical wisdom—in the Greek, *phronēsis*; and (c) appropriate affect. Some philosophers who follow Aristotle also invoke the conception of *eudaimonia*, or flourishing. For eudaimonists, being virtuous is necessary, but not sufficient, for *eudaimonia*, which is sometimes translated as "happiness." For Aristotle, external goods, such as good family, friends, wealth, good children, noble birth, and good looks, are also required. Neo-Aristotelians can update these goods for our day and age; for example, even virtuous people need clean air and water, the ability to feel and be safe, and food and economic security in order to flourish.

I comment further on eudaimonist virtue ethics later in this chapter, but for now let me introduce, if only briefly, the ecumenical conception of virtue with which most contemporary virtue ethicists work. Agents possessing virtuous dispositions typically choose to act virtuously when they can. As noted, neither virtuous dispositions nor virtuous actions are possible without appropriate motivation (one exception is discussed in the Two Alternatives to Neo-Aristotelian Virtue Ethics section). For example, if a student volunteers at a nursing home simply because she wants an entry for her resumé, her behavior could be considered prosocial, but it is not virtuous. It is instead motivated by self-interest. Similarly, if I give you a gift simply in order to ingratiate myself with you, this act is not virtuous but self-interested. I do not mean to imply by these examples that self-interested motivation is the only alternative to virtuous motivation. Vicious motivation, too, is an alternative to virtuous. In the film *The Help*, for example, the character played by Octavia Spencer gave her former employers, who had treated her disrespectfully and rudely dismissed her, a chocolate pie made from very unsavory ingredients. She did this out of spite and a desire for revenge.[2] So, for the most part, philosophers are united in the view that *virtuous motivation* is

---

[2]Viewers of the film might want to debate the motivations I've attributed to the character, as well as the question of whether the act was justified in light of her former employers' cruelty. Without delving further into these questions, the main point is that motivations of spite, revenge, malice, etc., are indeed vicious, and inform vicious dispositions and actions. Her former employers' dispositions to cruelty and callous disrespect are surely vicious by this standard.

necessary, but not sufficient, for virtue. By "necessary but not sufficient" I mean to indicate that virtuous motivation is not enough for a disposition or an action to be considered virtuous.

As noted, virtuous dispositions must also be informed by a second element, *practical wisdom*, and virtuous actions must be guided by it. Practical wisdom is a complex form of reasoning that has multiple roles to play in enabling one to be virtuous. Foremost among these roles is the successful guidance of virtuous action; important, too, is adjudicating among possibly competing virtues in cases of conflict. To illustrate how practical wisdom guides action stemming from a single virtue, consider that my compassion in helping an unemployed friend should be thoughtful and deliberate. Perhaps, given that I do not want to wound his pride, I should not offer him financial assistance outright but should instead provide him with work for which I compensate him. Practical wisdom helps me to arrive at this plan. Practical wisdom also helps the virtuous person to decide which of a possible suite of virtues is the most appropriate in any given circumstance. Should I be merciful toward a student who asks for an extension on turning in her paper and allow her to submit it late, or deny the request in an effort to be fair to other students who have submitted theirs on time? Here again, practical wisdom guides my deliberations.

Finally, the third component of virtue is *appropriate affect*. If I give a gift because I care for you, but I do so grudgingly, the action is not virtuous, even though the motivation might be. The action is not done with the appropriate emotion—wholehearted care and concern for the other.

Significant variations can be found within this framework. I spend the rest of the chapter discussing some of these. In the first section, I explain the distinction between *virtue ethics* and *virtue theory* and its implications for the role of motivation in virtue. Here I discuss neo-Aristotelianism, the main type of approach to virtue ethical theory currently on offer, by taking up the important work of Rosalind Hursthouse (1999). I then briefly take up two contemporary alternatives to neo-Aristotelianism in the work of philosophers Michael Slote and Linda Zagzebski. Some colleagues and I recently published a book, *Understanding Virtue: Theory and Measurement* (Wright et al., 2021), in which we adapt whole trait theory (WTT), a social-cognitivist approach to traits, to a broadly neo-Aristotelian approach to virtue with the hope of facilitating efforts in virtue measurement. Next, I review the main features of WTT and explain how my coauthors and I integrate it with neo-Aristotelianism. In all of these discussions my focus will be on highlighting various theoretical approaches to motivation. As we will see, in all but one case motivation is of paramount importance for virtue.

VIRTUE ETHICS AND VIRTUE THEORY

Studies of virtue have an ancient philosophical pedigree, going back to Plato (1961) and Aristotle (1985) in the Western philosophical tradition and to Confucius and Buddhism in the Eastern.[3] In the West, interest in virtue continued through the Middle Ages, finding a central place in the work of Christian theologians such as St. Thomas Aquinas (on virtue in Aquinas, see Vogler, 2018). It fell into abeyance during the modern period with the rise of ethical theories such as deontology and consequentialism. *Deontological theories*, such as that advanced during the modern period by Immanuel Kant (1993), take concepts such as rules, principles, or duties to have pride of place. *Consequentialist theories*, such as those put forward by John Stuart Mill (2002) during the modern period, take the promotion of pleasure or happiness as central to ethics and believe that the moral worth of an act depends on its having overall better consequences than any alternative that is available to the agent at the time of acting.

Sustained philosophical interest in virtue did not reappear until the 20th century. The precipitating factor was a seminal article by Elizabeth Anscombe, "Modern Moral Philosophy" (1958), in which she lamented that neither deontology nor consequentialism provides an adequate philosophical psychology and urges a return to Aristotle to fill this gap. Although a number of important books and papers on virtue were published during the next 20 years, the focus of our concern, and what triggered the present deluge of books and articles on virtue, was the publication in 1999 of Rosalind Hursthouse's *On Virtue Ethics*. The book is noteworthy because Hursthouse developed virtue ethics as an alternative theory type to deontology and consequentialism; that is, she offered a neo-Aristotelian theory according to which virtue is the central ethical concept in terms of which other concepts, such as rules and right action, are understood and derived. By contrast, as I have noted, deontological theories take concepts such as rules, principles, or duties to have preeminence, and consequentialist theories believe that good consequences—those that maximize pleasure or happiness (otherwise known as *utility*)—have moral primacy.

Deontological and consequentialist theories can include theories of virtue, according to which virtue is situated vis-à-vis the central ethical concept of the overarching theory type. For example, Kant believed that virtue is the strength of will needed to do our duty, and contemporary consequentialists

---

[3]For an overview of Confucian and Buddhist virtue ethics, see Tiwald (2018) and MacKenzie (2018), respectively.

such as Julia Driver (2001) believe that virtues are traits that typically bring about good consequences. In both examples, virtue is defined in terms of another, more primary concept. When virtue is presented as the central concept of a type of theory that is meant to stand as an alternative to deontology or consequentialism, the theory is known as a *theory of virtue ethics*. By contrast, the term *virtue theory* is used to refer to theories of virtues that have subordinate places within other ethical theory types, as in deontological virtue theories, such as Kant's, or consequentialist virtue theories, such as Driver's. I raise the distinction between virtue ethics and virtue theory because it is important for understanding how different theorists interpret the nature and importance of the motivation to act virtuously.

Hursthouse, as a neo-Aristotelian, is adamant that both dispositions and actions must be appropriately motivated to be virtuous. What does it mean to be appropriately motivated? In essence, this: A virtuous person sees a fact in the world as a reason to act in a certain way (i.e., in accordance with a certain virtue), desires to act accordingly, and, other things being equal, does act accordingly. A person who is disposed to be virtuous has become habituated to see facts in the world in a certain way, that is, as requiring virtuous responses. The qualifier "other things being equal" refers to the absence of conditions that might defeat the virtuous person's reason to act, such as an insurmountable obstacle that prevents them from acting, a stronger virtuous reason to act that outweighs the initial reason, or some factor that would render the virtuous act unnecessary, such as the intervention of another person. To illustrate, suppose (following the previous example) that Anna's friend has recently lost his job. Anna sees her friend's lack of income as a reason for acting, and she desires to help. Her motivation is appropriately virtuous provided that it is genuinely directed to the other's good. Anna might express this to herself in any number of ways, for example, "He needs my help," "It is what friends do for each other," "It is the generous/decent/kind thing to do," "It is what charity requires," "It is the right thing to do," and so on. Anna's motivation is virtuous because it expresses a commitment to the value of her virtuous act (see Hursthouse, 1999, Chapter 6, especially pp. 135–136).

Further points should be noted. For one thing, Anna's act can be defeated by countervailing reasons. As I said, an insurmountable obstacle might prevent her from acting, for she, too, could be unemployed and thus unable to render financial assistance. Alternatively, she might realize that her friend needs to prove to himself that he can be financially stable on his own and decide not to offer assistance for fear of wounding his pride and undermining his self-confidence. Finally, her act of assistance might be made otiose by another's coming to his aid before she has a chance to do so. In these cases, even though Anna did not or could not act, she is still considered virtuous because she has the appropriate mental state.

What, exactly, is the appropriate mental state? For Aristotle and neo-Aristotelians, the mental states of virtuous people can be described as *phronetic*, that is, as characterized by practical wisdom. Practical wisdom is a kind of reasoning that informs virtue. Although a full elucidation of this complex notion is beyond the scope of this chapter, we can say that one cannot have virtue without *phronēsis*, and one cannot have *phronēsis* without virtue. To be virtuous in this rich Aristotelian sense is to be able to perceive facts that call for a virtuous response, to be able to use practical wisdom to decide what to do in the circumstances, to be motivated from a desire to be virtuous, and to feel appropriately, that is, to have emotional responses aligned with virtue. In order to be virtuous, specific actions must proceed from this kind of mental state. The virtuous person is one for whom virtues have become entrenched states of character—the generous person is one who is disposed to see the world as the generous person would, readily perceiving occasions that call for generosity, being adept at using practical wisdom to form and execute generous plans that will be successful in expressing generosity, desiring to be generous, and acting generously in a wholehearted way. From these brief remarks, we can see that, for Aristotle and neo-Aristotelians, we can fail to be virtuous in many ways: by failing to perceive occasions that call for virtue; by failing to reason well enough to successfully hit the target of virtue—perhaps by not noticing that a well-intended gift will wound a friend's pride; by having the wrong kinds of motivations; or by having the wrong kinds of feelings.

Let me note one final point regarding eudaimonia and virtuous motivation. Hursthouse (1999), as a neo-Aristotelian, endorsed the view that virtue is necessary for human flourishing. For Aristotle and those inspired by him, such as Hursthouse, we should choose to be virtuous not in order to become *eudaimon*, that is, not for the sake of flourishing, though being virtuous is our best bet to lead a flourishing life (see Hursthouse, 1999, pp. 172–173). We should choose virtue for its own sake, not for the sake of good consequences it might bring, such as pleasure or happiness. However, it is through choosing and being virtuous that a flourishing life is most likely to be attained.[4]

---

[4]Like Aristotle, neo-Aristotelians admit the possibility that bad luck or misfortune can derail one's best efforts to flourish. For example, despite being virtuous, a parent's child could die, thereby marring his or her life. Or a virtuous person could become caught up in a war or other social circumstances that ruin her chances of flourishing.

Let us briefly take stock. Hursthouse (1999), a neo-Aristotelian, developed an approach called *virtue ethics*, which purports to set virtue ethics on the same footing as deontology and consequentialism, as an alternative theory type. Virtue ethics takes virtue to be the central ethical concept in terms of which other ethical concepts should be understood, and it is structurally similar to deontology, which takes duties, rules, or principles to be central, and consequentialism, which takes good consequences that maximize utility, to have pride of place. Hursthouse adopted and expanded central tenets of Aristotle's approach to virtue, including the idea that appropriate motivation, summed up as the desire to be virtuous, is required for virtuous dispositions and actions.

Let us contrast this sketch of the neo-Aristotelian approach to virtue and virtuous motivation with those offered by Kantian and utilitarian theories of virtue, considering Kant's theory first and then turning to utilitarian accounts.[5]

Hill and Cureton (2018) aptly explained Kant's virtue theory, in which virtue is situated as a subsidiary concept among a nexus of more fundamental concepts. In Kant's theory, the *moral law*, or *categorical imperative*, has pride of place. The first version of the categorical imperative, the *formula of universal law*, states that we should always act so that the maxim of our action could become a universal law.[6] This principle allows us to identify our moral duties, such as perfect duties to tell the truth and imperfect duties to cultivate our talents.[7] It gives rise to moral rules, such as "Do not lie," and "Improve one's talents when possible." Kant defined *virtue* as "a kind of strength and resoluteness of will to resist and overcome obstacles that oppose fulfilling our moral duties" (Hill & Cureton, 2018, p. 263). The obstacles to duty are our "tendencies to indulge our natural desires, impulses, and inclinations when

---

[5]Hill and Cureton (2018) offer an excellent overview of Kant's theory of virtue. See Grenberg (2005) and Baxley (2010) for two contemporary accounts of Kantian virtue. Utilitarianism, a group of theories that take as central the principle of utility (roughly, maximize the greatest good for the greatest number), is the most common type of consequentialism. For the purposes of this chapter, I use the terms *utilitarianism* and *consequentialism* interchangeably.

[6]Three versions of the Categorical Imperative appear in *The Grounding of the Metaphysics of Morals* (Kant, 1993). Kant regards them as equivalent. Scholars debate this.

[7]For Kant, perfect duties are those that we must perform on every occasion on which the opportunity arises. By contrast, we have some latitude of choice about when to fulfill imperfect duties. For example, because of my perfect duty to tell the truth, I may never lie, even when presented with an opportunity to do so. Because I have an imperfect duty to cultivate my talents, I may on occasion fail to do so, provided that I have the general end of cultivating my talents and make it a policy to do so on occasion. See Kant (1993).

they tempt us to act in ways that conflict with moral demands" (Hill & Cureton, 2018, p. 263). Although we may speak of many virtues (corresponding to different kinds of duty), there is only one true virtue: "the wholehearted commitment and effective capacity to fulfill our moral duties out of respect for the moral law, despite our tendencies to indulge our opposing natural desires" (Hill & Cureton, 2018, p. 263).

For Kant, then, the moral law and our duty to obey it are of primary importance. The only kind of motivation that has moral worth is the desire to act from our duty or, to put the point another way, out of reverence for the moral law. When we do this, we have a good will. The good will is a rational will, born of recognition of, and respect for, the moral law. When we have and act from a good will, we express the purely rational side of our natures and are self-legislating autonomous beings, that is, rational beings who give the moral law to ourselves. Kant acknowledged, however, that we are not purely rational beings. We have natural inclinations; for example, we seek our self-interest, we have sympathy for others, and we are emotional beings. These are called *heteronomous* influences because they pull us away from the dictates of our rational nature. None of these motivations—the desire for self-interest; sympathy for others; or emotional inclinations toward others, such as love—has moral worth for Kant. Consequently, standard virtuous motivations in the Aristotelian sense, such as the desire for another's good, compassion for another, or the desire for another's welfare, do not count as morally worthy motives. At best, they are morally neutral. The only true virtue is the strength of will that bolsters our commitment to the moral law.[8]

Let us again pause to take stock. We should note that, within Kant's theory, virtue does not have pride of place but is defined in terms of its ability to help us abide by the moral law and do our duties. This stands in contrast to Hursthouse (1999), for whom virtue is the central ethical concept. For Hursthouse, virtue is done for its own sake, and virtuous motivation expresses the agent's recognition of virtue's value. For Kant, virtue and virtuous motivation ultimately express our commitment to the moral law. If we desire to act compassionately toward another in need and not from our commitment to the moral law, our desire is not a virtuous motivation.

---

[8]There is more complexity in Kant's view that I will not consider here. For example, consistently with Kant's remarks, we might regard honesty as the specific virtue that helps us to do our duty of truth-telling. Kant also regards pity as an emotion that can help move us to perform our duty, thus indicating that sometimes emotional motivations can assist us in doing our duty and needn't always distract us from it. See Kant (1980).

Let us now consider consequentialist, or utilitarian, theories of virtue. Bradley (2018) examined several. For all of these conceptions, virtues are traits or dispositions that are thought to promote good consequences. For example, in his discussion of virtue consequentialism, Bradley quoted G. E. Moore's *Principia Ethica* (1903, p. 172): "A virtue may be defined as a habitual disposition to perform certain actions, which generally produce the best possible results" (p. 399). As Bradley explained,

> Moore's view is adapted from his consequentialism about moral duties: an act is morally required if and only if its consequences are better than those of any alternatives. According to Moore, ". . . virtues are dispositions to perform actions we're morally required to do." (p. 399)

For example, keeping our promises is thought to be a moral duty, other things being equal. Consequently, a disposition to keep promises, other things being equal, would, on Moore's view, be a virtue. The phrase, "other things being equal," is meant to provide an escape clause so that we can justify breaking promises in the face of truly pressing demands, such as more important moral duties. In other words, the virtue of keeping our promises is flexible enough to allow us to make the decision to break a promise, such as the promise to meet a friend for lunch on a specific date, at a specific time, and in a specific place, if a more important duty arises, say, our child becomes sick and we need to pick her up from school and take her to the doctor's office.

Bradley (2018, pp. 399–400) also discussed *maximizing virtue consequentialism* (MVC), *scalar virtue consequentialism* (SVC), and Julia Driver (2001)'s *virtue consequentialism*. According to MVC, "A character trait is a virtue if and only if its consequences are at least as good any alternative character trait," and "two traits are alternatives if and only if it is impossible to have both at the same time" (Bradley, 2018, p. 400). Bradley (2018, p. 400) underscored an important feature of MVC: Whether a trait counts as a virtue is determined not in isolation but by comparison with alternative traits. To illustrate, consider a case in which a teacher possesses the traits of justice and mercy and is confronted with a case in which a student asks for an extension of the deadline for an important paper for a course. Surely, it's the case that the teacher has the two traits at the same time, but what Bradley must mean, I think, is that if both are truly alternatives—that is, if exercising both would maximize utility by producing the same quantity of goodness— then both cannot be exercised at the same time. The teacher must consider the consequences of each course of action: acting *justly* or *mercifully*. There are reasons for acting justly and for acting mercifully. Acting justly by refusing to alter the deadline would bring about good consequences for the student: encouraging greater responsibility by forcing him to pay more attention to deadlines, to learn the lessons of good time management, and so on, and would, in addition, be fair to other members of the class who do not get the benefit of an extension. Acting mercifully could also have good consequences, such as giving the student enough time to do good work, acknowledging the legitimacy of his reasons, and so on. Suppose that the teacher decides that acting in either way would maximize the same amount of utility. In that case, justice and mercy are alternatives in the sense that it would be impossible for both to be exercised at the same time. It is up to the teacher to choose whether to act justly or to act mercifully and here, it seems, MVC would give no guidance because each course of action brings about the same amount of utility. The teacher's decision to act either justly or mercifully would be arbitrary because reasons for doing either are not decisive. The decision could, perhaps, be decided by flipping a coin.

According to SVC: "One character trait is more of a virtue (vice) than another if it has better (worse) consequences" (Bradley, 2018, p. 400). As Bradley (2018, pp. 400–401) noted, SVC does not tell us which traits are virtues or vices; neither does it specify a threshold separating the two categories. Thus, on SVC one trait could be more of a virtue than another—it could result in better consequences than another, even though both are vices. To illustrate this interesting situation, suppose that I have a disposition to be rude to people—commonly thought a vice. Suppose that I also have the disposition to lie—also thought a vice. Suppose, in addition, that my disposition to be rude only annoys people, whereas my disposition to lie results in harm, or property loss—as when I lie to someone by denying that I have stolen his phone charger. My disposition to be rude, according to SVC, would be more of a virtue than my disposition to lie because it results in better consequences.

Bradley (2018, p. 401) noted that Driver (2001)'s virtue consequentialism attempts to address this concern, specifying that "a trait is a virtue if and only if it has on balance good consequences" (see Driver, 2001, p. 82). But this, Bradley (p. 401) remarked, is far from clear. Driver cannot mean that the consequences brought about by a virtue on balance are intrinsically good, for the value of some virtues consists in bringing about what is intrinsically good and that of others consists in preventing what is intrinsically bad. The distinction is important, he observed, in cases in which circumstances make it impossible to bring about consequences that are on balance intrinsically good and the best that can be done is to make things less bad. To illustrate this point, consider a case in which a loved one is dying of cancer. We are powerless to bring about an intrinsically good outcome, such as radical remission; the best we can do is to make things less bad for her, perhaps by alleviating her suffering through pain medication. A controversial point should be noted. One might think that alleviating suffering is intrinsically good. Bradley would be inclined to say, I believe, that in the circumstances, alleviating suffering does not, on balance, bring about intrinsically good consequences. The alleviation of suffering is not, on balance, an intrinsically good consequence in the circumstances, for it is no more than a means of bringing about a less bad end—a death with less pain than the patient would suffer without the pain medication. The consequence, in other words, is instrumentally good for making the patient's situation less bad, but not intrinsically good, that is, good in and of itself.

I should note that none of these consequentialist theories really cares much about the motivation to be virtuous. What is essential, from the consequentialist point of view, is whether the consequences that a virtuous disposition promotes are, on balance, good. This is compatible with fanciful scenarios in which someone who typically has bad motivations, such as malice or the desire for revenge, somehow produces actions that, on balance, create more happiness than unhappiness. No other type of virtue theory or virtue ethical theory countenances such laxity about the nature of virtuous motivation.

To sum up the main points of this section, I should note that both virtue ethics as developed by Hursthouse (1999) and Kantian theories of virtue take positions on what virtuous motivation is and its importance for being virtuous. For Hursthouse, virtuous motivation expresses the agent's commitment to the value of virtue. For Kant, it expresses her commitment to the moral law. For consequentialists, virtuous motivation is not centrally important; instead, it is the overall consequences of our dispositions for maximizing utility that make our dispositions virtuous or vicious.

TWO ALTERNATIVES TO NEO-ARISTOTELIAN VIRTUE ETHICS

In this discussion of virtue ethics, I delved into key features of neo-Aristotelian virtue ethics. In this section, I wish to turn, if only briefly, to the work of two philosophers who have departed from neo-Aristotelian virtue ethics in significant respects: Michael Slote and Linda Zagzebski. Both developed early approaches to virtue, then changed in interesting ways in their later writings.[9] Both provide interesting alternatives to neo-Aristotelianism by stressing the importance of emotions as virtuous motivations. By contrast, neo-Aristotelians emphasize the desire to be virtuous in some way, for example,

---

[9]My discussion of Slote and Zagzebski draws on passages from Snow (2020, pp. 24–28).

the desire to be compassionate or courageous, and, more globally, the desire to be a virtuous person, as essential motivations for virtue.

Slote (1997, 2001) began his work on virtue ethics with what has been called "agent-based" virtue ethics, then departed from that perspective in interesting ways (Slote, 2010, 2018), thereby championing moral sentimentalism.

Approaches to virtue ethics typically are agent focused in that they are interested in agents and their characteristics. However, agent-basing "treats the moral status of acts as derivative from independent and fundamental aretaic (as opposed to deontic) characterizations of motives, character traits or individuals" (Slote, 2001, p. 5, and 1997, p. 206; quoted in Pettigrove, 2018, p. 360; see also Slote, 1992, pp. 83–84). What matters are the actual motives and dispositions of agents; in other words, the goodness of an action is derived from the agent's motives when she performs the action (see also Hursthouse & Pettigrove, 2018). Slote's earlier work emphasizes head-on the importance of motives for virtue.

In later work, Slote (2010, 2018) shifted to a sentimentalist approach in which empathy is the central concepts: "The virtue-ethical sentimentalist holds, very roughly, that normative distinctions and motivations derive from emotion or sentiment rather than (practical) reason" (Slote, 2018, p. 344). This is, of course, at loggerheads with Aristotle's emphasis on practical wisdom. His later approach invokes the sentimentalist tradition of Francis Hutcheson and David Hume (he noted that Hutcheson was influenced by the Judeo–Christian tradition) and reminds us of the importance of the philosopher Hume as an alternative to Aristotle as a source for inspiration about virtue (see Hutcheson, 1991, and Hume, 1975, 1978). Hume famously thought that reason is, or ought to be, the slave of the passions, and held that virtues are those dispositions of character that either are, or would be, useful or agreeable to oneself or to others.[10]

To take stock, we can see that Slote, while embracing the ecumenical conception of virtue outlined at the outset of this chapter, moves in his work toward the importance of emotions—specifically, empathy—as the basis of virtue and virtuous motivation. In contrast with neo-Aristotelianism, the importance of practical wisdom for virtue is downplayed in this scheme.

Turning now to Zagzebski, let us note that in early work she, like Slote, developed a version of agent-based virtue ethics that she called "motivation-based" (Zagzebski, 1996, p. 82). The concept of a motivation is fundamental,

---

[10]See Hume (1975, 1978). Slote (2018, 344–345) also discusses Buddhist and Confucian influences as part of the historical background of contemporary virtue-ethical sentimentalism.

and the concept of a virtue is defined in terms of a good motivation. The concept of a right act is then defined in terms of a virtue. A motive is a feeling or emotion that initiates and directs action toward an end (Zagzebski, 1996, p. 131). *Virtue* is defined as "a deep and enduring acquired excellence of a person, involving a characteristic motivation to produce a certain desired end and reliable success in bringing about that end" (Zagzebski, 1996, p. 137). She then defined "right act" as an act that "a virtuous person might do in certain circumstances," where "might" stands in for "would" (Zagzebski, 1996, p. 233). One can see that Zagzebski (1996) adopted the ecumenical conception of virtue sketched earlier but emphasized emotion as the basis of virtuous motivation.

In later work, she developed *exemplarist moral theory* (e.g., Zagzebski, 2017). Moral theories simplify, systematize, and justify moral beliefs and practices, using a variety of moral concepts. As we have seen, different theories emphasize different moral concepts, working primarily with three main concepts: the right, the good, and virtue. Deontological theories prioritize the right, giving both the good and virtue subsidiary roles, whereas consequentialist theories accord the good (construed as happiness or pleasure) pride of place, defining right actions and virtuous traits as those that bring about the good. Virtue ethics takes virtue to be the primary concept in terms of which goodness (flourishing) is obtained, and in terms of which right action might be defined. Each of these theory types is foundationalist in structure, identifying one fundamental concept—the right, the good, and virtue, respectively—as the basis in terms of which the others are defined.

Exemplar theory is also foundationalist, but the foundation is not a concept. It is, instead, exemplars of moral goodness. We identify figures such as Confucius, Jesus Christ, and others as exemplars of moral goodness through our feelings of admiration for them (Zagzebski, 2017, p. 10). Thus, unlike other types of moral theory, Zagzebski's proceeds by identifying morally exemplary individuals as foundational and defining moral terms, such as "right act," as what they would do, and moral properties, such as "virtues," as their admirable traits (Zagzebski, 2017, pp. 21–22). The feeling of admiration, she contended, not only allow us to identify exemplars but also motivates us to be like them. It "is a kind of attraction that carries with it the desire to imitate or emulate" (Zagzebski, 2017, p. 20).

Thus, for Zagzebski (2017), a specific emotion—namely, reflective admiration for exemplars—is essential for virtue, for it carries with it a desire to be like the exemplar who is admired. If, for example, I admire Mother Teresa because of her compassion, that admiration, Zagzebski thinks, includes the desire to be like Mother Teresa. Consequently, I should want to emulate

Mother Teresa by being compassionate. The emotion of admiration for an exemplar—someone I directly identify through my emotion as possessing goodness—motivates me to be virtuous myself.

What if my admiration is misplaced? Zagzebski (2017, pp. 16–17) thinks that moral communities help people successfully identify moral exemplars. In other words, our emotional reactions can be judged by our communities. We can be given guidance if our admiration misses the mark. Is it possible for communities to radically disagree about who is exemplary? Zagzebski (2017, p. 17) thinks not. Humans have the same nature, the same emotional dispositions, psychological tendencies, and so on. If one community consistently admired people who were nasty and brutish, Zagzebski (p. 17) thinks it would be doubtful that they would be in the same natural kind as us.

I, for one, think this is too swift a move. Not only isolated individuals but also entire communities seem to have a tendency to admire very dubious characters. The rise of "strongmen" such as Hitler; Mussolini; Stalin; and, more recently, Viktor Orbán in Hungary, Narendra Modi in India, and Jair Bolsanaro in Brazil indicates that communities of people who are undeniably members of the human species tend to admire individuals who embrace power; racism; and illiberal, authoritarian political positions. Despite Zagzebski (2017)'s detailed analyses of admiration, emulation, exemplars, virtue, and other concepts, the extent to which humans are capable of admiring vicious people without being corrected by their communities remains a nagging issue for anyone inclined to embrace exemplarism.

That said, exemplarism is bolstered by psychological studies of the emotions that people experience upon considering stories about good and bad deeds done to someone else (Haidt & Algoe, 2004). Research suggests that it is elevation—feeling moved by a good deed done for others—and not mere admiration—awe for a display of competence—that is the moral emotion that people feel upon contemplating morally exemplary acts. Haidt and Algoe (2004, p. 330) contended that research participants in a "good deed" condition reported motivations suggesting that a moral emotion was operative that made them "care about the state of the social world, . . . and want to do something to improve it." The authors continued: "Participants reported wanting to do good deeds themselves and wanting to tell other people about the good-deed doer" (p. 330). By contrast, those in the "bad deed" conditions experienced self-reported anger and disgust, reported wanting to tell others about the bad-deed doer, and wanted to directly criticize the person (Haidt & Algoe, 2004, pp. 330–331). Haidt and Algoe drew an important conclusion:

> Importantly, people experiencing these emotions did their part to amplify the distinctions between good and bad through their behaviors and motivations.

Not only did they want to praise or vilify the other publically [*sic*], they thought about their relationships with the others in new ways. Good deeds often gave rise to the desire for stronger relationships with the virtuous other, while bad deeds did the opposite. If we assume that people sometimes do act on these motivations, at least by gossiping, then we can see how emotions such as elevation, admiration, disgust, and anger help to churn the waters of social relationships, encouraging those who did not witness the original act to choose sides and update their moral registers for the people involved. (pp. 331–332)

This provides a model for how communities can act to correct misplaced admiration for bad actors. We should also note that my examples are of leaders who have sought or are seeking to quash free speech and action that would be critical of their wrongdoing, such that community critiques of their bad deeds are likely to be suppressed. For example, according to Human Rights Watch, Bolsonaro blocked critics on social media, violating the rights to free speech and information (see Human Rights Watch, 2021). More recently, however, thousands protested, calling for his removal (see BBC, 2021).

The foregoing observations indicate that the emotions, judgments, and actions operative in our confrontation with good and bad actors and deeds are complex. Their influences on our communities are also complex, subject to a variety of competing forces, and worthy of further study.

WHOLE TRAIT THEORY

In Snow (2010), I advanced a theory of virtue that draws on the resources of Mischel and Shoda's (1995) theory of traits.[11] Known as CAPS (cognitive–affective processing system), the theory conceptualizes traits in terms of social-cognitive units, such as beliefs, desires, goals, plans, and regulatory strategies. I argued that virtues are subsets of CAPS traits. The aim was to respond to the situationist challenge to neo-Aristotelian virtue ethics. In the late 1990s and early 2000s, several philosophers, calling themselves *situationists*, drew upon work in empirical psychology to argue that global or robust traits, that is, traits that manifest across different situation types, either do not exist or exist in such scarcity that they have little, if anything, to do with producing behavior.[12] Their attack on Aristotelian virtues was

---

[11]See, for example, Mischel (1973, 1984, and 1990), and Mischel and Shoda (1995, 1998). The neo-Aristotelian philosopher Daniel C. Russell (2009) takes a similar approach to mine.

[12]Prominent in this debate are Harman (1999, 2000, and 2003), Doris (1998 and 2002), and Merritt (2000).

direct: If virtues are global traits, and global traits either do not exist or have little effect on behavior, then we cannot become the kinds of people that neo-Aristotelian virtue ethicists believe we should be. The larger point is that neo-Aristotelian virtue ethics lacks an adequate empirical psychology. I drew upon the CAPS theory in order to argue that global traits can and do exist and that virtue ethics can indeed be adequately grounded in empirical psychology.

Prevailed upon by colleagues in psychology, I subsequently abandoned CAPS in favor of a more recent and better developed empirical approach to traits: WTT.[13] I then worked with colleagues in psychology to integrate WTT and a broadly neo-Aristotelian approach to virtue. The resulting theory is explained and defended in detail in Wright et al.'s (2021) book. In the rest of this section, I furnish a brief overview of aspects of WTT that bear on how it approaches motivation; I then delve into the integration of WTT with an Aristotelian approach to virtue with a focus on motivation.[14]

WTT is called "whole trait theory" because it unites the *descriptive side* of a trait, represented by the frequency with which a person behaves in a trait-appropriate manner over time and in different situations, and the *explanatory side*, which involves the underlying social-cognitive systems that are responsible for producing this person-specific distribution of trait-appropriate responses.

WTT describes the kinds of people we are by measuring the degree to which people possess traits, contending that the degree to which a person possesses a trait is determined by the density distribution of their trait-appropriate responses. *Density distribution* refers to the range of situations in which those responses are produced and the frequency with which the responses occur. Snow et al. (2020, p. 284) stated that density distributions are best understood as a function of both consistency and habituality, where *consistency* is the extent to which a person has trait-appropriate responses to trait-relevant stimuli and *habituality* is the extent to which trait-appropriate responses have become a dynamically automatic response to trait-relevant stimuli. To illustrate, consider the virtue of kindness. Many occasions in daily life provide opportunities for being kind, or the opposite. For example, I can be kind, rude, or oblivious to the cashier in a grocery store; I can hold the door for a person who is entering or exiting a building behind me, or I can

---

[13]For the development of WTT, see, for example, Fleeson (2007), Fleeson and Gallagher (2009), Fleeson and Jayawickreme (2015), Jayawickreme and Fleeson (2017), and Jayawickreme et al. (2019).

[14]The subsequent discussion (in the next two sections) draws on Snow et al. (2020).

let it close in her face; I can turn away solicitors from my house with a polite "No thank you" or slam the door; I can help someone with a heavy bag or ignore her. If a person frequently acts with kindness when a variety of situations calling for kindness arise, their density distribution, that is, the frequency with which they manifest the state of being kind in daily life, will display consistency. Some people act so frequently and are so consistently kind that their responses and actions become habitual. Kindness for them has become so routinized that it has become part of their nonconscious psyches. They no longer need to think about whether or how to be kind—they do it automatically.[15]

The explanatory side of WTT regards traits as robust dispositional capacities for trait-appropriate behavior. As with neo-Aristotelian accounts of virtue, trait-appropriate behavior typically depends on whether features of a situation call for the exercise of a trait. According to neo-Aristotelian accounts, virtuous agents see these features as reasons calling for the exercise of a specific virtue, or, if the situation calls for it, several virtues. The perception of these features is crucial for both WTT and neo-Aristotelian theories; WTT calls these features *inputs*. Inputs are processed, according to WTT, by social-cognitive systems called *intermediates*, and trait-appropriate actions or emotional responses are known as *outputs*.

The social-cognitive systems are organized into five subsystem types: (a) interpretative, (b) motivational, (c) stability-inducing, (d) temporal, and (e) random processes. None of these function in isolation but instead operate as an interconnected, dynamic system. Because the two most important types for our purposes are the interpretative and motivational, I leave aside an explanation of the others.

The interpretative system comprises interrelated perceptual, cognitive, and affective states, mechanisms, processes, capacities, and structures that determine how trait-relevant information is analyzed and interpreted. This system provides the background knowledge that enables a person to make sense of the world and supplies a repository of schemas and scripts for action. For example, the interpretative system enables someone to discern situations in which honesty is called for. Suppose, for example, that I see that someone has dropped her wallet, and I am the only person in a crowd who notices. The interpretative system allows me to access a variety of scripts for possible behavior, for example, "say nothing and pocket the money," or "alert the person who dropped the wallet and return it to her."

---

[15]For an explanation of how this can occur, see Snow (2010), especially Chapter 2.

The motivational system also comes into play. What I decide to do will likely depend on what I have most reason to do—perhaps I need the money and decide to keep the wallet, or perhaps honesty is of greater importance to me and I return it. The motivational system is composed of a broad range of states, mechanisms, processes, capacities, and structures associated with various end states, both those for which I strive and those that I seek to avoid. They create the directions for trait manifestation. One can think of end states as goals. If my goal is to be honest (I seek to be honest and to avoid theft), I have reason to return the wallet. On the other hand, if my goal is to get as much as I can for myself and honesty is of little value to me, I have reason to keep the wallet. People have many goals, but whichever is activated most strongly in any given situation is the most likely to guide behavior.

WHOLE TRAIT THEORY AND VIRTUOUS MOTIVATION

The similarities of WTT with a broadly neo-Aristotelian approach to virtue should be evident: Each draws on underlying cognitive and motivational processes, structures, and mechanisms to explain how and why people manifest trait-relevant behavior. On the issue of motivation, however, I must note an important difference between WTT and Aristotelian views.

For Aristotle, virtuous action must be appropriately motivated, that is, done for the right reasons. As noted earlier, this can take a variety of forms, but the key point is that truly virtuous action, from the Aristotelian perspective, is chosen because it is virtuous. WTT, by contrast, makes no judgments about the kinds of motives that are appropriate for traits, other than that they be relevant to a person's perception and interpretation of the stimuli that activate a trait.

Despite this, the WTT framework is broadly consistent with the motivational structure of virtues. In the integrated approach to virtue taken by Snow et al. (2020) and Wright et al. (2021), motivation looms large in four distinct respects. Motivation (1) is necessary for having and acting from specific virtues, such as generosity, courage, and so on; (2) is necessary if one wants to be virtuous overall, that is, to have good character; (3) individuates specific virtues from other virtues and from nonvirtuous elements that can help or hinder virtuous actions, such as schemas, scripts, and other traits; and (4) provides internal structure to specific virtues by influencing and organizing cognitions that follow in the train of virtuous motivation.

I now address each point in turn. In regard to Point 1, my colleagues and I follow Aristotle in thinking that appropriate motivation is necessary, but not sufficient, for having and acting from specific virtues. This point was explained earlier. Point 2 is different. We also believe that, to be virtuous in a strong sense, one must want to possess an overall good character. Many people want to be merciful as well as just, courageous as well as generous, and so on. Consequently, Point 2 addresses the desire to be a certain kind of person. To do this successfully, practical wisdom needs to operate at a level higher than simply guiding action stemming from a single virtue. At this higher level, practical wisdom is needed to regulate different virtues, checking and balancing their operation in one's life. For example, as mentioned in the beginning of this chapter, practical wisdom enables us to adjudicate between potentially conflicting virtues, knowing in particular cases when to be just and when to be merciful, for example. This is by no means easy, and the solution to cases in which virtues conflict is not always obvious. Yet, following Aristotle, we believe that virtuous motivation works hand in hand with practical wisdom in such cases.

Points 3 and 4 are about the structural roles that virtuous motivation plays. These points follow Snow (2010 and 2013) and offer a view of the motivational structure of virtues that differs both from WTT and from Aristotle's conception of virtue. Point 3 mentions two respects in which motivations individuate specific virtues—from each other and from elements external to virtue that can either help or hinder it. As for the first respect, my colleagues and I contend that specific virtues each have a characteristic motivation; that is, unlike WTT, we think that a specific motivational core is internal to and characteristic of each virtue. For example, compassion requires benevolence toward another in need and the desire to help; generosity requires that we wholeheartedly give to others for their own sake, without expecting something in return; and courage requires us to overcome fear in the face of what we perceive as danger or a threat. Absent such central motivations, we do not see how virtue can be ascribed to a person in an Aristotelian sense.

Following Snow (2013), we further contend that the central motivation that is characteristic of each virtue distinguishes it from external elements, such as scripts, schemas, and other traits, that can help or hinder virtue and its exercise. In other words, we believe that the motivation characteristic to compassion—the desire to help another in need—differs from the scripts and schemas that allow one to put that desire into action when confronted with the fact of another's need. To be sure, the line here can be blurry, for it is surely the case that the nature of our desire is shaped by the scripts and schemas that are available to us; we have culturally influenced scripts of how compassionate people help others, and exposure to those can deepen and shape our desire and how we express it. Nevertheless, we maintain that those scripts and schemas, influential though they may be, differ from the actual desire to compassionately help others. Similarly, we believe that the motivation that is intrinsic to virtue differs from other personality traits that could help or hinder virtue and virtuous action. If I am naturally impulsive, for example, this could hinder my efforts to be courageous—very likely by undermining my practical wisdom—causing me to act rashly instead of courageously. The motivation central to courage—the desire to overcome fear in the face of a threat or danger—is then skewed by my impulsiveness.

Point 4 clearly differs from Aristotle's view. Following Snow (2010), my colleagues and I maintain that the motivations that are central to each virtue structure the other elements of the virtue such that, were the motivations removed or altered, the other elements, including the cognitions central to each virtue, would also be changed. In other words, we view virtues as more or less tightly integrated bundles of social-cognitive units that are conjointly activated in response to our perceptions of features of situations, with the motivations characteristic of each virtue playing a key role in influencing the cognitions and affect that follow in train. For example, compassion is structured by the desire to help another perceived to be in need, and this desire puts in train beliefs such as "She needs help; I should do something," plans such as "I'll offer assistance by going over to her," and similar thoughts and desires. If the motivation central to compassion, the desire to help another in need, is changed, the ensuing cognitions would also change. Consider that a cruel person would have a very different motivation, perhaps the desire to have malicious fun at another's expense. The cognitions set in train from this motivation would be very different from those of the compassionate person. Thus, we regard virtues as more or less tightly structured bundles of social-cognitive units, with motivations playing a central unifying role in distinguishing virtues from each other and from other kinds of traits. We also believe that virtues, conceived in this way, can be distinguished from external structures, such as scripts or schemas, that help to facilitate or impede virtuous action.

To be sure, Aristotle did not make such explicit claims about the unifying role of motivations in structuring virtues. That said, we believe that our view is broadly neo-Aristotelian, and we defend this claim by adding that in a virtue as we conceive of it, the cognitions that are shaped by motivations are reasons in the Aristotelian sense. In other words, the cognitions found in virtuous actions and responses and shaped by virtuous motivations are the workings of *phronēsis*—Aristotelian practical wisdom. In addition, our conception of virtue is broadly compatible with WTT in the sense that virtues as we conceive of them could be considered a subset of traits in the sense explained by WTT.

CONCLUSION

In this excursus into virtuous motivation I have sought to establish several points. Most philosophers view motivation as essential for being virtuous and acting virtuously. Even within this camp, however, there are interesting variations, such as are found in the work of Slote and Zagzebski. I (a philosopher) and my colleagues in psychology have sought to integrate a broadly Aristotelian conception of virtue with the social-cognitivist theory of traits provided by WTT. This has the advantage of showing how this important philosophical perspective on virtue ethics can have adequate empirical grounding. The discussion has also shown how motivation looms large in our integrated perspective on virtue. This is by no means the last word on virtuous motivation. In particular, my colleagues and I hope that the measurement of virtuous motivation is facilitated by our integration of philosophy and empirical psychology. Far more work remains to be done.

REFERENCES

Anscombe, G. E. M. (1958). Modern moral philosophy. *Philosophy*, *33*(124), 1–19. https://doi.org/10.1017/S0031819100037943

Aristotle. (1985). *The Nicomachean ethics* (T. Irwin, Trans.). Hackett.

Baxley, A. M. (2010). *Kant's theory of virtue: The value of autocracy*. Cambridge University Press. https://doi.org/10.1017/CBO9780511779466

BBC. (2021, October 2). *Brazil Bolsonaro: Thousands protest calling for president's removal*. https://www.bbc.com/news/world-latin-america-58777244

Bradley, B. (2018). Contemporary consequentialist theories of virtue. In N. E. Snow (Ed.), *The Oxford handbook of virtue* (pp. 398–412). Oxford University Press.

Cushman, F. (2013). Action, outcome, and value: A dual-system framework for morality. *Personality and Social Psychology Review*, *17*(3), 273–292. https://doi.org/10.1177/1088868313495594

Doris, J. M. (1998). Persons, situations, and virtue ethics. *Noûs*, *32*(4), 504–530. https://doi.org/10.1111/0029-4624.00136

Doris, J. M. (2002). *Lack of character: Personality and moral behavior*. Cambridge University Press. https://doi.org/10.1017/CBO9781139878364

Driver, J. (2001). *Uneasy virtue*. Cambridge University Press. https://doi.org/10.1017/CBO9780511498770

Ellemers, N. (2017). *Morality and the regulation of social behavior: Groups as moral anchors*. Routledge. https://doi.org/10.4324/9781315661322

Ellemers, N., van der Toorn, J., Paunov, Y., & van Leeuwen, T. (2019). The psychology of morality: A review and analysis of empirical studies published from 1940 through 2017. *Personality and Social Psychology Review*, *23*(4), 332–366. https://doi.org/10.1177/1088868318811759

Fleeson, W. (2007). Studying personality processes: Explaining change in between-persons longitudinal and within-person multilevel models. In R. W. Robins, R. C. Fraley, & R. F. Krueger (Eds.), *Handbook of research methods in personality psychology* (pp. 523–542). Guilford Press.

Fleeson, W., & Gallagher, P. (2009). The implications of Big Five standing for the distribution of trait manifestation in behavior: Fifteen experience-sampling studies and a meta-analysis. *Journal of Personality and Social Psychology, 97*(6), 1097–1114. https://doi.org/10.1037/a0016786

Fleeson, W., & Jayawickreme, E. (2015). Whole trait theory. *Journal of Research in Personality, 56*, 82–92. https://doi.org/10.1016/j.jrp.2014.10.009

Goodwin, G. (2015). Moral character in person perception. *Current Directions in Psychological Science, 24*(1), 38–44. https://doi.org/10.1177/0963721414550709

Goodwin, G. P., Piazza, J., & Rozin, P. (2014). Moral character predominates in person perception and evaluation. *Journal of Personality and Social Psychology, 106*(1), 148–168. https://doi.org/10.1037/a0034726

Goodwin, G., Piazza, J., & Rozin, P. (2015). Understanding the importance and perceived structure of moral character. In C. Miller, R. M. Furr, K. Knobel, & W. Fleeson (Eds.), *Character: New directions from philosophy, psychology, and theology* (pp. 100–126). Oxford University Press. https://doi.org/10.1093/acprof:oso/9780190204600.003.0005

Grenberg, J. (2005). *Kant and the ethics of humility: A story of dependence, corruption, and virtue.* Cambridge University Press. https://doi.org/10.1017/CBO9780511627859

Haidt, J., & Algoe, S. (2004). Moral amplification and the emotions that attach us to saints and demons. In J. Greenberg, S. Koole, & T. Pyszczynsji (Eds.), *Handbook of experimental existential psychology* (pp. 322–335). Guilford Press.

Harman, G. (1999). Moral philosophy meets social psychology: Virtue ethics and the fundamental attribution error. *Proceedings of the Aristotelian Society, 99*(3), 315–331. https://doi.org/10.1111/1467-9264.00062

Harman, G. (2000). The nonexistence of character traits. *Proceedings of the Aristotelian Society, 100*(1), 223–226. https://doi.org/10.1111/j.0066-7372.2003.00013.x

Harman, G. (2003). No character or personality. *Business Ethics Quarterly, 13*(1), 87–94. https://doi.org/10.5840/beq20031316

Hill, T. E., Jr., & Cureton, A. (2018). Kant on virtue: Seeking the ideal in human conditions. In N. E. Snow (Ed.), *The Oxford handbook of virtue* (pp. 263–280). Oxford University Press.

Human Rights Watch. (2021, August 19). *Brazil: Bolsonaro blocks thousands of critics on social media.* https://www.hrw.org/news/2021/08/19/brazil-bolsonaro-blocks-critics-social-media

Hume, D. (1975). *Enquiries concerning human understanding and concerning the principles of morals* (3rd ed., L. A. Selby-Bigge & P. H. Nidditch, Eds.). Clarendon Press.

Hume, D. (1978). *A treatise of human nature* (2nd ed., L. A. Selby-Bigge & P. H. Nidditch, Eds.). Clarendon Press.

Hursthouse, R. (1999). *On virtue ethics.* Oxford University Press.

Hursthouse, R., & Pettigrove, G. (2018), Virtue ethics. In E. N. Zalta (Ed.), *The Stanford encyclopedia of philosophy* (Winter 2018 ed.). Stanford University. https://plato.stanford.edu/archives/win2018/entries/ethics-virtue/

Hutcheson, F. (1991). An inquiry concerning the original of our ideas of virtue or moral good. In D. D. Raphael (Ed.), *British moralists 1650–1800* (Vol. 1, pp. 261–299). Hackett.

Jayawickreme, E., & Fleeson, W. (2017). Does whole trait theory work for the virtues? In W. Sinnott-Armstrong & C. B. Miller (Eds.), *Moral psychology: Virtue and character* (pp. 75–104). MIT Press. https://doi.org/10.2307/j.ctt1n2tvzm.9

Jayawickreme, E., Zachry, C., & Fleeson, W. (2019). Whole trait theory: An integrative approach to examining personality structure and process. *Personality and Individual Differences, 136*, 2–11. https://doi.org/10.1016/j.paid.2018.06.045

Kant, I. (1980). *Lectures on ethics* (L. Infield, Trans.). Hackett.

Kant, I. (1993). *Grounding for the metaphysics of morals with on the supposed right to lie because of philanthropic concerns* (3rd ed., J. Ellington, Ed.). Hackett.

MacKenzie, M. (2018). Buddhism and the virtues. In N. E. Snow (Ed.), *The Oxford handbook of virtue* (pp. 153–170). Oxford University Press.

Merritt, M. (2000). Virtue ethics and situationist personality psychology. *Ethical Theory and Moral Practice, 3*(4), 365–383. https://doi.org/10.1023/A:1009926720584

Mill, J. S. (2002). *Utilitarianism* (2nd ed., G. Sher, Ed.). Hackett.

Mischel, W. (1973). Toward a cognitive social learning reconceptualization of personality. *Psychological Review, 80*(4), 252–283. https://doi.org/10.1037/h0035002

Mischel, W. (1984). Convergences and challenges in the search for consistency. *American Psychologist, 39*(4), 351–364. https://doi.org/10.1037/0003-066X.39.4.351

Mischel, W. (1990). Personality dispositions revisited and revised: A view after three decades. In L. A. Pervin (Ed.), *Handbook of personality: Theory and research* (pp. 111–134). Guilford Press.

Mischel, W., & Shoda, Y. (1995). A cognitive–affective system theory of personality: Reconceptualizing situations, dispositions, dynamics, and invariance in personality structure. *Psychological Review, 102*(2), 246–268. https://doi.org/10.1037/0033-295X.102.2.246

Mischel, W., & Shoda, Y. (1998). Reconciling processing dynamics and personality dispositions. *Annual Review of Psychology, 49*(1), 229–258. https://doi.org/10.1146/annurev.psych.49.1.229

Moore, G. E. (1903). *Principia ethica*. Cambridge University Press.

Pettigrove, G. (2018). Alternatives to Neo-Aristotelian virtue ethics. In N. E. Snow (Ed.), *The Oxford handbook of virtue* (pp. 259–376). Oxford University Press.

Piazza, J., Goodwin, G., Rozin, P., & Royzman, E. (2014). When a virtue is not a virtue: Conditional virtues in moral evaluation. *Social Cognition, 32*(6), 528–558. https://doi.org/10.1521/soco.2014.32.6.528

Pizarro, D., & Tannenbaum, D. (2012). Bringing character back: How the motivation to evaluate character influences judgments of moral blame. In M. Milkulincer & P. Shaver (Eds.), *The social psychology of morality: Exploring the causes of good and evil* (pp. 91–108). American Psychological Association. https://doi.org/10.1037/13091-005

Plato. (1961). *The collected dialogues of Plato* (E. Hamilton, Ed.). Princeton University Press.

Russell, D. C. (2009). *Practical intelligence and the virtues*. Oxford University Press.

Slote, M. (1992). *From morality to virtue*. Oxford University Press.

Slote, M. (1997). Virtue ethics. In M. Baron, P. Pettit, & M. Slote (Eds.), *Three methods of ethics* (pp. 175–238). Blackwell.

Slote, M. (2001). *Morals from motives*. Oxford University Press. https://doi.org/10.1093/0195138376.001.0001

Slote, M. (2010). *Moral sentimentalism*. Oxford University Press.

Slote, M. (2018). Sentimentalist virtue ethics. In N. E. Snow (Ed.), *The Oxford handbook of virtue* (pp. 343–358). Oxford University Press.

Snow, N. (2010). *Virtue as social intelligence: An empirically grounded theory*. Routledge. https://doi.org/10.4324/9780203880579

Snow, N. (2013). Notes toward an empirical psychology of virtue: Exploring the personality scaffolding of virtue. In J. Peters (Ed.), *Aristotelian ethics in contemporary perspective* (pp. 130–144). Routledge.

Snow, N. (2020). *Contemporary virtue ethics*. Cambridge University Press. https://doi.org/10.1017/9781108580496

Snow, N., Wright, J., & Warren, M. (2020). Virtue measurement: Theory and applications. *Ethical Theory and Moral Practice, 23*(2), 277–293. https://doi.org/10.1007/s10677-019-10050-6

Strohminger, N., & Nichols, S. (2014). The essential moral self. *Cognition, 131*(1), 159–171. https://doi.org/10.1016/j.cognition.2013.12.005

Tiwald, J. (2018). Confucianism and neo-Confucianism. In N. E. Snow (Ed.), *The Oxford handbook of virtue* (pp. 171–189). Oxford University Press.

Uhlmann, E. L., Pizarro, D. A., & Diermeier, D. (2015). A person-centered approach to moral judgment. *Perspectives on Psychological Science, 10*(1), 72–81. https://doi.org/10.1177/1745691614556679

Vogler, C. (2018). Turning to Aquinas on virtue. In N. E. Snow (Ed.), *The Oxford handbook of virtue* (pp. 224–240). Oxford University Press.

Wright, J., Warren, M., & Snow, N. (2021). *Understanding virtue: Theory and measurement*. Oxford University Press.

Zagzebski, L. (1996). *Virtues of the mind: An inquiry into the nature of virtue and the ethical foundations of knowledge*. Cambridge University Press. https://doi.org/10.1017/CBO9781139174763

Zagzebski, L. (2017). *Exemplarist moral theory*. Oxford University Press. https://doi.org/10.1093/acprof:oso/9780190655846.001.0001

6 LEARNING TO WEIGH COMPETING MORAL MOTIVATIONS

ORIEL FELDMANHALL AND AMRITA LAMBA

Our human moral sense is colored by a fusion of self-serving biases and other-orientated preferences. On the one hand, we want to maximize self-benefit, and thus we work toward achieving outcomes that increase our pleasure, wealth, prestige, power, and reputation. On the other hand, because we care about those around us, we also behave in ways that help others, even when it comes at a cost to the self.

We exist at a nexus point in human history at which morally fraught issues, such as legal access to abortion, restricting gun ownership, race and gender disparity, and wealth inequality, just to name a few, are becoming ever-polarizing moral issues that we each must find ways to navigate through. For example, deciding whether we should lie to a loved one to spare their feelings over a political impasse, or figuring out whether to distance ourselves from a family member who harbors an unwavering racist worldview, have become common fodder in our everyday lives. Moral tensions need not be restricted to lofty armchair thought experiments in which individuals can cogently reason through the pros and cons of each outcome. Instead, weighing up competing moral motivations spans a rich social space. Indeed,

https://doi.org/10.1037/0000342-007
Motivation and Morality: A Multidisciplinary Approach, M. K. Berg and E. C. Chang (Editors)

during every interaction we have with others, we make inferences about their beliefs regarding a wide spectrum of topics that touch on both moral and nonmoral issues, gleaning insight from imperfect information and then using this knowledge to construct our own views about the world. In this chapter, we ask, "How do humans learn to weigh information to learn what is right and just?"

In the past 20 years there has been a seismic shift toward understanding how people wade through the messy space of moral inference and decision making. Armed with philosophical vignettes that aim to map the contexts of when it is appropriate to engage in a moral behavior (e.g., I might pull the lever in the trolley dilemma, but I will not push the person off the footbridge to save five others), researchers have accumulated a trove of evidence illuminating the intricacies of the moral mind (Greene et al., 2001; Ruff & Fehr, 2014; Van Bavel et al., 2015; Yoder & Decety, 2018). Although this class of moral vignette can be useful for understanding why humans make meaningful distinctions between certain moral situations, the results of such extreme, unlikely hypotheticals do not lend themselves to being generalized across situations. Furthermore, a moral decision (or any decision, for that matter) is rarely made in isolation. Although moral beliefs and choices often feel deeply personal and self-actualized, they are often learned from those around us. As people move about their worlds engaging with people in both superficial and intimate ways, they make a series of decisions that inform and shape their mental model of the world (Wheatley et al., 2019). These decisions guide the probability of making a similar decision in the future. A choice to stand up for a colleague who is being mistreated might be repeated if the colleague is appreciative and the intervention results in a safer work environment, but not if the colleague is ungracious and the decision leads to backlash. A young adolescent may emulate a moral stance embodied by their favorite celebrity role model or by a group of peers and thus learns to adopt a set of moral beliefs by observing others. This feedback loop, and the ability to integrate information from the environment to help guide subsequent moral decisions is called *social learning*.

In this chapter, we take the perspective that one promising avenue for understanding how humans learn to weigh competing moral motivations is by decomposing the moral inference process into a set of fundamental building blocks that include rewards and punishments. In particular, we take the approach of reasoning through a set of first principles borrowed from the learning domain to characterize the core cognitive and environmental factors that shape the way humans learn *from* and *about* others. We thus adopt the framework that although moral norms may be largely culturally contextualized, these fundamental learning blocks operate universally to shape our moral preferences and choices.

Cognitive neuroscience has made immense strides in understanding how humans learn (Bassett & Mattar, 2017; Cohen et al., 2012; Fiorillo et al., 2003; Glimcher, 2011; Shamay-Tsoory & Mendelsohn, 2019). The computational models leveraged to interrogate how humans learn about value—whether learning occurs from monetary rewards, accuracy, tasty treats, and so on—provide a useful framework that describes *how* people make decisions to maximize reward and minimize punishment (Daw et al., 2011; Frank et al., 2004; Niv, 2009). More recently, these models have been co-opted to explain the mechanisms that drive social behaviors, such as learning to trust or cooperate with a stranger (Behrens et al., 2008; FeldmanHall, Otto, & Phelps, 2018; Hackel & Amodio, 2018; Hackel et al., 2015; van Baar et al., 2022). Applying formal learning frameworks to complicated social behaviors, including how we learn to trust or when we empathize, has been beneficial for gaining mathematical tractability in a fuzzy and complex psychological space (Cushman & Gershman, 2019). Indeed, the most striking examples of how formal learning models map onto sophisticated moral beliefs occur by carefully crafting learning algorithms and applying them to moral content (FeldmanHall & Nassar, 2021; Griffiths et al., 2010; Park et al., 2019; Steixner-Kumar et al., 2020; van Baar et al., 2022), ideally in ways that shape real-world issues, such as political polarization (Rathje et al., 2021). The success of such models in capturing learning as it relates to moral phenomena highlights the need for researchers across disciplines to embrace the role of social learning in shaping moral beliefs and the role of reward learning algorithms in reinforcing increasingly extreme moral judgments. We touch on some of these algorithms later in the chapter.

In the following sections, we address the big picture connections between human morality and social learning by first describing who we tend to learn from and the circumstances humans exploit when observing other people navigating the world. After this, we describe how we learn about other people, centering our discussion on the unique environmental constraints and cognitive demands that often encumber adaptive inference when trying to figure out what another person is like (e.g., are they trustworthy?). In the final section of this chapter, we introduce formal learning models that describe the mechanisms by which humans integrate social, moral, and emotional information to create useful mental models of their social worlds to both learn from and about others. We argue that these learning mechanisms form the backbone of our moral beliefs to guide our choices.

WHOM DO WE LEARN *FROM*?

Scholars have long discussed the origins of human moral inference. Where, for example, do young children learn the types of moral norms that govern how they should interact with others? The question of whom we learn from was initially tackled in a now-famous study involving children punching an inflatable toy known as the Bobo doll (Bandura et al., 1963). Bandura et al. (1963) set up a series of experiments in which he could measure patterns of aggressive behavior in children after they observed an adult modeling aggressive behavior. The results were just what you would imagine: Three- and 4-year-old children who observed a violent adult attacking a doll mimicked those violent behaviors themselves, even when the adult was no longer present. This finding—that children learn to interact with the world by observing those around them—shifted our understanding of how social learning occurs. Rather than learning by directly experiencing everything, people can observe others and use that information to make decisions, even those that are fraught with moral tensions. We now know that people routinely learn by observing others, across many different contexts, and with many different types of behaviors (Burke et al., 2010; Shafto et al., 2012; Smith & Sørensen, 2000). Children, who have much to learn about the world, appear to be faithful imitators, even when some observed actions (e.g., punching a doll) are clearly superfluous to achieving the desired outcome (Lyons et al., 2007).

People, however, do not indiscriminately learn from just anyone. After relatively short observation periods, people can swiftly figure out who is an expert and who is a novice (Boorman et al., 2013), and they can use that knowledge in a flexible manner (Vélez & Gweon, 2019). Even when observing two expert advice-givers, people are adept at picking up latent behavioral patterns that could be more informative during learning (e.g., being risk-seeking or risk-averse). People also prefer to learn from those who are confident (Campbell-Meiklejohn et al., 2017) and not overly informative or instructive in their teaching style, which allows for some level of exploration to still occur (Bridgers et al., 2020). When it comes to moral phenomena, people learn how to be moral or immoral simply by observing their own ingroup members and conforming to their (im)moral behaviors (Abrams et al., 1990; Stein, 2017). An interesting bias that has emerged from this research is that people apply different thresholds to ingroups and outgroups when it comes to condoning immoral behavior. Research shows, for example, that people readily turn the other cheek when observing immoral ingroup behavior (Aquino et al., 2007), and they are even more likely to become dishonest themselves after watching a dishonest ingroup member (Gino et al., 2009).

Of interest is that outgroup members who behave in particularly moral or noteworthy ways—for example, not cheating despite being given ample opportunity—reveal a similar relationship, fueled by intergroup competition. In this case, the observing outgroup member strives to be perceived as even more morally virtuous than the outgroup member (Vives et al., 2022).

When learning by observing others, there are different strategies an individual can deploy, including emulation and imitation. *Emulation* is when the underlying structure that gives rise to people's actions must be inferred, which means that there can be a dissociation between the action and the outcome. For example, children pay close attention to what a teacher demonstrates and use the observed behavior to help build a mental model of the environment that goes beyond the taught behavior—that is, inferring a causal reason for behaviors that extends beyond what meets the eye (Goodman et al., 2011). In contrast, *imitation* is the simple strategy of copying another's actions exactly, the behaviors that were observed in Bandura et al.'s (1963) famous Bobo doll experiment. More recent work has made progress in understanding when one of these strategies dominates, revealing that the level of uncertainty in the environment governs which of these two strategies gets implemented during observational learning (Charpentier et al., 2020). If uncertainty about the action–outcome pairing is high, emulation is the favored strategy; elsewise, imitation is favored.

People bring other assumptions to the table that help speed learning, including the belief that people act in goal-directed (S. Liu et al., 2017) and efficient (S. Liu & Spelke, 2017) ways that aim to maximize rewards and minimize punishments (Jara-Ettinger et al., 2016). This can be understood by the type of information people attend to when observing others. For example, when a teacher explains and demonstrates that a particular toy can play music, preschoolers not only learn that the toy is musical, but they also infer that this is the toy's only function, and thus they do not continue to explore whether the toy has any other capabilities (Bonawitz et al., 2011). This is because children assume that they are being taught the most important information; if information is not taught, then there must not be any additional useful information to learn (Gweon et al., 2014; Gweon & Asaba, 2018; Shafto et al., 2014). When learning from others, an individual also jointly attends to the teacher's emotional expressions and depth of knowledge (Wu & Gweon, 2021) because these are useful metrics that make learning more efficient. In other words, not all observed information is treated equally during the learning process (Vélez & Gweon, 2021). Finally, social feedback, such as praise, is intrinsically rewarding and is used to shore up learning (Ho et al., 2017, 2019). However, it is not treated in the same way that other types of rewards are typically treated, as social feedback becomes valued even more when it is given by those who are frugal with their praise (Asaba et al., 2018).

Across a variety of contexts, such as learning how to interact with an inflatable doll or how to behave in an educational setting, we seek out competent others and emulate the types of behaviors we believe to be rewarding. Although much of this work has not been in the domain of morality per se (given the difficulties associated with testing real moral content in a laboratory setting), these data reveal that humans acquire much of their behavioral repertoire from others, allowing us to extrapolate to make clear predictions about where our moral templates are learned from. Given that we carefully attend to and learn from confident experts about nonmoral content, it is likely that these particular individuals are also the ones to distill insight into which action or knowledge is morally appropriate or not. Of course, there are also many other settings in which we cannot directly learn moral knowledge because it must be inferred. In the next section, we outline the inference mechanisms that we use to learn about others and the types of cognitive biases that shape our emergent beliefs.

HOW DO WE LEARN *ABOUT* OTHERS?

One of the greatest challenges about social learning is figuring out how to value other people (FeldmanHall & Nassar, 2021). No two humans are ever exactly alike. This poses a problem when trying to learn about others, such as whether a person is trustworthy or generous. Moreover, social relationships (even the most superficial ones) require that we try to accurately infer the hidden intentions and motivations of others. To infer another's unobservable intentions, we must decode uncertain and multidimensional social cues (e.g., silence after a joke is told), mentally stitching together past and present outcomes from different circumstances and using relevant social knowledge to form accurate predictions about strangers or known others in novel scenarios. Although seemingly trivial, learning about others comes with a host of unique obstacles that may result in social friction when even minor miscalibrations occur.

Let us take the example of new friends grabbing a cup of coffee. As they sit down to chat, they gather information about the preferences, intentions, beliefs, and opinions of the other. This process is done in the absence of having a cheat sheet about the other's likes and dislikes, their past histories, experiences, and future desires. Preferences must be gleaned from imperfect emotional cues (e.g., smiles, frowns, nods) and verbal descriptions that do not always reveal a veridical preference.

This example illustrates how we are constantly being bombarded with uncertainty on a multitude of levels (FeldmanHall & Shenhav, 2019). *Uncertainty* refers to a prediction's precision given the available information (Hirsh et al., 2012). At their core, social interactions hinge on dynamic, hidden states, for example, the intentions or motivations of another. Critically, these intentions and motivations cannot be directly observed. What transpires at the surface is not necessarily the same as what is happening underneath the smiles and nods (e.g., is her smile genuine or a polite gesture?). On top of this, because people typically share only partial information about themselves, much remains unknown about the preferences and beliefs of those with whom we engage. The fact that most people's preferences and beliefs are only partially observable affects how we respond in turn. For example, whether a smile is perceived as genuine or a polite gesture may dictate just how long two people go on bantering. Because there is uncertainty about what another person is like, there is also uncertainty about what action to take and how the chosen action will ultimately be received by the other person (FeldmanHall & Nassar, 2021).

Social information is also usually multidimensional, which adds another hurdle when trying to successfully navigate the social world. People have many idiosyncratic wants and feelings. For example, I may declare that I love ice cream, but what I really mean is that I love coffee hazelnut almond chip and abhor vanilla, and I will only eat ice cream if it is above 80 degrees outside. From this standpoint, my love for ice cream is nuanced (because I do not love all ice cream flavors) and highly context dependent (it must be warm outside). When another person is trying to infer my predilections about ice cream, all these considerations come into play. It is rarely as simple as loving ice cream writ large. This is, of course, a toy example, but the logic can be extended to far more complex and everyday moral phenomena, such as aggression, fairness, trustworthiness, and so forth. I may swear to a friend that I am entirely trustworthy and I always keep her secrets, but when I find that it might actually be beneficial (for me and her) to expose some of this confidential information, I hesitate for but a moment before spilling the beans. The fact that social information is inherently multidimensional influences how we learn about the social value of other individuals. Although categorical judgments might be easy to make (e.g., he is aggressive), they would not reflect a one-to-one mapping with how that individual likely engages with the world (e.g., he is aggressive when he feels attacked). Moreover, when refracted through one's own perspective, relational schemas and self-anchoring can distort how social information is integrated, updated, and ultimately valued (Baldwin, 1992; Tamir & Mitchell, 2013; Tversky & Kahneman, 1974; van den Berg & Wenseleers, 2018).

These social inference challenges are compounded by the fact that feedback about others is not always delivered at the moment that a choice is made. Imagine running into a friend at the grocery store. You excitedly say hi, but he gives you the cold shoulder and walks away. Why did he ignore you? You rack your brain and remember that months before you told two friends a juicy piece of gossip about him, breaking your own moral code not to gossip. Then you also remember that the last time you saw him you were in a rush and did not stop to chat. The problem you are now faced with is figuring out why your friend ignored you: Is it because you ignored him first, or is it because he found out that you were gossiping about him—and, if it is the latter, which one of your friends cannot be trusted? This example illustrates the timescale along which many social learning problems unfold. Feedback is not always immediate, and it can be difficult to figure out which behavior or cue to even assign credit to—a challenge known as the *credit assignment problem* (Akaishi et al., 2016; Hamid et al., 2021; Sutton, 1984). In the social world, it would be hard to learn whom to trust if we are unable to properly assign feedback to the behaviors or cue that sparked it, even when they have occurred in the distant past.

Finally, learning about others requires that information gleaned be integrated across experiences to enable generalization—the hallmark of successful learning (FeldmanHall & Dunsmoor, 2018; FeldmanHall, Dunsmoor, et al., 2018). When a person can take the principles learned in one context and apply it to another, they have successfully cut down the amount of learning they need to do, a critical feature of adaptive behavior (Chumbley et al., 2012; Dymond et al., 2015; Lashley & Wade 1946). For example, should an apple cause an allergic reaction when you eat it at home, it is likely that it will cause an allergic reaction if you are eating it on a bus. In the social–moral world, however, there are rarely two situations that are alike (because people are dynamic), and local moral norms (Bicchieri, 2005; Everett et al., 2017) can dictate whether a behavior is successful (or not) in a certain context. You might, for example, observe someone telling a lie when defending a friend. From this experience, have you learned that he is untrustworthy and thus he should be avoided the next time you see him? Learning how to execute the appropriate social behavior across social contexts therefore requires retrieving the relevant information from prior experiences, attending to the most revealing moral cues, and adaptively adjusting one's behavior, even when only partial social information is available (Mastroianni et al., 2021; van Baar et al., 2022). Clearly people can do this, and they are even able to generalize moral traits such as trustworthiness from perceptual features alone (FeldmanHall, Dunsmoor, et al., 2018).

As we navigate our social worlds, we are constantly integrating pieces of knowledge about how we should we behave toward others and how we believe others should behave with us in turn. These constructed beliefs help to define our own moral calculus (Cushman, 2015; Kim et al., 2020; Mende-Siedlecki et al., 2013). Someone may, for example, observe a colleague using another colleague's material as if it were their own. Does the observer perceive this as an immoral action? Because we cannot directly observe another's intentions and motivations, our own biases and miscalibrations in reading the intentions of others can lead us to draw faulty moral inferences (Cameron et al., 2010; Correll et al., 2007; Frank et al., 2019; Hirozawa et al., 2020; Kleiman-Weiner et al., 2015; Siegel et al., 2017). For example, instead of plagiarizing, perhaps the colleague was experiencing source misattribution or was given permission to use the material. The problem is that social learning requires a tremendous degree of inference over hidden mental states, which can lead to many errors during the learning process and can even contribute to stereotype bias (Olsson et al., 2016). In the next section, we outline a set of learning mechanisms people use to overcome these challenges. The goal of this section is not to outline all the various algorithms used during moral inference but rather to provide readers with a cursory overview of how standard reward learning models borrowed from cognitive neuroscience can be applied to the moral domain. By delineating a set of first principles, our hope is to center our discussion on the ways in which human moral inference emerges through a set of domain general learning mechanisms.

MECHANISMS FOR SOCIAL LEARNING

When we are either learning from or about other people in our social worlds, we use information and cues gained from the experience to update an existing mental model of what will happen next. In other words, when we think through the consequences of our actions, such as contemplating whether to trust a friend, lie to another, or help a stranger, we use previously acquired experiences to make educated guesses about behavior given the relevant inputs (e.g., if I say x, they will do y). Within the cognitive science literature, this process is conceptualized as maintaining an *internal generative model of the environment*—in essence, distilling multidimensional environmental inputs into a relatively small number of one-dimensional parameters (e.g., randomness, degree of inequity between parties) that can be used to mentally simulate future outcomes.

Although the complexity of our social worlds can be plausibly and intelligently structured in infinite ways, much of our social experience can be considered in terms of value. This is often thought of through the lens of expected rewards and losses. Did trusting my friend result in a generally positive or negative outcome? Did this outcome deviate or match my predictions? Given the computational revolution (Bossaerts & Murawski, 2017), we now have a clearer understanding of how humans learn from reward and punishment, especially for simpler behaviors, such as learned associations between stimuli and actions, which have also been recently applied to moral stimuli and actions as well (FeldmanHall & Dunsmoor, 2018). Reinforcement learning (RL) theory and Bayesian belief models have provided immensely useful frameworks that detail at the mechanistic level how humans leverage past experiences to enable efficient decision making.

Although these models are relatively simple algorithmically, social psychologists and neuroscientists are increasingly turning to formal computational models to inform how learning unfolds in the social and moral domains (Charpentier & O'Doherty, 2018, Vélez & Gweon, 2021), primarily because computational models offer the unique ability to augment standard statistical analyses by providing a formalized description of the underlying process driving a particular behavioral response (Daw, 2014; Nassar & Frank, 2016; Wilson & Collins, 2019). Computational models also allow researchers to explicitly decompose theoretically and empirically meaningful aspects of the experimental paradigm into subject- or group-specific parameters. For example, researchers can capture choice randomness and sensitivity to uncertainty in a probabilistic learning task and use the resulting parameters as regressors to examine differences across individuals or task settings. Here we describe two main computational frameworks—RL and Bayesian—that have been used to describe social and moral behaviors, enumerating both their strengths and weaknesses for capturing social learning. We introduce the underlying logic of RL and Bayesian algorithms and detail how each model can be used to better identify how humans learn in their social–moral worlds.

Reinforcement Learning Models

RL models are particularly appealing to researchers in social psychology (Lockwood & Klein-Flügge, 2021), given their computational simplicity and because they neatly map onto well-characterized stimulus–response mechanisms (e.g., operant conditioning and associative learning) that have long been examined in the classic learning and memory literature. The fundamental and underlying assumptions of RL models are that agents strive to maximize accumulated rewards while minimizing surprise and punishment. RL uses a relatively simple computational architecture to stitch together past outcomes in order to accurately predict future outcomes. When applied to human cognition, RL frameworks are often integrated with theories of active inference (Friston et al., 2009) and Bayesian brain theories (Friston, 2010; Mathys et al., 2011), which postulate that homeostatic neural mechanisms drive humans and organisms to constantly seek reward (Pessiglione et al., 2006) and minimize uncertainty (Friston, 2010; Rushworth & Behrens, 2008).

The most elementary form of RL is defined as a finite *Markov decision process*, in which the state of the world is pared down to a finite set of states, actions, and rewards that jointly occur at a given moment in time, which greatly reduces the representational complexity of any specific learning problem (Sutton & Barto, 1998). In RL, the learning problem is further simplified by discretizing time steps, such that learning is chunked into individual state–action–reward episodes (e.g., trial type × choice + feedback pairing in a learning task). Furthermore, the finite Markov decision process becomes particularly efficient because all relevant information that is needed to make an optimal decision in the moment (assuming sufficient training has already occurred) is quantified and summarized in the previous time step as cached values, which facilitates efficient learning.

To visualize how reinforcement learning models work, imagine the process of deciding whether or not you want to have dinner at your favorite restaurant, which is located about 45 minutes from your house, or whether you will have dinner at your second-favorite restaurant, which is only 15 minutes away. When making your dinner choice, the value of each place may be informed by (a) how much you enjoy the food and (b) the travel costs of getting there. Using a simple RL approach, you do not necessarily need to retrieve every dining experience you have ever had, or the exact travel times to and from each place, to form a decision; instead, you may implicitly conjure up an approximate value representation of each restaurant that in many ways is a gestalt summary of your past experiences. After making a presumably value-maximizing choice, you may then reevaluate whether you made the best choice (e.g., maybe you drove 45 minutes to your favorite restaurant, and the food was not nearly as good as you remembered) and will then factor this experience into your stored value representation of that restaurant for next time.

Keeping this example in mind, model-free RL algorithms can capture most aspects of the restaurant decision-making process while explicitly lacking a representation of the structure of the environment (hence the term *model-free*). This drastically reduces the computational complexity of the algorithm and allows model-free RL mechanisms to generalize across a broad array of contexts. The Rescorla–Wagner (RW) equation defined below tabulates the presumed value of executing a given action (V[A], e.g., eating at each restaurant) at the next decision opportunity or time point, $V(A)_{t+1}$, as a function of $V(A)$ on previous time points (e.g., how much you liked eating at your favorite restaurant the last few times you went there), which is known as the reward expectation (Rescorla & Wagner, 1972). The reward expectation on the next time step, $V(A)_{t+1}$, is adjusted through the joint combination of a reward, R, received on the current time step (how much you enjoyed the most recent dining experience) minus expected rewards, $V(A)$, (was the current dining experience better, worse, or the same compared with your prior experiences?), which produces the scalar value δ.

$$\delta = R - V(A)$$

The δ on the current time step computes the relative *reward prediction error* (RPE), or the degree to which the reward expectation, $V(A)$, deviates from actual reward outcomes (did your restaurant experience exceed your expectations or lead to disappointment?). The RPE value allows for a simple form of error-driven learning to appropriately calibrate future predictions through the fixed learning rate parameter, α, which governs the degree to which RPEs drive reward expectation, $V(A)_{t+1}$ (how much does disappointment, or having your expectations exceeded, factor into your decision to go to the restaurant again in the future?):

$$V(A)_{t+1} \leftarrow V(A) + \alpha \times \delta$$

$$\delta = R - V(A)$$

Alternative forms of RL have also been proposed, such as the Pearce–Hall model of Pavlovian learning (Pearce & Hall, 1980). The Pearce–Hall model includes an additional component—associability—that parametrizes the strength of the relationship between the intensity of an unconditioned response (λ; e.g., salivating when you arrive at your favorite restaurant) and the associative strength of all stimuli on previous trials (ΣV; e.g., to what degree are past dining experiences at the restaurants you dine at predictive of future dining experiences?). Associability therefore tracks the degree to which reinforcers in the environment reliably predict future reward or punishment.

Though simplistic computationally, RL algorithms can be scaled up through modern machine learning methods and through recurrent neural network architectures to accomplish exceedingly complex learning tasks (Schaeffer et al., 2001; Schraudolph et al., 1994). Given the relative computational trade-off between accuracy and efficiency associated with model-free learning algorithms, RL has long been an appealing candidate mechanism of learning in humans and animals (Montague et al., 1996; Schultz et al., 1997).

Reinforcement Learning in Moral Contexts

The application of RL to social and moral contexts has reaped a number of important insights into human moral behavior, mainly that, much like classic reward learning, social and moral learning can be explained in terms of prediction errors. Some of the earliest social RL research revealed that humans learn social value—such as whether a person is competent and can be relied upon—through prediction errors (Behrens et al., 2008; Burke et al., 2010; van den Bos et al., 2013). Once this basic premise was established, researchers began digging into whether certain morally fraught contexts affected how prediction errors were used (Boorman et al., 2013; FeldmanHall, Otto, & Phelps, 2018; Koster-Hale & Saxe, 2013; Lockwood et al., 2016), and whether there is a true one-to-one mapping between nonsocial learning algorithms and moral learning algorithms (Apps et al., 2015; Olsson et al., 2020). For example, Hackel et al. (2015) found that when participants were required to learn the reward dynamics of a human partner and a slot machine, there are distinct learning profiles for figuring out that a person is generous versus a machine merely dispenses rewards. Although learning in both tasks did evoke much of the same neural circuitry that is typically observed in standard nonsocial reward learning paradigms, learning about an altruistic human partner recruited an additional set of brain regions known for computing higher level moral inference. In a subsequent decision-making task that probed for inductive biases acquired from the previous learning phase, Hackel et al. further found that participants were more likely to use trait-level information, such as generosity or altruism (i.e., the proportion of possible returns that was given back to the subject), rather than actual monetary rewards received, when predicting the future behavior of partners. In short, although reward itself was informative, the moral information about a partner (i.e., their generosity even when less money was offered) was far more useful for navigating social inference problems.

RL frameworks have also been successful in describing how people dynamically adjust their moral beliefs about others. Chang and colleagues (2010) modeled beliefs about another's trustworthiness and found evidence that people use past monetary rewards (e.g., the number of times that a person was trustworthy in an investment task) to make inferences about the likelihood that a person will engage in prosocial behaviors in the future. Critically, beliefs about another's trustworthiness were not stagnant but instead were dynamically adjusted on the basis of new evidence. In contrast, previously learned probabilities about slot machines were not dynamically adjusted at the same rate, suggesting that when we learn about the moral value of others we may use increased representational flexibility. Similar findings of context-dependent moral computations have been borne out across numerous other experiments since then, suggesting that humans may use a distinct and computationally characterizable set of cognitive mechanisms when learning about the social or moral value of others (Charpentier & O'Doherty, 2018; Lamba et al., 2020; Lockwood et al., 2016; Olsson et al., 2020). Collectively, studies that have examined moral learning through RL frameworks provide considerable evidence that humans engage in error-driven learning to infer moral value (e.g., generosity and trustworthiness) and that these learning mechanisms both diverge and overlap with nonsocial learning processes.

Although novel approaches to understanding human social learning from an RL perspective expands the scope of computational modeling work to more ecologically valid contexts, RL alone—especially when the models take the form of model-free algorithms—struggles to fully describe social learning processes. This is largely because model-free algorithms are computationally insensitive to many of the core features that define social or moral learning problems. For example, model-free RL algorithms assume that every observation provides the agent with the necessary information to update the value of representations of the current state–action pairing (S,A) and the value of future (i.e., successor) states. Receiving reward in state Y after executing action X should allow the agent to increase the value of (S,A) at the next time step. *Perceptual aliasing* occurs in situations in which several states in the learning space are equally implicated by the current set of observations. In other words, the elements of the moral environment that are predictive of outcome "My friend and I will agree on who the next political candidate should be" versus "My friend and I will disagree about abortion rights" may share many of the same features, making it difficult for the individual to execute the appropriate actions. When multiple states are indistinguishable at the current time step it becomes difficult to predict the value of successor states and to assign credit to actions in the current state (e.g., if my friend continues to have a neutral expression after I said X, does this indicate a positive, negative, or neutral outcome?; Crook & Hayes, 2003; Gershman & Daw, 2017; Hasino, 2003). In this example, the individual would not learn because value representations (e.g., value of performing action X) cannot be mapped to the appropriate state representations (e.g., when my friend is in mood *Y*), which is required for error-driven learning.

At first blush, model-based RL algorithms would seem to solve this problem; however, although this problem can be reformulated as a partially observable Markov decision process, or POMDP (Kaelbling et al., 1998), model-based RL algorithms that involve POMDP solutions can be computationally intractable in experimental settings because the state–action space is far too large to allow efficient learning. A strength of the computational approach is that models are applied to relatively minimalistic experimental environments, in which optimal solutions (e.g., how an "optimal" agent would perform the task) can be derived (Daw, 2014). In other words, computational models are most successfully used in tasks in which subject-specific parameters can be compared with performance benchmarks derived from a simulated optimal learner. These performance benchmarks can be very difficult to figure out when scaled to more complex environments, in which multiple learning algorithms or combinations of parameters may produce reasonable or even "optimal" performance—a problem that often arises during moral dilemmas, especially those that have no clear optimal outcome.

A solution to this problem that has emerged in recent years is to leverage *inverse reinforcement learning* (IRL; Baker et al., 2009; Collette et al., 2017). In IRL, an individual can observe the behaviors of another and use this information to infer what that person is trying to achieve, what their goals are, and ultimately what their (perhaps latent) preferences are (Jern et al., 2017). The idea of IRL basically flips the logic of RL because the reward function must be discovered by observing another person's behavior. If we were relying on traditional RL to learn in moral contexts, the reward function would have to include an exhaustive list of all the human behaviors we might see and the list of weights that describe how important or trivial each behavior is—an almost impossible endeavor. This is where more basic, model-free RL algorithms break down. IRL has a number of benefits that extend beyond its tractability, including describing a mechanism for what seems to be a very basic social skill often used in moral contexts: the ability to figure out another's moral preferences even when they deviate from our own. IRL has also been posited as a useful tool to capture how people reason about other people's mental states (Jara-Ettinger, 2019), an everyday occurrence on which we all rely, known as *theory of mind*, which are crucial for trying to work through a moral dilemma. The past 10 years have revealed that IRL algorithms can capture an array of social learning problems, from figuring out another person's food preferences (Baker et al., 2017) to how others make moral trade-offs (Kleiman-Weiner et al., 2017).

Bayesian Models

Although computationally tractable and elegant in their simplicity, RL algorithms—especially those of the model-free variety—cannot on their own account for the broad range of flexible and dynamic behaviors that characterize human learning and decision making (Chang et al., 2010; Daw et al., 2011; Dayan & Berridge, 2014; McGuire et al., 2014; Nassar et al., 2010). For example, real-world learning problems require a well-honed set of inference mechanisms to navigate through highly uncertain situations. Borrowing from RL terminology, uncertainty at the most rudimentary level occurs when mappings among states, actions, and reward are unknown. Although RPE minimization reduces surprise in environments where the mappings between actions and states are known and fixed (i.e., stationary), the statistics of the real world are fundamentally ambiguous, noisy, and often rapidly evolve (Behrens et al., 2007, 2008), especially when it comes to moral and social phenomenon (FeldmanHall & Shenhav, 2019).

To adaptively learn in a nonstationary world, humans need to flexibly update their internal models (e.g., their beliefs about the world) with new observations that counteract existing beliefs (Behrens et al., 2007; Yu & Dayan, 2005). This view stems from Bayesian brain theories of learning, in which the value of information itself must be dynamic (Courville et al., 2006; Friston, 2010; Mathys et al., 2011). According to Bayesian learning theory, organisms can thrive and flourish only if the following conditions hold: The organism has a useful generative model of the environment (i.e., a set of beliefs about what outcomes to expect given specific environmental conditions) and the organism strives to minimize entropy (i.e., uncertainty) through its interactions with the environment. The implications of these tenets are broad, such that the organism in this case might be a species of bird that has a generative model of how to fly under particular wind conditions that it has acquired over an evolutionary timescale, to holding a generative model of how to embezzle money from your employer. Regardless, the idea that people have internal models of the environment that are used to navigate the world and, ultimately, to survive, is impeded by the uncertainty encountered in the environment and in the system (e.g., confidence).

Bayesian models are appealing because they offer the ability to model beliefs about the world around us probabilistically rather than deterministically, and they can capture important dynamics that govern how and when we go about updating these beliefs. One particular advantage of using Bayesian models to capture learning processes is the ability to capitalize on the link between learning and uncertainty. If an organism is learning in a stable environment, then after initial action–reward pairings are learned and δ is consistently 0 (i.e., no reward prediction error because learning should eventually reach an asymptote), then learning rates should also be low to avoid wasted cognitive effort. However, sudden changes in δ should increase the salience of information because it signifies that something has changed. If the agent updated their beliefs about the world, such that this new observation was weighted equally to past observations, the organism would be too slow to respond to imminent threats or might miss out on large rewards. Adaptive learning should therefore require dynamically adjusting one's learning rate, such that RPEs are weighted by the degree of uncertainty in the environment. This idea has been supported by computational modeling and neuroimaging work, demonstrating that when humans are tasked to learn in volatile reward environments in which the structure of rewards frequently reverses, they dynamically adjust their learning rates from low to high after incurring a new set of RPEs (Franklin & Frank, 2015; Nassar et al., 2010, 2019).

Bayesian Models in Moral Contexts

In the social world, Bayesian belief models are particularly useful for describing learning problems because they allow researchers to formalize how previously learned representations (e.g., priors) bias learning, especially when contradictory evidence is presented (Griffiths et al., 2010; Hessel et al., 2019). In moral situations, perceived uncertainty is also often elevated because we do not have access to the mental states of others and need to infer these hidden states (FeldmanHall & Shenhav, 2019). This increase in social uncertainty should normatively result in faster learning (Behrens et al., 2007; Franklin & Frank, 2015; Nassar et al., 2010). Recent work from our lab suggests that changes in moral uncertainty do in fact prompt humans to dynamically adjust their beliefs about the reward statistics of social partners more efficiently than they adjust their beliefs about nonsocial agents (e.g., slot machines)—in particular when the social interactions begin to elicit negative RPEs (Lamba et al., 2020). In this case, participants must learn how much money to entrust to three different social partners, who either begin the game by (a) being very trustworthy and reciprocating back much of the entrusted money, (b) being untrustworthy by not sharing back any of the entrusted money, or (c) being neither highly trustworthy or untrustworthy (the "neutral" partner; in reality, each partner is a preprogrammed agent). The participants must learn, over time, that the partners' moral behaviors are not static, but rather each partner subtly and gradually reverses their behavior over the course of the task (e.g., trustworthy → untrustworthy).

In essence, this requires participants to continually adjust their beliefs about each partner's trustworthiness. We find that humans exploit the degree of uncertainty in the environment to enable more efficient updating: When uncertainty is low because a partner's moral behavior is stable and consistent, participants develop strong beliefs about how their partner will respond in future interactions. However, when these beliefs are challenged (i.e., a trustworthy partner begins to behave in a more selfish manner) and uncertainty increases, participants are able to use that information to update their beliefs accordingly.

To better understand how participants leverage uncertainty to guide moral learning and decision making, we fit participants' data to a Bayesian model, allowing us to examine how moral beliefs about trustworthiness were adjusted between each interaction (Lamba et al., 2020). The results suggested that participants rely on the relative uncertainty in the environment to govern how much they should update their beliefs, such that low uncertainty about moral outcomes enabled participants to form strong expectations. In contrast, greater uncertainty about a partner prompted participants to effectively override their prior beliefs and forget previous interactions that no longer fit with current behaviors. This is one way in which people can minimize the impact of previously learned behaviors so that current beliefs stay up to date. In short, participants weighed current moral information more heavily than prior moral information when uncertainty was high, allowing new moral beliefs to form that are more aligned with current outcomes.

Returning to our previous example, imagine that Friend A is on one side of the political aisle and Friend B is on the other. We all know how this social interaction is going to go. Friend A may begin the interaction with positive expectations about the friendship (a peaked prior distribution over positive values), but as evidence mounts that the friendship may not be as solid as previously thought (as Friend B espouses fringe conspiracy theories), Friend A must update their beliefs about the friendship. Bayesian models offer the ability to examine belief updating while taking into account relevant cognitive factors that inform how this moral updating occurs (i.e., the speed and strength by which it occurs). For example, the way new contradictory evidence overcomes previous beliefs can be captured through a decay parameter, which measures how much a person effectively "forgets" previously learned experiences when presented with contradictory ones (Franklin & Frank, 2015).

It is also plausible that a person may increase their learning in moments of uncertainty by simply attending more to unexpected moral outcomes, but they may fail to weigh this evidence in their beliefs about the friendship because perhaps the current situation is not reflective of previous or anticipated future outcomes. This would require a Bayesian model of the environment that weighs surprising outcomes relative to the degree to which the individual believes this surprising outcome is reflective of changes in the underlying causal statistics of the environment (i.e., the degree to which Friend A believes the argument is likely to lead to other negative interactions in the future or is simply a one-off incident; Nassar et al., 2019). For these reasons, Bayesian models lend themselves particularly well to capturing complex moral dynamics, in which reward contingencies are constantly changing and our internal models of the world (and, by extension, the actions we should take) are constantly evolving.

We have outlined a set of learning models borrowed from cognitive neuroscience that have shown impressive success in capturing behavior across a variety of domains, such as value-based decision making, statistical learning, and moral learning. Though elegant in their simplicity, RL and Bayesian models hinge on the idea that human inference and beliefs are constantly shifting targets, sculpted from preexisting biases and incoming streams of social and moral knowledge. As we increasingly confront a bombardment of moral issues on the national and international stage, from how we deal with an emerging climate crisis to social justice issues such as racial reparations, it has never been more important to understand the ways in which human moral judgments systematically emerge and are updated from the social inputs around us. Although social computational models of learning are still in their infancy, formal models of learning are becoming increasingly sophisticated in their ability to capture the building blocks of human learning and reasoning that are relevant to the moral domain, such as concept abstraction (Gershman et al., 2015; R. G. Liu & Frank, 2021; Tenenbaum et al., 2011) and mental simulation (Ho et al., 2022). These models are likely the next frontier in furthering our understanding of how humans develop, learn, and refine their nuanced and rich moral beliefs about the world around us.

CONCLUSION

Our social words are rich with hidden clues about how we should behave, what types of responses will help us succeed, and what others need from us. We integrate and weigh this information by relying on multiple learning mechanisms, each of which allows us to encapsulate the intricate complexities of the social world around us into compact and functional representations to facilitate adaptive behavior. As a tool, computational modeling has enabled unprecedented access to the biological mechanisms that govern human social behavior. This flourish in the natural sciences has brought momentum to understanding the social mind and has produced many novel and intriguing insights about how humans navigate their social and moral worlds.

REFERENCES

Abrams, D., Wetherell, M., Cochrane, S., Hogg, M. A., & Turner, J. C. (1990). Knowing what to think by knowing who you are: Self-categorization and the nature of norm formation, conformity and group polarization. *British Journal of Social Psychology*, *29*(2), 97–119. https://doi.org/10.1111/j.2044-8309.1990.tb00892.x

Akaishi, R., Kolling, N., Brown, J. W., & Rushworth, M. (2016). Neural mechanisms of credit assignment in a multicue environment. *The Journal of Neuroscience, 36*(4), 1096–1112. https://doi.org/10.1523/JNEUROSCI.3159-15.2016

Apps, M. A. J., Lesage, E., & Ramnani, N. (2015). Vicarious reinforcement learning signals when instructing others. *The Journal of Neuroscience, 35*(7), 2904–2913. https://doi.org/10.1523/JNEUROSCI.3669-14.2015

Aquino, K., Reed, I. I. A., II, Thau, S., & Freeman, D. (2007). A grotesque and dark beauty: How moral identity and mechanisms of moral disengagement influence cognitive and emotional reactions to war. *Journal of Experimental Social Psychology*, *43*(3), 385–392. https://doi.org/10.1016/j.jesp.2006.05.013

Asaba, M., Hembacher, E., Qiu, H., Anderson, B., Frank, M. C., & Gweon, H. (2018). Young children use statistical evidence to infer the informativeness of praise. *Cognitive Science*. https://langcog.stanford.edu/papers_new/asaba-2018-cogsci.pdf

Baker, C. L., Jara-Ettinger, J., Saxe, R., & Tenenbaum, J. B. (2017). Rational quantitative attribution of beliefs, desires and percepts in human mentalizing. *Nature Human Behaviour, 1*(4), Article 0064. https://doi.org/10.1038/s41562-017-0064

Baker, C. L., Saxe, R., & Tenenbaum, J. B. (2009). Action understanding as inverse planning. *Cognition, 113*(3), 329–349. https://doi.org/10.1016/j.cognition.2009.07.005

Baldwin, M. W. (1992). Relational schemas and the processing of social information. *Psychological Bulletin, 112*(3), 461–484. https://doi.org/10.1037/0033-2909.112.3.461

Bandura, A., Ross, D., & Ross, S. A. (1963). Imitation of film-mediated aggressive models. *Journal of Abnormal and Social Psychology, 66*(1), 3–11. https://doi.org/10.1037/h0048687

Bassett, D. S., & Mattar, M. G. (2017). A network neuroscience of human learning: Potential to inform quantitative theories of brain and behavior. *Trends in Cognitive Sciences, 21*(4), 250–264. https://doi.org/10.1016/j.tics.2017.01.010

Behrens, T. E., Hunt, L. T., Woolrich, M. W., & Rushworth, M. F. (2008). Associative learning of social value. *Nature, 456*(7219), 245–249. https://doi.org/10.1038/nature07538

Behrens, T. E., Woolrich, M. W., Walton, M. E., & Rushworth, M. F. (2007). Learning the value of information in an uncertain world. *Nature Neuroscience, 10*(9), 1214–1221. https://doi.org/10.1038/nn1954

Bicchieri, C. (2005). *The grammar of society: The nature and dynamics of social norms*. Cambridge University Press. https://doi.org/10.1017/CBO9780511616037

Bonawitz, E., Shafto, P., Gweon, H., Goodman, N. D., Spelke, E., & Schulz, L. (2011). The double-edged sword of pedagogy: Instruction limits spontaneous exploration and discovery. *Cognition, 120*(3), 322–330. https://doi.org/10.1016/j.cognition. 2010.10.001

Boorman, E. D., O'Doherty, J. P., Adolphs, R., & Rangel, A. (2013). The behavioral and neural mechanisms underlying the tracking of expertise. *Neuron, 80*(6), 1558–1571. https://doi.org/10.1016/j.neuron.2013.10.024

Bossaerts, P., & Murawski, C. (2017). Computational complexity and human decision-making. *Trends in Cognitive Sciences, 21*(12), 917–929. https://doi.org/10.1016/j.tics.2017.09.005

Bridgers, S., Jara-Ettinger, J., & Gweon, H. (2020). Young children consider the expected utility of others' learning to decide what to teach. *Nature Human Behaviour, 4*(2), 144–152. https://doi.org/10.1038/s41562-019-0748-6

Burke, C. J., Tobler, P. N., Baddeley, M., & Schultz, W. (2010). Neural mechanisms of observational learning. *Proceedings of the National Academy of Sciences of the United States of America, 107*(32), 14431–14436. https://doi.org/10.1073/pnas. 1003111107

Cameron, C. D., Payne, B. K., & Knobe, J. (2010). Do theories of implicit race bias change moral judgments? *Social Justice Research, 23*(4), 272–289. https://doi.org/10.1007/s11211-010-0118-z

Campbell-Meiklejohn, D., Simonsen, A., Frith, C. D., & Daw, N. D. (2017). Independent neural computation of value from other people's confidence. *The Journal of Neuroscience, 37*(3), 673–684. https://doi.org/10.1523/JNEUROSCI.4490-15.2016

Chang, L. J., Doll, B. B., van 't Wout, M., Frank, M. J., & Sanfey, A. G. (2010). Seeing is believing: Trustworthiness as a dynamic belief. *Cognitive Psychology, 61*(2), 87–105. https://doi.org/10.1016/j.cogpsych.2010.03.001

Charpentier, C. J., Iigaya, K., & O'Doherty, J. P. (2020). A neuro-computational account of arbitration between choice imitation and goal emulation during human observational learning. *Neuron, 106*(4), P687–P99.E7. https://doi.org/10.1016/j.neuron. 2020.02.028

Charpentier, C. J., & O'Doherty, J. P. (2018). The application of computational models to social neuroscience: Promises and pitfalls. *Social Neuroscience, 13*(6), 637–647. https://doi.org/10.1080/17470919.2018.1518834

Chumbley, J. R., Flandin, G., Bach, D. R., Daunizeau, J., Fehr, E., Dolan, R. J., & Friston, K. J. (2012). Learning and generalization under ambiguity: An fMRI study. *PLOS Computational Biology, 8*(1), e1002346. https://doi.org/10.1371/journal. pcbi.1002346

Cohen, J. Y., Haesler, S., Vong, L., Lowell, B. B., & Uchida, N. (2012). Neuron-type–specific signals for reward and punishment in the ventral tegmental area. *Nature, 482*(7383), 85–88. https://doi.org/10.1038/nature10754

Collette, S., Pauli, W. M., Bossaerts, P., & O'Doherty, J. (2017). Neural computations underlying inverse reinforcement learning in the human brain. *eLife, 6*, e29718. https://doi.org/10.7554/eLife.29718

Correll, J., Park, B., Judd, C. M., Wittenbrink, B., Sadler, M. S., & Keesee, T. (2007). Across the thin blue line: Police officers and racial bias in the decision to shoot. *Journal of Personality and Social Psychology, 92*(6), 1006–1023. https://doi.org/10.1037/0022-3514.92.6.1006

Courville, A. C., Daw, N. D., & Touretzky, D. S. (2006). Bayesian theories of conditioning in a changing world. *Trends in Cognitive Sciences*, *10*(7), 294–300. https://doi.org/10.1016/j.tics.2006.05.004

Crook, P. A., & Hayes, G. (2003). Learning in a state of confusion: Perceptual aliasing in grid world navigation. In *Proceedings of Towards Intelligent Mobile Robots (TIMR 2003) 4th British Conference on (Mobile) Robotics*. https://studylib.net/doc/8654226/learning-in-a-state-of-confusion--perceptual-aliasing-in-...Bristol2003

Cushman, F. (2015). Deconstructing intent to reconstruct morality. *Current Opinion in Psychology*, *6*, 97–103. https://doi.org/10.1016/j.copsyc.2015.06.003

Cushman, F., & Gershman, S. (2019). Computational approaches to social cognition. *Topics in Cognitive Science*, *11*(2), 281–298. https://doi.org/10.1111/tops.12424

Daw, N. D. (2014). Advanced reinforcement learning. In P. W. Glimcher & E. Fehr (Eds.), *Neuroeconomics* (2nd ed., pp. 299–320). Academic Press. https://doi.org/10.1016/C2011-0-05512-6

Daw, N. D., Gershman, S. J., Seymour, B., Dayan, P., & Dolan, R. J. (2011). Model-based influences on humans' choices and striatal prediction errors. *Neuron*, *69*(6), 1204–1215. https://doi.org/10.1016/j.neuron.2011.02.027

Dayan, P., & Berridge, K. C. (2014). Model-based and model-free Pavlovian reward learning: Revaluation, revision, and revelation. *Cognitive, Affective & Behavioral Neuroscience*, *14*(2), 473–492. https://doi.org/10.3758/s13415-014-0277-8

Dymond, S., Dunsmoor, J. E., Vervliet, B., Roche, B., & Hermans, D. (2015). Fear generalization in humans: Systematic review and implications for anxiety disorder research. *Behavior Therapy*, *46*(5), 561–582. https://doi.org/10.1016/j.beth.2014.10.001

Everett, J. A., Ingbretsen, Z., Cushman, F., & Cikara, M. (2017). Deliberation erodes cooperative behavior—Even towards competitive out-groups, even when using a control condition, and even when eliminating selection bias. *Journal of Experimental Social Psychology*, *73*, 76–81. https://doi.org/10.1016/j.jesp.2017.06.014

FeldmanHall, O., & Dunsmoor, J. E. (2018). Viewing adaptive social choice through the lens of associative learning. *Perspectives on Psychological Science*, *14*(2), 175–196. https://doi.org/10.1177/1745691618792261

FeldmanHall, O., Dunsmoor, J. E., Tompary, A., Hunter, L. E., Todorov, A., & Phelps, E. A. (2018). Stimulus generalization as a mechanism for learning to trust. *Proceedings of the National Academy of Sciences of the United States of America*, *115*(7), E1690–E1697. https://doi.org/10.1073/pnas.1715227115

FeldmanHall, O., & Nassar, M. R. (2021). The computational challenges of social learning. *Trends in Cognitive Sciences*, *25*(12), P1045–1057. https://doi.org/10.1016/j.tics.2021.09.002

FeldmanHall, O., Otto, A. R., & Phelps, E. A. (2018). Learning moral values: Another's desire to punish enhances one's own punitive behavior. *Journal of Experimental Psychology: General*, *147*(8), 1211–1224. https://doi.org/10.1037/xge0000405

FeldmanHall, O., & Shenhav, A. (2019). Resolving uncertainty in a social world. *Nature Human Behaviour*, *3*(5), 426–435. https://doi.org/10.1038/s41562-019-0590-x

Fiorillo, C. D., Tobler, P. N., & Schultz, W. (2003). Discrete coding of reward probability and uncertainty by dopamine neurons. *Science*, *299*(5614), 1898–1902. https://doi.org/10.1126/science.1077349

Frank, D. A., Chrysochou, P., Mitkidis, P., & Ariely, D. (2019). Human decision-making biases in the moral dilemmas of autonomous vehicles. *Scientific Reports*, *9*(1), Article 13080. https://doi.org/10.1038/s41598-019-49411-7

Frank, M. J., Seeberger, L. C., & O'Reilly, R. C. (2004). By carrot or by stick: Cognitive reinforcement learning in parkinsonism. *Science*, *306*(5703), 1940–1943. https://doi.org/10.1126/science.1102941

Franklin, N. T., & Frank, M. J. (2015). A cholinergic feedback circuit to regulate striatal population uncertainty and optimize reinforcement learning. *eLife*, *4*, e12029. https://doi.org/10.7554/eLife.12029

Friston, K. (2010). The free-energy principle: A unified brain theory? *Nature Reviews Neuroscience*, *11*(2), 127–138. https://doi.org/10.1038/nrn2787

Friston, K. J., Daunizeau, J., & Kiebel, S. J. (2009). Reinforcement learning or active inference? *PLOS ONE*, *4*(7), e6421. https://doi.org/10.1371/journal.pone.0006421

Gershman, S. J., & Daw, N. D. (2017). Reinforcement learning and episodic memory in humans and animals: An integrative framework. *Annual Review of Psychology*, *68*(1), 101–128. https://doi.org/10.1146/annurev-psych-122414-033625

Gershman, S. J., Horvitz, E. J., & Tenenbaum, J. B. (2015). Computational rationality: A converging paradigm for intelligence in brains, minds, and machines. *Science*, *349*(6245), 273–278. https://doi.org/10.1126/science.aac6076

Gino, F., Ayal, S., & Ariely, D. (2009). Contagion and differentiation in unethical behavior: The effect of one bad apple on the barrel. *Psychological Science*, *20*(3), 393–398. https://doi.org/10.1111/j.1467-9280.2009.02306.x

Glimcher, P. W. (2011). Understanding dopamine and reinforcement learning: The dopamine reward prediction error hypothesis. *Proceedings of the National Academy of Sciences of the United States of America*, *108*(Suppl. 3), 15647–15654. https://doi.org/10.1073/pnas.1014269108

Goodman, N. D., Ullman, T. D., & Tenenbaum, J. B. (2011). Learning a theory of causality. *Psychological Review*, *118*(1), 110–119. https://doi.org/10.1037/a0021336

Greene, J. D., Sommerville, R. B., Nystrom, L. E., Darley, J. M., & Cohen, J. D. (2001, September 14). An fMRI investigation of emotional engagement in moral judgment. *Science*, *293*(5537), 2105–2108. https://doi.org/10.1126/science.1062872

Griffiths, T. L., Chater, N., Kemp, C., Perfors, A., & Tenenbaum, J. B. (2010). Probabilistic models of cognition: Exploring representations and inductive biases. *Trends in Cognitive Sciences*, *14*(8), 357–364. https://doi.org/10.1016/j.tics.2010.05.004

Gweon, H., & Asaba, M. (2018). Order matters: Children's evaluation of under-informative teachers depends on context. *Child Development*, *89*(3), e278–e292. https://doi.org/10.1111/cdev.12825

Gweon, H., Pelton, H., Konopka, J. A., & Schulz, L. E. (2014). Sins of omission: Children selectively explore when teachers are under-informative. *Cognition*, *132*(3), 335–341. https://doi.org/10.1016/j.cognition.2014.04.013

Hackel, L. M., & Amodio, D. M. (2018). Computational neuroscience approaches to social cognition. *Current Opinion in Psychology*, *24*, 92–97. https://doi.org/10.1016/j.copsyc.2018.09.001

Hackel, L. M., Doll, B. B., & Amodio, D. M. (2015). Instrumental learning of traits versus rewards: Dissociable neural correlates and effects on choice. *Nature Neuroscience*, *18*(9), 1233–1235. https://doi.org/10.1038/nn.4080

Hamid, A., Frank, M. J., & Moore, C. I. (2021). Dopamine waves as a mechanism for spatiotemporal credit assignment. *Cell*, *184*(10), 2733–2749. https://doi.org/10.1016/j.cell.2021.03.046

Hasino, S. (2003). *Reinforcement learning for problems with hidden state*. https://people.csail.mit.edu/hasinoff/pubs/hasinoff-rlhidden-2002.pdf

Hessel, M., van Hasselt, H., Modayil, J., & Silver, D. (2019). *On inductive biases in deep reinforcement learning*. https://arxiv.org/pdf/1907.02908.pdf%3C/p%3E

Hirozawa, P. Y., Karasawa, M., & Matsuo, A. (2020). Intention matters to make you (im)moral: Positive–negative asymmetry in moral character evaluations. *The Journal of Social Psychology*, *160*(4), 401–415. https://doi.org/10.1080/00224545.2019.1653254

Hirsh, J. B., Mar, R. A., & Peterson, J. B. (2012). Psychological entropy: A framework for understanding uncertainty-related anxiety. *Psychological Review*, *119*(2), 304–320. https://doi.org/10.1037/a0026767

Ho, M. K., Abel, D., Correa, C. G., Littman, M. L., Cohen, J. D., & Griffiths, T. L. (2022). People construct simplified mental representations to plan. *Nature*, *606*(7912), 129–136. https://doi.org/10.1038/s41586-022-04743-9

Ho, M. K., Cushman, F., Littman, M. L., & Austerweil, J. L. (2019). People teach with rewards and punishments as communication, not reinforcements. *Journal of Experimental Psychology: General*, *148*(3), 520–549. https://doi.org/10.1037/xge0000569

Ho, M. K., MacGlashan, J., Littman, M. L., & Cushman, F. (2017). Social is special: A normative framework for teaching with and learning from evaluative feedback. *Cognition*, *167*, 91–106. https://doi.org/10.1016/j.cognition.2017.03.006

Jara-Ettinger, J. (2019). Theory of mind as inverse reinforcement learning. *Current Opinion in Behavioral Sciences*, *29*, 105–110. https://doi.org/10.1016/j.cobeha.2019.04.010

Jara-Ettinger, J., Gweon, H., Schulz, L. E., & Tenenbaum, J. B. (2016). The naïve utility calculus: Computational principles underlying commonsense psychology. *Trends in Cognitive Sciences*, *20*(8), 589–604. https://doi.org/10.1016/j.tics.2016.05.011

Jern, A., Lucas, C. G., & Kemp, C. (2017). People learn other people's preferences through inverse decision-making. *Cognition*, *168*, 46–64. https://doi.org/10.1016/j.cognition.2017.06.017

Kaelbling, L. P., Littman, M. L., & Cassandra, A. R. (1998). Planning and acting in partially observable stochastic domains. *Artificial Intelligence*, *101*(1–2), 99–134. https://doi.org/10.1016/S0004-3702(98)00023-X

Kim, M., Park, B., & Young, L. (2020). The psychology of motivated versus rational impression updating. *Trends in Cognitive Sciences*, *24*(2), 101–111. https://doi.org/10.1016/j.tics.2019.12.001

Kleiman-Weiner, M., Gerstenberg, T., Levine, S., & Tenenbaum, J. B. (2015). Inference of intention and permissibility in moral decision making. *Cognitive Science*. https://www.mit.edu/~maxkw/pdfs/kleiman2015inference.pdf

Kleiman-Weiner, M., Saxe, R., & Tenenbaum, J. B. (2017). Learning a commonsense moral theory. *Cognition*, *167*, 107–123. https://doi.org/10.1016/j.cognition.2017.03.005

Koster-Hale, J., & Saxe, R. (2013). Theory of mind: A neural prediction problem. *Neuron*, *79*(5), 836–848. https://doi.org/10.1016/j.neuron.2013.08.020

Lamba, A., Frank, M. J., & FeldmanHall, O. (2020). Anxiety impedes adaptive social learning under uncertainty. *Psychological Science, 31*(5), 592–603. https://doi.org/10.1177/0956797620910993

Lashley, K. S., & Wade, M. (1946). The Pavlovian theory of generalization. *Psychological Review, 53*(2), 72–87. https://doi.org/10.1037/h0059999

Liu, R. G., & Frank, M. J. (2021). *Hierarchical clustering optimizes the tradeoff between compositionality and expressivity of task structures in reinforcement learning.* bioRxiv. https://doi.org/10.1101/2021.07.20.453122

Liu, S., & Spelke, E. S. (2017). Six-month-old infants expect agents to minimize the cost of their actions. *Cognition, 160,* 35–42. https://doi.org/10.1016/j.cognition.2016.12.007

Liu, S., Ullman, T. D., Tenenbaum, J. B., & Spelke, E. S. (2017, November 24). Ten-month-old infants infer the value of goals from the costs of actions. *Science, 358*(6366), 1038–1041. https://doi.org/10.1126/science.aag2132

Lockwood, P. L., Apps, M. A. J., Valton, V., Viding, E., & Roiser, J. P. (2016). Neurocomputational mechanisms of prosocial learning and links to empathy. *Proceedings of the National Academy of Sciences of the United States of America, 113*(35), 9763–9768. https://doi.org/10.1073/pnas.1603198113

Lockwood, P. L., & Klein-Flügge, M. C. (2021). Computational modelling of social cognition and behaviour—A reinforcement learning primer. *Social Cognitive and Affective Neuroscience, 16*(8), 761–771. https://doi.org/10.1093/scan/nsaa040

Lyons, D. E., Young, A. G., & Keil, F. C. (2007). The hidden structure of overimitation. *Proceedings of the National Academy of Sciences of the United States of America, 104*(50), 19751–19756. https://doi.org/10.1073/pnas.0704452104

Mastroianni, A. M., Gilbert, D. T., Cooney, G., & Wilson, T. D. (2021). Do conversations end when people want them to? *Proceedings of the National Academy of Sciences of the United States of America, 118*(10), e2011809118. https://doi.org/10.1073/pnas.2011809118

Mathys, C., Daunizeau, J., Friston, K. J., & Stephan, K. E. (2011). A Bayesian foundation for individual learning under uncertainty. *Frontiers in Human Neuroscience, 5,* Article 39. https://doi.org/10.3389/fnhum.2011.00039

McGuire, J. T., Nassar, M. R., Gold, J. I., & Kable, J. W. (2014). Functionally dissociable influences on learning rate in a dynamic environment. *Neuron, 84*(4), 870–881. https://doi.org/10.1016/j.neuron.2014.10.013

Mende-Siedlecki, P., Baron, S. G., & Todorov, A. (2013). Diagnostic value underlies asymmetric updating of impressions in the morality and ability domains. *The Journal of Neuroscience, 33*(50), 19406–19415. https://doi.org/10.1523/JNEUROSCI.2334-13.2013

Montague, P. R., Dayan, P., & Sejnowski, T. J. (1996). A framework for mesencephalic dopamine systems based on predictive Hebbian learning. *The Journal of Neuroscience, 16*(5), 1936–1947. https://doi.org/10.1523/JNEUROSCI.16-05-01936.1996

Nassar, M. R., Bruckner, R., & Frank, M. J. (2019). Statistical context dictates the relationship between feedback-related EEG signals and learning. *eLife, 8,* e46975. https://doi.org/10.7554/eLife.46975

Nassar, M. R., & Frank, M. J. (2016). Taming the beast: Extracting generalizable knowledge from computational models of cognition. *Current Opinion in Behavioral Sciences, 11,* 49–54. https://doi.org/10.1016/j.cobeha.2016.04.003

Nassar, M. R., Wilson, R. C., Heasly, B., & Gold, J. I. (2010). An approximately Bayesian delta-rule model explains the dynamics of belief updating in a changing environment. *The Journal of Neuroscience, 30*(37), 12366–12378. https://doi.org/10.1523/JNEUROSCI.0822-10.2010

Niv, Y. (2009). Reinforcement learning in the brain. *Journal of Mathematical Psychology, 53*(3), 139–154. https://doi.org/10.1016/j.jmp.2008.12.005

Olsson, A., Knapska, E., & Lindström, B. (2020). The neural and computational systems of social learning. *Nature Reviews Neuroscience, 21*(4), 197–212. https://doi.org/10.1038/s41583-020-0276-4

Olsson, A., McMahon, K., Papenberg, G., Zaki, J., Bolger, N., & Ochsner, K. N. (2016). Vicarious fear learning depends on empathic appraisals and trait empathy. *Psychological Science, 27*(1), 25–33. https://doi.org/10.1177/0956797615604124

Park, S. A., Sestito, M., Boorman, E. D., & Dreher, J. C. (2019). Neural computations underlying strategic social decision-making in groups. *Nature Communications, 10*(1), Article 5287. https://doi.org/10.1038/s41467-019-12937-5

Pearce, J. M., & Hall, G. (1980). A model for Pavlovian learning: Variations in the effectiveness of conditioned but not of unconditioned stimuli. *Psychological Review, 87*(6), 532–552. https://doi.org/10.1037/0033-295X.87.6.532

Pessiglione, M., Seymour, B., Flandin, G., Dolan, R. J., & Frith, C. D. (2006). Dopamine-dependent prediction errors underpin reward-seeking behaviour in humans. *Nature, 442*(7106), 1042–1045. https://doi.org/10.1038/nature05051

Rathje, S., Van Bavel, J. J., & van der Linden, S. (2021). Out-group animosity drives engagement on social media. *Proceedings of the National Academy of Sciences of the United States of America, 118*(26), e2024292118. https://doi.org/10.1073/pnas.2024292118

Rescorla, R. A., & Wagner, A. (1972). A theory of Pavlovian conditioning: Variations in the effectiveness of reinforcement and nonreinforcement In H. Black & W. F. Prokasy (Eds.), *Classical conditioning II: Current research and theory* (pp. 64–99). Appleton-Century-Crofts.

Ruff, C. C., & Fehr, E. (2014). The neurobiology of rewards and values in social decision making. *Nature Reviews Neuroscience, 15*(8), 549–562. https://doi.org/10.1038/nrn3776

Rushworth, M. F., & Behrens, T. E. (2008). Choice, uncertainty and value in prefrontal and cingulate cortex. *Nature Neuroscience, 11*(4), 389–397. https://doi.org/10.1038/nn2066

Schaeffer, J., Hlynka, M., & Jussila, V. (2001). Temporal difference learning applied to a high-performance game-playing program. In *IJCAI'01: Proceedings of the 17th International Joint Conference on Artificial Intelligence* (Vol. 11, pp. 529–534). Association for Computing Machinery.

Schraudolph, N., Dayan, P., & Sejnowski, T. (1994). Temporal difference learning of position evaluation in the game of Go. In J. Cowan, G. Tesauro, & J. Alspector (Eds.), *Advances in Neural Information Processing 6: NIPS 1993.* https://proceedings.neurips.cc/paper/1993/file/e2a2dcc36a08a345332c751b2f2e476c-Paper.pdf

Schultz, W., Dayan, P., & Montague, P. R. (1997, March 14). A neural substrate of prediction and reward. *Science, 275*(5306), 1593–1599. https://doi.org/10.1126/science.275.5306.1593

Shafto, P., Goodman, N. D., & Frank, M. C. (2012). Learning from others: The consequences of psychological reasoning for human learning. *Perspectives on Psychological Science*, *7*(4), 341–351. https://doi.org/10.1177/1745691612448481

Shafto, P., Goodman, N. D., & Griffiths, T. L. (2014). A rational account of pedagogical reasoning: Teaching by, and learning from, examples. *Cognitive Psychology*, *71*, 55–89. https://doi.org/10.1016/j.cogpsych.2013.12.004

Shamay-Tsoory, S. G., & Mendelsohn, A. (2019). Real-life neuroscience: An ecological approach to brain and behavior research. *Perspectives on Psychological Science*, *14*(5), 841–859. https://doi.org/10.1177/1745691619856350

Siegel, J. Z., Crockett, M. J., & Dolan, R. J. (2017). Inferences about moral character moderate the impact of consequences on blame and praise. *Cognition*, *167*, 201–211. https://doi.org/10.1016/j.cognition.2017.05.004

Smith, L., & Sørensen, P. (2000). Pathological outcomes of observational learning. *Econometrica*, *68*(2), 371–398. https://doi.org/10.1111/1468-0262.00113

Stein, R. (2017). "Trumping" conformity: Urges towards conformity to ingroups and nonconformity to morally opposed outgroups. *Journal of Experimental Social Psychology*, *70*, 34–40. https://doi.org/10.1016/j.jesp.2016.12.007

Steixner-Kumar, S., Rusch, T., Doshi, P., Gläscher, J., & Spezio, M. (2020). Humans depart from optimal computational models of socially interactive decision-making under partial information. *Scientific Reports*, *12*(1), 289. https://doi.org/10.31234/osf.io/rcq25

Sutton, R. S. (1984). *Temporal credit assignment in reinforcement learning* [Unpublished doctoral dissertation]. University of Massachusetts Amherst.

Sutton, R. S., & Barto, A. G. (1998). *Introduction to reinforcement learning* (Vol. 135). MIT Press.

Tamir, D. I., & Mitchell, J. P. (2013). Anchoring and adjustment during social inferences. *Journal of Experimental Psychology: General*, *142*(1), 151–162. https://doi.org/10.1037/a0028232

Tenenbaum, J. B., Kemp, C., Griffiths, T. L., & Goodman, N. D. (2011, March 11). How to grow a mind: Statistics, structure, and abstraction. *Science*, *331*(6022), 1279–1285. https://doi.org/10.1126/science.1192788

Tversky, A., & Kahneman, D. (1974). Judgment under uncertainty: Heuristics and biases. *Science*, *185*(4157), 1124–1131. https://doi.org/10.1126/science.185.4157.1124

van Baar, J. M., Nassar, M. W., Deng, W., & FeldmanHall, O. (2022). Latent motives guide structure learning during adaptive social choice. *Nature Human Behaviour*, *6*, 404–414. https://doi.org/10.1038/s41562-021-01207-4

Van Bavel, J. J., FeldmanHall, O., & Mende-Siedlecki, P. (2015). The neuroscience of moral cognition: From dual processes to dynamic systems. *Current Opinion in Psychology*, *6*, 167–172. https://doi.org/10.1016/j.copsyc.2015.08.009

van den Berg, P., & Wenseleers, T. (2018). Uncertainty about social interactions leads to the evolution of social heuristics. *Nature Communications*, *9*(1), 2151. https://doi.org/10.1038/s41467-018-04493-1

van den Bos, W., Talwar, A., & McClure, S. M. (2013). Neural correlates of reinforcement learning and social preferences in competitive bidding. *The Journal of Neuroscience*, *33*(5), 2137–2146. https://doi.org/10.1523/JNEUROSCI.3095-12.2013

Vélez, N., & Gweon, H. (2019). Integrating incomplete information with imperfect advice. *Topics in Cognitive Science, 11*(2), 299–315. https://doi.org/10.1111/tops.12388

Vélez, N., & Gweon, H. (2021). Learning from other minds: An optimistic critique of reinforcement learning models of social learning. *Current Opinion in Behavioral Sciences, 38*, 110–115. https://doi.org/10.1016/j.cobeha.2021.01.006

Vives, M. L., Cikara, M., & FeldmanHall, O. (2022). Following your group or your morals? The in-group promotes immoral behavior while the out-group buffers against it. *Social Psychology and Personality Science, 13*(1), 139–149. https://doi.org/10.1177/19485506211001217

Wheatley, T., Boncz, A., Toni, I., & Stolk, A. (2019). Beyond the isolated brain: The promise and challenge of interacting minds. *Neuron, 103*(2), 186–188. https://doi.org/10.1016/j.neuron.2019.05.009

Wilson, R. C., & Collins, A. G. (2019). Ten simple rules for the computational modeling of behavioral data. *eLife, 8*, e49547. https://doi.org/10.7554/eLife.49547

Wu, Y., & Gweon, H. (2021). Preschool-aged children jointly consider others' emotional expressions and prior knowledge to decide when to explore. *Child Development, 92*(3), 862–870. https://doi.org/10.1111/cdev.13585

Yoder, K. J., & Decety, J. (2018). The neuroscience of morality and social decision-making. *Psychology, Crime & Law, 24*(3), 279–295. https://doi.org/10.1080/1068316X.2017.1414817

Yu, A. J., & Dayan, P. (2005). Uncertainty, neuromodulation, and attention. *Neuron, 46*(4), 681–692. https://doi.org/10.1016/j.neuron.2005.04.026

PART III

BIOLOGICAL ORIGINS AND MARKERS OF MORAL MOTIVATION

7 THE DEVELOPMENTAL NEUROBIOLOGY OF MORAL MINDSETS

Basic Needs and Childhood Experience

MARY S. TARSHA AND DARCIA NARVAEZ

In this chapter, we describe the formation of neurobiological systems that are critical not only for well-being but also motivation—moral motivation in particular. We examine humanity's basic needs; the communal practices that humanity evolved to meet those needs; and the effects of need satisfaction or nonsatisfaction on the development of moral capacities, including dispositional mindsets. Basic needs, their satisfaction, and the resulting capacities are intertwined with motivation generally: We have innate motivations for basic need satisfaction to help us grow optimally; satisfaction of these needs early in life sets up capacities that contrast with impaired formation of capacities related to moral motivations that results from nonsatisfaction of these needs.

BASIC NEEDS AND WELL-BEING

Basic needs are built-in motivations for optimizing one's development and well-being. Several theorists have postulate multiple basic needs. Basic needs fundamental for *physical* well-being include food, shelter, sleep (Maslow, 1970),

https://doi.org/10.1037/0000342-008
Motivation and Morality: A Multidisciplinary Approach, M. K. Berg and E. C. Chang (Editors)

and positive touch, the latter being especially important for healthy physiological development, particularly during infancy (Field, 2002; Hertenstein, 2002; Montagu, 1986). Conversely, bodily integrity (Nussbaum, 2013) is violated not only by sexual abuse but also by corporal punishment (e.g., Gershoff & Grogan-Kaylor, 2016). In addition to physical basic needs, *psychological* well-being is facilitated by a sense of safety (Maslow, 1970), trust (Erikson, 1950), belonging, love (Maslow, 1970; Nussbaum, 2013), autonomy (Deci & Ryan, 1985), control (Fiske, 2004), competence (Deci & Ryan, 1985), and connection to the natural world (Louv, 2005), as well as self-actualization (Maslow, 1970), and play (Burghardt, 2005).

There are disagreements about which basic needs are most fundamental. For example, Erik Erikson (1950) identified trust (vs. mistrust) as a fundamental stage in the first year of life; recent empirical evidence demonstrates that positive touch from caregivers builds a healthy neurobiology (Field, 2002), which is fundamental to social trust in part through the mechanism of a well-functioning vagus nerve (Porges, 2011). When development goes well—that is, because of quality of the relational care received—the child establishes an inner state of trusting the world. However, if seeds of distrust have been planted in early life, a sense of disconnection and distrust may follow the individual throughout life, mitigated only if an intervention reshapes neurobiologically based attitudes.

In terms of basic need fulfillment, infants (before age 4 years) differ from older children because they are brain-immature, with rapid growth underway. To develop their biopsychosocial well-being, they need the simultaneous meeting of all aforementioned basic needs (as observed in our ancestral environment, small-band hunter–gatherers; Narvaez, 2013b, 2018a). Later in this chapter, we discuss how our ancestral environment provided for the basic needs of young children.

The shift to more cognitive capacities throughout childhood, adolescence, and adulthood brings to the fore additional basic needs. As development proceeds, cognitive advances yield a greater need to understand the surrounding world (Fiske, 2004), as demonstrated by children's favored question of "Why?" As they develop, growing children and adults have a need to experience a sense of purpose—Why am I here? (Staub, 2003). Answers to these questions are best grounded in safe, stable, and nurturing relationships (Garner et al., 2021) that provide the type of support needed to explore and make positive meaning of the world throughout the course of development (Benson et al., 2011; Bronfenbrenner, 1979).

Converging evidence suggests that meeting basic needs fosters the kinds of mindsets that promote prosociality and capacities for relational attunement and communal imagination that undergird compassion (Narvaez, 2014). To understand further how basic needs promote prosociality, we begin with the Evolved Developmental Niche, the system of care that evolved to meet the basic needs of developing persons.

MEETING BASIC NEEDS: THE EVOLVED DEVELOPMENTAL NICHE

The human genus spent 99% of its history in small-band hunter–gatherer communities, or nomadic foragers, some of which are still in existence and have been studied by anthropologists (Hewlett & Lamb, 2005). The non-civilized, nonindustrialized, "preconquest" lifestyle, worldview, and conscious-ness apparent in these and similar societies are quite different from those of advanced industrialized societies (e.g., Narvaez, 2013b; Narvaez & Tarsha, 2021; Sorenson, 1998).

One of the most striking commonalities found among foragers worldwide is the developmental system for raising the young (Hewlett & Lamb, 2005), what we call the evolved nest or *evolved developmental niche* (EDN; Narvaez, Gleason, et al., 2013). The EDN is the ecological system of care that evolved to meet basic needs and optimize early life development, when human brains are highly immature and rapidly develop in response to physical and social experience. The EDN is provisioned by a community and includes seven components: (a) soothing perinatal experiences; (b) touch, being held, or kept near others constantly; (c) caregiver prompt and appropriate responses to keep the baby optimally aroused; (d) breastfeeding on request frequently (two to three times/hour initially) and, on average, for 4 years; (e) multiple *allomothers*—frequent care by responsive individuals other than mothers (fathers and grandmothers, in particular); (f) multiage, self-directed free play in nature; and (g) high social embeddedness. Converging evidence from developmental psychology (Kim et al., 2011), neuroscience (Schore, 2003), evolutionary biology (Carter & Porges, 2013), and epigenetics (Champagne, 2018) suggests that each component of the EDN is a critical variable in shaping neurobiological processes that undergird an individual's health and well-being, as well as sociomorality (Narvaez, 2014). Although there are differences in specifics, nomadic foragers live with considerable physical stress (from our perspective) but low social stress because throughout their lives they receive generous support from other members of the community (Ingold, 2005). The ancestral context is relationally rich, providing for all basic needs in a communally oriented, mutually responsive sharing culture (Widlok, 2017)—companionship care (Narvaez, 2014), allowing each to develop in a species-normal manner.

Early care quality influences how well the child's right brain hemisphere develops, which grows more rapidly than the left hemisphere over the first 3 years of life (Schore, 2019a). Until age 3, neuronal blood flow and activity in the brain are primarily in the right side (Chiron et al., 1997; Schore, 2011). At 6 weeks of age (postnatal)—the same time many U.S. infants are placed in day care, where allomothering is minimally provided—the subcortical and cortical circuits in the right basolateral amygdala and right anterior cingulate begin a period of critical maturation (Schore, 2019a). Both structures are part of the limbic system and are critical for emotion-processing behaviors (Schore, 2019b). Like other neurobiological components, they develop in an experience-dependent manner and require implicit maternal sensitivity and responsivity for proper development (Schore, 2019b).

Infant studies have demonstrated that *other-consciousness sympathy* is fundamental to human nature (Trevarthen, 2002). Newborns show an innate readiness for companionship, "a need and a skill for exchange of motive states" that gives rise to "moral relating, in which the infant and his or her companion show concern for one another" (Trevarthen, 2002, p. 109). In the exchange of emotions, they sense one another, valuing one another's feelings. The human spirit and its sympathies, so well documented by infant studies, can be thwarted by unresponsive care, promoting instead alienation, humiliation, and shame.

Implicit maternal sensitivity, which supports infant right brain development, requires activation of the parent's right brain hemisphere. Kringelbach and colleagues (2008) used magnetoencephalography to investigate the neural signature of parental instinct, the part of the brain that responds visually and perceptually to their infants' changing cues. They found that the right hemisphere—specifically, the right fusiform gyrus—mediated parenting and perception. Additional studies have also affirmed the asymmetric role of the right brain in perceiving gestures, voices, faces, smells, and even pheromones (Brancucci et al., 2009). In short, responsive care depends on healthy implicit social processing precisely because responding to ongoing affective cues from the infant, in the moment, is an integral part of responsive parenting.

Apart from neuroimaging studies, mounting evidence from clinical research demonstrates the importance of quality relationships in shaping child outcomes. For example, in a large cross-cultural sample ($N = 3,523$ children between ages 6 and 13), Hambrick and colleagues (2019) investigated the relation among clinical ratings using the neurosequential model of therapeutics, which assesses four aspects of child development: (a) developmental adversity, (b) developmental relational health, (c) current relational health, and (d) central nervous system (CNS) functioning (capabilities across several brain-mediated developmental functions). Relational ill health in the first 2 months of life more strongly predicted negative current CNS functioning than at any other time point. In addition, *relational health* at 0 to 2 months—that is, the quality of caregiving and overall social support—was a stronger predictor of CNS functioning than was developmental adversity. Other studies have underscored the importance of this time period as relationally sensitive (Schneider-Hassloff et al., 2016; Turecki & Meaney, 2016) and its correspondence with healthy neurobiological functioning and right hemisphere functioning across development.

Responsive caregiving contributes to relational health, a broad outcome of the type of caregiver–child relationship that comprises EDN-consistent care. Although responsiveness is integral for neurobiological development, each of the other components of the EDN may also be vital (Narvaez, Panksepp, et al., 2013). We provide an extended example about the importance of positive touch, whose effects have been isolated in studies, because touch is intrinsic to the other EDN components and is fundamental in early life, with a lack of it leading to failure to thrive and numerous other adverse outcomes across the lifespan (Barnett, 2005).

Positive touch in infancy promotes healthy functioning in multiple systems, including healthy serotonin and dopamine levels (Field et al., 2005) and stress response (Feldman et al., 2010). Within the mother–father–infant triad, coordinated movement between physical proximity and affectionate touch coupled with synchronized social gaze increases plasma oxytocin, the social bonding hormone (Gordon et al., 2010). In addition, positive maternal touch generally supports the "social brain," the neuronal networks dedicated to interacting and processing the social world, such as practicing the capacity to be sensitive to the emotions, thoughts, and interests of others and the ability to engage in meaningful social interactions. In a functional magnetic resonance study, maternal positive touch supported both resting brain networks and neuronal connectivity in 5-year-old children; those with mothers who provided low or minimal touch had lower brain connections in their right dorsal medial prefrontal cortex, an important part of the social brain that controls mentalizing (Brauer et al., 2016). James Prescott (1990, 1996), formerly of the National Institutes of Health, has examined data from more than 400 societies, observing that cultures that provided more physical touch (carrying) and breastfeeding in infancy had lower levels of aggression and violence in adulthood, an association that has been supported by others (e.g., Field, 1999). In contrast to positive touch, the detrimental effects of corporal punishment are well documented, with numerous cross-cultural studies, longitudinal investigations (Berlin et al., 2009; Gershoff et al., 2012), and large meta-analyses (Gershoff, 2002; Gershoff & Grogan-Kaylor, 2016) over a span of 5 decades that have identified the long-term consequences of harsh touch (e.g., spanking), including aggression.

In general, when the EDN is not provided, or trauma is experienced at sensitive times in development, such as unresponsive, distressing care; harsh touch; or corporal punishment, species-normal development may be thwarted. Lack of EDN provision equates to deprivation of children's needs, what we call *undercare*, shifting a child from an optimal trajectory to being at risk for dysregulation and disconnection. For example, undercare exacerbates the stress response system: the hypothalamic–pituitary–adrenocortical axis, which fosters stress reactivity (Lupien et al., 2009). The burgeoning field of stress research has shown the importance of continually meeting young children's needs for support in order to properly regulate and shape the hypothalamic–pituitary–adrenocortical axis (Gunnar & Quevedo, 2007). Thus, the social environment becomes embedded within the developing stress response system, a major component of self-regulation and sociality (Dich et al., 2015; McEwen, 2019; Schore, 2002). In this way, healthy physical and neurobiological processes, along with the basic building blocks of socio-emotional intelligence, self-regulation and morality, can become impaired (Narvaez, 2014; Schore, 1997, 2002).

MOTIVATED MINDS

Basic needs fulfillment through EDN provision also influences the type of motivations that direct and drive a wide span of human behavior. Higgins (2011) suggested that motivation means "to have preferences that direct choices" (p. 41). He identified three types of motivations: (a) seeking to survive, (b) maximizing pleasure, and (c) being effective in life pursuits. Converging evidence suggests that each of these motivations is influenced by early life experience. For example, undercare in early life can enhance a *survival* motivation, from neurobiological shaping described earlier, one that is stress reactive, altering blood flow, attention, and perception. *Pleasure* focus is also shaped by early life experience. Human brains are set up to be addicted to people and to experience great pleasure from social relationships (Zellner et al., 2011). Thus, when the EDN is not provided, such as when an infant is routinely denied positive touch and responsive care (and instead consistently isolated in a crib or playpen for hours), the social pleasure systems can emerge underdeveloped (e.g., oxytocin system). A socially impoverished early childhood may replace social with nonsocial pleasure seeking, which is abnormal for a social mammal.

In addition to seeking survival and pleasure, Higgins (2011) found a third type of motivation by answering the question "What do people really want?" He concluded that individuals want to be *effective in life pursuits*. This requires all sorts of tacit knowledge for getting along well in the world, including well-functioning executive functions, which are seeded in the first year of life (Schore, 2019a), are typically the last cognitive function to reach adult levels (in the third decade of life), and are the first to show decline in aging adults (Wiebe & Karbach, 2017). Life pursuits can be colored by the settings of the other two motives, even moral pursuits.

RELATING NEUROBIOLOGY TO MORAL MOTIVATION: ETHICAL MINDSETS

Triune ethics metatheory (Narvaez, 2008, 2014, 2016, 2018a) examines *ethogenesis*, moral ontology from an evolutionary developmental systems standpoint (Narvaez, 2018b). This metatheory integrates neuroscience, evolutionary systems theory, and developmental and clinical research, postulating multiple potential ethical mindsets that shift based on the situation. Mindsets emerge from individualized neuroception and neurobiological functions, involving social approach and avoidance in ways patterned in early life through epigenetics and plasticity (differing from ontological developmental patterns that distinguish humans from other apes; Tomasello, 2019). A mindset shapes motivation in the moment, affecting perception, affordances, and actions; when guiding behavior, it becomes an ethic (Narvaez, 2013a). Mindsets are situational but can become dispositional based on early life experience when neurobiological structures are tailored. Species-normal dispositional mindsets are shaped by the EDN and are evident among nomadic foragers. These include *social engagement*—enjoyable, flexible, relational attunement in the moment—and *communal imagination*: the use of abstraction toward benevolent, connected planning that is inclusive of the wider community. On the other hand, routine undercare (lack of the EDN) and significant trauma can lead to a self-protectionist orientation to the social life, characterized by aggression and oppositionalism, and withdrawal and subordination, based in various forms of dysregulation (Narvaez, 2014). Face-to-face self-protectionism can be helpful for acute situations but becomes antisocial when dispositional. Self-protectionist dispositions undergird corresponding abstracting mindsets such as calculating protectionism, which is built-on oppositionalism, used to manipulate or harm others; and a relationally and emotionally detached imagination, which is built on disconnected withdrawal.

Some might argue that it would be helpful to have a stress-reactive brain in a dangerous, uncertain world. A little vigilance certainly may be good for today's world, but not the sustained vigilance that is commonplace in hyper-reactive individuals. Stress reactivity from early trauma can imprison and impair an individual over the long term. In this case, the individual is conditioned to react instead of freely choosing to act.

Triune ethics metatheory provides an explanation for how cooperative sociality and morality are embodied, dynamic processes (Narvaez, 2014). Both require the integration of and interplay between reasoning and emotions, between neurobiology and perception of context (Narvaez, 2010, 2016). The interplay among these systems requires extensive flexibility, not only on the inside, among neurobiological systems, but also, on the outside, via flexible responsiveness to changing contexts and situations. The neurobiological ability to shift and adapt to changing contexts is grounded in multiple systems. One system involves the vagus nerve, the 10th cranial nerve, a branch of the parasympathetic nervous system of the CNS that controls rest, digestion, social engagement and feelings of safety (Porges, 2011). The name *vagus* is Latin for "wandering," indicating the vast length and trajectory of the nerve as it begins in the brainstem and travels throughout the body to innervate the heart, lungs, liver, digestive tract, and immune system (Mazzone & Undem, 2016).

There are two types of vagal functioning: (a) *vagal tone* (baseline functioning) and (b) *vagal flexibility* (contextual functioning). The connection between vagal baseline functioning and socioemotional development makes sense when one considers that one vagal pathway is a neuroanatomical and neurophysiological link between the regulation of the striated muscles of the face (via the brain stem), the larynx, and the regulation of the autonomic nervous system. The muscles of the face and larynx are connected to the heart by means of the vagus nerve, which lends itself to social interaction. The connections among heart, voice, emotion, and face make it possible to express emotional states on the face and in the voice, thereby conveying one's emotions to others. In this way, the vagus nerve provides the neuromechanical connections needed for social and emotional expression and perception. The vagus nerve is a critical neurobiological component needed to support physiological states and feelings of prosocial behavior such as empathy, compassion, social attachment (social bonds), feelings of safety (Porges, 2017), and emotional regulation (Bryant & Hutanamon, 2018; Carter & Porges, 2013; Flores & Porges, 2017; Movahed Abtahi & Kerns, 2017). Thus, baseline functioning or vagal tone is considered a biomarker for sociality (Carter & Porges, 2013); feelings of safety (Porges, 2017); and prosocial behaviors, such as empathy and compassion (Diamond et al., 2012).

Similar to other neurobiological systems, the development of vagus nerve functioning is sensitive to social environmental influences and caregiving environments. Early experiences that are rich in responsive care shape the functioning of the vagus nerve to operate in a regulated, adaptive manner (Clark et al., 2016; Musser et al., 2011; Shahrestani et al., 2014). Conversely, early experiences deprived of responsive care yield children with dysregulated vagal functioning (Skowron et al., 2014). Vagus nerve functioning is relatively stable across development and can influence sociomoral capacities. For example, in the first months of life, greater vagal tone (healthy functioning) predicted greater emotional regulation, attention, and self-control and decreased behavior problems at age 5 years (Feldman, 2009). At 3 years of age, children with lower resting baseline vagal tone and stronger recovery from stress demonstrated greater sympathy in subsequent years (ages 6 and 7; Taylor et al., 2015). Vagal tone functioning in infancy and early childhood predicts development of adaptive skills related to morality in middle childhood, including sympathy, emotional regulation, attention, behavior problems, and self-control (Feldman, 2009; Taylor et al., 2015). Childhood experiences have also been associated with vagal tone in adult samples. In a recent vagal tone study, women ($N = 78$) reported on childhood EDN history and adverse childhood experiences (Tarsha & Narvaez, 2022). EDN history moderated the negative influences of adverse childhood experiences on women's vagal regulation, suggesting that the EDN buffers adversity by supporting the physiological building blocks of health and resilience.

Vagal tone has been identified as a neural pathway to compassion (Porges, 2017; Stellar et al., 2015) and cooperative behavior (Beffara et al., 2016), including prosociality (Kogan et al., 2014). In adults, moral judgment has been linked with neuro–visceral integration, such that individuals with high vagal tone report higher deontology scores (emphasis on duty-based morality) compared with those with low vagal tone, who report higher scores of utilitarianism (Park et al., 2016).

CONNECTING THE EVOLVED DEVELOPMENTAL NICHE, BASIC NEEDS, AND SOCIOMORAL FUNCTIONING

In our work, we are beginning to delineate the connections among EDN-consistent childhoods, moral behavior, and vagal functioning. For example, in our analyses with 6-year-old children, EDN-consistent experiences supported physiological functioning, as measured via vagal functioning, and this, in turn, mediated moral behavior (Tarsha et al., 2022). Put more specifically, experience of frequency of free play in the last week, an indicator of EDN-consistent experience, predicted higher vagal functioning (more parasympathetic activation), which mediated social oppositional behavior. This suggests that play, a critical component of the EDN, may shape physiological regulation and buffer against social oppositional behavior. However, maternal sociomoral behavior may also influence how children physiologically react. In separate analyses, maternal self-protectionist behavior was associated with children's parasympathetic regulation, in other words, lower vagal tone (Tarsha et al., 2020). In one cross-cultural study (United States: $N = 525$, China: $N = 379$), child well-being, sociality, and sociomoral temperament (protectionism or engagement) were examined (Narvaez et al., 2021). Mediation analyses demonstrated that sociomoral temperament mediated relations between well-being (happiness, thriving, depression, and anxiety) and social outcomes (empathy, concern after wrongdoing, internalized conduct, inhibitory control, and misbehavior) in both samples, with engagement slightly outperforming protectionism. The findings suggest that fostering early well-being may influence social outcomes through a child's developing sociomoral temperament. Taken together, the findings suggest that childhood experiences influence the development of moral behavior and physiological regulation in children in whose environments EDN consistency is associated with engagement and EDN inconsistency is associated with indicators of self-protectionism.

Investigations of each EDN component and its relationship to socioemotional processing are still being conducted, but several connections have emerged. For example, in a recent study (Narvaez et al., 2019) that used cross-cultural samples (United States, $n = 574$; Switzerland, $n = 96$; China, $n = 382$), parents reported on young children's EDN-consistent experience in the past week. The EDN components included experiences of positive and negative touch, indoor and outdoor free play, and family togetherness inside and outside the home. Frequency of EDN component experience in the last week predicted children's social thriving, including social engagement with others, in all three countries.

In a survey study of U.S. adults (Narvaez, Wang et al., 2016; $N = 606$), a retrospective report of an EDN-consistent childhood predicted a social engagement orientation via a pathway through secure attachment, mental health (less anxiety and depression), and perspective taking. The less healthy paths linked lower scores on EDN-consistent childhoods to low secure attachment, worse mental health (higher anxiety and depression) predicting a reactive protectionism orientation[1] via low perspective taking, or, in a second

---

[1]In Narvaez et al.'s (2016) article, the term *social opposition* was used. The term used now is *reactive protectionism*.

path, predicting social withdrawal orientation via personal distress. In another survey of adults (Narvaez, Thiel et al., 2016; $N = 295$), the role of an EDN-consistent childhood history was examined regarding outcomes of moral behavior, in particular communal engagement behavior and social withdrawal behavior. In mediation analyses, EDN history predicted both types of moral behavior through secure attachment: a measure of psychological and physical health. For communal engagement behavior, the path included the social capacity of perspective taking; for social withdrawal, the social capacity mediator was personal distress. Of interest is that the direct path from EDN history to adult communal engagement behavior was also significant, demonstrating that the mediators contributed to, and were shaped by, EDN history, but the strength of EDN experience in childhood maintained direct effects on adult moral behavior. EDN history scores shaped, both directly and indirectly, forms of adult moral behavior in expected directions.

However, as we mentioned earlier, the role of basic needs in childhood is also an important contributor to developing moral capacities and moral behaviors. To examine this relationship, two additional studies were conducted with U.S. adults (Kurth & Narvaez, 2018). In the first sample ($N = 350$), EDN history and basic needs fulfillment history were investigated as they related to a social engagement orientation. Basic needs fulfillment was measured according to the Basic Needs Satisfaction Scale (Noble et al., 2018) with items corresponding to Fiske's (2004) BUCET list: belonging, understanding, control, enhancing self, and trust. Two factors resulted: Effectance and Discouragement. Using mediation analyses, EDN history predicted adult social engagement orientation positively through Effectance and negatively through Discouragement in separate models. Of interest is that only the model with Effectance reduced the direct path from EDN history to engagement, indicating the importance of fulfilled childhood basic needs when examining adult social engagement orientation. In a second study of adults ($N = 400$), childhood histories of effectance and discouragement were investigated with regard to moral personality outcomes (honesty, forgiveness, distrust), orientation (communal, protectionist) and moral behavior (social engagement, communal, reactive protectionist, social withdrawal). In regression analyses controlling for EDN history and adult attachment, basic needs fulfillment predicted, in the expected directions, honesty, forgiveness, distrust, a communal imagination orientation, reactive protectionist behavior, and withdrawal protectionist behavior. Taken together, such evidence suggests that basic needs satisfaction in childhood leads to the development of capacities oriented toward communal relationality and social engagement.

CONCLUSION

Moral mindsets emerge from early experiences that shape neurobiological functioning for a lifetime, barring intervention. When basic needs are met and the EDN is provided in early childhood, a well-functioning interpersonal neurobiology facilitates the development of flexible sociality, as found in social engagement and communal orientations. In contrast, undercare from a degraded EDN and unmet basic needs impairs neurobiological development, enhancing innate survival systems. Consequently, the individual is more easily triggered, exhibiting protectionist mindsets and corresponding behaviors. In this case, motivation systems can be flavored by protectionism in situations of perceived threat, whether the motivation is surviving, maximizing pleasure, or being effective in life pursuits.

Because of their mutual influence, childhood experiences and interpersonal neurobiological development can be seen as pillars of adult well-being and moral functioning. Childhood experiences of support (basic needs met and EDN provided) lead to neurobiological structures that are apparent in physiological well-being and social well-being. For example, relational attunement relies on a regulated stress response system, and compassion relies on a well-functioning vagus nerve. On the other hand, dysregulated systems can impair health and sociality, boosting self-protective social orientations.

Considering the converging evidence regarding the connections among basic needs, EDN provision, well-being, and moral motivation, it seems appropriate that both researchers and practitioners examine these constructs together. Separating them can—and often does—lead to a skewed understanding of sociomoral development. For example, examining reactive or calculating protectionism without also investigating childhood experiences might lead to the conclusion that self-protectionist (self-centered) behavior is species normal rather than emergent from particular life histories.

In a world currently overwhelmed with self-protectionist attitudes and behaviors likely rooted in part in early undercare, restoring our species' EDN may be imperative. Self-calming capacities, as well-functioning stress response and vagus nerve allow, ground the flexible social intelligence sorely needed to address the numerous crises we face.

REFERENCES

Barnett, L. (2005). Keep in touch: The importance of touch in infant development. *Infant Observation*, 8(2), 115–123. https://doi.org/10.1080/13698030500171530

Beffara, B., Bret, A. G., Vermeulen, N., & Mermillod, M. (2016). Resting high frequency heart rate variability selectively predicts cooperative behavior. *Physiology & Behavior*, *164*(Pt. A), 417–428. https://doi.org/10.1016/j.physbeh.2016.06.011

Benson, P. L., Scales, P. C., & Syvertsen, A. K. (2011). The contribution of the developmental assets framework to positive youth development theory and practice. *Advances in Child Development and Behavior, 41*, 197–230. https://doi.org/10.1016/B978-0-12-386492-5.00008-7

Berlin, L. J., Ispa, J. M., Fine, M. A., Malone, P. S., Brooks-Gunn, J., Brady-Smith, C., Ayoub, C., & Bai, Y. (2009). Correlates and consequences of spanking and verbal punishment for low-income White, African American, and Mexican American toddlers. *Child Development, 80*(5), 1403–1420. https://doi.org/10.1111/j.1467-8624.2009.01341.x

Brancucci, A., Lucci, G., Mazzatenta, A., & Tommasi, L. (2009). Asymmetries of the human social brain in the visual, auditory and chemical modalities. *Philosophical Transactions of the Royal Society of London: Series B, Biological Sciences, 364*(1519), 895–914. https://doi.org/10.1098/rstb.2008.0279

Brauer, J., Xiao, Y., Poulain, T., Friederici, A. D., & Schirmer, A. (2016). Frequency of maternal touch predicts resting activity and connectivity of the developing social brain. *Cerebral Cortex, 26*(8), 3544–3552. https://doi.org/10.1093/cercor/bhw137

Bronfenbrenner, U. (1979). *The ecology of human development.* Harvard University Press.

Bryant, R. A., & Hutanamon, T. (2018). Activating attachments enhances heart rate variability. *PLOS ONE, 13*(2), e0151747. https://doi.org/10.1371/journal.pone.0151747

Burghardt, G. M. (2005). *The genesis of animal play: Testing the limits.* MIT Press.

Carter, C. S., & Porges, S. W. (2013). Neurobiology and the evolution of mammalian social behavior. In D. Narvaez, J. Panksepp, A. N. Schore, & T. Gleason (Eds.), *Evolution, early experience and human development* (pp. 132–151). Oxford University Press.

Champagne, F. A. (2018). Beyond the maternal epigenetic legacy. *Nature Neuroscience, 21*(6), 773–774. https://doi.org/10.1038/s41593-018-0157-6

Chiron, C., Jambaque, I., Nabbout, R., Lounes, R., Syrota, A., & Dulac, O. (1997). The right brain hemisphere is dominant in human infants. *Brain: A Journal of Neurology, 120*(6), 1057–1065. https://doi.org/10.1093/brain/120.6.1057

Clark, C. A., Skowron, E. A., Giuliano, R. J., & Fisher, P. A. (2016). Intersections between cardiac physiology, emotion regulation and interpersonal warmth in preschoolers: Implications for drug abuse prevention from translational neuroscience. *Drug and Alcohol Dependence, 163*(Suppl. 1), S60–S69. https://doi.org/10.1016/j.drugalcdep.2016.01.033

Deci, E., & Ryan, R. (1985). *Intrinsic motivation and self-determination in human behavior.* Academic Press. https://doi.org/10.1007/978-1-4899-2271-7

Diamond, L. M., Fagundes, C. P., & Butterworth, M. R. (2012). Attachment style, vagal tone, and empathy during mother–adolescent interactions. *Journal of Research on Adolescence, 22*(1), 165–184. https://doi.org/10.1111/j.1532-7795.2011.00762.x

Dich, N., Hansen, Å. M., Avlund, K., Lund, R., Mortensen, E. L., Bruunsgaard, H., & Rod, N. H. (2015). Early life adversity potentiates the effects of later life stress on cumulative physiological dysregulation. *Anxiety, Stress, and Coping, 28*(4), 372–390. https://doi.org/10.1080/10615806.2014.969720

Erikson, E. H. (1950). *Childhood and society.* W. W. Norton.

Feldman, R. (2009). The development of regulatory functions from birth to 5 years: Insights from premature infants. *Child Development, 80*(2), 544–561. https://doi.org/10.1111/j.1467-8624.2009.01278.x

Feldman, R., Singer, M., & Zagoory, O. (2010). Touch attenuates infants' physiological reactivity to stress. *Developmental Science, 13*(2), 271–278. https://doi.org/10.1111/j.1467-7687.2009.00890.x

Field, T. (1999). American adolescents touch each other less and are more aggressive toward their peers as compared with French adolescents. *Adolescence, 34*(136), 753–758.

Field, T. (2002). Infants' need for touch. *Human Development, 45*(2), 100–103. https://doi.org/10.1159/000048156

Field, T., Hernandez-Reif, M., Diego, M., Schanberg, S., & Kuhn, C. (2005). Cortisol decreases and serotonin and dopamine increase following massage therapy. *The International Journal of Neuroscience, 115*(10), 1397–1413. https://doi.org/10.1080/00207450590956459

Fiske, S.T. (2004). *Social beings: A core motives approach to social psychology.* Wiley.

Flores, P. J., & Porges, S. W. (2017). Group psychotherapy as a neural exercise: Bridging polyvagal theory and attachment theory. *International Journal of Group Psychotherapy, 67*(2), 202–222. https://doi.org/10.1080/00207284.2016.1263544

Garner, A., Yogman, M., & The Committee on Psychosocial Aspects of Child and Family Health, Section on Developmental and Behavioral Pediatrics, Council on Early Childhood. (2021). Preventing childhood toxic stress: Partnering with families and communities to promote relational health. *Pediatrics, 148*(2), e2021052582. https://doi.org/10.1542/peds.2021-052582

Gershoff, E. T. (2002). Corporal punishment by parents and associated child behaviors and experiences: A meta-analytic and theoretical review. *Psychological Bulletin, 128*(4), 539–579. https://doi.org/10.1037/0033-2909.128.4.539

Gershoff, E. T., & Grogan-Kaylor, A. (2016). Spanking and child outcomes: Old controversies and new meta-analyses. *Journal of Family Psychology, 30*(4), 453–469. https://doi.org/10.1037/fam0000191

Gershoff, E. T., Lansford, J. E., Sexton, H. R., Davis-Kean, P., & Sameroff, A. J. (2012). Longitudinal links between spanking and children's externalizing behaviors in a national sample of White, Black, Hispanic, and Asian American families. *Child Development, 83*(3), 838–843. https://doi.org/10.1111/j.1467-8624.2011.01732.x

Gordon, I., Zagoory-Sharon, O., Leckman, J. F., & Feldman, R. (2010). Oxytocin, cortisol, and triadic family interactions. *Physiology & Behavior, 101*(5), 679–684. https://doi.org/10.1016/j.physbeh.2010.08.008

Gunnar, M. R., & Quevedo, K. M. (2007). Early care experiences and HPA axis regulation in children: A mechanism for later trauma vulnerability. *Progress in Brain Research, 167*, 137–149. https://doi.org/10.1016/S0079-6123(07)67010-1

Hambrick, E. P., Brawner, T. W., Perry, B. D., Brandt, K., Hofmeister, C., & Collins, J. O. (2019). Beyond the ACE score: Examining relationships between timing of developmental adversity, relational health and developmental outcomes in children. *Archives of Psychiatric Nursing, 33*(3), 238–247. https://doi.org/10.1016/j.apnu.2018.11.001

Hertenstein, M. J. (2002). Touch: Its communicative functions in infancy. *Human Development, 45*(2), 70–94. https://doi.org/10.1159/000048154

Hewlett, B. S., & Lamb, M. E. (2005). *Hunter–gatherer childhoods: Evolutionary, developmental and cultural perspectives.* Aldine.

Higgins, E. T. (2011). *Beyond pleasure and pain.* Oxford University Press.

Ingold, T. (2005). On the social relations of the hunter–gatherer band. In R. B. Lee & R. Daly (Eds.), *The Cambridge encyclopedia of hunters and gatherers* (pp. 399–410). Cambridge University Press.

Kim, P., Feldman, R., Mayes, L. C., Eicher, V., Thompson, N., Leckman, J. F., & Swain, J. E. (2011). Breastfeeding, brain activation to own infant cry, and maternal sensitivity. *The Journal of Child Psychology and Psychiatry, 52*(8), 907–915. https://doi.org/10.1111/j.1469-7610.2011.02406.x

Kogan, A., Oveis, C., Carr, E. W., Gruber, J., Mauss, I. B., Shallcross, A., Impett, E. A., van der Lowe, I., Hui, B., Cheng, C., & Keltner, D. (2014). Vagal activity is quadratically related to prosocial traits, prosocial emotions, and observer perceptions of prosociality. *Journal of Personality and Social Psychology, 107*(6), 1051–1063. https://doi.org/10.1037/a0037509

Kringelbach, M. L., Lehtonen, A., Squire, S., Harvey, A. G., Craske, M. G., Holliday, I. E., Green, A. L., Aziz, T. Z., Hansen, P. C., Cornelissen, P. L., & Stein, A. (2008). A specific and rapid neural signature for parental instinct. *PLOS ONE, 3*(2), e1664. https://doi.org/10.1371/journal.pone.0001664

Kurth, A., & Narvaez, D. (2018). Basic needs satisfaction and its relation to sociomorality capacities and behavior. In D. Narvaez (Ed.), *Basic needs, wellbeing and morality: Fulfilling human potential* (pp. 91–133). Palgrave-MacMillan.

Louv, R. (2005). *Last child in the woods: Saving our children from nature deficit disorder.* Workman.

Lupien, S. J., McEwen, B. S., Gunnar, M. R., & Heim, C. (2009). Effects of stress throughout the lifespan on the brain, behaviour and cognition. *Nature Reviews Neuroscience, 10*(6), 434–445. https://doi.org/10.1038/nrn2639

Maslow, A. (1970). *Motivation and personality* (2nd ed.). Harper & Row.

Mazzone, S. B., & Undem, B. J. (2016). Vagal afferent innervation of the airways in health and disease. *Physiological Reviews, 96*(3), 975–1024. https://doi.org/10.1152/physrev.00039.2015

McEwen, B. S. (2019). Prenatal programming of neuropsychiatric disorders: An epigenetic perspective across the lifespan. *Biological Psychiatry, 85*(2), 91–93. https://doi.org/10.1016/j.biopsych.2018.10.005

Montagu, A. (1986). *Touching: The human significance of the skin.* Harper & Row.

Movahed Abtahi, M., & Kerns, K. A. (2017). Attachment and emotion regulation in middle childhood: Changes in affect and vagal tone during a social stress task. *Attachment & Human Development, 19*(3), 221–242. https://doi.org/10.1080/14616734.2017.1291696

Musser, E. D., Backs, R. W., Schmitt, C. F., Ablow, J. C., Measelle, J. R., & Nigg, J. T. (2011). Emotion regulation via the autonomic nervous system in children with attention-deficit/hyperactivity disorder (ADHD). *Journal of Abnormal Child Psychology, 39*(6), 841–852. https://doi.org/10.1007/s10802-011-9499-1

Narvaez, D. (2008). Triune ethics: The neurobiological roots of our multiple moralities. *New Ideas in Psychology, 26*(1), 95–119. https://doi.org/10.1016/j.newideapsych.2007.07.008

Narvaez, D. (2010). Moral complexity: The fatal attraction of truthiness and the importance of mature moral functioning. *Perspectives on Psychological Science, 5*(2), 163–181. https://doi.org/10.1177/1745691610362351

Narvaez, D. (2013a). Neurobiology and moral mindsets. In K. Heinrichs & F. Oser (Eds.), *Moral and immoral behavior: Theoretical and empirical perspectives on moral motivation* (pp. 289–307). Sense.

Narvaez, D. (2013b). The 99%—Development and socialization within an evolutionary context: Growing up to become "A good and useful human being." In D. Fry (Ed.), *War, peace and human nature: The convergence of evolutionary and cultural views* (pp. 643–672). Oxford University Press.

Narvaez, D. (2014). *Neurobiology and the development of human morality: Evolution, culture and wisdom.* W. W. Norton.

Narvaez, D. (2016). *Embodied morality: Protectionism, engagement and imagination.* Palgrave-MacMillan. https://doi.org/10.1057/978-1-137-55399-7

Narvaez, D. (Ed.). (2018a). *Basic needs, wellbeing and morality: Fulfilling human potential.* Palgrave-MacMillan. https://doi.org/10.1007/978-3-319-97734-8

Narvaez, D. (2018b). Ethogenesis: Evolution, early experience and moral becoming. In J. Graham & K. Gray (Eds.), *The atlas of moral psychology* (pp. 451–464). Guilford Press.

Narvaez, D., Gleason, T., Tarsha, M., Woodbury, R., Cheng, Y., & Wang, L. (2021). Sociomoral temperament: A mediator between wellbeing and social outcomes in young children. *Frontiers in Psychology, 12,* 742199. https://doi.org/10.3389/fpsyg.2021.742199

Narvaez, D., Gleason, T., Wang, L., Brooks, J., Lefever, J., Cheng, A., & The Centers for the Prevention of Child Neglect. (2013). The evolved development niche: Longitudinal effects of caregiving practices on early childhood psychosocial development. *Early Childhood Research Quarterly, 28*(4), 759–773. https://doi.org/10.1016/j.ecresq.2013.07.003

Narvaez, D., Panksepp, J., Schore, A., & Gleason, T. (Eds.). (2013). *Evolution, early experience and human development: From research to practice and policy.* Oxford University Press.

Narvaez, D., & Tarsha, M. (2021). The missing mind: Contrasting civilization with non-civilization development and functioning. In T. Henley & M. Rossano (Eds.), *Psychology and cognitive archaeology: An Interdisciplinary approach to the study of the human mind* (pp. 55–69). Routledge.

Narvaez, D., Thiel, A., Kurth, A., & Renfus, K. (2016). Past moral action and ethical orientation. In D. Narvaez, *Embodied morality: Protectionism, engagement and imagination* (pp. 99–118). Palgrave-Macmillan.

Narvaez, D., Wang, L., & Cheng, A. (2016). Evolved developmental niche history: Relation to adult psychopathology and morality. *Applied Developmental Science, 20*(4), 294–309. https://doi.org/10.1080/10888691.2015.1128835

Narvaez, D., Woodbury, R., Gleason, T., Kurth, A., Cheng, A., Wang, L., Deng, L., Gutzwiller-Helfenfinger, E., Christen, M., & Näpflin, C. (2019). Evolved development niche provision: Moral socialization, social maladaptation and social thriving in three countries. *SAGE Open, 9*(2). https://doi.org/10.1177/2158244019840123

Noble, R., Kurth, A., & Narvaez, D. (2018). Measuring basic needs satisfaction and its relation to health and wellbeing. In D. Narvaez (Ed.), *Basic needs, wellbeing and morality: Fulfilling human potential* (pp. 17–49). Palgrave-Macmillan.

Nussbaum, M. (2013). *Political emotions: Why love matters for justice.* Belknap.

Panksepp, J. (2004). *Affective neuroscience: The foundations of human and animal emotions.* Oxford University Press.

Park, G., Kappes, A., Rho, Y., & Van Bavel, J. J. (2016). At the heart of morality lies neuro–visceral integration: Lower cardiac vagal tone predicts utilitarian moral judgment. *Social Cognitive and Affective Neuroscience, 11*(10), 1588–1596. https://doi.org/10.1093/scan/nsw077

Porges, S. (2011). *Polyvagal theory.* W. W. Norton.

Porges, S. W. (2017). *The pocket guide to the polyvagal theory: The transformative power of feeling safe.* W. W. Norton.

Prescott, J. W. (1990). Affectional bonding for the prevention of violent behaviors: Neurobiological, psychological and religious/spiritual determinants. In L. J. Hertzberg, G. F. Astrum, et al. (Eds.), *Violent behavior: Vol. 1. Assessment and intervention* (pp. 125–150). PMA Publishing. https://www.ojp.gov/ncjrs/virtual-library/abstracts/social-and-economic-context-violent-behavior-violent-behavior

Prescott, J. W. (1996). The origins of human love and violence. *Pre- and Perinatal Psychology Journal, 10*(3), 143–188.

Schneider-Hassloff, H., Straube, B., Jansen, A., Nuscheler, B., Wemken, G., Witt, S. H., Rietschel, M., & Kircher, T. (2016). Oxytocin receptor polymorphism and childhood social experiences shape adult personality, brain structure and neural correlates of mentalizing. *NeuroImage, 134*, 671–684. https://doi.org/10.1016/j.neuroimage.2016.04.009

Schore, A. N. (1997). Early organization of the nonlinear right brain and development of a predisposition to psychiatric disorders. *Development and Psychopathology, 9*(4), 595–631. https://doi.org/10.1017/S0954579497001363

Schore, A. N. (2002). Dysregulation of the right brain: A fundamental mechanism of traumatic attachment and the psychopathogenesis of posttraumatic stress disorder. *The Australian and New Zealand Journal of Psychiatry, 36*(1), 9–30. https://doi.org/10.1046/j.1440-1614.2002.00996.x

Schore, A. N. (2003). Early relational trauma, disorganized attachment, and the development of a predisposition to violence. In D. Siegel & M. Solomon (Eds.), *Healing trauma: Attachment, mind, body, and brain* (pp. 101–167). W. W. Norton.

Schore, A. N. (2011). The right brain implicit self lies at the core of psychoanalysis. *Psychoanalytic Dialogues, 21*(1), 75–100. https://doi.org/10.1080/10481885.2011.545329

Schore, A. N. (2019a). *The development of the unconscious mind.* W. W. Norton.

Schore, A. N. (2019b). *Right brain psychotherapy.* W. W. Norton.

Shahrestani, S., Stewart, E. M., Quintana, D. S., Hickie, I. B., & Guastella, A. J. (2014). Heart rate variability during social interactions in children with and without psychopathology: A meta-analysis. *The Journal of Child Psychology and Psychiatry, 55*(9), 981–989. https://doi.org/10.1111/jcpp.12226

Skowron, E. A., Cipriano-Essel, E., Gatzke-Kopp, L. M., Teti, D. M., & Ammerman, R. T. (2014). Early adversity, RSA, and inhibitory control: Evidence of children's neurobiological sensitivity to social context. *Developmental Psychobiology, 56*(5), 964–978. https://doi.org/10.1002/dev.21175

Sorenson, E. R. (1998). Preconquest consciousness. In H. Wautischer (Ed.), *Tribal epistemologies* (pp. 79–115). Ashgate.

Staub, E. (2003). *The psychology of good and evil: Why children, adults, and groups help and harm others.* Cambridge University Press. https://doi.org/10.1017/CBO9780511615795

Stellar, J. E., Cohen, A., Oveis, C., & Keltner, D. (2015). Affective and physiological responses to the suffering of others: Compassion and vagal activity. *Journal of*

Personality and Social Psychology, 108(4), 572–585. https://doi.org/10.1037/pspi0000010

Tarsha, M. S., Gleason, T., Cheng, Y., Wang, L., & Narvaez, D. (2022, April 1–2). *Play predicts sociomoral learning mediated by respiratory sinus arrhythmia* [Paper]. Special Topics Meeting: Learning Through Play and Imagination: Expanding Perspectives (Society for Research in Child Development), St. Louis, MO, United States.

Tarsha, M. S., Kurth, A., Gleason, T., Cheng, A., & Narvaez, D. (2020). Maternal antisocial behavior and age 6 child vagal tone across three conditions [Abstracts from the 53rd Annual Meeting of the International Society for Developmental Psychobiology]. *Developmental Psychobiology, 62*(Suppl. 1), S4–S71. https://doi.org/10.1002/dev.22051

Tarsha, M. S., & Narvaez, D. (2022). Effects of adverse childhood experience on physiological regulation are moderated by evolved developmental niche history. *Anxiety, Stress, and Coping, 35*(4), 488–500. https://doi.org/10.1080/10615806.2021.1989419

Taylor, Z. E., Eisenberg, N., & Spinrad, T. L. (2015). Respiratory sinus arrhythmia, effortful control, and parenting as predictors of children's sympathy across early childhood. *Developmental Psychology, 51*(1), 17–25. https://doi.org/10.1037/a0038189

Tomasello, M. (2019). *Becoming human: A theory of ontogeny*. Harvard University Press.

Trevarthen, C. (2002). Proof of sympathy: Scientific evidence on the co-operative personality of the infant, and evaluation of John MacMurray's "Mother and Child." In D. Fergusson & N. Dower (Eds.), *John MacMurray: Critical perspectives* (pp. 77–117). Peter Lang.

Turecki, G., & Meaney, M. J. (2016). Effects of the social environment and stress on glucocorticoid receptor gene methylation: A systematic review. *Biological Psychiatry, 79*(2), 87–96. https://doi.org/10.1016/j.biopsych.2014.11.022

Widlok, T. (2017). *Anthropology and the economy of sharing*. Routledge.

Wiebe, S. A., & Karbach, J. (Eds.). (2017). *Executive function: Development across the life span*. Routledge. https://doi.org/10.4324/9781315160719

Zellner, M. R., Watt, D. F., Solms, M., & Panksepp, J. (2011). Affective neuroscientific and neuropsychoanalytic approaches to two intractable psychiatric problems: Why depression feels so bad and what addicts really want. *Neuroscience and Biobehavioral Reviews, 35*(9), 2000–2008. https://doi.org/10.1016/j.neubiorev.2011.01.003

8 MORALITY AND MODEL COHERENCE

A Constructivist and Biologically Tractable Account of Moral Motivation

JORDAN E. THERIAULT

[Their] complaint is that we have made no effort to seek consilience with neuroscience and genetics. We agree with their claim but cannot see how this counts as a mark against [moral foundations theory]. If their "expectation" about the requirements for nativist theories were to become widespread, there would be no more nativist theories. And that, we suspect, is why they have proposed an impossibly high bar. (Haidt & Joseph, 2011, p. 2119; in response to Suhler & Churchland, 2011)

Formulating a biologically tractable account of moral psychology is daunting. In fact, this task has been called an impossibly high bar for popular nativist accounts like the moral foundations theory. Although linking complex psychological experiences with their underlying biology is a "hard problem"

I would like to thank the editors of this volume, Martha Berg and Edward Chang, as well as John Barresi, Amelia Brown, Joseph Jebari, Ditte Marie Munch-Jurisic, Liane Young, and Evan Westra for their generous feedback. I would also like to thank Lisa Feldman Barrett, Dana Brooks, Katie Hoemann, Daniel Kelly, David Melnikoff, Tage Rai, Ajay Satpute, Karen Quigley, and all members of the Animal Normativity Workshop for conversations that inspired this work. Funding for this research was provided by an experiential artificial intelligence postdoctoral fellowship from the Roux Institute at Northeastern University.

https://doi.org/10.1037/0000342-009
Motivation and Morality: A Multidisciplinary Approach, M. K. Berg and E. C. Chang (Editors)

(Chalmers, 1995; but see Churchland, 1996; Varela, 1996), this chapter suggests that recent theoretical advances in understanding brain-based information processing and emotion can help dissolve some of this apparent intractability when it comes to moral motivation. In particular, this chapter suggests that moral motivation—ranging from social pressure to conform to norms to a felt obligation to uphold moral principles—can be explained by domain-general aspects of brain–body interactions combined with metabolic incentives to regulate local and global social environments.

The present account of moral motivation removes the requirement for innate moral intuitions (i.e., innate moral knowledge), which have impacted moral psychology (Graham et al., 2013; Haidt, 2001, 2012; Haidt & Joseph, 2004, 2008) but been criticized on the basis of their biological plausibility (Suhler & Churchland, 2011). As a theoretical construct, moral intuitions stand in for a fully mechanistic explanation of why moral judgment feels as it does and why moral judgments occur in response to particular kinds of violations. Moral intuitions are described as

> the sudden appearance in consciousness, or at the fringe of consciousness, of an *evaluative feeling* (like–dislike, good–bad) about the character or actions of a person, without any conscious awareness of having gone through steps of search, weighing evidence, or inferring a conclusion. (emphasis added; Haidt & Bjorklund, 2008, p. 188; modified from Haidt, 2001, p. 818)

These intuitions are considered innate in the sense that they are a "first draft," which is later modified by culture (Graham et al., 2013, p. 61); however, for the purposes of moral psychology, the most critical aspect of these intuitions is that they provide a simple answer to the "hard problem" of linking physical events (like morally relevant stimuli) to affective experience—in other words, "human beings come equipped with an intuitive ethics, an innate prepared-ness to feel flashes of approval or disapproval toward certain patterns of events involving other human beings" (Haidt & Joseph, 2004, p. 56). However, this simple answer gives no mechanistic account of how emotional experience is created; it only stipulates that particular stimuli elicit particular prewired responses (with brain biology, presumably, doing the prewiring). Further, recent research in affective neuroscience suggests that there is no simple stimulus–response link between external events and emotional experience (Barrett, 2017a, 2017b). Moral intuitions, then, obscure the causal forces that mediate between environmental events and emotional experience when our objective as scientists should be to understand these forces.

This chapter outlines a biologically tractable, nonnativist account of moral motivation and sketches how it might emerge from more general pro-cesses in human brains and bodies. To accomplish this goal, the chapter relates normative motivation to a sense of moral obligation. Normative motivation is a sense that one should do something, or that a certain behavior is correct or normal, as opposed to it being merely rewarding or personally advantageous. A sense of moral obligation is when one feels that one should or ought to take a moral stand and behave a particular way, regardless of what other people think. Both feel subjectively similar (a *sense of should*), but they bring about opposite behaviors: conforming to norms versus taking a moral stand against them. I have previously proposed that normative motivation can be understood by the principle that through action—and critically, through inaction—humans can exercise control over their social environment (see Theriault et al., 2021a, 2021b). Specifically, when an individual adjusts their behavior to conform to others' expectations, they can make others' behavior more predictable for themselves, which has knock-on benefits for regulating their own affective experience and the metabolic costs of information processing in the local social environment.[1] The chapter first reviews the theoretical and empirical assumptions that this account depends on, then explains how this form of social control works to produce a normative sense of should, which motivates an individual to conform to others' expectations and keep the local social environment predictable. Next, the chapter describes how a sense of moral obligation might motivate nonconformist behavior while nonetheless producing a similar subjective experience as in normative conformity—in other words, a sense of should. Specifically, I hypothesize that nonconformist moral behavior may be organized around features of human social expectations that are ubiquitous in an individual's global social environment. These ubiquitous social expectations produce generalized *social maxims* that inform how one should behave across local social contexts, and violating these social maxims could disrupt social relationships globally, meaning that local nonconformity (i.e., morally principled behavior) may sometimes be motivated by the benefits of more global social stability. Finally, the last part of the chapter briefly elaborates on how topics in modern moral psychology, such as moral dumbfounding and moral foundations theory, can be revisited and reinterpreted from this new perspective. Overall, this account clarifies how complex social processes may emerge from simpler biological ones while also demonstrating how culturally inherited social expectations (i.e., social reality; Berger & Luckmann, 1966/2011; Hacking, 1986; Searle, 1995) become biologically relevant for both brains and bodies.

---

[1]Exceptions to this general principle are also informative and are more fully explored in Theriault et al. (2021a) and its commentary and responses (Constant et al., 2021; Fotopoulou, 2021; Jebari, 2021; Rai, 2021; Theriault et al., 2021b; Tsakiris, 2021; Tummolini & Pezzulo, 2021).

BACKGROUND

Developing a biologically tractable account of moral psychology requires some initial link between psychological experience and brain biology. Traditional neuroscientific accounts sometimes obscure how complex psychological phenomena (e.g., mental inference, affective experience, hallucinations) connect to the biological mechanisms underlying them. Recent predictive processing models have put psychology in computational terms that are more biologically tractable, advancing a generalized framework for understanding cognition and cortical organization (Barrett & Simmons, 2015; Clark, 2013, 2015; Denève & Jardri, 2016; Friston, 2010; Friston et al., 2017; Hohwy, 2013; Hutchinson & Barrett, 2019; Keller & Mrsic-Flogel, 2018; Rao & Ballard, 1999; Sengupta et al., 2013; Seth, 2015; Shadmehr et al., 2010). These approaches provide novel computational accounts of cognition, which can succinctly explain well-known phenomena from cognitive and clinical psychology in terms of the dynamics between top-down prediction and bottom-up prediction error computations—for example, habituation and learning (Friston et al., 2016; Ramaswami, 2014), delusion and hallucination in schizophrenia (Corlett, 2017; Feeney et al., 2017; Jardri et al., 2017), and developmental dysfunction in autism (Lawson et al., 2014, 2015; Palmer et al., 2017; Van de Cruys et al., 2014). Closely related to this work is the theory of constructed emotion (Barrett, 2017a, 2017b) where the brain is thought to cluster top-down predictions into conceptual categories as it navigates through and learns from the environment that it inhabits (Barsalou, 1999). For example, the concept of "bird" clusters a variety of physically distinct organisms into one conceptual category on the basis of particular points of similarity, and, depending on the context, "bird" may call one image or another to mind (Barsalou & Sewell, 1984; Yeh & Barsalou, 2006). Critically, the theory of constructed emotion proposes that emotion concepts combine information about the state of the body (i.e., interoception) with the surrounding context, providing an account of psychological motivation that is closely related to the body's prospective state.

The Brain Predictively Regulates the Internal Environment

Considered generally, the brain mediates between sensory experience received from the environment and behaviors enacted to change that environment (see Figure 8.1; Cisek, 1999, 2019; Ross Ashby, 1960). Sensory experience is both interoceptive (i.e., from the internal state of the body; e.g., metabolic, visceral, or immune status) and exteroceptive (i.e., from outside the body; e.g., sights, sounds, smells). Extensive interdisciplinary work in neuroscience and

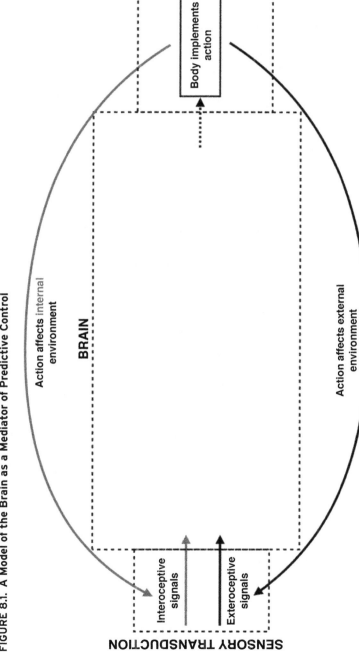

FIGURE 8.1. A Model of the Brain as a Mediator of Predictive Control

Note. The brain mediates between interoceptive and exteroceptive sensory experience and the enactment of behaviors that reciprocally affect incoming sensory signals. The brain is left as a blank box in this figure, which will be filled out in the figures that follow.

engineering suggests that the brain's fundamental job is to "[regulate] the internal milieu [to help] the organism survive and reproduce" (Sterling & Laughlin, 2015, p. 11). Thus, regulating an organism's interoceptive status through its interactions with the environment is fundamentally what the brain evolved to do.

Predictive processing models describe how the brain might efficiently encode interoceptive and exteroceptive sensory information (see Figure 8.2). Such models propose that the brain as a whole uses prior experience to build a predictive, roughly hierarchical model of the world (i.e., the body in its environment; Allen & Tsakiris, 2018; Barrett, 2017a, 2017b; Conant & Ross Ashby, 1970). Note that this framework is an alternative to traditional feature detection theories in neuroscience, where "the activity of neurons in sensory pathways . . . [represent] the presence of a feature or an object in the environment" (Keller & Mrsic-Flogel, 2018, p. 424). Instead, cortical organization is thought to consist of a predictive hierarchy, where prior experience generates top-down predictions that constrain bottom-up encoding to forward only what was unpredicted. This concept is known as *prediction error*. At the bottom of this hierarchy, signals are closely related to sensation (e.g., sights, sounds, visceral status), but as they ascend the hierarchy, bottom-up signals become increasingly compressed, abstract, and multimodal. For example, an apple is recognized as an apple because of its combination of color, smell, and texture, and the brain is thought to predict this multimodal combination of features when an individual opens their packed lunch (or even when they call an apple to mind; Barrett, 2017a). Critically, prediction error modifies top-down predictions in the next instant, which makes learning possible. For example, if an individual holds the apple in front of their face, its color one moment ago is highly predictive of its color now, allowing bottom-up encoding to be limited to changes. Predictive processing models, then, suggest that prior experience filters bottom-up signals, and that a bottom-up signal is informative if and only if it was unpredicted. A perfectly predictable signal means the internal model has no reason to change, and hence, there is no information to be encoded (Shannon & Weaver, 1949/1964).[2]

---

[2]To avoid confusion, it is important to make a subtle distinction between data and information. *Data* about an apple could include a list of all features that we think to record, such as color, texture, and taste. A large list of features would mean that we have a large amount of data about the apple. *Information* modifies or adds to the data that we already have. For example, if I had seen and touched apples before but never eaten one, then biting an apple provides information (i.e., new data) about its taste.

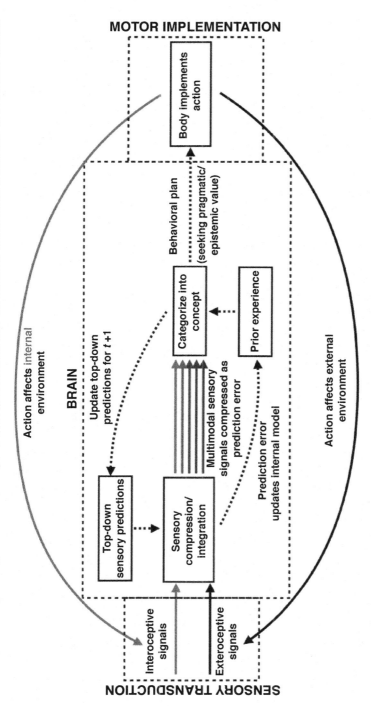

FIGURE 8.2. Incorporating Predictive Coding and Conceptualization Into the Model of the Brain as a Mediator of Predictive Control

Note. Interoceptive and exteroceptive signals are received by the animal via sensory transduction and passed to the brain. In the brain, predictable components of these signals are filtered and integrated across sensory modalities. These multimodal signals both update the internal model and are categorized using concepts available from prior experience. Concepts generate predictions that both filter incoming sensory signals in the next instant (*t* +1) and implement motor plans for behavior. The purpose of behavior is to regulate the interoceptive environment, either by gaining resources (i.e., pursuing pragmatic value) or gaining information to improve the internal model (i.e., gaining epistemic value). Implementing actions affects the internal and external environment, generating interoceptive and exteroceptive signals and repeating the cycle.

212 • *Jordan E. Theriault*

Why filter bottom-up signals? Among other benefits (e.g., rapid error correction via forward models; Shadmehr et al., 2010), such filtering could reduce the metabolic costs of bottom-up signaling. Across species, and across levels of cortical activity, the metabolic costs of neuronal signaling form approximately 70% to 75% of the total energy costs in the brain (Attwell & Laughlin, 2001; Hyder et al., 2013; Sengupta et al., 2010; Yu et al., 2018). These costs stem almost entirely from the cost of repolarizing neurons via Na^+/K^+ pumps after action potentials or synaptic transmission (Attwell & Laughlin, 2001; Harris & Attwell, 2012). By encoding information as prediction error, these information transmission costs can potentially be regulated. Further, I have suggested elsewhere that the neuronal channels responsible for encoding prediction error may be fueled by a metabolic pathway that is substantially less efficient at converting glucose to cellular energy compared to cellular respiration (i.e., aerobic glycolysis; Theriault et al., 2022), meaning that prediction error encoding may draw heavily on metabolic resources (and on compensatory mechanisms to account for this heavy usage; Sennesh et al., 2022). Thus, limiting encoding to unpredictable signals provides a potential route for maintaining metabolic efficiency (Sengupta et al., 2013; Theriault et al., 2021a; Zénon et al., 2019), which would significantly improve evolutionary fitness given that natural selection acts to "economize in every part of the organization" (Darwin, 1859/2001, p. 137).

A brain organized around prediction can also prepare context-sensitive responses to challenges (e.g., predators) before it encounters them (Barrett & Finlay, 2018; Sterling, 2012). This means that relatively few responses need to be innately prepared, and their "triggers" can be quite simple. Simple preprogrammed reflexes (i.e., stimulus–response reactions) do exist—for example, when a zebra fish sees a predator (stimulus), it flips 180° and swims in the opposite direction (response)—but with even a small amount of time, a brain can prepare a more complex and adaptive response. If the zebra fish has > 50 milliseconds to react, then the direction of its escape turn becomes more random; if it has > 200 milliseconds to react, then it becomes more likely to hide or use the environment to its advantage (Barrett & Finlay, 2018; Catania, 2009; Dunn et al., 2016). With respect to innate moral intuitions, some stimulus features may evoke an automatic response (e.g., auditory vibrations trigger a startle response in zebra fish; Eaton & Farley, 1975), but, for the complex sets of physical and social events thought to trigger moral intuitions, it is unlikely that the triggering features are recognized in the absence of experience (e.g., recall that above, even "apple" was an abstract combination of features; Barrett, 2017a). In other words, although animals can implement simple stimulus–response reactions, in the complex and temporally extended environments that humans inhabit, adaptive behavior is generally more likely to incorporate predictive and contextually sensitive nuance. Indeed, incorporating this contextual sensitivity instead of relying on preprogrammed stimulus–response reactions is one reason why a large brain is worth its energetic investment (Sterling & Laughlin, 2015).

Predictive processing frameworks, then, have at least two relevant implications for moral psychology: (a) The brain is predictive, not reactive, and (b) bottom-up encoding, and its metabolic costs, can be regulated by either an accurate internal model or a predictable environment (Sengupta et al., 2013; Theriault et al., 2021a; Zénon et al., 2019). The first implication suggests that the brain's role is to prospectively regulate the health of the animal (Sterling, 2012), rather than react to challenges as they occur, and the second implication suggests that it can be epistemically valuable to make the internal model accurate or to select behaviors that make (or keep) the external world predictable (Friston et al., 2017; Pezzulo et al., 2015; Tummolini & Pezzulo, 2021). The ideas of prospective regulation and epistemic value have played critical roles in prior accounts of normative motivation (Theriault et al., 2021a, 2021b; Tummolini & Pezzulo, 2021).

The Theory of Constructed Emotion: Emotions Are Concepts, and Concepts Are Predictions

An account of morality must, at some point, describe what motivates people to perform one action instead of another. As discussed in the introduction, emotions (or moral intuitions) have often fulfilled this role in moral psychology, where emotions and moral intuitions are thought to be behavioral and psychological reactions to evolutionarily relevant stimuli or situations. In the context of moral psychology, emotions are thought to produce feelings and motivations, which drive behaviors, such as approaching, avoiding, forgiving, and retaliating (e.g., Fehr & Gächter, 2002; Graham et al., 2009; Gray & Wegner, 2011; Greene, 2013; Haidt, 2001; Haidt & Joseph, 2004). According to Haidt and Joseph (2004),

> It seems that in all human cultures, individuals often react with flashes of feeling linked to moral intuitions when they perceive certain events in their social worlds: when they see others (particularly young others) suffering, and others causing that suffering [but see our discussion of hazing rituals below]; when they see others cheat or fail to repay favors; and when they see others

who are disrespectful or who do not behave in a manner befitting their status in the group. (p. 58)

The view that emotions are evolutionarily prepared reactions to emotion-evoking stimuli has long been orthodoxy (Ekman, 1992; Fanselow, 2018; Panksepp, 1998, 2011); however, as discussed earlier, the features that the brain is innately prepared to detect are almost certainly simpler than complex, abstract, and temporally extended emotion-evoking stimuli. The theory of constructed emotion (Barrett, 2017a, 2017b) offers an alternative account of emotion that is consistent with the emerging consensus from neuro-science: it proposes that emotions like fear, anger, or sadness are abstract categorizations—or concepts (like "apples" or "birds")—that structure and guide prediction and behavior in the moments to follow.

In the theory of constructed emotion, an emotion is created by concep-tualizing affective experience in an exteroceptive context. Affect is the low dimensional subjective experience that corresponds to the bodily, interoceptive state (Barrett, 2017b; Barrett & Bliss-Moreau, 2009; Chanes & Barrett, 2016; Craig, 2015; Seth, 2013). It consists of two dimensions: valence (i.e., feeling good or bad) and arousal (i.e., feeling alert or tired; Barrett, 2017a; Damasio, 1999; James, 1890/1931; Wundt, 1896). Any emotion is accompanied by affective experience (Barrett, 2006; Barrett & Bliss-Moreau, 2009; Russell, 2003; Russell & Barrett, 1999; Wundt, 1896), and by carrying information about the internal state of the body, affect gives emotions their motivational force and drives adaptive behavior.

To say that emotions are concepts, then, is to say that emotions are group-ings of top-down predictions and action plans made by the brain's internal model (Figure 8.2; Barrett, 2017a, 2017b). Such concepts organize interocep-tive and exteroceptive sensory signals by using prior experience to categorize them. For example, the concept of an apple includes its color, smell, texture, taste, and how to eat it. An "apple" concept carries information about which combinations of sensory signals make an object an "apple" or not, and what kinds of motor plans should be enacted when an "apple" is encountered. Emotion concepts are hypothesized to work similarly, but a greater degree of interoceptive information (and their conscious experience as affect) is involved in the process of emotion concept categorization. On this account, then, emotions are not reactions; rather, they are interoception (and affective experience) in an external context, which has been categorized in accor-dance with prior experience to generate prospectively adaptive behavior. Because every individual's prior experience is unique, variability in how people respond to an emotional stimulus (or a moral scenario) is meaningful and reflects differences in their internal models. That is, one person's experience will lead them to categorize situations differently than another person, making learning and development essential to emotion, and by extension, moral motivation.[3]

The Subjective Experience of Moral Motivation

Prior accounts of moral psychology have grounded moral motivation in emotional reactions to particular stimuli or situations (e.g., Fehr & Gächter, 2002; Graham et al., 2009; Gray & Wegner, 2011; Greene, 2013; Haidt, 2001; Haidt & Joseph, 2004). However, by doing this, they have missed an important part of the puzzle: moral motivation has a particular subjective sensation—a feeling that one should or ought to do something, which is distinct from a feeling that a behavior will be rewarded or punished. Solomon Asch (1952/1962) drew attention to this problem in his textbook for social psychology:

> It is understandable that rewards and punishments produce desire and fear, but there is no way of seeing how they can produce the experience of "should". . . . [W]hen we are determined to tell the truth even if it is painful . . . we are granting recognition to certain properties of action that are not described in the current categories of habit and desire. (p. 356)

This distinction is easily missed in emotional reaction accounts because the subjective experience involved in the emotional response is a part of the reaction—that is, morally relevant emotional stimuli evoke morally relevant emotional responses, as opposed to nonmoral desire or aversion. On these accounts, why moral motivation feels different than other kinds of desires or aversions is no mystery: the triggering stimuli are different, so the triggered emotions will be different too. However, if the hypothesis that emotions are stimulus–response reactions is rejected as biologically implausible, then at least two problems emerge: (a) Why are interoceptive signals sometimes conceptualized as emotions and at other times as a subjective sense that one should do something—in other words, a sense of should—and (b) why do some moral motivations appear to be universal among humans without being innately specified (e.g., an aversion to causing suffering)? I return to

---

[3]The role of interoception and its interpretation is actually present in Kohlberg's account of moral psychology although the implicit constructivism has generally not been emphasized in reviews of this work. For example, Kohlberg (1971) wrote, "Two adolescents, thinking of stealing, may have the same feeling of anxiety in the pit of their stomachs. One . . . interprets the feeling as 'being chicken' and ignores it. The other . . . interprets the feeling as 'the warning of my conscience' and decides accordingly" (pp. 189–190).

the second problem in the last part of this chapter when I discuss implications for moral psychology, but I address the first problem next, reviewing a previously developed account of how morality could be interoceptively relevant (Theriault et al., 2021a, 2021b). That is, how could other people's expectations, or one's own moral principles, affect the body?

A SENSE OF SHOULD IN NORMATIVE MOTIVATION

Elsewhere, my colleagues and I developed an account to explain how people's expectations, through their relationship with interoception, produce an affective experience that pressures individuals to conform to norms. This affective experience is called normative motivation, or a sense of should (Theriault et al., 2021a, 2021b). This account hinged on how individuals conform to others' expectations to control both prediction error in their social environment and the metabolic costs of encoding prediction error.

Normative motivation stems from a relationship between other people's expectations and their interoceptive consequences for an individual. Social norms are standards for behavior that stem from people's expectations (Bicchieri, 2006). For example, some norms include observing social customs (e.g., wearing makeup if female, or not if male), avoiding social disruptions (e.g., remaining silent during a film), or obeying commands (e.g., passing the salt when asked). Norms set standards for how people should behave in social settings, and norm conformity is so ubiquitous it largely passes beneath anyone's notice except when someone violates those norms or when someone considers violating them.

Normative motivation is the sense that one should (or ought to) conform to these expectations and is experienced as affectively distinct from the pursuit/avoidance of pleasant/unpleasant outcomes (Asch, 1952/1962, Chapter 12; Smith, 1790/2010, Part 3, Chapter 2; Theriault et al., 2021a). For example, when considering whether to buy a scarf, a person might try it on, see whether they like it, then decide "nah, I don't feel like it." However, when their mother asks them to pass the salt at Thanksgiving dinner, they rarely weigh the costs and benefits; they just obey and pass the salt (see also Fiske & Rai, 2015; Fiske & Tetlock, 1997; Rai & Fiske, 2011). Refusing to pass the salt—"Nah, I don't feel like it"—would require them to overcome an anticipatory aversion felt at the prospect of violating their mother's expectation. Critically, this anticipatory aversion is an anxious aversion. That is, it is not just an anticipatory disliking but an anticipatory anxiety (involving both negative valence and high arousal; Barrett, 2006; Barrett & Bliss-Moreau, 2009; Russell, 2003;

Russell & Barrett, 1999). A person may even be able to trigger this anticipatory anxiety in themselves if they come to the brink of violating a social norm (e.g., seriously preparing to scream in a crowded room). In the context of normative motivation, then, a sense of should is the anticipatory anxiety felt toward violating people's expectations, and anxiety is a conceptualization of interoceptive signals (Barrett, 2017a, 2017b). But how does the relationship between one's behavior and other people's expectations have interoceptive consequences?

The answer relies on three premises: (a) Encoding prediction error carries a metabolic cost (see background); (b) on average, when animals receive prediction error (i.e., information), they are more likely to change their behavior; and (c) concepts are learned to generate adaptive behavior and regulate the internal milieu (Barrett, 2017a, 2017b; Sterling & Laughlin, 2015), including metabolic efficiency and the metabolic costs of processing prediction error (Figure 8.3). From these premises, it follows that when Amelia (one person) violates the expectations of Bob (another person), on average, the violation causes Bob to change his behavior. When Bob changes his behavior in ways that Amelia cannot easily predict, the metabolic costs Amelia must pay toward prediction error encoding increase. If Amelia's concepts organize predictions to help her select adaptive behaviors (as in the theory of constructed emotion; see background), then Amelia's concepts about social norms may help her select adaptive behaviors in social settings—in this case, behaviors that satisfy Bob's expectations and control the metabolic costs of prediction error in her local social environment. By conforming to norms, Amelia gains epistemic value by promoting a better fit between her internal model and the external environment; however, she gains this epistemic value by keeping the environment predictable. In other words, conforming maintains a status quo, and a status quo can relax the metabolic costs of prediction error encoding.

The anxious character of a sense of should is thought to stem from the established relationship between prediction error, norepinephrine release, and arousal. When an animal is surprised by unexpected sensory signals, autonomic activity produces arousal (e.g., Critchley et al., 2005; Dayan & Yu, 2006; Hajcak et al., 2003; Spruit et al., 2018). For a sense of should, we proposed that individuals learn that violating other people's expectations will, on average, create social uncertainty (Theriault et al., 2021a, 2021b). As a consequence, an individual anticipates the anxiety this uncertainty will generate when they consider violating someone else's expectations (e.g., their mother's) or shared expectations (i.e., norms). A sense of should, then, is a motivation felt as an anticipatory anxiety, but it is adaptive in that it motivates behaviors that minimize metabolic costs of prediction error encoding.

FIGURE 8.3. The Sense of Should in the Model of the Brain as a Mediator of Predictive Control

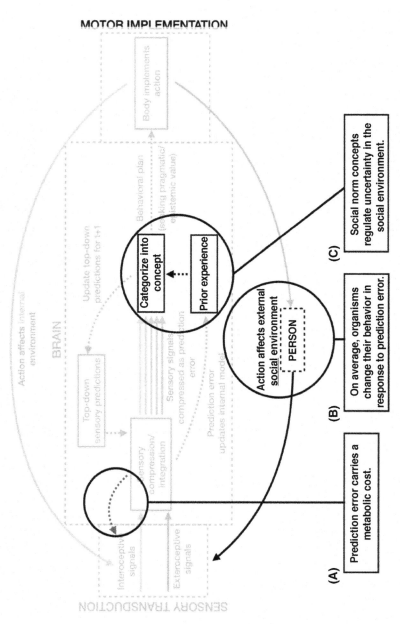

Note. (A) The bottom-up signaling of prediction error is assumed to carry a metabolic cost, which is decreased in a predictable environment. (B) On average, other animals (i.e., the social environment) will change their behavior in response to prediction error. (C) Social norm concepts can be learned and used to anticipate which behaviors will violate other people's predictions, allowing animals to control the prediction error returned to them from the social environment—and, by extension, its metabolic costs and their interoceptive consequences. For another illustration of the sense of should, see Figure 1 in Theriault et al. (2021a).

This account explains normative motivation as a process using simple principles of metabolism and cortical organization (in the predictive processing model), but its implications for behavior are flexible. In other words, the content of normative motivation is context dependent, and different social contexts—with their different social expectations—will motivate an individual to perform different behaviors. For example, someone might avoid swearing around their grandmother but avoid acting too formally around their closest friends. Note that this account is distinct from most previous accounts, which have grounded norm compliance in reputational pursuit (e.g., Cialdini et al., 1990; Constant et al., 2019; FeldmanHall & Shenhav, 2019; Kelley, 1952; Paluck et al., 2016; Toelch & Dolan, 2015). The point to conforming is not to maximize reputation or its material benefits in the future; rather, the point to conforming is to regulate the costs of one's social environment in the very near future (for more discussion, see Theriault et al., 2021a). This is not to say that people never act to gain social esteem—a sense of should describes one motivation among many—but it is worth considering that, anecdotally, some of the most popular people are nonconformists (Moscovici, 1976, Chapter 4).

Normative motivation, then, is not the only factor involved in selecting a behavior. Normative motivation creates epistemic value by keeping the external environment predictable, but one could also gain epistemic value by learning to make better predictions (Friston et al., 2017; Theriault et al., 2021a). However, to make better predictions, one needs to encode prediction error. Therefore, exploiting and exploring contains a tradeoff—one can exploit a social environment by conforming to people's expectations and keeping environment predictable, but one could also explore a social environment by intentionally violating people's expectations to see how they react (Theriault et al., 2021a; Tummolini & Pezzulo, 2021). Even conversational language could be considered a controlled form of social exploration, where syntax provides a predictable scaffold but semantic content feeds people information (i.e., prediction error) in a controlled way, eliciting interpretable reactions (see also Reber & Norenzayan, 2018). We suggested that normative motivation (and its paired affective experience, a sense of should) is one tool among many for regulating the social environment, but its ability to help many individuals mutually stabilize a shared social environment makes it a useful default. That is, we hypothesized that most aspects of an individual's behavior are selected to conform to other people's expectations even when alternative actions that could more immediately satisfy pragmatic needs (e.g., for food, sex) are available (Theriault et al., 2021a, 2021b).

To return to the motivating question: If emotions are not stimulus–response reactions but concepts that combine interoceptive signals and an exteroceptive context (Barrett, 2017a, 2017b), then why are interoceptive signals (experienced as affect) sometimes conceptualized as valenced "fears" and "desires" (Asch, 1952/1962, p. 356) while at other times conceptualized as anticipatory anxiety in a sense of should? The answer is that a sense of should involves a particular kind of interoceptive signal and a particular kind of exteroceptive context. The interoceptive signal is an increase (or anticipated increase) in sensory prediction error (which increases arousal; e.g., Critchley et al., 2005; Spruit et al., 2018), and the exteroceptive context is the social dynamic where conforming to people's expectations can maintain a status quo in the local social environment. A concept forms when abstract relationships among sensory signals can be used to guide behavior. A sense of should is a concept that emerges from the dynamics of social organisms having both mutual expectations about each other and brains that pay a metabolic cost to encode prediction error. This explanation shows how the normative experience of a sense of should could emerge without being innately specified (e.g., by an emotional reaction or a moral intuition).

This sense of should motivates behaviors that conform to expectations—and in many cases, this sense of should could promote prosocial behavior (or moral behavior, if prosocial and moral are equated; but see Fiske & Rai, 2015). However, some of the most striking (and sometimes admirable) examples of morally motivated behavior fly in the face of conformity, where acting morally means resisting social pressure and doing the "right" thing even at a cost to one's reputation or comfort. How might a sense of should, despite being shaped by an aversion to social uncertainty, produce non-conformist morally motivated behavior?

A SENSE OF SHOULD IN MORAL MOTIVATION AND MODEL COHERENCE

Historically, moral cognition has been difficult to define. Some of the most popular proposals in moral psychology have emphasized the role of moral content. For example, moral cognition may relate to intuitions and behaviors surrounding harm, fairness, loyalty, authority, and purity (Graham et al., 2009, 2011; Haidt & Joseph, 2004, 2011). Other work has focused on particular categories of morally relevant behavior, such as altruistic punishment or the fair distribution of goods (e.g., Blake et al., 2015; Fehr & Gächter, 2002; Kurzban et al., 2015; McAuliffe et al., 2017). The approach in this section is different; it focuses on process over content. As with normative motivation above, I hypothesize that the content of moral concepts is flexible and contextually dependent; that is, people in different cultures will feel morally motivated to behave in different ways (Cameron et al., 2015). However, more so than in normative motivation, the nature of human social organization makes some moral concepts more likely to develop than others (Jebari, 2019), which means that moral motivation, as a process, does produce some constraints for moral content. This section develops a process-based account of moral motivation, building on the previously developed principles of predictive processing and a sense of should. In this section, I introduce a hypothesis that moral motivation involves conforming to social expectations about behavior that generalize across social contexts (i.e., social maxims) and that doing so may help to maintain a coherent internal model of the social environment, considered globally.

Moral motivation may help maintain a coherent model of the global social environment. Normative and moral motivation both involve a sense of should—a felt obligation to do something because it is correct, normal, or right rather than just rewarding or advantageous. However, normative motivation stabilizes a local social environment (for an individual's own metabolic benefit) by motivating individuals to conform to other people's expectations whereas moral motivation does not necessarily create local stability and may even demand nonconformity. Indeed, what some would consider paradigmatically morally principled behavior can involve violating people's expectations, destabilizing the social environment, or even self-destruction—for example, refusing to lie even when it would save lives (Kant, 1785/1998), giving all nonessential income to charity (Singer, 1999), or dying for a cause (Atran, 2010). We might respect and admire someone who takes a moral stand, but taking such a stand can be risky.[4] How could such strong moral motivation be explained from an interoceptively grounded motivational framework? That is, how could someone value a particular behavior so highly that they would follow through with it in spite of, for example, the undesirable or destabilizing consequences of strict deontology, utilitarian self-sacrifice, or martyrdom?

To answer this, we need to distinguish between the local and global social environment. The local social environment includes agents in the present

---

[4]We might also fear someone who acts on moral principle. For example, ideological militants or terrorist organizations may be willing to kill others or sacrifice themselves out of moral motivation (Atran, 2010; Fiske & Rai, 2014). Of course, what motivates a particular person—moral motivation, normative motivation (i.e., social pressure), or simply the pursuit of desirable ends (e.g., anticipated heavenly rewards)—cannot be answered without knowing how the person feels. Nevertheless, it remains true that differences between these motives are recognized as meaningful: if someone claimed to have felt obliged to act on moral principle, then one way to denigrate them would be to say they had an ulterior material motive (Fiske & Tetlock, 1997; Tetlock, 2003).

context and near future. The global social environment includes stable and important social relationships (and corresponding expectations) that persist across local social contexts—for example, relationships with close friends, romantic partners, colleagues, and communities. The local social environment contributes to normative motivation: when someone violates local expectations, they cause the local social environment to change in ways that their internal model may not be able to predict, and normative motivation is an anticipatory anxiety toward the consequences of those unpredictable changes. However, some behaviors that would conform to local expectations could also change social relationships that are central to the global social environment. For example, if an attractive and interested stranger strikes up a conversation with someone at a bar, that person may feel pressured to cheat on a romantic partner (i.e., normative motivation in a local context); nevertheless, they may remain faithful, anticipating that, if found out, this knowledge would change that existing romantic relationship[5] (a core part of one's global social environment). Further, even if their partner never discovered that unfaithfulness, that individual would reconceptualize their relationship with their partner, and all the behaviors and feelings that concept implies might change.[6] In either case, an important part of one's global social environment, which was once predictable, is now thrown into question. These fundamental predictions (or equivalently, concepts) about the global social environment could be called *social maxims*.

I hypothesize, then, that behaviors that violate social maxims can force those social maxims to be revised and that the anticipated metabolic and affective consequences of such revisions can generate a sense of should supporting moral motivation. This hypothesis rests on the premises that (a) structural features of human physiology and social organization create emergent social maxims, (b) these social maxims become core predictions in the brain's predictive internal model, and (c) violating core social maxims could force individuals to revise their predictions about relationships between themselves and others in their global social environment. In the context of moral motivation, then,

---

[5]Note that this model contains no commitment to the anticipation being explicit or conscious. An internal model issues many predictions, but the question of how predictions become conscious is a second issue beyond the scope of this paper.
[6]This account is subtly different from a reputational account. On this account, moral motivation does not directly stem from the anticipated costs of losing a relationship (i.e., pragmatic costs). Rather, on this account, moral motivation stems from the anticipated costs of having to learn and modify the internal model in order to adjust to a "new normal" in these relationships (i.e., epistemic costs).

a sense of should is an anticipatory anxiety felt toward violating social maxims because doing so would threaten to disrupt core relationships in the global social context, and by extension, disrupt elements of the global (and local) social environment that depend on these relationships (see discussion below on how social maxims might relate to other social predictions). Moral motivation, then, does involve conforming, but it involves conforming to social maxims that generalize across social situations, meaning that local nonconformity may be a cost worth paying to maintain a more global correspondence between one's social environment and internal model.

Social maxims are a product of other people's persistent social expectations about one's behavior, meaning that social maxims, as expectations, can compel both normative and moral motivation. The difference between normative and moral motivation is in *why* the social maxim motivates: normative motivation keeps the local social environment predictable whereas moral motivation maintains the integrity of one's internal model of the global social environment.[7] An interesting consequence of this hypothesis is that it may be difficult for one to introspect whether one's own behavior is morally or normatively motivated, for both normative and moral motivations produce the same subjective experience—a sense of should. That is, without knowing one's subjective experience, an external observer cannot identify whether one's behavior (e.g., sharing) was motivated by an anticipated reward (e.g., reputation) or by a sense of should. Likewise, if one cannot know the exact causes of their own behavior, then it may be difficult for one to identify whether one's behavior was morally or normatively motivated, as subjective experience does not differentiate between the two. Moral and normative motivation, then, would be indistinguishable to an individual so long as expectations in the immediate social environment align with the social maxim— the moral behavior is also the expected behavior. In other words, to know that one is really motivated by a moral principle, one may need to be "tested" by a situation where moral motivation requires local nonconformity.[8] The

---

[7]The difference between normative and moral motivation is a difference in degree, not kind, as local and global social environments exist along a spectrum.

[8]This claim implies that desire-based motivation, normative motivation, and moral motivation can be empirically distinguished, but they cannot be distinguished by observing behavior or even by phenomenological reporting on subjective experience. Discriminating between motivation by desire versus a sense of should would require information about the agent's subjective experience. Discriminating between normative and moral motivation (both experienced as a sense of should) would require a situation where distinct behaviors satisfy local social expectations and global social maxims.

examples developed below, which report on subjective experience and conflicting moral and normative motives, will help to clarify this difference.

How Might Social Maxims Form?

That the brain's internal model would organize itself around social maxims is an extension of the idea that evolutionary and behavioral adaptation orient themselves around constant constraints (Lewontin, 2001; Ross Ashby, 1960; Sterling & Laughlin, 2015). That is, animals can adjust to environmental regularities through evolutionary adaptation (changing physiology across generations) or through behavioral adaptation (changing behavior within one lifetime; Lewontin, 2001; Ross Ashby, 1960; Skinner, 1990; Sterling & Laughlin, 2015). For example, from sea to land, the mechanical load exerted by gravity increases by approximately 1,000× (Volkmann & Baluška, 2006), and as a consequence, in sea- and land-dwelling snakes, properties of the circulatory system vary drastically (e.g., placement of the heart; Lillywhite, 1988). Warm-blooded animals offer another example: They use metabolically generated heat to keep their body temperature constant, allowing other physical parameters to be optimized around this constant value (e.g., axon diameter in the brain; Faisal et al., 2005). Evolution adapts physiology to predictable environmental parameters, but behavioral adaptation can leverage predictable parameters as well, meaning that under different conditions (e.g., low gravity) the brain's internal model must reinvest in learning sensorimotor contingencies it had previously mastered.

What social maxims for behavior could human physiology and social organization produce? An answer could begin by asking whether any behaviors are socially disruptive across nearly all social contexts—that is, are there expectations that, if violated, almost always disrupt the social environment? Actions causing physical harm are a reasonable first candidate, as human and nonhuman animals have evolved fight-or-flight responses to change their behavior in response to physical pain. If violating someone's expectations increases the likelihood of an unpredictable reaction (see Figure 8.3), then the same logic applies to harming them (perhaps even more so). For this reason, prior accounts have suggested that aversions to physical violence (J. Blair et al., 2006; R. J. Blair, 1995) or to intentionally causing suffering (Gray et al., 2012, 2014) are fundamental to moral motivation. Avoiding harm to other animals, then, may be an emergent social maxim, where across contexts the brain's internal model orients itself around the prediction that harming other animals will be socially disruptive. Indeed, this anticipatory aversion to harm appears to be so well trained that knowingly pantomiming violence (e.g., stabbing someone with a realistic fake knife) creates anticipatory arousal (Cushman et al., 2012), or a sense of should.

However, humans often do live in violent environments and can overcome an aversion to violence (Collins, 2008, Chapter 2; Fiske & Rai, 2015; Munch-Jurisic, 2022; Waller, 2007). Initially, being involved in violence may produce affective and interoceptive consequences. For example,

> A wide range of perpetrator accounts reveal that initial involvement in killing often led to nightmares, anxiety attacks, debilitating guilt, depression, gastrointestinal problems, temporary impotence, hallucinations, substance abuse, numerous bodily complaints, and many other signs of stress reactions. (Waller, 2007, p. 73; quoted and discussed in Munch-Jurisic, 2022)

However, the present account suggests that anticipatory anxiety felt toward social uncertainty, including toward the consequences of violence, can be unlearned through practice (Theriault et al., 2021b; Tummolini & Pezzulo, 2021). Consistent with this, firsthand reports suggest that perpetrators can even enjoy violence after the aversion is overcome:

> Flying over a group of civilians in a helicopter, he was ordered to fire at them, an order he did not obey. The helicopter circled over the area and again he was ordered to fire, which again he did not do. The officer in charge then threatened him with court martial, which led him to fire the next time around. He vomited, felt profoundly distressed. The veteran reported that in a fairly short time firing at civilians became like an experience at a target-shooting gallery, and he began to enjoy it. (Staub, 1992, p. 134; quoted and discussed in Munch-Jurisic, 2022)

Thus, even if an aversion to physical harm is likely to emerge as a social maxim, it likely can be overcome with practice. Once the consequences of violence become familiar, and as one's internal model adapts to make predictions within a new set of social expectations, an anxious aversion to practiced forms of physical harm may begin to dissipate.

Conversely, some people may override an aversion to receiving physical pain from others, on account of normative or moral motivation (Fiske & Rai, 2015). That is, they expect to receive violence and conform to the expectation. Whether their reasons for doing so are normative (i.e., regulating the local social environment) or moral (i.e., regulating the global social environment) may be hard to articulate, even to themselves. For example, in hazing rituals, new members of a group are expected to be initiated and senior members are expected to the carry violent initiations out (Fiske & Rai, 2015, Chapter 13). A former high school athlete, interviewed in university, described his expectations and experiences:

> You knew you had it coming; it's a right [sic] of passage. I mean, the seniors were older and I expected it. I saw it with my sisters and brothers going through

school and they'd tell me stories. It just went with the territory. . . . I think hazing is a way of finding status between those who are inferior and those who are superior. Usually the people that did the hazing were the hot shots of the team—you know, the big players, the star players, or whatnot. And since they don't really know you as a freshman, once you get hazed, then you could hang out with them. It's just easier for you to get to know them. After being hazed, then they're your friends. (Waldron et al., 2011, pp. 117–118)

Thus, even ubiquitous social contingencies, like reactions to physical harm, can be at odds with widespread social expectations in cultures or social groups. If a social group forms a large part of one's social environment (e.g., during a military deployment), then its collective expectations likely form social maxims around which one's internal model will be constructed. For the brain to adaptively regulate behavior in an environment, its internal model should be structured around widespread social expectations of the environment in which it finds itself. Social maxims, then, will be highly dependent on the culture that an individual occupies (but see the discussion of moral foundations theory in the section Implications for Moral Psychology).

How Might Social Maxims Relate to Other Social Predictions?

If the brain implements a hierarchical, predictive model of the world (Barrett, 2017a; Cisek, 2019; Ross Ashby, 1960; Sterling & Laughlin, 2015), then some predictions will depend on others. Just as gravity can structure physiology, social maxims may structure other dependent social predictions. Unlike gravity, however, people are physically capable of violating social maxims. Further, social maxims are not a stable constraint: if maxims are violated, one's relationship to others could permanently change, and one may find that they now relate differently to the global social environment (which may now produce different social maxims). For example, someone could punch a stranger in the face and undermine core social predictions (for both individuals involved) that people are safe from physical harm. But if someone did this, then they may find it difficult to return to the same equilibrium with the global social environment that they previously occupied. That is, others may act differently toward them, and they may not be able to return to previous norms of interaction. In this case, that person would need to invest in reconstructing their model of the social environment and its relation to themselves. Our existence as social animals and the means we have available to meet our material needs (e.g., purchasing food with money, receiving money for labor) rely on assumptions that our behavior and the behavior of others will adhere to social maxims (e.g., that money will be accepted to mediate an exchange of goods; Marx, 1867/1992).[9] Social maxims may differ between cultures, but for stable forms of social interaction to emerge, some features of social organization must remain predictable.

Some social predictions are more central than others. Quine and Ullian (1978) provided a metaphor for this web of dependencies in their "web of belief":

> Some beliefs, like [that Hannibal crossed the Alps], we shall probably retain while we live. Some, like our belief in the dependability of our neighborhood cobbler, we may abandon tomorrow in the face of adverse evidence. And some, like the belief that a bird chirped within earshot, will simply die of unimportance forthwith. (p. 10)

Quine and Ullian were concerned with representational beliefs, but the metaphor applies equally to prediction: some abstract predictions are retained across contexts, like that violence will disrupt our social environment, while other predictions are strong but can be abandoned in the face of evidence, like that being insistent always makes others comply, and sensory predictions (e.g., birds chirping) can exist in the moment but drop away shortly after (see Figure 8.4). As reviewed in the background section, predictions that are higher in the cortical hierarchy are abstract compressions of sensory signals (i.e., concepts; Barrett, 2017a), and as predictions reach the sensory periphery, they become increasingly short-term and specific.

Critically, predictions (or beliefs, for Quine & Ullian, 1978) can conflict. In the face of conflicting predictions, the web of belief's internal consistency can only be maintained by abandoning one belief or another. According to Quine and Ullian (1978),

> When a set of beliefs has accumulated to the point of contradiction, find the smallest selection of them you can that still involves contradiction. . . . For we can be sure that we are going to have to drop some of the beliefs in that subset, whatever else we do. (p. 18)

On a predictive interpretation of Quine and Ullian, internal consistency would be defined as not predicting inconsistent sensory signals and not enacting physically inconsistent motor plans. As with beliefs, contradictions among predictions could be removed by modifying the internal model—in essence, dropping some predictions or modifying them to be consistent with others.

---

[9]Our behavior as individuals cannot change the social fact that money mediates exchanges, but if we keep using fake bills at a particular store, then we may no longer be trusted to make purchases at it.

FIGURE 8.4. Web of Belief/Prediction

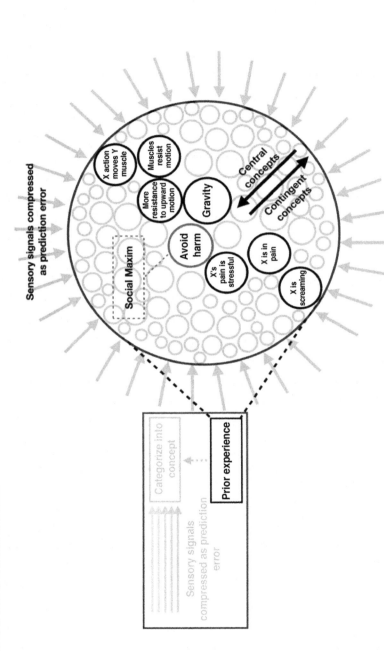

Note. Quine and Ullian's (1978) metaphor of the "web of belief" applies equally well to the hierarchical dependencies of the brain's predictive model. Some core predictions (e.g., about the force of gravity, or the social consequences of intentional harm) can occupy a central position in the web, and more context dependent or sensory specific predictions can occupy the periphery, but these peripheral predictions depend on more central nodes. If a central prediction is abandoned (e.g., because it conflicts with another), then peripheral predictions must be modified as well. I hypothesize that moral motivation stems from an anticipatory aversion to behaviors that would threaten reorganization of the internal model by violating central social maxims whereas normative motivation is an anticipatory aversion to disrupting the external social environment.

For example, a teenager that participates in hazing rituals might drop, modify, or rationalize inconsistency between their behavior and a social maxim against intentional harm.[10]

Social maxims, then, are hypothesized to be core predictions about the social world, and their revision will have downstream consequences for other social predictions. When a central belief must be abandoned, peripheral beliefs that depend on it must be revised as well (Quine & Ullian, 1978). Likewise, when someone violates a social maxim (or find that social maxims conflict), they might be forced to revise the predictions made by their internal model. This means that when someone behaves "immorally," there are potentially two costs: (a) the costs of physical or reputational punishments that other people might levy against them and (b) the costs of revising their understanding of the social world and their place within it.[11] That is, violating social maxims can place one into a new equilibrium with the global social environment, in which case one's internal model of the social environment will need to be modified. Avoiding the costs of model revision may motivate morally principled nonconformity in the local social environment, where someone resists social pressure (e.g., to join a hazing) even under the threat of physical or reputational punishment. That is, some people may be unable to reconcile moral violations with a continuity of their existing social relationships (e.g., with family, friends, church), and so, motivated by global model coherence, they might violate local social norms—in other words, they might take a moral stand against local social pressure.

How Might Social Maxims Vary Across Individuals?

The present account may be able to connect predictive theories of cortical organization (e.g., Clark, 2013; Hutchinson & Barrett, 2019; Keller &

---

[10]Another former high school athlete described their participation in hazing rituals and appeared to rationalize to himself how hazing violence is consistent with other positive social relationships, and actually prosocial in the end:

Some of the guys took it more seriously than others, and a couple kids got hurt. Not from what I did. I mean I did participate in throwing some balloons and whacking some kids. But two specific guys that were with me actually hurt a couple kids. Like, one kid went to the hospital because he thought his tailbone was broken. He couldn't sit down. . . . He was really embarrassed and angry and kind of shocked, really, that it went that far. But, after that happened, we really treated him well. And he finally did get to the point where he joked around about it, but for a couple weeks he was pretty upset about it. (Waldron et al., 2011, p. 119)

[11]These ideas share much in common with cognitive dissonance (or inconsistency) theory and its extensions (Festinger, 1962; Gawronski & Brannon, 2019; Gawronski & Strack, 2012; C. Harmon-Jones & Harmon-Jones, 2018; E. Harmon-Jones et al., 2009). A point of particular importance to refine is how arousal, generated by prediction error, receives its affective valence (e.g., Kruglanski et al., 2018).

Mrsic-Flogel, 2018; Pezzulo et al., 2015) to the drastic variability observed in the moral behavior of individuals. That is, by virtue of each individual's different developmental environment and social relationships, they will have formed a unique internal model of their own global social environment. That is, sets of social maxims might differ across cultures and the individuals within them. It is not surprising, then, that individuals drastically differ in what they do, or do not, feel obligated to do. This variability is missed when moral motivation is grounded in innate "moral intuitions" (Haidt, 2001; Haidt & Joseph, 2011). The present account—where moral motivation stems from model coherence—suggests that this individual variability can be captured by considering (a) how individuals uniquely construct their internal model through personal experience and (b) how interoceptive information about the body is received and experienced as affect by the brain. Both nature and nurture have a place—nature in how an individual's brain is wired to process interoception and affect, and nurture in how their internal model is constructed.

Behaviors that are exclusively morally motivated—behaviors with the sub-jective experience of a sense of should, selected over a conflicting normatively motivated behavior—might also be rare. Most often, both moral and normative motivations align and proscribe the same behavior (especially if someone is in the social environment that their internal model was trained in).[12] However, in cases where moral and normative motivation are opposed, choosing to seriously disrupt local norms to act purely on moral principle could be risky (e.g., consider Joan of Arc). This risk is especially salient if easier ways to maintain an internally consistent internal model are available (e.g., making an excuse to oneself to rationalize inconsistency, or removing oneself from the local social environment). For example, another student interviewed by Waldron et al. (2011) quit soccer after being hazed. This allowed him to maintain a consistent internal model by changing his environment, which in turn removed the source of the contradiction. However, the example also

---

[12]That moral and normative motivations frequently proscribe the same behaviors raises an interesting question about moral motivation and normative motivation when someone is culturally transplanted. If local expectations (i.e., norms) are unknown, then that individual will continue to disrupt their social environment through unintentional norm violations until they learn them. This is a case of that individual's behavior being guided by more general social predictions within their internal model (i.e., habits learned from their original culture), but we might hesitate to call this moral motivation. Moral motivation, then, might require that one both knows what is required by local norms, but chooses to violate them in favor of more global model coherence.

demonstrates that an opportunity may have existed for him to act out of pure moral obligation, as this chapter has defined it:

> On the soccer team, after the first game all of the freshmen had to be at one of the guy's houses. . . . So, I wanted to go and prove that I belonged. Once there, they made the freshmen take eight shots. . . . I was pretty sheltered, went to a Catholic grade school and junior high, so I had never had alcohol in my life. . . . [W]e went along with it and one kid actually ended up going to the hospital 'cause he was so drunk. I ended up throwing up because I had never had alcohol before. . . . After I puked, I was embarrassed and angry. I was like, why am I here? This is stupid. *I really wanted to get them in trouble, but I wouldn't dare ever do that.* But I was really angry. That's pretty much what made me quit soccer at the end of the season. I didn't play after that 'cause I was really upset about how they went about stuff, how they initiated you. (Waldron et al., 2011, p. 118; emphasis added)

From the perspective of reputation, physical safety, or social stability, getting seniors in trouble could be potentially disastrous; yet, the student still felt motivated to do it. The account of moral motivation that this chapter developed attempts to explain how he might come to feel this way and provides a framework for assessing the contributions of biological and environmental factors in future work.

IMPLICATIONS FOR MORAL PSYCHOLOGY

This final section briefly revisits two major topics in moral psychology, which have shaped the research agenda of the last 2 decades: moral dumbfounding (Haidt, 2001) and moral foundations theory (Graham et al., 2009, 2011, 2013; Haidt & Graham, 2007; Haidt & Joseph, 2004, 2008, 2011). Using the account developed in this chapter, *moral dumbfounding* can be interpreted as a resistance to experimenter-based social pressure aimed at changing moral judgments that were reinforced as social maxims outside the lab. *Moral foundations theory* can be understood as a descriptive account of some general classes of emergent social maxims, but this description provides little insight into the fundamental mechanisms that produce these maxims. The processes that produce both normative and moral motivation are agnostic to the specific content of social norms and maxims, meaning that if universal patterns in moral judgment and motivation are identified (as in moral foundations theory), then the cause of those patterns cannot be assumed to be innate. Indeed, other work has demonstrated that social organizations can converge on similar normative standards without those standards being specified in advance (for a review, see Jebari, 2019).

232 • *Jordan E. Theriault*

Moral Dumbfounding Exerts Local Social Pressure for Logical Consistency in Opposition to a Globally Coherent Moral Understanding

Moral dumbfounding is one of the most well-known observations used to motivate social intuitionist theories of morality, where innately specified moral intuitions are thought to drive "automatic moral judgment" in response to "complex social stimuli" (Haidt, 2001, p. 819). The classic example describes Mark and Julie, a brother and sister who secretly commit incest, use multiple forms of birth control, and both subsequently agree that they enjoyed the experience, that it brought them closer, and that they will keep it secret (Haidt, 2001; Haidt et al., 2000). After participants were told this story, they were asked to make a moral judgment, and most said that incest was morally wrong. But every reason a participant could give for why incest is wrong was ruled out in the example. Incest could create birth defects, but they used birth control. Incest could cause emotional harm, but it did not. Others could find out and ostracize them, but they kept it a secret. Eventually, participants gave up but continued to insist that incest is wrong, and they just could not explain why. Participant reactions to this incest example were taken as evidence against rationalist approaches to morality (e.g., Kohlberg, 1971), where moral judgments are "reached primarily by a process of reason and reflection" (Haidt, 2001, p. 814; but see Jebari, 2019).

However, in the description above, the same stimulus–response logic (or "feature-detection" logic; Keller & Mrsic-Flogel, 2018) criticized in the Background section is on clear display. People give a negative moral judgment, but they cannot identify a reason for it; therefore, it is concluded that some feature of the stimulus (e.g., descriptions of incest) triggers an evaluative moral intuition. The leap from a morally relevant social stimuli to an evaluative outcome obscures the mechanistic steps that intervene between the two; or in other words, moral intuitions do not provide any explanation of how moral motivation actually works. This chapter proposed an alternative: (a) that affect and interoception, combined with a predictive brain in a social environment, can produce a subjective sense of should, (b) that this sense of should can motivate individuals to conform to expectations in the local social environment (normative motivation), and (c) that in some cases this sense of should can motivate individuals to behave in ways that are consistent with social maxims learned from general expectations within the global social environment. Normative and moral motivations are often aligned, but when in opposition, an adherence to moral motivation could explain striking instances of morally motivated nonconformity.

From this perspective, then, an alternative explanation could account for moral dumbfounding: In their prior experience, people have developed an internal model of their global social environment, which includes predictions that incest is immoral, that it will bring about negative consequences, and perhaps most important, that they should judge that incest is wrong. Thus, when a participant is presented with an unusual case of safe, consensual, consequence-free incest, they may maintain their social maxim to insist that the incest is wrong even when pressured to be logically consistent by the experimenter. Indeed, rather than jettison this social maxim to accommodate one exception, the participant can ignore the contradiction ("It's just wrong, and I can't explain why") or just wait for the experiment to end, at which point the social pressure from the experimenter is removed. In a sense, then, moral dumbfounding is an interesting case where people actually defend their answer out of moral motivation, as this chapter has defined it. A social maxim to condemn incest was previously learned, and social pressure is exerted in opposition from the experimenter (to logically justify their moral judgment). In upholding the social maxim to condemn incest, participants feel social pressure (i.e., a sense of should) and act in opposition to it—meaning that one interpretation of this work is that participants are not "morally dumbfounded" but are actually upholding their condemnation of incest out of moral principle.

Moral Foundations Theory May Provide a Taxonomy of Probable Social Maxims

Moral foundations theory is an elaboration on social intuitionist models and suggests that several kinds of social stimuli can trigger the social intuitions underlying moral judgment (Graham et al., 2009, 2011, 2013; Haidt & Graham, 2007; Haidt & Joseph, 2004, 2008, 2011). The most widely embraced set of moral foundations includes foundations related to harm/care, fairness/reciprocity, ingroup/loyalty, authority/respect, and purity/sanctity. These foundations are embraced differently by political liberals and conservatives (Graham et al., 2009). Other subtly different taxonomies have been provided as well, for example, separating proscriptive and prescriptive moral motives for the self, other individuals, and the social group (Janoff-Bulman & Carnes, 2013).

There is extensive evidence that moral concepts can be roughly broken down into this taxonomy (Graham et al., 2011), but the present account of moral motivation offers an alternative explanation of the underlying mechanism. Rather than tapping innate intuitions and their modification by culture, moral foundations theory may provide a taxonomy of social maxims that are likely to emerge as a consequence of the social structures in which people are embedded (see Jebari, 2019). The example of harm was worked out earlier, but even then, it was shown that a single social maxim against harm is unlikely to avoid contradictions across all social contexts. Contradictions between social maxims, and the model corrections that they necessitate, do not occur at random—meaning that the internal model within each person as it develops over time will increasingly reflect structural regularities in their social environment. The structure of each individual's internal model is not predetermined, but it will be biased to reflect the social environment within which they grew up. In turn, that social environment will be biased to have certain structural properties in its social organization, given that some forms of social organization persist and others collapse (Henrich, 2015; Muthukrishna et al., 2014). Indeed, it has been argued that this moral structuralism, where certain forms of social organization are objectively more likely to occur than others, is the most coherent way to interpret the original project of moral rationalism (see Jebari, 2019).[13]

However, regardless of what social organizations emerge, the present account suggests that processes responsible for both normative and moral motivation are agnostic to the specific content of norms and social maxims (as opposed to accounts centered on moral intuition; Graham et al., 2013; Haidt, 2001, 2012; Haidt & Joseph, 2004, 2008). That is, widespread social expectations are self-reinforcing parts of social reality even if they are arbitrary (Berger & Luckmann, 1966/2011; Hacking, 1986; Searle, 1995), and these expectations motivate us through interacting processes in our brains and bodies. Thus, on the one hand, the expectations in the social environment exert a real motivational force on individuals. However, on the other hand, our individual biology contains very few innate specifications that would stop us from collectively changing social reality.

CONCLUSION

Defining moral cognition remains a difficult problem, and the problem has been exacerbated by disagreements among moral psychologists on what constitutes the moral cognition they want to study. For example, on different

---

[13]Put briefly, moral psychologists and empirical moral philosophers interested in social intuitionist theories have interpreted rationalist accounts to be concerned with the use of "reflective or deliberative reasoning . . . contrasted with the exercise of affective or intuitive capacities" (Jebari, 2019, p. 2432). In reality, rationalist accounts are concerned with finding objective moral principles without reifying them, such as objective properties of how social networks are organized, and the behavioral requirements placed on individuals if that network is to be maintained (Jebari, 2019).

accounts, moral cognition is grounded in development (Kohlberg, 1971), relational commitments (Fiske & Rai, 2015), a universal agent/patient template of harm (Gray et al., 2012), innate emotional intuitions (Haidt, 2001), or the elaboration of these intuitions by culture into distinct domains (e.g., individualizing vs. binding foundations; Graham et al., 2009). This chapter aimed to describe moral motivation, and in doing so, it separated the culturally and historically contingent moral content (e.g., harm aversion, ingroup preferences) from more general and universal biological and social processes whose interactions make moral psychology possible. This use of the term *moral* may not have satisfied all readers, but the strategy taken here was to identify a recognizable subjective experience (i.e., a sense of should), explain it from simple principles of embodied motivation and predictive cortical organization, and show how it could motivate morally principled nonconformity. To this end, I proposed that the brain constructs an internal model of the social environment it occupies and that violating global social expectations in that social environment (i.e., social maxims) would threaten to disrupt an individual's equilibrium with their social environment, forcing them to revise their internal model of the world to accommodate the change. Future work should elaborate on the metabolic costs of model construction and reorganization, but the present work was intended to show that a rich account of moral motivation can be developed from simple biological premises. Of particular promise, this account of moral motivation builds on a general account of normative motivation (Theriault et al., 2021a, 2021b), which explains how people's expectations, regardless of any explicit intention to enforce compliance with them, generate social rules for behavior. Thus, from biological principles, psychologists can start to build an explanation of not only moral motivation, but also the rich web of norms that structure social reality.

REFERENCES

Allen, M., & Tsakiris, M. (2018). The body as first prior: Interoceptive predictive processing and the primacy of self-models. In M. Tsakiris & H. De Preester (Eds.), *The interoceptive mind: From homeostasis to awareness* (pp. 27–45). Oxford University Press.

Asch, S. (1962). *Social psychology* (7th ed.). Prentice-Hall. (Original work published 1952)

Atran, S. (2010). *Talking to the enemy: Faith, brotherhood, and the (un)making of terrorists* (Reprint edition). HarperCollins e-books.

Attwell, D., & Laughlin, S. B. (2001). An energy budget for signaling in the grey matter of the brain. *Journal of Cerebral Blood Flow and Metabolism*, *21*(10), 1133–1145. https://doi.org/10.1097/00004647-200110000-00001

Barrett, L. F. (2006). Valence is a basic building block of emotional life. *Journal of Research in Personality*, *40*(1), 35–55. https://doi.org/10.1016/j.jrp.2005.08.006

Barrett, L. F. (2017a). *How emotions are made: The secret life of the brain*. Pan Macmillan.

Barrett, L. F. (2017b). The theory of constructed emotion: An active inference account of interoception and categorization. *Social Cognitive and Affective Neuroscience, 12*(1), 1–23. https://doi.org/10.1093/scan/nsx060

Barrett, L. F., & Bliss-Moreau, E. (2009). Affect as a psychological primitive. *Advances in Experimental Social Psychology 41*, 167–218. https://doi.org/10.1016/S0065-2601(08)00404-8

Barrett, L. F., & Finlay, B. L. (2018). Concepts, goals and the control of survival-related behaviors. *Current Opinion in Behavioral Sciences, 24*, 172–179. https://doi.org/10.1016/j.cobeha.2018.10.001

Barrett, L. F., & Simmons, W. K. (2015). Interoceptive predictions in the brain. *Nature Reviews Neuroscience, 16*(7), 419–429. https://doi.org/10.1038/nrn3950

Barsalou, L. W. (1999). Perceptual symbol systems. *Behavioral and Brain Sciences, 22*(4), 577–660. https://doi.org/10.1017/S0140525X99002149

Barsalou, L. W., & Sewell, D. R. (1984). *Constructing representations of categories from different points of view* (Technical Report No. 2; Emory Cognition Project). Emory University.

Berger, P. L., & Luckmann, T. (2011). *The social construction of reality: A treatise in the sociology of knowledge*. Open Road Media. (Original work published 1966)

Bicchieri, C. (2006). *The grammar of society: The nature and dynamics of social norms*. Cambridge University Press.

Blair, J., Marsh, A. A., Finger, E., Blair, K. S., & Luo, J. (2006). Neuro-cognitive systems involved in morality. *Philosophical Explorations, 9*(1), 13–27. https://doi.org/10.1080/13869790500492359

Blair, R. J. R. (1995). A cognitive developmental approach to mortality: Investigating the psychopath. *Cognition, 57*(1), 1–29. https://doi.org/10.1016/0010-0277(95)00676-P

Blake, P. R., McAuliffe, K., Corbit, J., Callaghan, T. C., Barry, O., Bowie, A., Kleutsch, L., Kramer, K. L., Ross, E., Vongsachang, H., Wrangham, R., & Warneken, F. (2015). The ontogeny of fairness in seven societies. *Nature, 528*(7581), 258–261. https://doi.org/10.1038/nature15703

Cameron, C. D., Lindquist, K. A., & Gray, K. (2015). A constructionist review of morality and emotions: No evidence for specific links between moral content and discrete emotions. *Personality and Social Psychology Review, 19*(4), 371–394. https://doi.org/10.1177/1088868314566683

Catania, K. C. (2009). Tentacled snakes turn C-starts to their advantage and predict future prey behavior. *Proceedings of the National Academy of Sciences of the United States of America, 106*(27), 11183–11187. https://doi.org/10.1073/pnas.0905183106

Chalmers, D. J. (1995). Facing up to the problem of consciousness. *Journal of Consciousness Studies, 2*(3), 200–219.

Chanes, L., & Barrett, L. F. (2016). Redefining the role of limbic areas in cortical processing. *Trends in Cognitive Sciences, 20*(2), 96–106. https://doi.org/10.1016/j.tics.2015.11.005

Churchland, P. S. (1996). The Hornswoggle problem. *Journal of Consciousness Studies, 3*(5–6), 402–408.

Cialdini, R. B., Reno, R. R., & Kalgren, C. A. (1990). A focus theory of normative conduct: Recycling the concept of norms to reduce littering in public places. *Journal of Personality and Social Psychology, 58*(6), 1015–1026. https://doi.org/10.1037/0022-3514.58.6.1015

Cisek, P. (1999). Beyond the computer metaphor: Behavior as interaction. *Journal of Consciousness Studies, 6*(11–12), 125–142.

Cisek, P. (2019). Resynthesizing behavior through phylogenetic refinement. *Attention, Perception & Psychophysics, 81*(7), 2265–2287. https://doi.org/10.3758/s13414-019-01760-1

Clark, A. (2013). Whatever next? Predictive brains, situated agents, and the future of cognitive science. *Behavioral and Brain Sciences, 36*(3), 181–204. https://doi.org/10.1017/S0140525X12000477

Clark, A. (2015). *Surfing uncertainty: Prediction, action, and the embodied mind.* Oxford University Press.

Collins, R. (2008). *Violence: A micro-sociological theory.* Princeton University Press. https://doi.org/10.1515/9781400831753

Conant, R. C., & Ross Ashby, W. (1970). Every good regulator of a system must be a model of that system. *International Journal of Systems Science, 1*(2), 89–97. https://doi.org/10.1080/00207727008920220

Constant, A., Friston, K. J., & Ramstead, M. J. D. (2021). What kind of explanation is the constructing and coasting strategy? Comment on: "The sense of should: A biologically-based framework for modeling social pressure" by Jordan E. Theriault, Liane Young, and Lisa Feldman Barrett. *Physics of Life Reviews, 36*, 80–82. https://doi.org/10.1016/j.plrev.2020.06.003

Constant, A., Ramstead, M. J. D., Veissière, S. P. L., & Friston, K. (2019). Regimes of expectations: An active inference model of social conformity and human decision making. *Frontiers in Psychology, 10*, Article 679. https://doi.org/10.3389/fpsyg.2019.00679

Corlett, P. R. (2017). I predict, therefore I am: Perturbed predictive coding under ketamine and in schizophrenia. *Biological Psychiatry, 81*(6), 465–466. https://doi.org/10.1016/j.biopsych.2016.12.007

Craig, A. D. (2015). *How do you feel? An interoceptive moment with your neurobiological self.* Princeton University Press. https://doi.org/10.23943/princeton/9780691156767.001.0001

Critchley, H. D., Tang, J., Glaser, D., Butterworth, B., & Dolan, R. J. (2005). Anterior cingulate activity during error and autonomic response. *NeuroImage, 27*(4), 885–895. https://doi.org/10.1016/j.neuroimage.2005.05.047

Cushman, F., Gray, K., Gaffey, A., & Mendes, W. B. (2012). Simulating murder: The aversion to harmful action. *Emotion, 12*(1), 2–7. https://doi.org/10.1037/a0025071

Damasio, A. R. (1999). *The feeling of what happens: Body and emotion in the making of consciousness.* Houghton Mifflin Harcourt.

Darwin, C. (2001). *On the origin of species by means of natural selection, or the preservation of favoured races in the struggle for life* (J. Manis, Ed.). Penn State University's Electronic Classics. (Original work published 1859)

Dayan, P., & Yu, A. J. (2006). Phasic norepinephrine: A neural interrupt signal for unexpected events. *Network: Computation in Neural Systems, 17*(4), 335–350. https://doi.org/10.1080/09548980601004024

Denève, S., & Jardri, R. (2016). Circular inference: Mistaken belief, misplaced trust. *Current Opinion in Behavioral Sciences, 11*, 40–48. https://doi.org/10.1016/j.cobeha.2016.04.001

Dunn, T. W., Gebhardt, C., Naumann, E. A., Riegler, C., Ahrens, M. B., Engert, F., & Del Bene, F. (2016). Neural circuits underlying visually evoked escapes in larval zebrafish. *Neuron, 89*(3), 613–628. https://doi.org/10.1016/j.neuron.2015.12.021

Eaton, R. C., & Farley, R. D. (1975). Mauthner neuron field potential in newly hatched larvae of the zebra fish. *Journal of Neurophysiology, 38*(3), 502–512. https://doi.org/10.1152/jn.1975.38.3.502

Ekman, P. (1992). An argument for basic emotions. *Cognition and Emotion, 6*(3–4), 169–200. https://doi.org/10.1080/02699939208411068

Faisal, A. A., White, J. A., & Laughlin, S. B. (2005). Ion-channel noise places limits on the miniaturization of the brain's wiring. *Current Biology, 15*(12), 1143–1149. https://doi.org/10.1016/j.cub.2005.05.056

Fanselow, M. S. (2018). Emotion, motivation and function. *Current Opinion in Behavioral Sciences, 19*, 105–109. https://doi.org/10.1016/j.cobeha.2017.12.013

Feeney, E. J., Groman, S. M., Taylor, J. R., & Corlett, P. R. (2017). Explaining delusions: Reducing uncertainty through basic and computational neuroscience. *Schizophrenia Bulletin, 43*(2), 263–272. https://doi.org/10.1093/schbul/sbw194

Fehr, E., & Gächter, S. (2002). Altruistic punishment in humans. *Nature, 415*(6868), 137–140. https://doi.org/10.1038/415137a

FeldmanHall, O., & Shenhav, A. (2019). Resolving uncertainty in a social world. *Nature Human Behaviour, 3*(5), 426–435. https://doi.org/10.1038/s41562-019-0590-x

Festinger, L. (1962). *A theory of cognitive dissonance.* Stanford University Press.

Fiske, A. P., & Rai, T. S. (2014). *Virtuous violence: Hurting and killing to create, sustain, end, and honor social relationships.* Cambridge University Press. https://doi.org/10.1017/CBO9781316104668

Fiske, A. P., & Tetlock, P. E. (1997). Taboo trade-offs: Reactions to transactions that transgress the spheres of justice. *Political Psychology, 18*(2), 255–297.

Fotopoulou, A. (2021). Mentalising allostasis: The sense that I should eat: Comment on "The sense of should: A biologically-based framework for modeling social pressure" by Jordan E. Theriault, Liane Young, and Lisa Feldman Barrett. *Physics of Life Reviews, 36*, 20–23. https://doi.org/10.1016/j.plrev.2020.09.002

Friston, K. (2010). The free-energy principle: A unified brain theory? *Nature Reviews Neuroscience, 11*(2), 127–138. https://doi.org/10.1038/nrn2787

Friston, K., FitzGerald, T., Rigoli, F., Schwartenbeck, P., O'Doherty, J., & Pezzulo, G. (2016). Active inference and learning. *Neuroscience and Biobehavioral Reviews, 68*, 862–879. https://doi.org/10.1016/j.neubiorev.2016.06.022

Friston, K., FitzGerald, T., Rigoli, F., Schwartenbeck, P., & Pezzulo, G. (2017). Active inference: A process theory. *Neural Computation, 29*(1), 1–49. https://doi.org/10.1162/NECO_a_00912

Gawronski, B., & Brannon, S. M. (2019). What is cognitive consistency, and why does it matter? In E. Harmon-Jones (Ed.), *Cognitive dissonance: Reexamining a pivotal theory in psychology* (2nd ed., pp. 91–116). American Psychological Association. https://doi.org/10.1037/0000135-005

Gawronski, B., & Strack, F. (2012). Cognitive consistency as a basic principle in social cognitive processing. In B. Gawronski & F. Strack (Eds.), *Cognitive consistency: A fundamental principle in social cognition* (pp. 1–16). Guilford Press.

Graham, J., Haidt, J., Koleva, S., Motyl, M., Iyer, R., Wojcik, S. P., & Ditto, P. H. (2013). Moral foundations theory: The pragmatic validity of moral pluralism. *Advances in*

Experimental Social Psychology, *47*, 55–130. https://doi.org/10.1016/B978-0-12-407236-7.00002-4

Graham, J., Haidt, J., & Nosek, B. A. (2009). Liberals and conservatives rely on different sets of moral foundations. *Journal of Personality and Social Psychology*, *96*(5), 1029–1046. https://doi.org/10.1037/a0015141

Graham, J., Nosek, B. A., Haidt, J., Iyer, R., Koleva, S., & Ditto, P. H. (2011). Mapping the moral domain. *Journal of Personality and Social Psychology*, *101*(2), 366–385. https://doi.org/10.1037/a0021847

Gray, K., Schein, C., & Ward, A. F. (2014). The myth of harmless wrongs in moral cognition: Automatic dyadic completion from sin to suffering. *Journal of Experimental Psychology: General*, *143*(4), 1600–1615. https://doi.org/10.1037/a0036149

Gray, K., & Wegner, D. M. (2011). Dimensions of moral emotions. *Emotion Review*, *3*(3), 258–260. https://doi.org/10.1177/1754073911402388

Gray, K., Young, L., & Waytz, A. (2012). Mind perception is the essence of morality. *Psychological Inquiry*, *23*(2), 101–124. https://doi.org/10.1080/1047840X.2012.651387

Greene, J. (2013). *Moral tribes: Emotion, reason, and the gap between us and them.* Penguin.

Hacking, I. (1986). Making up people. In T. C. Heller (Ed.), *Reconstructing individualism: Autonomy, individuality, and the self in Western thought* (pp. 222–236). Stanford University Press.

Haidt, J. (2001). The emotional dog and its rational tail: A social intuitionist approach to moral judgment. *Psychological Review*, *108*(4), 814–834. https://doi.org/10.1037/0033-295X.108.4.814

Haidt, J. (2012). *The righteous mind: Why good people are divided by politics and religion.* Penguin Books Limited.

Haidt, J., & Bjorklund, F. (2008). Social intuitionists answer six questions about moral psychology. In W. Sinnott-Armstrong (Ed.), *Moral psychology: Vol. 2. The cognitive science of morality: Intuition and diversity* (pp. 181–217). MIT Press.

Haidt, J., Björklund, F., & Murphy, S. (2000). *Moral dumbfounding: When intuition finds no reason* [Unpublished manuscript]. University of Virginia.

Haidt, J., & Graham, J. (2007). When morality opposes justice: Conservatives have moral intuitions that liberals may not recognize. *Social Justice Research*, *20*(1), 98–116. https://doi.org/10.1007/s11211-007-0034-z

Haidt, J., & Joseph, C. (2004). Intuitive ethics: How innately prepared intuitions generate culturally variable virtues. *Daedalus*, *133*(4), 55–66. https://doi.org/10.1162/0011526042365555

Haidt, J., & Joseph, C. (2008). The moral mind: How five sets of innate intuitions guide the development of many culture-specific virtues, and perhaps even modules. In *The innate mind: Vol. 3. Foundations and the future* (pp. 367–391). Oxford University Press.

Haidt, J., & Joseph, C. (2011). How moral foundations theory succeeded in building on sand: A response to Suhler and Churchland. *Journal of Cognitive Neuroscience*, *23*(9), 2117–2122. https://doi.org/10.1162/jocn.2011.21638

Hajcak, G., McDonald, N., & Simons, R. F. (2003). To err is autonomic: Error-related brain potentials, ANS activity, and post-error compensatory behavior. *Psychophysiology*, *40*(6), 895–903. https://doi.org/10.1111/1469-8986.00107

Harmon-Jones, C., & Harmon-Jones, E. (2018). Toward an increased understanding of dissonance processes: A response to the target article by Kruglanski et al. *Psychological Inquiry*, *29*(2), 74–81. https://doi.org/10.1080/1047840X.2018.1480691

Harmon-Jones, E., Amodio, D. M., & Harmon-Jones, C. (2009). Action-based model of dissonance: A review, integration, and expansion of conceptions of cognitive conflict. In M. P. Zanna (Ed.), *Advances in Experimental Social Psychology* (Vol. 41, pp. 119–166). Elsevier Academic Press.

Harris, J. J., & Attwell, D. (2012). The energetics of CNS white matter. *The Journal of Neuroscience*, *32*(1), 356–371. https://doi.org/10.1523/JNEUROSCI.3430-11.2012

Henrich, J. (2015). *The secret of our success: How culture is driving human evolution, domesticating our species, and making us smarter*. Princeton University Press. https://doi.org/10.2307/j.ctvc77f0d

Hohwy, J. (2013). *The predictive mind*. Oxford University Press. https://doi.org/10.1093/acprof:oso/9780199682737.001.0001

Hutchinson, J. B., & Barrett, L. F. (2019). The power of predictions: An emerging paradigm for psychological research. *Current Directions in Psychological Science*, *28*(3), 280–291. https://doi.org/10.1177/0963721419831992

Hyder, F., Rothman, D. L., & Bennett, M. R. (2013). Cortical energy demands of signaling and nonsignaling components in brain are conserved across mammalian species and activity levels. *Proceedings of the National Academy of Sciences of the United States of America*, *110*(9), 3549–3554. https://doi.org/10.1073/pnas.1214912110

James, W. (1931). *The principles of psychology: Vol. 1*. Holt. https://archive.org/details/theprinciplesofp01jameuoft (Original work published 1890)

Janoff-Bulman, R., & Carnes, N. C. (2013). Surveying the moral landscape: Moral motives and group-based moralities. *Personality and Social Psychology Review*, *17*(3), 219–236. https://doi.org/10.1177/1088868313480274

Jardri, R., Duverne, S., Litvinova, A. S., & Denève, S. (2017). Experimental evidence for circular inference in schizophrenia. *Nature Communications*, *8*(1), Article 14218. https://doi.org/10.1038/ncomms14218

Jebari, J. (2019). Empirical moral rationalism and the social constitution of normativity. *Philosophical Studies*, *176*(9), 2429–2453. https://doi.org/10.1007/s11098-018-1134-3

Jebari, J. (2021). Beyond the metabolic costs of prediction error: Comments on "The sense of should: A biologically-based framework for modeling social pressure" by Jordan E. Theriault, Liane Young, and Lisa Feldman Barrett. *Physics of Life Reviews*, *36*, 18–19. https://doi.org/10.1016/j.plrev.2020.11.001

Kant, I. (1998). *Groundwork of the metaphysics of morals* (M. Gregor, Ed.). Cambridge University Press. https://doi.org/10.1017/CBO9780511809590.004 (Original work published 1785)

Keller, G. B., & Mrsic-Flogel, T. D. (2018). Predictive processing: A canonical cortical computation. *Neuron*, *100*(2), 424–435. https://doi.org/10.1016/j.neuron.2018.10.003

Kelley, H. H. (1952). Two functions of reference groups. In G. E. Swanson, T. M. Newcomb, & E. L. Hartley (Eds.), *Readings in social psychology* (2nd ed., pp. 410–414). Holt, Rinehart & Winston.

Kohlberg, L. (1971). From is to ought: How to commit the naturalistic fallacy and get away with it in the study of moral development. In T. Mischel (Ed.), *Cognitive development and epistemology* (pp. 151–235). Academic Press. https://doi.org/10.1016/B978-0-12-498640-4.50011-1

Kruglanski, A. W., Jasko, K., Milyavsky, M., Chernikova, M., Webber, D., Pierro, A., & di Santo, D. (2018). Cognitive consistency theory in social psychology: A paradigm reconsidered. *Psychological Inquiry, 29*(2), 45–59. https://doi.org/10.1080/1047840X.2018.1480619

Kurzban, R., Burton-Chellew, M. N., & West, S. A. (2015). The evolution of altruism in humans. *Annual Review of Psychology, 66*(1), 575–599. https://doi.org/10.1146/annurev-psych-010814-015355

Lawson, R. P., Friston, K. J., & Rees, G. (2015). A more precise look at context in autism. *Proceedings of the National Academy of Sciences of the United States of America, 112*(38), Article E5226. https://doi.org/10.1073/pnas.1514212112

Lawson, R. P., Rees, G., & Friston, K. J. (2014). An aberrant precision account of autism. *Frontiers in Human Neuroscience, 8*, Article 302. https://doi.org/10.3389/fnhum.2014.00302

Lewontin, R. C. (2001). *The triple helix: Gene, organism, and environment.* Harvard University Press.

Lillywhite, H. B. (1988). Snakes, blood circulation and gravity. *Scientific American, 259*(6), 92–98. https://doi.org/10.1038/scientificamerican1288-92

Marx, K. (1992). *Capital: Vol. 1. A critique of political economy* (B. Fowkes, Trans.; Illustrated edition). Penguin Classics. (Original work published 1867)

McAuliffe, K., Blake, P. R., Steinbeis, N., & Warneken, F. (2017). The developmental foundations of human fairness. *Nature Human Behaviour, 1*(2), Article 0042. https://doi.org/10.1038/s41562-016-0042

Moscovici, S. (1976). *Social influence and social change.* Academic Press.

Munch-Jurisic, D. (2022). *Perpetrator disgust: The moral limits of gut feelings.* Oxford University Press.

Muthukrishna, M., Shulman, B. W., Vasilescu, V., & Henrich, J. (2014). Sociality influences cultural complexity. *Proceedings of the Royal Society B: Biological Sciences, 281*(1774), Article 20132511. https://doi.org/10.1098/rspb.2013.2511

Palmer, C. J., Lawson, R. P., & Hohwy, J. (2017). Bayesian approaches to autism: Towards volatility, action, and behavior. *Psychological Bulletin, 143*(5), 521–542. https://doi.org/10.1037/bul0000097

Paluck, E. L., Shepherd, H., & Aronow, P. M. (2016). Changing climates of conflict: A social network experiment in 56 schools. *Proceedings of the National Academy of Sciences of the United States of America, 113*(3), 566–571. https://doi.org/10.1073/pnas.1514483113

Panksepp, J. (1998). *Affective neuroscience: The foundations of human and animal emotions.* Oxford University Press.

Panksepp, J. (2011). The basic emotional circuits of mammalian brains: Do animals have affective lives? *Neuroscience and Biobehavioral Reviews, 35*(9), 1791–1804. https://doi.org/10.1016/j.neubiorev.2011.08.003

Pezzulo, G., Rigoli, F., & Friston, K. (2015). Active Inference, homeostatic regulation and adaptive behavioural control. *Progress in Neurobiology, 134*, 17–35. https://doi.org/10.1016/j.pneurobio.2015.09.001

Quine, W. V., & Ullian, J. S. (1978). *The web of belief* (2nd ed.). McGraw-Hill.

Rai, T. S. (2021). Toward a moral psychology untethered from long-term cooperation: Comment on "The sense of should: A biologically-based framework for modeling social pressure" by Jordan E. Theriault, Liane Young, and Lisa Feldman Barrett. *Physics of Life Reviews, 36,* 7–8. https://doi.org/10.1016/j.plrev.2020.12.002

Rai, T. S., & Fiske, A. P. (2011). Moral psychology is relationship regulation: Moral motives for unity, hierarchy, equality, and proportionality. *Psychological Review, 118*(1), 57–75. https://doi.org/10.1037/a0021867

Ramaswami, M. (2014). Network plasticity in adaptive filtering and behavioral habituation. *Neuron, 82*(6), 1216–1229. https://doi.org/10.1016/j.neuron.2014.04.035

Rao, R. P. N., & Ballard, D. H. (1999). Predictive coding in the visual cortex: A functional interpretation of some extra-classical receptive-field effects. *Nature Neuroscience, 2*(1), 79–87. https://doi.org/10.1038/4580

Reber, R., & Norenzayan, A. (2018). Shared fluency theory of social cohesiveness: How the metacognitive feeling of processing fluency contributes to group processes. In J. Proust & M. Fortier (Eds.), *Metacognitive diversity: An interdisciplinary approach* (pp. 47–67). Oxford University Press.

Ross Ashby, W. (1960). *Design for a brain: The origin of adaptive behavior.* Chapman & Hall.

Russell, J. A. (2003). Core affect and the psychological construction of emotion. *Psychological Review, 110*(1), 145–172. https://doi.org/10.1037/0033-295X.110.1.145

Russell, J. A., & Barrett, L. F. (1999). Core affect, prototypical emotional episodes, and other things called emotion: Dissecting the elephant. *Journal of Personality and Social Psychology, 76*(5), 805–819. https://doi.org/10.1037/0022-3514.76.5.805

Searle, J. R. (1995). *The construction of social reality.* The Free Press.

Sengupta, B., Stemmler, M. B., & Friston, K. J. (2013). Information and efficiency in the nervous system—A synthesis. *PLoS Computational Biology, 9*(7), Article e1003157. https://doi.org/10.1371/journal.pcbi.1003157

Sengupta, B., Stemmler, M., Laughlin, S. B., & Niven, J. E. (2010). Action potential energy efficiency varies among neuron types in vertebrates and invertebrates. *PLOS Computational Biology, 6*(7), Article e1000840. https://doi.org/10.1371/journal.pcbi.1000840

Sennesh, E., Theriault, J., Brooks, D., van de Meent, J.-W., Barrett, L. F., & Quigley, K. S. (2022). Interoception as modeling, allostasis as control. *Biological Psychology, 167,* Article 108242. https://doi.org/10.1016/j.biopsycho.2021.108242

Seth, A. K. (2013). Interoceptive inference, emotion, and the embodied self. *Trends in Cognitive Sciences, 17*(11), 565–573. https://doi.org/10.1016/j.tics.2013.09.007

Seth, A. K. (2015). The cybernetic Bayesian brain: From interoceptive inference to sensorimotor contingencies. In T. Metzinger & J. M. Windt (Eds.), *Open MIND* (pp. 1–24). MIND Group. https://doi.org/10.15502/9783958570108

Shadmehr, R., Smith, M. A., & Krakauer, J. W. (2010). Error correction, sensory prediction, and adaptation in motor control. *Annual Review of Neuroscience, 33*(1), 89–108. https://doi.org/10.1146/annurev-neuro-060909-153135

Shannon, C., & Weaver, W. (1964). *The mathematical theory of communication* (10th ed.). The University of Illinois Press. (Original work published 1949)

Singer, P. (1999, September 5). The Singer solution to world poverty. *The New York Times.* https://www.nytimes.com/1999/09/05/magazine/the-singer-solution-to-world-poverty.html

Skinner, B. F. (1990). *B.F. Skinner at the APA Annual Convention (8/10/1990)* [Video]. YouTube. https://www.youtube.com/watch?v=Bf-GKbcSFNo

Smith, A. (2010). *The theory of moral sentiments* (R. P. Hanley, Ed.). Penguin Classics. (Original work published 1790)

Spruit, I. M., Wilderjans, T. F., & van Steenbergen, H. (2018). Heart work after errors: Behavioral adjustment following error commission involves cardiac effort. *Cognitive, Affective & Behavioral Neuroscience, 18*(2), 375–388. https://doi.org/10.3758/s13415-018-0576-6

Staub, E. (1992). *The roots of evil: The origins of genocide and other group violence* (Rev. ed.). Cambridge University Press.

Sterling, P. (2012). Allostasis: A model of predictive regulation. *Physiology & Behavior, 106*(1), 5–15. https://doi.org/10.1016/j.physbeh.2011.06.004

Sterling, P., & Laughlin, S. (2015). *Principles of neural design.* MIT Press.

Suhler, C. L., & Churchland, P. (2011). Can innate, modular "foundations" explain morality? Challenges for Haidt's moral foundations theory. *Journal of Cognitive Neuroscience, 23*(9), 2103–2116. https://doi.org/10.1162/jocn.2011.21637

Tetlock, P. E. (2003). Thinking the unthinkable: Sacred values and taboo cognitions. *Trends in Cognitive Sciences, 7*(7), 320–324. https://doi.org/10.1016/S1364-6613(03)00135-9

Theriault, J. E., Shaffer, C., Dienel, G. A., Sander, C. Y., Hooker, J. M., Dickerson, B. C., Barrett, L. F., & Quigley, K. S. (2022). *Aerobic glycolysis, the efficiency tradeoff hypothesis, and the biological basis of neuroimaging: A solution to a metabolic mystery at the heart of neuroscience.* https://doi.org/10.31234/osf.io/pkzr8

Theriault, J. E., Young, L., & Barrett, L. F. (2021a). The sense of should: A biologically-based framework for modeling social pressure. *Physics of Life Reviews, 36*, 100–136. https://doi.org/10.1016/j.plrev.2020.01.004

Theriault, J. E., Young, L., & Barrett, L. F. (2021b). *Situating and extending the sense of should. Reply to comments on "The sense of should: A biologically based framework for modeling social pressure."* PsyArXiv. https://doi.org/10.31234/osf.io/yfdb7

Toelch, U., & Dolan, R. J. (2015). Informational and normative influences in conformity from a neurocomputational perspective. *Trends in Cognitive Sciences, 19*(10), 579–589. https://doi.org/10.1016/j.tics.2015.07.007

Tsakiris, M. (2021). How should the political animals of the 21st century feel?: Comment on "The sense of should: A biologically-based framework for modelling social pressure" by J. E. Theriault et al. *Physics of Life Reviews, 36*, 77–79. https://doi.org/10.1016/j.plrev.2020.06.008

Tummolini, L., & Pezzulo, G. (2021). The epistemic value of conformity: Comment on "The sense of should: A biologically-based framework for modeling social pressure" by Jordan E. Theriault, Liane Young, and Lisa Feldman Barrett. *Physics of Life Reviews, 36*, 74–76. https://doi.org/10.1016/j.plrev.2020.06.010

Van de Cruys, S., Evers, K., Van der Hallen, R., Van Eylen, L., Boets, B., de-Wit, L., & Wagemans, J. (2014). Precise minds in uncertain worlds: Predictive coding in autism. *Psychological Review, 121*(4), 649–675. https://doi.org/10.1037/a0037665

Varela, F. J. (1996). Neurophenomenology: A methodological remedy for the hard problem. *Journal of Consciousness Studies, 3*(4), 330–349.

Volkmann, D., & Baluška, F. (2006). Gravity: One of the driving forces for evolution. *Protoplasma, 229*(2–4), 143–148. https://doi.org/10.1007/s00709-006-0200-4

Waldron, J. J., Lynn, Q., & Krane, V. (2011). Duct tape, Icy Hot and paddles: Narratives of initiation onto US male sport teams. *Sport, Education and Society, 16*(1), 111–125. https://doi.org/10.1080/13573322.2011.531965

Waller, J. E. (2007). *Becoming evil: How ordinary people commit genocide and mass killing*. Oxford University Press.

Wundt, W. (1896). *Outlines of psychology* (C. H. Judd, Trans.). Gustav E. Stechert.

Yeh, W., & Barsalou, L. W. (2006). The situated nature of concepts. *The American Journal of Psychology, 119*(3), 349–384. https://doi.org/10.2307/20445349

Yu, Y., Herman, P., Rothman, D. L., Agarwal, D., & Hyder, F. (2018). Evaluating the gray and white matter energy budgets of human brain function. *Journal of Cerebral Blood Flow and Metabolism, 38*(8), 1339–1353. https://doi.org/10.1177/0271678X17708691

Zénon, A., Solopchuk, O., & Pezzulo, G. (2019). An information-theoretic perspective on the costs of cognition. *Neuropsychologia, 123*, 5–18. https://doi.org/10.1016/j.neuropsychologia.2018.09.013

CONCLUSION

Emerging Themes and Avenues for Future Work

KRISTIN LAURIN AND IREIN ANN THOMAS

This volume showcases attempts to answer different questions about moral motivation using different levels of analysis. In this conclusion, we summarize the major takeaways from the preceding chapters. We also highlight the various assumptions the individual chapters make, implicitly or explicitly, about the nature of morality, about how moral motivations relate to other kinds of motivations, and about the most appropriate ways of assessing these motivations. Finally, we draw out the chapters' collective implications for the kinds of work that would best advance the field.

SUMMARY OF KEY TAKEAWAYS

To help jog readers' memories, in case they have not read the preceding pages in recent days or weeks, the first three chapters collectively emphasize the importance of norms in determining moral motivations and the importance of understanding morality by examining concrete situations rather than abstract principles. Chapter 1 (Hitlin) portrays moral motivation as a consequence

https://doi.org/10.1037/0000342-010
Motivation and Morality: A Multidisciplinary Approach, M. K. Berg and E. C. Chang (Editors)

of the desire to fit into one's local social environment. Chapter 2 (Malle) also emphasizes the importance of people's perceptions of the expectations of their local environment but goes further to describe how individuals and societies operate to ensure that moral motivations translate into corresponding behavior. Chapter 3 (Miller and Engelbrecht) points out that cultures sometimes hold drastically different moral expectations or norms and provides examples that illustrate the danger of trying to abstract those differences into overarching similarities.

The next two chapters together delve into the guiding principles that can motivate individual moral decision making. Chapter 4 (Gawronski et al.) argues for three such principles—a desire to comply with moral norms, but also a desire to maximize universal positive outcomes and a preference for action versus inaction—and provides an elegant method for identifying individual differences in these three drivers; the authors go on to use its tripartite model to account for findings in the existing literature. Chapter 5 (Snow) adds an alternative principle to the mix: In addition to doing the right thing out of a sense of duty to norms, a desire to maximize outcomes, or a proclivity for (in)action, a person can do the right thing because of their pure motivation to be virtuous.

The final three chapters offer perspectives on how we (fail to) learn to act morally. Chapter 6 (FeldmanHall and Lamba) develops a Bayesian account of social learning that can be applied to the learning of moral norms; this account explains how, with sufficient learning, we can maintain our understanding of these norms in spite of occasional violations while retaining the flexibility to recognize the need to learn anew if norms fundamentally shift. Chapter 7 (Tarsha and Narvaez) highlights one set of constraints on the kinds of norms we can learn, arguing that when a person's early developmental needs are not met they learn to look out for Number 1: to prioritize their own needs over those of others. Chapter 8 (Theriault) elaborates further on one mechanism of social learning, arguing that, on an evolutionary biological level, our motivation to act morally is really a motivation to avoid violating others' expectations so that we do not trigger them into unpredictable behavior.

THREE EMERGING THEMES

The preceding summary offers a narrative for how this volume's chapters fit together if one organizes them around the concepts of norms, expectations, local environments, and social learning. At the same time, together they offer conflicting answers to three important questions about morality and moral motivation.

Question 1: Is Morality Universal or Culturally Determined?

Is there is a universally true definition of what is moral? Or is morality relative, such that each culture, or even subculture, creates its own equally legitimate rules for moral behavior? From a psychological point of view, the answer to this philosophical question (e.g., Gowans, 2021) determines what behaviors researchers study when they want to understand morality and the cognitive processes that underlie it: Do we all have to study cooperation and altruism (or whatever behaviors are deemed moral across time and geography)? Or can we also study how and when, for example, people follow culturally specific rules about processing meat before eating it? Although few contemporary scholars would deny the existence of some cultural variation in what counts as moral, the chapters in this volume imply different limits on that variation.

Implied Universalism

At least three chapters in this volume assume, at least implicitly, a common or universal morality, typically one that emphasizes care and concern for other people. Gawronski and colleagues' mathematical method for mapping individual differences in concern with following moral norms versus with maximizing overall consequences takes for granted what the moral norms are—for example, it assumes that when people say they would prevent the use of torture to acquire information, or that they would not help another person end their life, they are demonstrating a sensitivity to moral norms. It only makes sense to bake the specific norms into the method if one assumes those norms are at least relatively universal. If one instead took the perspective that there are cultures (and subcultures) in which torture and suicide are not considered immoral, it becomes apparent that the model would mistake that cultural variation in norm content for cultural variation in sensitivity to norms.

Similarly, although Snow's concepts of virtue and vice could in principle flexibly refer to different traits and behaviors from culture to culture, her chapter implies they are a universal given. For example, she gives a prototypical example of the vicious individual as a racist authoritarian. Moreover, she dismisses the possibility that such individuals could operate as moral exemplars, even if their entire community admires them, because their traits and behaviors disqualify them from the label "moral." These views imply that morality (or at least virtue) has a certain universal meaning, one that by definition cannot include racism or authoritarianism.

Finally, Tarsha and Narvaez's work on the long-term effects of experiences in early development also implies (though rather indirectly) universalist assumptions. To make sense of their chapter's place in a book on morality, one has to assume that their key measures of social engagement and relational attunement are unquestionably facets of morality. The implication is again that morality must always revolve around care and concern for other people.

Explicit Cultural Relativism

Other chapters instead ascribe a central role to culture in shaping what counts as morality. Most obviously, take Miller and Engelbrecht's chapter on cultural norms. They criticize ideas like moral foundations theory (Graham et al., 2013)—a theory whose goal is to explain variation in how people conceive of morality—for not going far enough, for reducing culture to being able only to influence a universal moral template. Miller and Engelbrecht argue that instead cultural differences should be understood in more deep and fundamental terms. For example, when Orthodox Hindu participants identify theft as wrong because of potential spiritual consequences, their choices should be seen not as an example of the universal harm/care foundation but rather as a completely different ethic derived from values about divinity.

At least two other chapters also highlight the importance of cultural variation. Malle argues that two important forces that guide our motivation toward (moral) behaviors are (a) the particular society in question and (b) the context in which a behavior takes place. Under this perspective, the same behavior may or may not be moral depending on the context and the society, and the same cognitive processes may drive radically different behaviors, depending on those around us. This view is echoed in Hitlin's sociological perspective, which conceptualizes individuals as embedded in a variety of contexts that influence their actions, with factors like culture, race, gender, socioeconomic status, and so forth, all contributing to determine what counts as moral.

These latter two chapters (i.e., Chapters 1 and 2), although they place a certain emphasis on cultural variation, are less insistent than Miller and Engelbrecht that nothing about morality is universal. Although they do not articulate this position in detail, both might, like the moral foundations theory we referenced earlier, be compatible with the view that certain universal principles adapt to different cultural environments to produce surface-level differences that nonetheless reflect deeper moral agreement.

Moving Forward

Scholars' assumptions about universality versus cultural relativity often go unspoken but frequently leak through in their approaches. To us, it seems unlikely that we will ever reach a consensus on this issue. On the one hand, this is a shame, because a consensus might help the field establish its boundaries: Should the study of morality and moral motivation focus on specific behaviors that the academy, and presumably the world, agrees are moral, or should it be the study of whatever behaviors and motivations a particular actor considers to be moral?

On the other hand, although the question of universality is philosophically interesting, it may be possible to make considerable advances without answering it. The chapters by FeldmanHall and Lamba (Bayesian learning and updating of social norms) and by Theriault (on evolutionary biological tuning to what others expect) describe learning processes driven by other people's reactions. Although these chapters' models do not formalize assumptions about whether these reactions are likely to differ culturally, this could presumably be built in. In turn, this could help generate important insights, for instance, what happens when a person leaves one moral community for another.

Question 2: What Is Motivation, and How Does Moral Motivation Relate to the Self's Other Motivations?

The chapters in this volume have different ways of conceiving of what motivation is, and of the relationship between moral motivations and the other motivations people experience, as well as of the interests that moral motivations ultimately serve.

In terms of defining motivations, consider the following dimensions. First, motivations may be defined by what people articulate as the reasons for their behavior or by the variables that researchers observe to be the actual drivers of people's behavior. Second, motivations can be considered at the level of the individual, as a property of a person's mind, or as embedded within that person's social and cultural environments. Some chapters portray motivations as being absorbed from the social environment and as outside of people's ability to articulate. Malle's ideas around the internalization of norms and Hitlin's sociological chapter are examples of these. Other chapters portray motivations as inherent to the individual but similarly difficult to articulate. Gawronski et al.'s method infers an individual person's latent motivations from their observed behavior, without relying on their self-reports and without regard to their social environment (although of course researchers can and have used his method to identify differences between cultural groups). The three chapters on social learning (Chapters 6–8) in some ways combine the cultural versus individual locus of motivations: On the one hand, all three are grounded in the idea that evolution confers on each individual certain motivations that help them survive (e.g., the motivation to reduce prediction error); on the other hand, those learning motivations inherent to each individual can teach them to adopt specific culturally or situationally appropriate motivations. The two remaining chapters, 3 and 5, are unique in implying that we might be interested in what people say motivates them. Beyond this point of commonality, these chapters differ rather dramatically. Miller and Engelbrecht describe a person's motivations as embedded in their culture context and emphasize that self-reported motivations may have no bearing on what actually motivates behavior and thus may be best interpreted as a reflection of the cultural context. Snow describes virtuous motivation as the property of an individual and seems to require that a truly virtuous motivation both accurately describe what drives a person's behavior and be evident in that person's self-reports.

Turning away from motivation broadly to moral motivation specifically, we first note that perhaps the most extreme position in this volume is one that Snow attributes to Aristotle: According to this Greek philosopher, if one is motivated to act morally for any reason other than morality's sake—for instance, if you help carry a neighbor's groceries because you want her to like you, or even because you want to feel like a good person—the action does not count as moral. Luckily, Snow rejects this position, which in our view would entail that more or less no humans have ever behaved morally. However, even if we accept that motivations to act morally often serve a superordinate function, there is a range of views on what this superordinate motive might be and on how conscious people are of it.

What Function Does Moral Action Serve?
One approach could try to explain morality through genetically evolved mechanisms. Under this approach, moral behavior would ultimately help individuals survive and reproduce. Theriault illustrates this approach well, arguing that we are driven to behave morally because we can more accurately predict others' responses to moral rather than immoral behavior. In turn, this spares us the metabolic costs of having to update our prediction models.

Several other authors in this volume also imply that there is some benefit to individuals to act morally, though few explicitly identify this benefit as an evolutionary one. For example, Malle's chapter, on social pressures, makes the case that people may act morally to avoid others' censure, and Tarsha and Narvaez's chapter, on early developmental experiences, makes the case that people may act *im*morally to protect themselves in an environment they perceive as hostile.

An alternative approach not represented in this volume would explain morality through culturally evolved mechanisms. Cultural evolution occurs when a cultural practice helps a society survive and grow and, as a result, becomes more widespread in the environment. One example of a cultural evolutionary perspective on moral behavior is Norenzayan and colleagues' (2016) theory of religion, which argues that societies need mechanisms that ensure members are honest and cooperative with each other if they are to grow beyond a few hundred members without imploding. This and other cultural evolutionary arguments suggest that moral behavior—in this case, specifically, honesty and cooperation—ultimately serves to benefit society.

How Distal Versus Proximate Are the Superordinate Motives That Morality Serves?

Couching moral motivations in evolutionary terms raises another question about superordinate motives: Even if moral behavior serves certain other functions—saving metabolic energy, helping one's society thrive, and so on—this may not be the most immediate driver of people's decisions about whether to act morally. This brings us to the distinction between distal and proximate motives (e.g., Scott-Phillips et al., 2011).

Proximate motives are the immediate causes of action of which people are often aware. As such, they are easy to intuit as the superordinate drivers of moral behavior. If you want to help your neighbor with her groceries because you want to befriend her, that is an example of a proximate motive. Indeed, wanting to feel like, or to appear to others as, a moral superstar can drive moral behavior: Hitlin's sociological perspective and Malle's model of the social drivers of moral motivation both explicitly note how seeking others' approval (or avoiding their censure) can motivate people to act morally. Snow's chapter on virtue also makes passing reference to this type of motivation.

The term *distal motives* refers to the ultimate and typically evolutionary functions that our actions serve. For example, if helping your neighbor with her groceries is likely to earn you a valuable ally to turn to in a crisis to increase your chances of survival, that survival is a distal motive. Although some people may at times be aware of their distal motives, there are many more times when they are not; as such, distal motives are interesting to psychologists because they can explain behavior in less obvious and intuitive ways. Clear illustrations of distal motives in this volume come from the chapters about learning. For example, FeldmanHall and Lamba argue that a person's moral motivation comes from a history of learning that moral behavior earns rewards. Thus, the distal motive is to accumulate rewards, even if one's subjective experience is that one desires to act morally out of pure altruism. Relatedly, Tarsha and Narvaez argue that immoral behavior comes from a need to protect oneself in a world where one cannot count on others to be sensitive and nurturing, making survival the distal motive. In Theriault's chapter, the distal motive for moral behavior is metabolic savings.

Defining What Counts as a Moral Motivation

Another question about the relationship between moral and other kinds of motives refers to how we define *moral motivation*. One simple definition is that it is any motivation toward a behavior that is moral. If helping your neighbor with her groceries is moral, then moral motivation could be simply your motivation to provide that help. This definition sidesteps the question of what behaviors are moral and whether this is universal or culturally determined; more relevant to this section, it also sidesteps the question of what other motives might be involved: It does not matter *why* you want to help your neighbor. With the possible exception of Snow, it is this definition under which authors in this volume generally operate.

But Snow at least indirectly raises the possibility that moral motivation could distinguish between the intrinsic desire to behave morally and extrinsic desires to behave morally in order to achieve another outcome. As we have noted, we find it unlikely that there exists a purely intrinsic moral motivation, completely separate from all other distal and proximal motives. However, it might nonetheless be possible to draw a distinction, for example, based on the motives of which people are aware. In that case, your motivation to help your neighbor carry her groceries would be moral if you experience it as purely altruistic (even if it arises from your distally motivated reinforcement learning), but not if you are aware that you are motivated to secure her gratitude or indebtedness.

Question 3: How Can We Assess Moral Motivations?

Motivations, unlike behavior, are internal states that cannot be directly observed; they must instead be inferred from some indirect marker. The chapters in this volume illustrate two common approaches to this task, each with its own strength and limitations. One is to simply ask people about their motivations, using their self-report as the indirect marker of motivation. The challenge with this approach is that talk is cheap: You might claim to be motivated to help your neighbor carry her groceries because it is socially desirable to do so, when in reality you have no intention of or desire to follow through. The problem is amplified if we require moral motivations to be to some degree intrinsic, because people may not always be able, even if they were willing, to report the full scope of their motivation. Even if your claim to want to help is truthful, you might not mention (or even realize) that you want to help because you might receive a $5 tip if you do so, or because, in return, she will agree to water your plants when you go on vacation.

The second common approach is to observe behavior and use that as an indirect marker of motivation. The challenge here is that behavior does not always follow motivation (e.g., Lobbestael, 2015). For example, Snow notes that traits orthogonal to morality, such as impulsivity, can interfere with motivation translating into behavior. You may be genuinely motivated to help your neighbor but rarely get the chance to because you are constantly distracted by interruptions in your immediate environment. Or you may be genuinely motivated to help, but your physical limitations may prevent it. Tarsha and Narvaez's chapter also illustrates how the absence of moral behavior, or even behavior they consider to be immoral, may be driven by orthogonal motivations, such as the need to protect oneself.

Gawronski and colleagues offer a creative way to measure motivation that, to some degree, avoids both aforementioned problems. They use multiple measurements across carefully constructed scenarios and apply mathematical modeling to establish the strength of various motives independent of each other. There is no single answer to their dilemmas that would unquestionably make the participant look moral, and its design rules out some orthogonal traits, such as tendencies toward action and inaction. However, even though this method uses scenarios that mirror real-world events, it relies on self-reported hypothetical intentions, which may not track actual behavior (e.g., Kormos & Gifford, 2014). Thus, more specific and sensitive tools for assessing moral motivations may continue to be developed, with an eye to how we choose to define moral motivations.

AVENUES FOR FUTURE RESEARCH

We close with some thoughts about potentially fruitful avenues for future research and theorizing in this realm.

Opportunities for Greater Conceptual and Operational Clarity

The preceding sections have illustrated that there are varying definitions of morality and of moral motivation; there is an opportunity here for the field to either unite around single consensual definitions or to develop an approach that more explicitly acknowledges and accounts for distinct perspectives. Here we identify two specific areas where researchers might consider sharpening their theoretical development.

Theriault's chapter distinguishes between two mental models: of (a) the social world and (b) the immediate environment. This distinction is crucial to differentiating between morality and conformity: *Conformity* is meeting others' expectations according to one's mental model of the immediate environment, whereas *morality* is meeting others' expectations according to one's mental model of the social world, even if that means violating expectations in the immediate environment. In drawing this distinction, Theriault raises intriguing questions about gray area cases that cannot be easily labeled as "social world" or "immediate environment." Consider the broadest possible social world (all humans on the planet) and the narrowest possible immediate environment (only the humans who are physically in front of me); here the distinction is obvious. But how would Theriault's model account for a person conforming to the entire circle of others who might learn about their behavior: Is that an immediate environment or a social world? He notes that one's social world can be constrained to one's cultural group, but how do we think about an extremely narrow cultural group, such as one's class of fellow eighth graders? Further clarifying what characteristics distinguish the two types of mental models will promote broader explorations of how individuals juggle the demands of the social world versus the immediate environment.

As another specific example, Miller and Engelbrecht distinguish between empirical findings that illustrate qualitative, rather than merely quantitative, cultural differences. In one case of the former, they argue that Hindu Indians' outlook on interpersonal responsibility is qualitatively different from European Americans' because it (a) is obligatory, (b) takes more precedence than justice concerns, and (c) is unaffected by preferential liking. The point about qualitative differences being distinct from quantitative differences is well taken. At the same time, it raises questions for future research about what stable principles we can use to determine whether any given between group (or between individual) difference in moral motivation is qualitative or quantitative. For example, take the finding that liberals are more universalist, whereas conservatives are more parochial, in terms of the social distance to which their care extends (Waytz et al., 2019). Would Miller and Engelbrecht's model call this difference merely a matter of degree, or something more fundamental? We look forward to future conceptual work on these important questions.

We certainly foresee no shortage of important conceptual work to come in the service of understanding moral motivations and even defining its terms. Consider our earlier discussion of universalism versus cultural relativism: We ourselves treated this distinction as clear-cut, but it may not be once one asks just how much cultural variation is enough to discount the possibility of universalism. If 99.99% of societies consider infanticide to be immoral, is that 0.01% enough to claim that there is no moral universal? If a moral universalist can explain away that tiny degree of variation by attributing it to likely measurement error, at what degree of variation does that attribution become implausible?

Greater Attention to Culture

The second potentially fruitful avenue we noticed would be to direct more effort toward understanding cultural differences and similarities. Conclusions of cultural difference can sometimes be mistaken when pains are not taken to make methodologies culturally specific. To use an example from Miller and Engelbrecht's chapter, if Western researchers assumed that stealing a train ticket would always be construed as immoral in any society, they might inadvertently conclude that Indians are on average less moral than Americans because the former are more willing to steal a train ticket to avoid missing an important event.

More broadly, most psychologists from Western countries have limited mental access to the moral content of other cultures. Using methodology that is not culturally specific could produce data that do not have cultural relevance, as Miller and Engelbrecht suggest. Vauclair and colleagues (2014) concur, pointing out that most researchers use expert-designed taxonomies and self-report measures that impress an external morality upon participants. As quantitative researchers, we are accustomed to empirical models that rely on abstract scenarios, imagined behaviors, and closed-ended responses by participants. These assessments do not allow us to readily notice errors in our assumptions about participants' interpretations of our materials; they also have limited external validity.

The correction of these errors is to ensure that study materials are culturally comparable—that is, that study participants understand them in the same terms. This requires an understanding of laypersons' conceptions of morality within different cultures, which calls for interdisciplinary work: Qualitative research can help quantitative researchers develop materials. For example, anthropologists have a rich history of documenting the lived experiences of different communities using qualitative methods, such as ethnographies, with the help of the community involved. Their work could help quantitative scholars better understand the moral content of different cultures and, in turn, create more sensitive measures. The examples from Miller and Engelbrecht's chapter provide some hints about some dimensions of cultural variation, but their overarching message is that our field is far from being able to provide a comprehensive map of cultural differences in how abstract moral values are translated into moral judgments and behaviors in concrete situations.

More Interdisciplinary Collaboration

The previous section touches on our final potentially fruitful avenue, which is more interdisciplinary collaboration. This volume offers levels of analysis that range from the broad societal level to the narrow level of cell metabolism. We hope to see more communication among these different levels in the future. As one example, consider the distinction we made before between distal and proximate motives. The reader may have noticed that the examples of proximate motives all came from chapters written at a relatively broad level of analysis, whereas the examples of distal motives all came from chapters written at a relatively narrow one. However, distal and proximate motives are not mutually exclusive—indeed, the two often coexist. People may (proximally) want to secure others' approval because (distally) doing so will allow them to survive. Or people may (proximally) want to elicit predictable reactions from others because (distally) doing so will allow them to economize metabolic resources. Exploring each of these possibilities will require cross-level collaboration. More generally, these cross-level collaborations would allow variables such as culture to be included within relatively detailed models of within-person processes such as social learning and mental models.

CONCLUSION

The authors of the chapters in this volume provide compelling contributions to the study of moral motivations, drawing from diverging disciplines, using different levels of analyses, and having differing research goals. There are many questions that remain to be answered in this research pursuit; with increased interdisciplinary collaboration, better operationalization of key terms, and culturally attuned scholarship, they can be explored to make for a strong study of morality.

REFERENCES

Gowans, C. (2021, March 10). Moral relativism. In E. N. Zalta (Ed.), *Stanford encyclopedia of philosophy*. Stanford University. https://plato.stanford.edu/archives/spr2021/entries/moral-relativism/

Graham, J., Haidt, J., Koleva, S., Motyl, M., Iyer, R., Wojcik, S., & Ditto, P. H. (2013). Moral foundations theory: The pragmatic validity of moral pluralism. *Advances in*

Experimental Social Psychology, *47*, 55–130. https://doi.org/10.1016/B978-0-12-407236-7.00002-4

Kormos, C., & Gifford, R. (2014). The validity of self-report measures of proenvironmental behavior: A meta-analytic review. *Journal of Environmental Psychology*, *40*, 359–371. https://doi.org/10.1016/j.jenvp.2014.09.003

Lobbestael, J. (2015). Challenges in aggression assessment: The gap between self-report and behavior, and a call for new valid behavioral paradigms. *Journal of Socialomics*, *5*(1), 359–371. https://doi.org/10.4172/2167-0358.1000141

Norenzayan, A., Shariff, A. F., Gervais, W. M., Willard, A. K., McNamara, R. A., Slingerland, E., & Henrich, J. (2016). The cultural evolution of prosocial religions. *Behavioral and Brain Sciences*, *39*, e1. https://doi.org/10.1017/S0140525X14001356

Scott-Phillips, T. C., Dickins, T. E., & West, S. A. (2011). Evolutionary theory and the ultimate–proximate distinction in the human behavioral sciences. *Perspectives on Psychological Science*, *6*(1), 38–47. https://doi.org/10.1177/1745691610393528

Vauclair, C., Wilson, M., & Fischer, R. (2014). Cultural conceptions of morality: Examining laypeople's associations of moral character. *Journal of Moral Education*, *43*(1), 54–74. https://doi.org/10.1080/03057240.2013.873365

Waytz, A., Iyer, R., Young, L., Haidt, J., & Graham, J. (2019). Ideological differences in the expanse of the moral circle. *Nature Communications*, *10*(1), 4389. https://doi.org/10.1038/s41467-019-12227-0

Index

A

Abend, G., 23, 27
Abortion, 89
Action. *See also* General preference for
    inaction vs. action *(I);* Moral behavior
    (moral action)
  CNI model predicting, 119
  costs and benefits of, 116, 117, 119
  occurrence vs., 93
  in traditional approach to studying
    dilemmas, 120
Action guides, norms vs., 48–49
Action plans, 214–215
Activation
  behavioral, 124
  norm, 46, 47, 54–55
Active interference, theories of, 167
Act/omission heuristic, 83
Adaptive behavior, in normative motivation,
  217
Admiration, 145–147
Affect (affective experience), 134, 135,
  214–216
Affinity, interpersonal responsibility and,
  95
African American men, values of self for,
  24
Agency, 25, 99
Agent-based virtue ethics, 144–145
Aggression, 160, 163–164, 191, 192
Agreeableness, 125
Aksan, N., 52
Alberts, J. K., 63
Algoe, S., 146–147
Allomothers, 189, 190

Altomonte, G., 23
Altruism
  empathy–altruism hypothesis, 6
  and intrinsic moral motivation, 252
  motivation and perception of, 8
  mutual agreement motivating, 32
  reciprocal, 5
  social status and, 24
Amygdala, 190
Anger, 6
Anscombe, Elizabeth, 136
Anterior cingulate cortex, 190
Anthropology, 255
Anticipated blame, 63
Anticipated guilt, 52–53
Anticipatory anxiety, 216–217, 223
Anticipatory aversion, to harm, 224–225
Anxiety, 216–217, 223
Appropriate affect, as component of virtue,
  134, 135
Approval seeking, 251
Aquino, K., 26
Aristotle, 134, 136, 138, 139, 144,
  150–152, 250
Arousal, 214, 217
Asch, Solomon, 215
Asia, 19, 33, 84. *See also specific countries*
Associability, 168
Assumptions, 161, 255
Attunement, relational, 198, 248
Authority/respect foundation, in MFT,
  84, 85, 87, 233
Autism, 208
Automatic moral judgment, 232

EDN-consistent experiences and
sociomoral functioning for,
195–196
effectiveness of punishment for, 59
impact of relational health on
development of, 190–191
learning of moral norms by, 160, 246
prosocial lying by, 98
right brain hemispheric development in,
190
sociomoral behavior of mothers and,
196
stage of moral development of, 79
undercare for, 192, 193
vagal tone and development of, 195
China, 34, 97–98
Choice, personal, 78, 80, 92, 95
Classical theory, in sociology, 31
Close relationships, 5–6, 55, 100
CNI model of moral decision making, 246
advantages over traditional approach,
127
described, 116
moral dilemmas in, 116–118
resolving ambiguities with, 118–120
studies of individual difference using,
121–126
CNS (central nervous system), 190–191
Cognition(s)
computational models of, 208
moral, 234–235
need for, 122
and virtues, 152
Cognitive affective processing system
(CAPS) theory of traits, 147–148
Cognitive developmental theory, 78–79,
87, 94
Cognitive dissonance, 229n11
Cognitive elaboration, 122
Cognitive neuroscience, learning research in,
159
Colby, A., 26
Collaboration, interdisciplinary, 256
Collective behavior
expectations of, 18–19, 30–31
theories of, 17–18
Collective habits, norms vs., 48
Collectivist societies, 19, 32, 83, 96, 99
Committed compliance, 52
Communal (social) engagement, 193,
197, 248
Communal imagination, 193

Community
benefits of norms for, 45–46, 50
in Big Three Ethics framework, 83
evolved developmental niche in, 189
identification of moral exemplars by,
146–147
judgment of justification by, 53, 54
specificity of norms to, 47–48
in transformative justice, 64
Comparisons, social, 5
Compassion, 151–152, 189, 195
Compensation, for victims, 57
Competence, need for, 188
Competing motivations, 4, 157–158.
See also Social learning
Computational models of cognition, 208
Computational models of social learning,
166–175
Bayesian, 172–175
reinforcement, 166–171
Concern for others, 6, 121–122, 157, 247
Confidence, 160
Conflicting motivations, 230–231
Conflicting predictions, 227
Conformity, 221, 254. *See also*
Nonconformist behavior
Confrontation, 57, 58, 62
Confucius and Confucian societies, 34,
98, 136
Consequences. *See also* Sensitivity to
consequences *(C)*
in CNI model, 116, 117, 119
in utilitarian moral outlook, 113–114
Consequentialism
the good, the right, and virtue in, 145
maximizing virtue, 141–142
political orientation and views of, 125
scalar virtue, 141, 142
virtue theory of, 136–137, 141–143
Conservatives, 85–86, 124–125
Consistency, density distributions and, 148
Constructed emotion, theory of, 208,
213–215
Context
for moral motivation, 25–26, 248
specificity of norms to, 48
Control, need for, 188
Conventional norms, 36, 49
Conventional stage of moral development,
78, 79
Conventions, in universalist theories,
78, 79

Individual differences in social maxims,
 229–231
Individualist societies, 19, 83, 96
Individual regulation of norm compliance,
 51–54
Individual rights, 78, 79, 81, 92
Inequality, 27, 34
Infanticide, 255
Infants
 basic needs of, 188
 other-consciousness sympathy for, 190
 parent–infant sleeping practices, 90
 pleasure motivation for, 192
 positive touch for, 191–192
 relational health and development of, 191
 vagal tone for, 195
Information, data vs., 210n2
Ingelhart, R., 34, 89
Ingroup/loyalty foundation, in MFT, 84,
 85, 87, 233
Ingroups, 28, 33, 100, 160–161
Inhibition, behavioral, 124
Injunctive norms, 50
Inputs, whole trait theory, 149
Instrumental harm, 123
Interactional context, 33, 48
Interaction order, 30
Interdisciplinary science of morality, 17,
 22–31
 boundaries in, 27–28
 collaboration in, 256
 emotion in, 26–27
 levels of, 23
 moral order in, 29–31
 pragmatism in, 28–29
 self and identity in, 25–26
 status and power in, 23–25
Intermediates, whole trait theory, 149–150
Internal consistency, 227, 229–231
Internal generative model of the
 environment, 165
Internalization
 of helping norms, 98–99
 of moral identity, 122–123
 punishment to encourage, 59
 regulating norm compliance with, 47,
 51–52
Internal model
 accuracy of, 213
 changing environment to maintain,
 230–231
 moral dumbfounding and, 233

revising, 229
 social environment and biasing of, 234
 social maxims and, 226, 229
Interoceptive sensory experience, 208–211,
 214, 215
Interpersonal responsibility, 92–96, 254
Interpretative subsystem, in WTT, 149
Intrinsically bad outcomes, 142–143
Intrinsically good outcomes, 142, 143
Intrinsic moral motivation, 252
Intuitions, moral, 206, 212–213, 230, 232
Inverse reinforcement learning (IRL), 171
Invisibility, immoral behavior and, 7–8

J

Jacquette, D., 6
Japan, 90, 96
Jealousy, 27
Jensen, L. A., 96
Johnson, Allan, 31
Joseph, C., 205, 213–214
Judgments. *See* Moral dilemma judgments
Justice
 cultural variation in views of, 91–94
 in developmental models of morality,
 78, 79
 mercy as alternative to, 141–142
 in moral grammar theory, 81
 morality of caring vs., 94
 restorative, 64
 in theory of dyadic morality, 88
 transformative, 64
Justice system, 59, 60, 64
Justification, 53–54, 63, 87–88

K

Kahane, G., 123
Kant, Immanuel, 92, 136, 137, 139–140,
 143
Keller, G. B., 210
Keller, M., 34
Kemper, T., 24
Kitayama, S., 33
Kiyonari, T., 58
Kochanska, G., 52
Kohlberg, L., 5–7, 18, 78, 81, 87, 94,
 215n3
Kringelbach, M. L., 190
Kroneisen, M., 125
Kruglanski, A. W., 85
Kurth, A., 197

About the Editors

Martha K. Berg, PhD, is an industry researcher. She received her BS in psychology with distinction and her MS in global health from Duke University, and her MS and PhD in social psychology from the University of Michigan. Dr. Berg has served as a student representative in the Society for Personality and Social Psychology, and as a student affiliate in the Center for the Science of Moral Understanding. She was selected to receive a Fulbright Research Grant in 2017, and her other awards and honors include the Robert B. Zajonc Scholars Award, the Ruth C. Hamill Graduate Student Research Award, and the Jerome S. Bruner Award for Excellence in Undergraduate Research.

Edward C. Chang, PhD, is a first-generation Korean American, born in Seoul, South Korea. He is a professor of clinical science and social work, and a faculty associate in Asian/Pacific Islander American Studies and in the Center for Positive Organizations, Ross School of Business, University of Michigan. Dr. Chang received his BA in psychology and philosophy, graduating summa cum laude, from the State University of New York at Buffalo, and his MA and PhD degrees from the State University of New York at Stony Brook. He completed his American Psychological Association–accredited clinical internship at Bellevue Hospital Center–New York University Medical Center. Dr. Chang served as a program evaluator for the Michigan Department of Community Health—Social Determinants of Health, working with the Asian Center Southeast Michigan. He is serving or has served as an associate editor of *Cognitive Therapy and Research,* the *International Journal of Existential Psychology and Psychotherapy*, the *Asian American Journal of Psychology*, and the *Journal of Personality and Social Psychology*. Dr. Chang has published more than 200 empirical and scholarly works focusing on optimism and pessimism, perfectionism, loneliness, social problem solving, and cultural influences on behavior. He is the editor of *Optimism and Pessimism: Implications for Theory, Research, and Practice* (2001) and *Self-Criticism and Self-Enhancement: Theory, Research, and Clinical Implications* (2007), and is a coeditor of *Virtue, Vice, and Personality: The Complexity of Behavior* (2003); *Social Problem Solving: Theory, Research, and Training* (2004); *Judgments Over Time: The Interplay of Thoughts, Feelings, and Behaviors* (2006); *Positive Psychology in Racial and Ethnic Groups: Theory, Research, and Practice* (2016); *Biopsychosocial Approaches to Understanding Health in South Asian Americans* (2018); *Treating Depression, Anxiety, and Stress in Ethnic and Racial Groups: Cognitive Behavioral Approaches* (2018); and *The International Handbook of Positive Psychology: A Global Perspective on the Science of Human Existence* (2022). He was recently identified as one of the 70 "top producers" of scholarly works in clinical psychology, from a pool of 1,927 core clinical faculty from PhD programs across the United States. His works have received wide media coverage, from *The Chronicles of Higher Education* to *The Wall Street Journal*. Dr. Chang has mentored one of the highest numbers of undergraduate students within the department. He has been recognized for his many years of teaching excellence at the University of Michigan by being selected for the *LSA Excellence in Education Award* in 2008 and by the *University Undergraduate Teaching Award* in 2011.